The Pastoral Epistles

The Pastoral Epistles

J. H. Bernard

BAKER BOOK HOUSE
Grand Rapids, Michigan

Reprinted 1980 by
Baker Book House Company
from the edition published by
Cambridge University Press
First published in 1899

ISBN: 0-8010-0797-6

PHOTOLITHOPRINTED BY CUSHING - MALLOY, INC.
ANN ARBOR, MICHIGAN, UNITED STATES OF AMERICA

EDITOR'S PREFACE

In the Notes and Introduction to this edition of the Pastoral Epistles I have thought it desirable to state the opinions which have been adopted after consideration, without, as a rule, giving references to the views of the many commentators who have travelled over the same ground. It is therefore necessary now to express my chief obligations. The problems of date and authorship are handled most fully by Holtzmann, whose edition is indispensable to the student who desires to learn the difficulties in the way of accepting St Paul as the writer. These are also stated, with brevity and candour, in Jülicher's *Einleitung in das N.T.* The *Introductions* of Dr Salmon and Dr Zahn should be read on the other side; and the chapter on the Pastoral Epistles in Dr Hort's *Judaistic Christianity* should not be overlooked. A more complete and elaborate statement of the conservative case is given by Weiss, whose edition of these Epistles is, on the whole, the best now accessible, whether for criticism or for exegesis. Of modern English commentaries Bishop Ellicott's is the most exact and trustworthy, in its detailed exposition of the text. Among the Patristic writers, St Chrysostom and St Jerome will often be found instructive; and Bengel's *Gnomon* can never be safely neglected.

I have to thank my friends, Dr Gwynn, and the General Editor, for their great kindness in reading the proofs and for much valuable criticism.

J. H. BERNARD.

21st *August*, 1899.

CONTENTS

INTRODUCTION

CHAPTER I.

THE LITERARY HISTORY OF THE PASTORAL EPISTLES.

THE interpretation of the several books of the Bible is necessarily affected in many directions by the view which is taken of their author and their date. In the case of some of St Paul's Epistles, those for instance addressed to the Romans, Galatians, and Corinthians, there is such a general consensus of opinion among scholars that they proceed from St Paul, that it is not necessary for an editor to spend much space in elaborating the proofs of what everyone who reads his commentary is likely to admit.

In the case of other Epistles, however, questions of date and authorship become of primary importance; the *data* may be uncertain, the phenomena which the documents present may have received widely different explanations; and it thus becomes a duty to present in detail all the evidence which is available. The Epistles to Timothy and Titus offer peculiar difficulties in these respects. They have been reckoned by the Church as canonical books, ever since the idea of a Canon of the N.T. came into clear consciousness; and they claim for themselves to have been written by St Paul, the Apostle of the Gentiles. But for various reasons which shall be explained as we proceed, serious difficulty has been felt by many in accepting the Pauline authorship; and critics are not in agreement as to whether we

are justified in believing them to have been written in the
Apostolic age.

We have to consider, then, at the outset, the problem of the
date and authorship of the Pastoral Epistles. The distribution
of the argument in this *Introduction* will be as follows. We
shall summarise (Chap. I.) the external evidence as to the
diffusion of these letters in the early Christian communities, and
consider how far this evidence justifies us in placing their origin
in the apostolic period. We go on (Chap. II.) to examine the
place which the Epistles must occupy in St Paul's life, if they are
to be regarded as the work of that Apostle. The arguments which
will here engage our attention will be mainly those derived from
the historical notices of events and individuals to be found in
the Epistles themselves. Chapter III. is devoted to a discussion
of the peculiar vocabulary, phraseology and style of these letters,
which admittedly vary much in this respect from the Pauline
letters universally conceded to be genuine. Chapter IV. treats
of the heresies which the writer had in his mind. In Chapter V.
an attempt is made to examine the nature of the ecclesiastical
organisation which the Pastoral Epistles reveal to us as existing
at the time of their composition.

To treat these large subjects exhaustively would require a
treatise ; and only a brief sketch can be attempted here. But
the main drift of the argument will be to shew that external
and internal evidence conspire to place the Epistles to Timothy
and Titus in a very early period of the history of the Christian
Society, and that, this being established, there is no good reason
for denying that their author was the Apostle whose name
they bear.

It will be convenient to remark in this place that these three
epistles are so closely linked together in thought, in phraseology,
and in the historical situation which they presuppose, that they
must be counted as having all come into being within a very
few years of each other. The general consent of critics allows
that they stand or fall together ; and it is therefore not always
necessary to distinguish the indications of the existence of one
from those of the existence of another. We may speak generally,

without loss of accuracy, of evidences of knowledge of the
Pastoral Epistles if we come upon reminiscences of any one of
them. And so, in investigating their literary history, we consider them not separately, but together.

Let us take, for clearness' sake, the testimony of the East
before we consider that of the West. In either case, we may
begin our enquiry about the year 180 of our era, after which
date there was no controversy as to the reception and authority
of our letters. We shall then work backwards as far as we
can.

§ I. *The testimony of the East.*

(i) Theophilus, Bishop of Antioch *circa* 181, may be our first
witness. Two passages from his apologetic treatise *ad Autolycum*
present certain traces of our letters:—

(a) *Ad Autol.* iii. 14 p. 389
ἔτι μὴν καὶ **περὶ τοῦ ὑποτάσσεσθαι
ἀρχαῖς καὶ ἐξουσίαις**, καὶ εὔχεσθαι
περὶ αὐτῶν, κελεύει ἡμᾶς θεῖος λόγος
ὅπως **ἤρεμον καὶ ἡσύχιον βίον
διάγωμεν**.

(b) *Ad Autol.* p. 95 **διὰ** ὕδατος
καὶ **λουτροῦ παλινγενεσίας** πάντας
τοὺς προσιόντας τῇ ἀληθείᾳ.

Tit. iii. 1 ὑπομίμνησκε αὐτοὺς
ἀρχαῖς ἐξουσίαις ὑποτίσσεσθαι.
1 Tim. ii. 2 ὑπὲρ βασιλέων
καὶ πάντων τῶν ἐν ὑπεροχῇ ὄντων,
ἵνα **ἤρεμον καὶ ἡσύχιον βίον
διάγωμεν**.

Tit. iii. 5 **διὰ λουτροῦ παλινγενεσίας** καὶ ἀνακαινώσεως πνεύματος ἁγίου.

It will be observed that Theophilus not only quotes the
Pastorals, but speaks of them as proceeding from 'the Divine
Word.'

(ii) An entirely different kind of witness may next be brought
into court. The apocryphal *Acts of Paul and Thecla*, a
romance setting forth certain legendary adventures of St Paul,
is believed by the best authorities to have been originated in
Asia Minor, and to have received its present form not later than
170 A.D.[1] Now these *Acta* depend for many details of their

[1] Some writers, e.g. Ramsay (*Church in the Roman Empire* p. 381)
hold that the nucleus of the book was a first century legend, which
was added to between 130 and 150. More recent investigations have
disclosed the fact that the *Acts of Paul and Thecla* is only one chapter
of a much larger work, the *Acts of Paul*, which is classed among the
antilegomena by Eusebius (*H. E.* iii. 25).

story upon 2 *Tim.* The romancer borrows phrases (λέγει οὗτος ἀνάστασιν γενέσθαι ὅτι ἤδη γέγονεν ἐφ᾽ οἷς ἔχομεν τέκνοις § 14; cp. 2 *Tim.* ii. 18), and names (Demas, Hermogenes, Onesiphorus) from that Epistle, and works them up into his tale. Whether these details were part of the original document, or were added by a reviser, is uncertain; but in any case we have here another indication of the circulation of 2 *Tim.* in Asia before the year 170.

(iii) Hegesippus, the earliest Church historian, may be cited next as an Eastern witness; for, though he travelled to Rome and to Corinth, his home was in Palestine. The date of his work, which we chiefly know from the citations in Eusebius, was probably about 170. In the following extract Eusebius seems to be incorporating the actual words of Hegesippus.

ap. Eus. *H. E.* iii. 32 διὰ τῆς **τῶν ἑτεροδιδασκάλων** ἀπάτης, οἳ καὶ, ἅτε μηδενὸς ἔτι τῶν ἀποστόλων λειπομένου, γυμνῇ λοιπὸν ἤδη κεφαλῇ τῷ τῆς ἀληθείας κηρύγματι τὴν **ψευδώνυμον γνῶσιν** ἀντικηρύττειν ἐπεχείρουν.

1 Tim. i. 3 ἵνα παραγγείλῃς τισὶν μὴ **ἑτεροδιδασκαλεῖν**. Cp. 1 Tim. vi. 3.

1 Tim. vi. 20 ἀντιθέσεις τῆς **ψευδωνύμου γνώσεως**.

The references to the ἑτεροδιδάσκαλοι and to their 'knowledge falsely so called' are unmistakeable.

(iv) Justin Martyr (*circa* 155) has two or three allusions to the phraseology of our letters.

(*a*) *Dial.* 7. 7 **τὰ τῆς πλάνης πνεύματα** καὶ **δαιμόνια** δοξολογοῦντα.
Dial. 35. 3 ἀπὸ τῶν **τῆς πλάνης πνευμάτων**.

1 Tim. iv. 1 **προσέχοντες πνεύμασιν πλάνοις** καὶ **διδασκαλίαις δαιμονίων**.

(*b*) *Dial.* 47. 15 ἡ γὰρ **χρηστότης** καὶ ἡ **φιλανθρωπία** τοῦ θεοῦ.

Tit. iii. 4 ὅτε δὲ ἡ **χρηστότης** καὶ ἡ **φιλανθρωπία** ἐπεφάνη τοῦ σωτῆρος ἡμῶν **θεοῦ**.

(v) The letter to the Philippians by Polycarp, bishop of Smyrna (*circa* 117), betrays several times a familiarity with the thought and language of the Pastorals.

(*a*) § 8 **προσκαρτερῶμεν τῇ ἐλπίδι ἡμῶν**...ὅς ἐστιν **Χριστὸς Ἰησοῦς**.

1 Tim. i. 1 ...καὶ **Χριστοῦ Ἰησοῦ τῆς ἐλπίδος ἡμῶν**.

See note on 1 Tim. i. 1 below.

(b) § 12 Orate etiam *pro regi-*
bus...ut fructus *vester manifestus*
sit in omnibus. [Fragment preserved only in Latin.]

(c) § 5 ὁμοίως διάκονοι ἄμεμ-
πτοι...μὴ διάβολοι, μὴ δίλογοι,
ἀφιλάργυροι...

1 Tim. ii. 1, 2 παρακαλῶ...
ποιεῖσθαι δεήσεις...ὑπὲρ βασιλέων.
1 Tim. iv. 15 ἵνα σου ἡ προκοπὴ
φανερὰ ᾖ πᾶσιν.
1 Tim. iii. 8 f. διακόνους...μὴ
διλόγους...μὴ αἰσχροκερδεῖς...γυ-
ναῖκας ὡσαύτως σεμνάς, μὴ διαβόλους.

The directions about deacons in these two passages are much
more closely parallel than even the above coincidences in language would suggest.

(d) § 4 ἀρχὴ δὲ πάντων χαλε-
πῶν φιλαργυρία...εἰδότες οὖν ὅτι
οὐδὲν εἰσηνέγκαμεν εἰς τὸν κόσμον
ἀλλ' οὐδὲ ἐξενεγκεῖν τι ἔχομεν.

1 Tim. vi. 10...ῥίζα γὰρ πάντων
τῶν κακῶν ἐστὶν ἡ φιλαργυρία.
1 Tim. vi. 7 οὐδὲν γὰρ εἰσηνέγκαμεν εἰς τὸν κόσμον, ὅτι οὐδὲ
ἐξενεγκεῖν τι δυνάμεθα.

This is an unmistakeable quotation.

(e) § 5 καὶ συνβασιλεύσομεν
αὐτῷ εἴγε πιστεύομεν.

2 Tim. ii. 12 εἰ ὑπομένομεν καὶ
συνβασιλεύσομεν.

It is just possible that in this passage Polycarp may be quoting,
not from 2 Tim. ii. 12, but from the hymn there quoted by St
Paul. See note *in loc.*

(f) § 9 οὐ γὰρ τὸν νῦν ἠγάπησαν αἰῶνα.

2 Tim. iv. 10 Δημᾶς γάρ με
ἐγκατέλιπεν ἀγαπήσας τὸν νῦν
αἰῶνα.

Note that Polycarp generally uses the phrase ὁ αἰὼν οὗτος, not
ὁ νῦν αἰών.

(vi) We turn from Polycarp, the disciple of St John, to
Ignatius, Bishop of Antioch (*circa* 116), of whose letters (in the
shorter Greek recension) Lightfoot's investigations may be taken
as having established the genuineness. There is no long quotation from the Pastorals in Ignatius as there is in Polycarp. But
the coincidences in phraseology can hardly be accidental.

(a) ad Magn. 11 &c. Ἰησοῦ
Χριστοῦ τῆς ἐλπίδος ἡμῶν.

1 Tim. i. 1 Χριστοῦ Ἰησοῦ
τῆς ἐλπίδος ἡμῶν.

So also *ad Trall.* inscr. and 2.

(b) ad Polyc. 6 ἀρέσκετε ᾧ στρατεύεσθε.

2 Tim. ii. 4 οὐδεὶς στρατευόμενος ἐμπλέκεται ταῖς τοῦ βίου πραγματίαις, ἵνα τῷ στρατολογήσαντι ἀρέσῃ.

(c) ad Eph. 2 καὶ Κρόκος... κατὰ πάντα με ἀνέπαυσεν ὡς καὶ αὐτὸν ὁ Πατὴρ Ἰησοῦ Χριστοῦ ἀναψύξαι.

2 Tim. i. 16 δῴη ἔλεος ὁ Κύριος τῷ Ὀνησιφόρου οἴκῳ, ὅτι πολλάκις με ἀνέψυξεν.

(d) ad Magn. 8 μὴ πλανᾶσθε ταῖς ἑτεροδοξίαις μηδὲ μυθεύμασιν τοῖς παλαιοῖς ἀνωφελέσιν οὖσιν· εἰ γὰρ μέχρι νῦν κατὰ Ἰουδαισμὸν ζῶμεν κ.τ.λ.

1 Tim. iv. 7 γραώδεις μύθους παραιτοῦ.
Tit. iii. 9 μωρὰς δὲ ζητήσεις... περιίστασο· εἰσὶν γὰρ ἀνωφελεῖς.
Tit. i. 14 μὴ προσέχοντες Ἰουδαϊκοῖς μύθοις.

(e) ad Magn. 3 καὶ ὑμῖν δὲ πρέπει μὴ συγχρᾶσθαι τῇ ἡλικίᾳ τοῦ ἐπισκόπου.

1 Tim. iv. 12 μηδείς σου τῆς νεότητος καταφρονείτω.

(f) We have some peculiar words in Ignatius only found elsewhere in the Pastoral Epistles, e.g. ἑτεροδιδασκαλεῖν (ad Polyc. 3; cp. 1 Tim. i. 3, vi. 3). Again κατάστημα (ad Trall. 3) is only found in N.T. at Tit. ii. 3, and πραϋπάθεια (ad Trall. 8) only at 1 Tim. vi. 11; and αἰχμαλωτίζειν is used by Ignatius of the machinations of heretical teachers (ad Philad. 2, Eph. 17) as it is at 2 Tim. iii. 6.

There is thus a continuous testimony to the circulation of the Pastoral Epistles in the East as far back as the year 116.

§ II. *The testimony of the West.*

(i) We begin with Irenaeus, bishop of Lyons (*cir.* 180), the disciple of Polycarp. The witness of his treatise *contra Haereses* is express and frequent to the *circulation*, the *authority*, and the *Pauline authorship* of the Pastoral Letters. The passages are familiar and need not be quoted. Cp. *Pref.* with 1 Tim. i. 4; iv. 16. 3 with 1 Tim. i. 9; ii. 14. 7 with 1 Tim. vi. 20; iii. 14. 1 with 2 Tim. iv. 9—11; iii. 2. 3 with 2 Tim. iv. 21; and i. 16. 3 with Tit. iii. 10. In the last-mentioned passage it is noteworthy that Irenaeus is appealing to the Epistle to Titus as written by St Paul, against *heretics*, who would certainly have denied the authority of the words quoted if they could have produced reasons for doing so.

(ii) Eusebius has preserved a remarkable Letter of the Churches of Vienne and Lyons to their brethren in Asia, written about the year 180 to acquaint them with the details of the great persecution in which they had recently lost their venerable bishop. Pothinus, the predecessor of Irenaeus, was martyred in the year 177, when he was ninety years of age. The witness of the Church over which he presided to the use of any N.T. book thus brings us a long way back into the second century. And the following phrases in the Letter betray a knowledge of the First Epistle to Timothy.

(a) Eus. *H. E.* v. i. 17 "Ατταλον …στῦλον καὶ ἑδραίωμα τῶν ἐνταῦθα ἀεὶ γεγονότα.

1 Tim. iii. 15 …ἥτις ἐστὶν ἐκκλησία θεοῦ ζῶντος, στῦλος καὶ ἑδραίωμα τῆς ἀληθείας.

(b) ap. Eus. *H. E.* v. iii. 2 Ἀλκιβιάδης μὴ χρώμενος τοῖς κτίσμασι τοῦ θεοῦ…πεισθεὶς δὲ… πάντων ἀνέδην μετελάμβανε καὶ ηὐχαρίστει τῷ θεῷ.

1 Tim. iv. 3, 4 …ἃ ὁ θεὸς ἔκτισεν εἰς μετάλημψιν μετὰ εὐχαριστίας.

(c) ap. Eus. *H. E.* v. i. 30 ὃς ὑπὸ τῶν στρατιωτῶν ἐπὶ τὸ βῆμα κομισθεὶς … ἐπιβοήσεις παντοίας ποιουμένων, ὡς αὐτοῦ ὄντος τοῦ Χριστοῦ, ἀπεδίδου τὴν καλὴν μαρτυρίαν.

1 Tim. vi. 13 Χριστοῦ Ἰησοῦ τοῦ μαρτυρήσαντος ἐπὶ Ποντίου Πειλάτου τὴν καλὴν ὁμολογίαν. (The vg. is *qui testimonium reddidit.*)

Dr Robinson has argued that the text of this Letter of the Churches of Vienne and Lyons betrays a familiarity with a Latin version of the N.T., rather than the Greek original[1]. If this could be regarded as established (and his arguments seem to me to be well founded), it would prove that by the year 180 the Pastoral Letters were so firmly received as canonical that a Latin version of them had been made and was current in Gaul.

(iii)   Contemporary with Irenaeus and the Letter from Vienne and Lyons is the work of Athenagoras of Athens (*cir.* 176); there is at least one remarkable parallel to a phrase in 1 *Tim.*

Legat. pro Christianis 16 p. 291 πάντα γὰρ ὁ θεός ἐστιν αὐτὸς αὐτῷ φῶς ἀπρόσιτον.

1 Tim. vi. 16 ὁ μόνος ἔχων ἀθανασίαν φῶς οἰκῶν ἀπρόσιτον.

Note that the word ἀπρόσιτος does not occur again in the Greek Bible, although it is used by Philo and Plutarch.

[1] *The Passion of St Perpetua,* p. 99.

(iv) Our next Western witness, Heracleon, must be placed a few years earlier (*cir.* 165); one phrase seems to recall 2 *Tim.*

ap. Clem. Alex. *Strom.* iv. 9	2 Tim. ii. 13 ἀρνήσασθαι γὰρ
διόπερ ἀρνήσασθαι ἑαυτὸν οὐδέποτε	ἑαυτὸν οὐ δύναται.
δύναται.	

See note below *in loc.*

(v) In the year 140 we find the heretic Marcion at Rome excluding the Pastoral Epistles from his Apostolicon, possibly on the ground (though this can be no more than conjecture) that they were only private letters and not on a par with formal declarations of doctrine. But whatever Marcion's reason for the omission, Tertullian who is our earliest authority for the fact cites it as a novel feature in his heretical teaching. "Miror tamen cum ad unum hominem literas factas receperit, quod ad Timotheum duas et unam ad Titum, de ecclesiastico statu compositas, recusaverit" are Tertullian's words (*adv. Marc.* v. 21). Thus Marcion may be counted as an unwilling witness to the traditional place which the Epistles to Timothy and Titus occupied in orthodox circles at Rome about the year 140.

The parallels to our letters in the 'Epistle to Diognetus' (a composite work of the second century) are not uninteresting (cp. e.g. §§ iv. xi. with 1 Tim. iii. 16 and § ix. with Tit. iii. 4), but inasmuch as the date of the piece is somewhat uncertain, and as the parallels are not verbally exact, we do not press them

(vi) The writer of the ancient homily which used to be called the Second Epistle of Clement, and which is a Western document composed not later than 140, was certainly familiar with the Pastorals.

(a) § 20 τῷ μόνῳ θεῷ ἀοράτῳ, πατρὶ τῆς ἀληθείας κ.τ.λ.

1 Tim. i. 17 τῷ δὲ βασιλεῖ τῶν αἰώνων, ἀφθάρτῳ, ἀοράτῳ μόνῳ θεῷ κ.τ.λ.

(b) § 7 οὐ πάντες στεφανοῦνται, εἰ μὴ οἱ πολλὰ κοπιάσαντες καὶ καλῶς ἀγωνισάμενοι.

1 Tim. iv. 10 εἰς τοῦτο γὰρ κοπιῶμεν καὶ ἀγωνιζόμεθα, ὅτι κ.τ.λ.

(c) § 8 τηρήσατε τὴν σάρκα ἁγνὴν καὶ τὴν σφραγῖδα ἄσπιλον ἵνα τὴν αἰώνιον ζωὴν ἀπολάβωμεν.

1 Tim. vi. 14 τηρῆσαί σε τὴν ἐντολὴν ἄσπιλον ἀνεπίλημπτον κ.τ.λ.

1 Tim. vi. 19 ἵνα ἐπιλάβωνται τῆς ὄντως ζωῆς.

The whole of §§ 6, 7, 8 recalls the language and thought of 1 Tim. vi. In addition to the above parallels there are noteworthy verbal coincidences, κοσμικαὶ ἐπιθυμίαι (§ 17 ; cp. Tit. ii. 12) ; κακοπαθεῖν (§ 19 ; cp. 2 Tim. i. 8, ii. 3, 9 ; iv. 5) ; and the word ἐπιφάνεια (§§ 12, 17) used as a synonym for the Parousia of Christ, a usage not found in the N.T. outside the Pastorals (see note on 1 Tim. vi. 14 below).

(vii) We may also with some degree of confidence cite Clement of Rome as a writer who was familiar with the phraseology of the Pastorals.

(a) § 2 ἕτοιμοι εἰς πᾶν ἔργον ἀγαθόν.

Tit. iii. 1 πρὸς πᾶν ἔργον ἀγαθὸν ἑτοίμους εἶναι. Cp. 2 Tim. ii. 21, iii. 17.

(b) § 29 προσέλθωμεν οὖν αὐτῷ ἐν ὁσιότητι ψυχῆς, ἁγνὰς καὶ ἀμιάντους χεῖρας αἴροντες πρὸς αὐτόν.

1 Tim. ii. 8 βούλομαι οὖν προσεύχεσθαι τοὺς ἄνδρας...ἐπαίροντας ὁσίους χεῖρας χωρὶς ὀργῆς καὶ διαλογισμοῦ.

(c) § 45 τῶν ἐν καθαρᾷ συνειδήσει λατρευόντων τῷ παναρέτῳ.

2 Tim. i. 3 ᾧ λατρεύω ἀπὸ προγόνων ἐν καθαρᾷ συνειδήσει.

(d) § 7 καὶ ἴδωμεν τί καλὸν καὶ τί τερπνὸν καὶ τί προσδεκτὸν ἐνώπιον τοῦ ποιήσαντος ἡμᾶς.

1 Tim. ii. 3 τοῦτο καλὸν καὶ ἀπόδεκτον ἐνώπιον τοῦ σωτῆρος ἡμῶν θεοῦ.

We may also compare § 54 with 1 Tim. iii. 13, § 21 with 1 Tim. v. 21, § 32 with Tit. iii. 5, and the title βασιλεῦ τῶν αἰώνων (§ 61) with 1 Tim. i. 17 (but cp. Tobit xiii. 6, Rev. xv. 3).

Holtzmann explains these coincidences between Clement and the Pastorals to be due to 'the common Church atmosphere' in which they all originated ; but it seems as if they were too close to admit of any other hypothesis save that Clement wrote with the language and thoughts of the Pastorals in his mind.

Holtzmann's explanation is sufficient, we think, of the parallels between the Pastorals and the Epistle of Barnabas, which occur for the most part in doctrinal phrases that may well have become stereotyped at a very early period. Thus we have (§ 7) μέλλων κρίνειν ζῶντας καὶ νεκρούς (cp. 2 Tim. iv. 1) and (§ 12) ἐν σαρκὶ φανερωθείς (cp. 1 Tim. iii. 16) ; but that two writers both use these expressions does not by itself prove that one borrowed from the other. See notes on 1 Tim. iii. 16, v. 17, 2 Tim. iv. 1 below.

The conclusion which we derive from this survey of the litera-ture of the period is that we find traces of the Pastoral Epistles in Gaul and Greece in 177, in Rome in 140 (certainly)—as far back as 95, if we accept Clement's testimony—and in Asia as early as 116. The remains of primitive Christian literature are so meagre for the first hundred years of the Church's life that we could hardly have expected *à priori* to have gathered testimonies from that period so numerous and so full to any book of the New Testament. And this attestation appears the more remarkable, both as to its range and its precision, if we consider the character of the letters under examination. They are not formal treatises addressed to Churches, like the Epistles to the Romans and the Galatians, but semi-private letters to individuals, provid-ing counsel and guidance which to some extent would only be applicable in special circumstances. And yet we find that their language is already familiar to the Bishop of Smyrna, who was St John's pupil, so familiar that he naturally falls into its use when he is speaking of the qualifications of Christian ministers. No subsequent Pastoral letters thus imprinted them-selves on the consciousness of the Church. Further, we observe that these Epistles claim to come from St Paul. There can be no mistake about that. Hence a writer who quotes from them as Polycarp does, indicates his belief in their apostolic author-ship.

External evidence, such as has been under review, is the most trustworthy of all; for, although men may differ as to the internal evidence,—the tone, the temper,—of a document, they rarely differ as to the fact of its citation by a subsequent writer. And so it has been worth giving in detail.

Finally, a word must be said as to the additional em-phasis that is given to the use of a New Testament Epistle when its words are used as authoritative or as familiar, not merely by individuals whose only claim to memory is that they have written books, but by bishops who represent the continuous tradition of their respective sees. Clement, Polycarp, Ignatius, are not single authorities. Their use of the Pastorals is not to be compared to the use by a literary man of our own day of a phrase or an argument that he has seen somewhere, and that has caught his fancy. It bears witness to the belief of the primitive Christian communities at Rome, at Smyrna, at Antioch, that the Pastoral letters were, at the least, documents "profitable for teaching, for reproof, for correction, for instruction which is in righteousness." When speaking of early Christian literature it must always be remembered that, however fragmentary it be, it is the outcome of the continuous life of a society, a society which has been ever jealous of change, for from the beginning it has claimed to be in possession of the truth of God. And thus we must read and interpret the literature in the light of the common faith which lies behind it.

From our study then of the evidence of the early and wide diffusion of the Pastoral Epistles, we are forced to conclude, that, if not genuine relics of the Apostolic age, they must have been forged in St Paul's name and accepted on St Paul's authority all over the Christian world, within fifty years of St Paul's death—within thirty years if we accept the testimony of Clement of Rome. At any rate, the documentary evidence forces them back to the first century. We have next to consider how far their internal witness agrees with the recorded tradition of the Church, the claim that they make for themselves, that they were written by St Paul, the Apostle of the Gentiles.

CHAPTER II.

THE PLACE OF THE PASTORAL EPISTLES IN ST PAUL'S LIFE.

We have now considered the evidence which history gives us of the diffusion of the Epistles to Timothy and Titus in the primitive Christian communities; and we have learned, from the traces of these letters which are to be found in the fragmentary remains of early Christian literature, more especially in the letter of Polycarp of Smyrna, that they were in the possession of the Church at the very beginning of the second century.

This conclusion, it will be borne in mind, is entirely independent of their authorship. Whether they were written by St Paul or not, at all events they were current in Christian circles, and were accepted as authoritative, within fifty years of his death.

We now proceed to interrogate the letters themselves, that we may determine how far their internal character corresponds with the early date that history demands for them; and we begin with the enquiry, as to how far they agree with what we know or can surmise of the facts of St Paul's life. Since they claim St Paul as their author, it is natural to expect that they will connect themselves with his troubled career. What then do they tell us about the circumstances of their composition, and about the history of the Apostle of the Gentiles?

Our chief authority for St Paul's life is, of course, the book of the Acts of the Apostles; but that book does not give us any account of St Paul's death. It brings him to Rome where he has appealed to the Emperor Nero; and it leaves him there, in custody, it is true, but yet permitted in his own hired house to enjoy the society of his friends and acquaintances. Whatever be the reason of his silence, St Luke does not tell us what happened as the result of that hazardous appeal. As far as St Luke's narrative is concerned, St Paul's subsequent history is a blank. We could not tell from the *Acts* whether that imprisonment in Rome was ended by death, or whether the great prisoner was released from his bonds and again permitted to pursue his missionary labours. The opinion on the subject most widely held among scholars is that the Epistles to the Philippians, Colossians, Ephesians and Philemon, were written during the period of St Paul's life at Rome of which St Luke gives us a glimpse in the closing verses of the *Acts;* just as it is agreed that the Epistles to the Churches of Thessalonica, Corinth, Galatia and Rome were written on previous missionary journeys. The question that comes before us now is: At what period of St Paul's life do the Pastoral Epistles claim to have been written? Is it when he was on his early missionary travels, or when he was in Rome expecting daily the issue of his appeal to the Emperor, or is it at a later period of his life of which we have no information from St Luke? We do not assume at this stage that they were written by St Paul; but we ask, At what period of his life do they profess to have been written, and is there any inherent difficulty as to the period which they claim for themselves?

Taking up the question in this form, we are soon forced to the conclusion that they cannot be fitted into St Paul's life as recorded in the *Acts*. Let us first examine the Second Epistle to Timothy. This letter might seem at first sight to be suitably placed in the period covered by the closing verses of St Luke's account, for the place of writing is plainly Rome, where the Apostle represents himself as calmly awaiting his martyrdom. He has finished his course; he has kept the faith; henceforth is laid up for him the crown of righteousness (2 Tim. iv. 7, 8). But a closer inspection reveals to us that the allusions to individuals and events in the Epistle do not harmonise with such an hypothesis. For we know from the *Acts* that before St Paul sailed for Italy he was two years in custody in Palestine (xxiv. 27), and that then he was at least two years longer in Rome (xxviii. 30). And yet here is a letter which alludes to events as quite recent that could only have taken place when he was a free man. Take for instance the words, "Erastus abode at Corinth, but Trophimus I left at Miletus sick " (2 Tim. iv. 20). This would be a strange way of telling news now some years old. As a matter of fact, on the last occasion that St Paul was at Miletus before he sailed for Italy, Timothy was with him, and would have been fully cognisant of all that had happened (Acts xx. 4, 17). And further on that occasion Trophimus was *not* left at Miletus sick, for we find him immediately afterwards in Jerusalem at the time of St Paul's arrest. Indeed St Luke tells us that it was because the Jews saw Trophimus the Ephesian in the city with him, that they made a disturbance on the ground that Paul was defiling the Temple by introducing a Greek into the holy place (Acts xxi. 29). It is impossible to suppose that the little piece of information given at 2 Tim. iv. 20 referred to an event so long past. It was evidently a recent occurrence. A like observation may be made on 2 Tim. iv. 13, "The cloke that I left at Troas with Carpus, bring when thou comest, and the books, especially the parchments." It is unnatural to imagine that St Paul's concern for the baggage that he had left behind at Troas was drawn out by the recollection of a travelling cloak and some books that had been parted from him years before. We cannot, then, with any plausibility place 2 Timothy in the period of imprisonment mentioned by St Luke. It presupposes a recent period of freedom.

Similar difficulties beset all theories by which it is attempted to place 1 *Tim.* or *Titus* in the years preceding the voyage to Rome. "I exhorted thee to tarry at Ephesus when I was going into Macedonia," are the opening words of the first letter to Timothy, following immediately after the customary salutation (1 Tim. i. 3). When could this have been? There are only two occasions on which St Paul was at Ephesus mentioned in the *Acts.* (i) On the first of these visits, which was very brief, he was on his way to Caesarea (Acts xviii. 19—22), not to Macedonia, so that this cannot be the visit alluded to in 1 *Tim.* (ii) The other visit was of longer duration. It is described in Acts xix. and lasted for some three years. And the suggestion has been made (though it is not adopted now by critics of any school) that we may find room in this period for both 1 *Tim.* and *Titus.* It is the case that after the termination of this long residence in Ephesus, St Paul journeyed to Macedonia (Acts xx. 1); but then he did not leave Timothy behind him. On the contrary he had sent Timothy and Erastus over to Macedonia beforehand (Acts xix. 22). *This* journey, then, cannot be the one alluded to in 1 Tim. i. 3. In short, if we are to suppose that the first letter to Timothy alludes to an expedition which started from Ephesus during St Paul's long stay there, some years before he visited Rome, we must recognise that St Luke tells us nothing about it. The same may be said of the visit of St Paul to Crete which is mentioned in the Epistle to Titus (i. 5). Now it is not improbable that the Apostle may have made several excursions from Ephesus of small extent, during the period mentioned in Acts xix., of which no information is given us by St Luke. It is likely, for instance, that he paid a brief visit to

Corinth during the three years (2 Cor. xii. 14, xiii. 1). But it is not possible to suppose that great and important journeys like those indicated in the Pastorals could have been passed over by the historian. Indeed there would hardly be time for them. We should have to take out of the three years not only a visit to Macedonia, of which we have no other record, but what would necessarily be a prolonged residence in Crete, when the Church was being organised there, and (apparently) a winter at Nicopolis (Tit. iii. 12). Events such as these are not the kind of events that are omitted by St Luke, who is especially careful to tell of the beginnings of missionary enterprise in new places, and of the "confirmation" of distant Churches. And further, if we are to take all these journeys out of the three years at Ephesus, St Paul's statement "By the space of three years I ceased not to admonish every one [sc. the elders of Ephesus] *night and day* with tears" (Acts xx. 31), becomes an absurd exaggeration[1].

Hence we come to the conclusion that the Pastoral Epistles do not fit into the life of St Paul as recorded in the Acts of the Apostles. They presuppose a period of activity subsequent to the imprisonment in Rome mentioned by St Luke; they indicate certain events in his life which are not mentioned and for which no room can be found in the *Acts*. 1 *Tim.* and *Titus* tell us of missionary enterprise of which we have no record in that book, so that they imply his release from his captivity; and 2 *Tim.*, inasmuch as it places him again at Rome, daily expecting death, presupposes a second imprisonment there.

Up to this point there is practically no difference of opinion

---

[1] Against a visit of St Paul to Ephesus after his release from imprisonment, it has been objected that his own words to the Ephesian elders at Miletus seem to preclude it: οἶδα ὅτι οὐκέτι ὄψεσθε τὸ πρόσωπόν μου ὑμεῖς πάντες....To this it may be said, (i) the language of Phil. i. 25 (τοῦτο πεποιθὼς οἶδα) expresses a like confident belief that he will be released from his bonds, and that he is strongly hopeful (ἐλπίζω γὰρ Philem. 22) of revisiting Colossae, so that in any case his own words do not forbid us to believe that he revisited the *neighbourhood* of Ephesus, which would be quite sufficient to justify the language of 1 Tim. i. 3. (ii) It is quite perverse to press the words of a presentiment, like that of Acts xx. 25, as if we certainly knew that they were justified by the issue. See Lightfoot, *Biblical Essays*, p. 422.

among scholars, whether they accept or deny the Pauline authorship of the Pastoral letters. The fact is admitted. The
Epistles to Timothy and Titus cannot be fitted into the history
of the *Acts*. But from this admitted fact widely different
inferences have been drawn. Those who accept the *prima
facie* evidence which the Pastoral Epistles afford, urge that
the assumptions underlying them, of St Paul's release from
captivity and his second imprisonment, afford no solid ground for
disputing their authenticity, inasmuch as the whole of St Paul's
life is not told in the *Acts*. If we take them as they stand they
give a quite conceivable though necessarily incomplete picture
of the later history of St Paul. It would be impossible that
they should receive direct verification from the *Acts* or from the
other Pauline letters, for they deal with a later period than do
those books. If they are consistent with themselves, that is all
that can be demanded.

Those, on the other hand, who deny the Pauline authorship of
the Pastorals begin by assuming that St Paul's first imprisonment at Rome under Nero was his only imprisonment, it being
terminated by his death, and that therefore there is no time
available in which we may place our letters. And it is insisted
that, in the absence of additional testimony, the inferential
witness of the Pastorals to a second imprisonment can only be
doubtful. From this the transition is easy to the statement
that such a second imprisonment is *unhistorical*. This is the
judgment of many writers of repute, and must receive detailed
examination. At the outset the criticism is obvious, that such
a method of historical enquiry, if pressed to extremes, would
result in discarding all documentary evidence for which direct
corroboration could not be produced ; and such procedure can
hardly be called scientific. Unless there is some better reason
for discarding the Pauline authorship of the Pastoral Epistles
than the reason that they tell us of events in his life, which,
without them, we should not know, they may still continue to
rank as authentic. It is not a sound maxim of law that a
single witness must necessarily mislead. But it is worth our
while to ask, Is there any corroboration forthcoming of the

testimony of the Pastoral letters to missionary labours of St Paul outside the period embraced by the Acts of the Apostles?

In the Epistle to the Philippians, written during his first sojourn in Rome, probably about the year 62 or 63 A.D., St Paul apparently anticipates that his captivity will not be prolonged much further. "I trust in the Lord," he says, "that I myself also shall come unto you shortly" (Phil. ii. 24). And, again, writing to Philemon under the same circumstances he bids him be ready to receive him: "Withal prepare me also a lodging, for I hope that through your prayers I shall be granted unto you" (Philemon 22). No doubt such anticipations might be falsified, but it is worth noticing that the tone of St Paul's letters at this period is quite different from the tone of a letter like 2 *Tim.*, which breathes throughout the spirit of resignation to inevitable martyrdom.

It ought not to be forgotten that there was no reason for anticipating that the issue of an appeal, such as that which St Paul made to Nero when he was brought before Festus (Acts xxv. 11), would be unsuccessful or unfavourable to the prisoner. On hearing the facts King Agrippa said that, had St Paul *not* appealed to the Emperor, his liberty would probably have been assured (Acts xxvi. 32), so little was there that could fairly be counted against him. And, although such appeals to the imperial jurisdiction might involve protracted delays, we cannot but suppose that they were on the whole fairly conducted. The stern justice of the imperial policy was, in large measure, independent of the personal character of the reigning Caesar. And it must be remembered that, although matters were different ten or twenty years later, there would be no question of putting a citizen on his trial merely *for being a Christian*, at as early a date as that of St Paul's first imprisonment in Rome. St Luke represents him as abiding "two whole years in his own hired dwelling," receiving all that visited him, "teaching the things concerning the Lord Jesus Christ with all boldness, none forbidding him" (Acts xxviii. 31). The specification of "two years" seems to indicate that the historian is conscious that at the end of that time a change in St Paul's circumstances was brought about, and this would most naturally be by his release.

St Paul at any rate did not despair of release; nay, at times he expected it. Was it granted to him? As we have seen, the New Testament does not tell us directly. The scanty fragments of information that survive must be gathered from subsequent Christian literature. Now in the letter of Clement, Bishop of Rome, addressed to the Corinthian Church about the year 95, there is a passage bearing on this question which is worthy of our careful attention. "Paul," says Clement (§ 5), "pointed out the prize of patient endurance. After that he had been seven times in bonds, had been driven into exile, had been stoned, had preached in the East and in the West, he won the noble renown which was the reward of his faith, having taught righteousness unto the whole world and having reached the bounds of the West; and when he had borne his testimony before the rulers, so he departed from the world and went unto the holy place." The passage is significant when the date and position of the writer are remembered. St Paul's long sojourn in Rome must have left an abiding impression on the members of the Church there, to whom indeed he had addressed before he saw them one of the most important and closely reasoned of his epistles. And we now find that the Bishop of Rome, writing less than thirty years after St Paul's death, seems to know of trials and adventures of the great Apostle of which we have no record in the New Testament. The phrase "seven times in bonds" may not perhaps be pressed; we do not know of precisely so many imprisonments of St Paul, but it is not impossible that Clement may be speaking in general terms, and the number *seven* serves well to round off a rhetorical sentence. But what is to be made of the phrase "having reached the boundary of the West" (ἐπὶ τὸ τέρμα τῆς δύσεως ἐλθών)? The place where the words were written was Rome, under whose dominion had now come Gaul, Spain, Britain. Rome itself, whatever it might seem to an Asiatic, was certainly not to a Roman the furthest Western limit of the Empire. Clement in this sentence distinctly implies that St Paul extended his missionary labours towards the western boundary of the then civilised world. But it is plain from the history in the *Acts* that he had not travelled further West than Rome before the year 63 A.D. His appeal to Nero was the occasion of his first visit to Italy. And thus it seems that Clement knew of some further journey of St Paul for which a place cannot be found in his life save by supposing that the result of the appeal was that he was set at liberty for a season. Clement's testimony is emphatic. He had the best opportunities for acquainting himself with the facts, and he mentions a journey of St Paul to the utmost limit of the West, not as if it were a little known expedition, but as if, on the contrary, it were one not needing fuller description in the summary that he is giving to the Corinthians of the labours of the Apostle of the Gentiles. Clement, then, is a witness for the release of St Paul from his first imprisonment.

What locality is meant by "the boundary of the West"? Whatever the phrase means, as we have seen, it must have reference to a place west of Italy. But we may bestow upon it a little closer scrutiny. The most natural meaning of the phrase τὸ τέρμα τῆς δύσεως in the first century would be the Pillars of Hercules at the Straits of Gibraltar, as Lightfoot has shewn[1] by quotations from Strabo and Velleius Paterculus; and if this be what Clement meant to convey, it indicates a visit of St Paul to Spain. Now we are not without evidence that such a visit was both planned and undertaken by St Paul. Writing to the Romans as far back as the year 58, he says (xv. 23, 24): "having these many years a desire to come unto you, whensoever I go unto Spain"; and again, "I will go on by you unto Spain" (xv. 28). There was, then, the intention in his mind to proceed, as soon as he could, from Rome to Spain, and there is every probability that if opportunity were given him he would carry out the intention.

There is, however, in Christian literature no direct assertion, for more than a century after St Paul's death, that such a visit to Spain was actually paid. Perhaps the earliest corroboration of Clement's hint is found in the interesting catalogue of books of

---

[1] *St Clement of Rome*, II. 30.

the New Testament, which is called, from the name of its discoverer, the Muratorian fragment on the Canon. The date of this is somewhere about the end of the second century; and the writer distinctly mentions a journey of Paul to Spain, although in a passage which is so corrupt that its meaning is not quite certain[1]. Like Clement, the author of the Muratorian fragment was probably a Roman; so that he had whatever benefit might be derived from local traditions about St Paul.

As we go later, the story becomes quite common. Quite a number of fourth and fifth century writers assert that St Paul visited Spain; and a still larger number speak of his release from captivity and his subsequent missionary labours, although they do not mention the quarter of the world which witnessed them[2]. Eusebius, for instance, one of the most trustworthy of these writers, introduces a probably erroneous interpretation of a verse in 2 *Tim.* by saying that "Report has it" (ὁ λόγος ἔχει) that St Paul's martyrdom took place on his second visit to Rome. But it does not seem safe to place reliance on any of

[1] The passage in Zahn's transcript reads as follows:

acta autem omniu*m* apostolorum
sub uno libro scribta sunt lucas obtime theofi-
le conprindit quia sub praesentia eius singula
gerebantur sicuti et semote passione*m* petri
euidentur declarat sed et profectione*m* pauli
ab urbe ab spaniam proficiscentis.

Zahn emends this so that the meaning will be that while Luke tells in the *Acts* the things of which he was a personal witness, he does *not* tell of the Martyrdom of Peter or of Paul's journey from Rome to Spain. This seems to be the best interpretation of the passage. But, on *any* interpretation, it is plain that the Muratorian writer had heard of this Spanish visit. It is probable, indeed (see James, *Apocrypha Anecdota*, II. xi.), that this writer derives some of his information, including this very point, from the Leucian *Actus Petri cum Simone*, which begin with the *profectio Pauli ab urbe in Spaniam*, and end with the *passio Petri*. These Acts, in their present form, are of uncertain date; but the latest date which is possible for them is the second half of the second century. Thus the argument in the text is not affected, if Dr James' theory of the sources of the Muratorian fragment be adopted; for we are then certain that the Muratorian writer is not inventing but borrowing from an older (apocryphal) document.

[2] See, for references, Lightfoot, *Biblical Essays*, pp. 425 f.

these writers.   There is no evidence that they were possessed of any information that we have not got; and most of them were quite capable of building up a superstructure of history on the verse in the Epistle to the Romans which speaks of St Paul's intention to go to Spain.   It would be easy to infer loosely from this, and state as a fact, that he did go.

To sum up, then, the results to which we have been led so far. We can find no place for the Pastorals in the life of St Paul as recorded in the *Acts*.   If they are genuine letters of his we must suppose that he was released from his first captivity at Rome, spent some years in missionary enterprise in the East and West, was again imprisoned at Rome, and met his death by martyrdom, the Second Epistle to Timothy containing the last words that he has for the Church.   There is nothing in any way inconsistent with any known fact in this supposition; it was put forward as history by the most competent of Christian scholars in the fourth and fifth centuries, when formal commentaries on Scripture became common.   That St Paul paid a visit to Spain is mentioned as early as the second century in the *Actus Petri cum Simone.*   It is in the highest degree probable that if released he would have done so.   But the only piece of early direct evidence, outside the Pastorals, which we have for a period of activity additional to that described by St Luke is the passage cited from Clement of Rome.

All attempts to reconstruct, from these scanty materials, the life of St Paul after the period covered by the *Acts* must be more or less conjectural.   But it is necessary to indicate the leading points brought out by the evidence, imperfect as it is.

We learn from Phil. ii. 24 and Philemon 22, as has been said, that St Paul proposed to proceed to Macedonia and to the churches of Asia Minor after his release.   We may therefore conclude that his steps were immediately turned eastward, and it is in no way improbable that he should have paid a short visit to Crete about the same time.   If he sailed from Ephesus on his long intended voyage to Spain (Rom. xv. 24, 28), Crete would lie on his way.   Of this voyage and visit we have no detailed knowledge whatever; although it probably lasted for some time.

If we are to translate Γαλατία in 2 Tim. iv. 10 by 'Gaul' (see note *in loc.*), he may have extended his journey to the towns along the Gulf of Lion.

Our next fixed point is that presented in 1 Tim. i. 3. Paul is at Ephesus again; he proceeds to Macedonia (i. 3), and at the moment of writing he intends to return to Ephesus shortly (iii. 14). We do not know the *place* from which this Epistle was written, but that it was from some town in Macedonia seems probable[1].

We then find him at Crete (Tit. i. 5), where he leaves Titus in charge of the infant Church. When he wrote this Epistle, he intended to pass the following winter (Tit. iii. 12) in Nicopolis (probably the city in Epirus of that name); and the letter was probably despatched from some of the towns on the coast of Asia Minor, which we hear of his visiting on his journey northward.

He is at Miletus (2 Tim. iv. 20) where he leaves Trophimus; he is at Troas (2 Tim. iv. 13) with Carpus; and then passes through Corinth (2 Tim. iv. 20). Not improbably he was arrested here and carried to Rome, his intention of going to Nicopolis being frustrated. Titus, who had been invited to Nicopolis (Tit. iii. 12), is with him at Rome for a time (2 Tim. iv. 10), but has left for Dalmatia when the Second Epistle to Timothy is written.

So far the Pastoral Epistles. Tradition adds one more fact, and that a kind of fact as to which its witness is hardly to be gainsaid, viz. in respect of the place and circumstances of St Paul's death. The concurrent testimony of many writers affirms that he ended his life by martyrdom at Rome, being beheaded under Nero. To Paul's martyrdom Clement (§ 5) is a witness, and, as Bishop of Rome, his testimony is peculiarly weighty. Tertullian[2] notes that the Apostle was beheaded, which is likely enough in itself, inasmuch as he was a Roman citizen, to whom the ignominious torture of crucifixion would

---

[1] The 'subscriptions' to the Epistles are of no authority; see note on 1 Tim. vi. 21.

[2] *De Praescr. Haer.* 36.

have been inappropriate. Dionysius of Corinth, writing about 170[1], says that Peter and Paul suffered at Rome "at the same time" (κατὰ τὸν αὐτὸν καιρόν), a perplexing phrase, which however does not necessarily imply that they perished in the same *year*. And Gaius the Roman presbyter[2], who lived about the year 200, mentions the grave of Peter on the Vatican and of Paul on the Ostian Way[3]. The force of this testimony is not to be evaded. A Church in whose early progress St Paul was so deeply interested, to which he had addressed the most elaborate and closely reasoned of his letters, many of whose members had been his personal friends—it is impossible to suppose that the tradition of such a Church could be mistaken about an event which must have affected it so deeply.

As to the exact year of St Paul's martyrdom we have no such certainty. We have no express evidence until the 4th century; the 13th year of Nero is the date registered by Eusebius in his Chronicle[4], and Jerome puts it a year later[5]. That is to say, according to these writers the date of St Paul's death is 67 or 68 A.D. There is nothing improbable in itself in this date. It is true that the great outbreak of persecution at Rome arose in July 64, being caused by the indignation directed against Christians as the supposed incendiaries; and the language of Clement of Rome (§ 5) suggests (though it does not explicitly assert) that it was in *this* persecution that Paul suffered. But it would be a grave mistake to suppose that persecution of Christians was not heard of again during Nero's reign. On the contrary it seems from that time forth to have been a standing matter, like the punishment of pirates or of brigands, to which Mommsen compares it. There would be nothing unusual or extraordinary in the execution of Christian believers at Rome in any year after that in which suspicion was directed to them on account of their alleged share

---

[1] ap. Euseb. *H. E.* II. 25.   [2] *Ib.*

[3] The concluding chapter of the *Acts of Paul* (see above p. xiii note) relates the return of Paul to Rome, and his martyrdom by decapitation at the hands of Nero. This early *apocryphon* implies at least a release of the Apostle from his first Roman imprisonment, and a further missionary journey.

[4] *Chr. Ann.* 2083.   [5] *Cat. Script. Eccl.* s.v. Paulus.

in the destruction of the city. Thus St Paul's martyrdom is quite as credible in the year 68 as in the year 64, although it is only of the persecutions of the earlier year that we possess a full account.

According to the received chronology, then, St Paul's death took place in 68 A.D., his first Roman imprisonment being terminated by release in the year 63. And this leaves a period of five years of which the only record in the N.T. is that to be found in the Pastoral Epistles[1]. The notices of St Paul's life found therein are in conflict with no known facts, and they are consistent with themselves. When we remember that admittedly apocryphal Pauline letters, such as the so-called Third Epistle to the Corinthians, invariably go astray when they deal with events and individuals, we find in this consistency a significant note of truth.

Further than this we cannot go with the evidence before us; but it is not too much to say that, if the only objections to the genuineness of the Pastoral Epistles were derived from the novelty of the information that they give as to the life of St Paul, there would be very little question as to their authorship. The really grave objections to them are based on their style and language, and these with kindred matters must now be considered in some detail.

---

[1] Mr Turner has recently discussed afresh the whole subject of the Chronology of St Paul's life (s.v. "Chronology" in Hastings' *Bible Dictionary*). He concludes that A.D. 62 is the true date of the end of the First Roman Captivity, and he accepts Clement's testimony to St Paul's martyrdom in the great persecution under Nero, which began in July 64 (Harnack takes the same view as to the date of the martyrdom). He thinks that Eusebius only worked backwards by means of the papal lists, and that he had no independent tradition for assigning the year 67 for the deaths of Peter and Paul. If Mr Turner's conclusions be adopted, we should have a period of two years only between the first and second imprisonments of Paul. This, however, would be a quite long enough period to contain the events recorded in the Pastorals and a journey to the West as well; and thus the argument in the text holds good.

CHAPTER III.

Adopting the received chronology, we must place the Second Epistle to Timothy, if genuine, in the year 68; for that letter purports to be written from Rome while St Paul was waiting for his end. It contains his last words to his friend and disciple, his son in the faith. And the First Epistle to Timothy and the Epistle to Titus cannot have been written many months before, for they allude to long journeys undertaken after St Paul's release in 63, which had been brought to a successful issue before the time of writing. We can thus hardly date either of these letters before 67. The marked similarities indeed between our three epistles, in respect alike of subject-matter and of style, forbid us to place any long interval between their several dates.

The Pastoral Letters constitute then a distinct group, differing from the other groups of Pauline Letters in various particulars. The following are the main points which it will be necessary to bear in mind. (1) They are addressed to individuals, not, like all the other letters (save the brief note to Philemon), addressed to Churches. (2) They were written some (possibly four or five) years later than any other letter from St Paul's hand, which has come down to us. (3) These intervening years were years of varied experience and of travel in many lands. It was in this period that, according to Clement, St Paul visited "the utmost limit of the West." These facts help us to meet the most serious difficulty in the way of accepting the Pastoral Epistles as genuine. Nothing has yet appeared in the course of our investigation which gives fair cause for suspicion; but it must now be pointed out that our three letters differ widely in point of vocabulary and style from the other letters which bear the name of Paul.

I. In each group of St Paul's writings, as in the writings of most authors, we find a number of words which he does not use elsewhere; but this tendency to a different vocabulary is especially marked in the Epistles to Timothy and Titus. It has been computed[1] that the number of words in the Pastoral Epistles which occur nowhere else in the New Testament is 176, a proportionately larger number of ἅπαξ λεγόμενα than we find in the earlier letters of St Paul. They are of all kinds; some, common Greek words, the use or neglect of which would depend largely on a man's peculiarities of style or the circumstances of his life; some, uncommon and curious, which might or might not come within his range of knowledge.

First, it is worth while to examine the value of such arguments in general. There are 77 *hapax legomena* in 1 *Tim.*, 49 in 2 *Tim.*, and 29 in *Titus* (all such words are indicated by an asterisk in the *Index Graecitatis* at the end of this volume). Mr Workman[2] has shewn that this means for *Titus* and 1 *Tim.* that there are 13 *hapax legomena* for every page of Westcott and Hort's edition, the figure for 2 *Tim.* being 11. In the case of the other epistles the figures become: Philippians 6·8, Colossians 6·3, 2 Corinthians 6·0, Ephesians 4·9, 1 Corinthians 4·6, Romans 4·3, 1 Thessalonians 4·2, Galatians 4·1, Philemon 4, 2 Thessalonians 3·6. Now this shews at once that the number of unusual words in the Pastorals is proportionately twice as great as in any other of St Paul's letters, and three times as great as in most of them. Upon this remarkable fact, Mr Workman makes two very interesting observations. (i) It appears from the figures that, speaking broadly, there are more *hapax legomena* in the later epistles than in the earlier ones, a circumstance which may be observed in the writings of many authors. As a man gains experience as a writer, his command over the language becomes greater, and his vocabulary is less limited to the words in common use among his associates. (ii) If a similar table of "relative frequency of *hapax legomena*" be drawn up for Shakespeare's plays, it is found that the frequency ranges from 3·4 in *The Two Gentlemen of Verona* to 10·4 in *Hamlet*, all

[1] These are the numbers resulting from an examination of the *Index Graecitatis* at the end of this volume. Holtzmann's computation is that there are 146 ἅπαξ λεγόμενα; but he follows a somewhat different method of numeration from ours.

[2] *Expository Times*, June 1896, p. 418. His figures are slightly different from those given above, but the argument remains unaffected.

the other plays lying between these limits. This shews that any argument based on the mere fact that *hapax legomena* occur in very large numbers in any given work must be applied with great caution, and that, indeed, by itself such a fact is no disproof of traditional authorship. Indeed the untrustworthiness of such a line of argument when applied to the particular case of the Pastoral Epistles becomes plain when we reflect that if we push it a little further, we should be driven to conclude that *each* of these epistles is by a different hand, for each has its own list of *hapax legomena*. Yet nothing can be more certainly shewn by internal evidence than that these letters form a group written by the same person about the same time.

Secondly, of the 176 *hapax legomena* which occur in the Pastorals, it must be observed that no less than 78 are found in the LXX. These were, therefore, entirely within St Paul's sphere of knowledge. And of the rest while some are strange words, uncommon or unknown in Greek literature, others are cognate to words elsewhere used by St Paul (e.g. ἀνάλυσις, cp. Phil. i. 23 ; or σώφρων, cp. Rom. xii. 3), or are words which must have been familiar to any educated man of his time. Examples will be given, as they occur, in the notes on the text.

The character of this peculiar vocabulary will be better understood by studying it under the heads suggested by Lightfoot[1]. We have, for instance, a new set of terms to describe moral and religious states; βέβηλος (see on 1 Tim. i. 9), εὐσέβεια and σεμνότης (see on 1 Tim. ii. 2), καλός which occurs with unusual frequency (see on 1 Tim. i. 8). Also a new set of terms relating to doctrine; διδασκαλία which is far more frequent in these letters than generally in St Paul (see on 1 Tim. i. 10), ἐκζήτησις, ζήτησις, μῦθος, λογομαχία, παραθήκη, and ὑγιής and its cognates as applied to doctrine (see on 1 Tim. i. 10). In considering such phenomena as these, we must not forget that the subject-matter of our letters is quite different from that of any other letter of St Paul. Now a difference in subject presupposes a certain change in vocabulary. In speaking of the qualifications of a deacon or a

---

[1] *Biblical Essays*, pp. 401 ff.

presbyter, or of the organisation and discipline of the early Christian communities, the writer is moving in a different ecclesiastical atmosphere from that of the days when he had to contend with opponents who counted the Jewish synagogue the only doorway of the Church. He has done with Judaism. He now recognises the existence of a distinctively Christian theology and the possibility of its development whether for good or for evil. And such a conception requires the use of words which did not naturally come in his way before. Words after all are only the expression of thoughts; as new thoughts arise in the mind, a new vocabulary is demanded[1].

We come now to consider the traces of liturgical formulae which the Pastorals present, of expressions, that is, which have become stereotyped through usage. Such are the five Faithful Sayings (πιστὸς ὁ λόγος, see on 1 Tim. i. 15), and the rhythmical confession of faith introduced by the words "Great is the mystery of Godliness" (1 Tim. iii. 16). Such passages teach us that at that moment of the Church's life when the letters were written, there had grown up a doctrinal and religious phraseology which would come naturally to the lips of a Christian teacher addressing a well-instructed Christian disciple and friend. By this St Paul would be influenced as much as another man and it is not extravagant to suppose that as time went on he would acquire phrases and words from the use of the society with which he associated which did not form part of his earlier style. The hypothesis which we have found necessary on other grounds, viz. that he spent the years immediately succeeding his release from captivity in wanderings both East and West, renders it in the highest degree probable that his later style would be modified by his more extended experience.

Stress has sometimes been laid on new ways of speaking of

---

[1] Mr Workman points out, in the Essay already cited, that similar phenomena occur in Shakespeare. "*Pulpit* occurs six times in one scene in *Julius Caesar*, and never elsewhere, not even in the Roman plays; *equivocator* four times and *equivocate* twice in the same scene in Macbeth and never elsewhere; *hovel* five times in *King Lear*; *mountaineer* four times in *Cymbeline*; *disposer* four times in *Troilus and Cressida*; *moon calf* five times in the *Tempest*, and so forth."

God, which appear in these letters. He is called e.g. σωτήρ (1 Tim. i. 1), μακάριος (1 Tim. i. 11), δυνάστης (1 Tim. vi. 15). But it is believed that the notes *in loc.* will help to remove the difficulty in these instances; and the like may be said of the use of ἐπιφάνεια for the παρουσία of Christ (see on 1 Tim. vi. 14 and cp. 2 Macc. xiv. 15)[1].

The salutation with which 1 and 2 *Tim.* open, viz. χάρις, ἔλεος, εἰρήνη, is not in the form adopted in all the other epistles ascribed to Paul, which is simply χάρις καὶ εἰρήνη (see on Tim. i. 1). Here, it has been urged, is an indication of a different hand. Such an argument is singularly unconvincing. For all through these investigations we are bound to consider not only the difficulties in the way of ascribing the Pastoral Epistles to St Paul, but the difficulties in the way of counter-hypothesis, viz. that they were forged in his name. Now it is all but certain that a forger would be careful to preserve so obvious a note of Pauline authorship as the salutation common to all his letters. He would not venture to change the familiar "Grace and peace." The one man who would have no scruple in changing his ordinary mode of address would be St Paul himself. The reasons for the change must remain conjectural; but the change itself is rather in favour of the Pauline authorship than against it.

II.   Not only are these traces of a new vocabulary important to notice, but we have also to take account of the absence from the Pastoral Epistles of a large number of familiar Pauline words

---

[1] It is easy to exaggerate the force of verbal coincidences, but a comparison of the vocabulary of the Pastoral Epistles and of the Second Book of the Maccabees shews striking resemblances. Thus God is called in both δυνάστης (1 Tim. vi. 15; 2 Macc. iii. 24, xii. 15), δεσπότης (1 Tim. vi. 1; 2 Macc. xv. 22), ὁ δίκαιος κριτής (2 Tim. iv. 8; 2 Macc. xii. 6); and the following words occur in St Paul's writings *only* in the Pastorals and in the LXX. *only* in 2 *Macc.*: ἀκατάγνωστος (Tit. ii. 8; 2 Macc. iv. 47), ἀνδροφόνος (1 Tim. i. 9; 2 Macc. ix. 28), βυθίζειν (1 Tim. vi. 9; 2 Macc. xii. 4), γυμνάζειν (1 Tim. iv. 8; 2 Macc. x. 15), ἔντευξις (1 Tim. ii. 1; 2 Macc. iv. 8), παρακολουθεῖν (1 Tim. iv. 6; 2 Macc. viii. 11), προδότης (2 Tim. iii. 4; 2 Macc. x. 13), σεμνότης (1 Tim. ii. 2; 2 Macc. iii. 12), στρατιώτης (2 Tim. ii. 3; 2 Macc. xiv. 39), σωφροσύνη (1 Tim. ii. 9; 2 Macc. iv. 37), ὑπόμνησις (2 Tim. i. 5; 2 Macc. vi. 17), φιλανθρωπία (Tit. iii. 4; 2 Macc. vi. 22).

and phrases. Some of these, indeed, could not be expected here. ἀκροβυστία does not occur, but then the controversy about circumcision had gone by ; διαθήκη does not occur, but the idea does not naturally enter into the argument of the Pastorals as it enters into Epistles like *Romans* and *Galatians* which deal with the burning questions about the permanent authority of the Jewish constitution. ἄδικος, ἀκαθαρσία, δικαίωμα, κατεργάζεσθαι, μείζων, μικρός, μωρία, παράδοσις, πείθειν, σῶμα, χαρίζεσθαι, χρηστός, appear in Holtzmann's list of Pauline words not found in the Pastorals, but in each case words cognate to them *are* found in the Pastorals. The other words in his list are hardly numerous enough to be significant, all things being considered ; the most interesting being καυχᾶσθαι and ἀποκαλύπτειν with their cognates, which are very prominent in St Paul's other letters and yet have no place in these.

Against such differences may be fairly set some undoubted resemblances to the earlier letters, to which attention is called in the notes. Holtzmann has endeavoured to minimise the significance of these by urging that the Pastorals agree better as to vocabulary with the Epistles of the Third Missionary Journey than with the Epistles of the First Captivity ; but, not to speak of the fact that the letters are all too short to permit of such arguments being regarded as trustworthy, the resemblances with *Philippians* (which is not improbably the last written of the letters of the First Captivity and therefore the nearest in time to the Pastorals) are unmistakeable[1]; cp. ἀνάλυσις (2 Tim. iv. 6) and ἀναλύειν (Phil. i. 23), σπένδεσθαι (2 Tim. iv. 6 ; Phil. ii. 17), σεμνός (1 Tim. iii. 8, and in St Paul only at Phil. iv. 8 outside the Pastorals), κέρδος (Tit. i. 11; Phil. i. 21), προκοπή (1 Tim. iv. 15; Phil. i. 12, 25).

III.   We pass to differences of syntax and structure of sentences. These, if present, would afford far better grounds for declaring in favour of difference of authorship than do differences of vocabulary. And there are a considerable number of such differences. The absence of connecting particles such as ἄρα,

---

[1] Cp. *Speaker's Comm.* on Philippians, p. 591.

διό, διότι (we have δι᾽ ἣν αἰτίαν three times, a form which does not
occur in any of the other Pauline writings), ἔπειτα, ἔτι, and many
others enumerated by Holtzmann, is curious, for St Paul is very
fond of connecting sentences together by means of such. The
sentences of the Pastorals are more rigidly constructed than
in the earlier letters, and the style has less of their ease and un-
conventionality. The prepositions ἀντί, ἄχρι, ἔμπροσθεν, παρά
with the accusative, and (a remarkable singularity) σύν are
never once used in our epistles[1]. The definite article is used
very sparingly. All this is very puzzling on any hypothesis.

Possibly the most plausible explanation that has yet been
offered of these differences between the earlier and the later
letters is that they are due to the employment after St Paul's
first captivity of a new amanuensis. That it was the Apostle's
habit to avail himself of such assistance we know (see Rom. xvi.
22; 1 Cor. xvi. 21; Gal. vi. 11; Col. iv. 18; 2 Thess. iii. 17); and
we can readily imagine that whoever wrote the Pastoral Letters
for him may have introduced some peculiarities of phrase and
diction, such as would have been foreign to the style of Tertius
(Rom. xvi. 22) or any former secretary.

At the same time, we must not exaggerate these differences
between the style of the Pastorals and that of the earlier letters.
The Pauline fashion of repeating and playing on a word appears
several times (1 Tim. i. 18, vi. 5, 6; 2 Tim. ii. 9, iii. 4, 17).
Sentences are strung together sometimes until grammar is lost,
quite in the Apostle's old manner, e.g. 1 Tim. i. 10; Titus i. 1—3
(cp. Eph. i. 3, iii. 1; Col. i. 3 ff.). It would not be easy, for
instance, to find a sentence more Pauline in its involved parenthesis and in its rough vigour than the following from 2 Tim. i.
8—11, "Suffer hardship with the gospel according to the power
of God: who saved us and called us with a holy calling, not
according to our works, but according to his own purpose and
grace, which was given us in Christ Jesus before times eternal,
but hath now been manifested by the appearing of our Saviour
Christ Jesus, who abolished death, and brought life and incorruption to light through the gospel, whereunto I was appointed a

---

[1] See note on Tit. iii. 15 *infra.*

herald, and an apostle, and a teacher." Again St Paul's thoughts often seem to travel so fast that they outstrip his powers of expression; there is in his confessedly genuine writings a marked tendency to leave sentences unfinished, to the occurrence of the figure which grammarians call *anacoluthon*. This is hardly a peculiarity that would occur to anyone writing in his name to reproduce; still less is it likely that a forger (and, if the Pastorals be not by St Paul, their author was nothing else, however well-intentioned) would *begin* a letter with an *anacoluthon*. And yet so one of the letters opens. The first sentence after the saluta-tion in 1 *Tim.* has no end; it is imperfect and ungrammatical. This is not a probable beginning to an epistle laboriously constructed by a literary artist simulating the manner of another. If the syntax and structural form of the letters be appealed to on the one side, they may also be appealed to on the other.

Such are some of the reasons which tend to diminish the force of the argument based on vocabulary and style. If there are traces of fresh experience in the language employed by the writer of these letters, that is what might have been expected; and it must not be forgotten that in many particulars the agree-ment with Pauline usage is remarkably close.

This topic of internal evidence may be examined from another point of view. If the letters were not written by St Paul, they must have been written by some one thoroughly imbued with his style and possessed of considerable insight into his ways of thinking. It is conceivable that the idea might have occurred to some enterprising person to compose letters in the name of the great Apostle with the laudable object of placing on an undis-puted basis the edifice of Church organisation. But as we read the Second Epistle to Timothy we can hardly persuade ourselves that it was so produced. The many personal salutations and references to slight incidents at the end of the letter are quite too lifelike to have been introduced for the sake of artistic effect. Even supposing that the minute knowledge which is displayed of St Paul's friends and associates does not point to anything more than intimate acquaintance on the part of the writer with the history of St Paul's last days at Rome, are we to admit that touches like the request that Timothy would not forget to bring with him the cloak and books that had been left behind at Troas (2 Tim. iv. 13) could have been due to a forger? Such a request is founded on no recorded incident, nor does it lead to any result. Or again, can the twice repeated "Do thy diligence to come shortly unto me" (2 Tim. iv. 9, 21) have any other explanation than that of the eager anxiety of the writer to see once more his best beloved son in the faith? Or to take one other instance which, curiously enough, has been appealed to by those who find indications of the spuriousness of our letters in their internal evidence. In the first letter to Timothy (iv. 12) the advice is given, "Let no man despise thy youth"; and again in the second letter (ii. 22), "Flee youthful lusts[1]." And all through both letters Timothy is addressed in language savouring somewhat of distrust and misgiving. All this, it has been said, implies that the writer conceives of Timothy as a very young man, young enough to be led away by passion, so young that he finds his legitimate authority difficult to enforce. And this is inconsistent not only with his implied position as head of an important Church, but also with the fact that he could not well have been less than 30 years old in the year 68, his association with St Paul having extended over 13 years. Here, it is urged, is an impossible use of language. The forger has but a confused notion of Timothy's age, and thinks of him at one moment as he is represented in the *Acts*, at another as old enough to be entrusted with the supervision of the Ephesian Church. It makes us view all arguments based on internal evidence with some suspicion when we find that a passage which to another is a token of spuriousness seems to ourselves a manifest note of genuineness. For it displays but a small experience of life and little knowledge of human nature to be surprised that an old and masterful man writing to one who had been his pupil and associate for thirteen years should continue to address him as if he were a youth. Timothy was, as a matter of fact, young for the responsible post which he filled; at this early period there were of necessity appointments of this sort; and St Paul's language

---

[1] See notes *in loc.* in each case.

might be justified from this point of view. And furthermore, the suspicion (underlying both letters) of Timothy's possible lapses into folly, whether it were well founded or not, is exactly what we might conjecture as present to the mind of the older man (see on 2 Tim. i. 6). He had seen Timothy grow up as it were; and to him therefore Timothy will for ever be in a condition of pupilage, needing the most minute directions on points of detail, likely to make false steps as soon as he begins to stand alone, not free from the hotheadedness which perhaps might have been his failing ten years before. To find in these directions, in this undercurrent of thought, anything but the most natural and affectionate anxiety is to display a perverted ingenuity.

The note of truth which appears in passages similar to those which have just been cited is so conspicuous that many critics[1], who, for various reasons, find it impossible to advocate the genuineness of the Pastoral Epistles as a whole, have put forward the hypothesis that in these interesting relics of an early Christian period are embedded precious fragments of true letters of St Paul. The hypothesis is not inconceivable in itself; but it is not easy to work out satisfactorily in detail, and it has not a shred of external evidence in its favour. Certainly the presence of such passages as 2 Tim. i. 15—18, iv. 13, 19—21, which fall in naturally with their context, makes it extremely difficult to doubt the genuineness of that epistle as a whole. And if 2 *Tim.* be from the hand of St Paul, it carries 1 *Tim.* and *Tit.* with it, to a very high degree of probability. It cannot be said that the attempts which have been made to dismember 1 *Tim.* are very convincing[2]; nor is there any general agreement among those who indulge in such critical exercises as to the passages that are to be counted genuine remains of St Paul.

[1] E.g. Credner, Ewald, von Soden, Knoke, Harnack, to mention only representative names.

[2] One of the most carefully considered of these analyses, that of Knoke, postulates three documents behind 1 Tim.; viz. (a) a private letter of instruction from Paul to Timothy, (b) a doctrinal letter, (c) fragments of a manual of Church Order. The reader may exercise his own ingenuity in determining how the dissections are to be made.

The result of the foregoing discussion may be thus summarised. The internal character of the Pastoral Epistles, their vocabulary and their style, presents a very perplexing literary problem. The peculiarities of vocabulary have not yet received full explanation. But, on the whole, these peculiarities are not of so anomalous a character as to outweigh the strong external testimony (see Chap. I.) to the Pauline authorship of the letters, supported as it is by the significant personal details in which the letters abound. The solution of our difficulties perhaps lies in facts of which we have no knowledge. We have already suggested (p. xli) that the employment of a new secretary by St Paul during his second imprisonment at Rome might account for a good many of the linguistic peculiarities which these Epistles present. No doubt this is only an hypothesis; but it is an hypothesis which contradicts no known facts, and, inasmuch as it serves to coordinate the phenomena, it deserves to be taken into serious consideration.

CHAPTER IV.

THE HERESIES CONTEMPLATED IN THE PASTORAL EPISTLES.

No discussion of the characteristics of the Pastoral Epistles would be complete which omitted to take notice of the warnings against heretical teachers with which the letters abound. The growth of vain, or irrelevant and useless, doctrine seems to have been present to the mind of the writer as a pressing danger to the Church; and he recurs again and again to the more prominent features of the teaching which he deprecates, that he may remind Timothy and Titus how serious is their danger when brought into contact with it. The Pastoral Epistles are, however, not controversial treatises; they are semi-private letters written for the guidance of friends. And thus it is not easy to discover the exact nature of the heresies that were prevalent at Ephesus and at Crete. The allusions are casual; and our knowledge of the conditions of Christian thought in the later

Apostolic and sub-Apostolic age is so imperfect, that it is not possible to arrive at conclusions more than probable on this and many kindred questions. In a former epistle of St Paul, the Epistle to the Colossians, we have a somewhat similar polemic directed against the innovating teachers at Colossae ; and it is possible that we may find in the earlier document hints by which we may interpret the latter. And, on the other hand, the letters of Ignatius written half a century later contain warnings against the strange doctrines then spreading in the cities of Asia Minor, which may perhaps shew us what the fruit was like of the seed which we see growing in the Pastoral Epistles.

But we shall begin by interrogating our epistles themselves, and then we may compare their witness with the information gained from other sources.

We notice first the direct advice which St Paul gives to Timothy and Titus as to the manner of their own teaching. They are not to teach anything new, in view of the new developments in the Churches entrusted to their care ; but they are to reiterate the doctrine that the Church has held from the beginning. "Abide thou in the things which thou hast learned and hast been assured of" (2 Tim. iii. 14). "Hold the pattern of sound words" (2 Tim. i. 13). "Guard that which is committed unto thee" (1 Tim. vi. 20). Positive statement of the main principles of the faith is suggested as the best safeguard against error. And such methods of meeting perversions of the truth seem to have been specially applicable to the circumstances of the Churches for whose benefit the Pastoral Epistles were written. For it will be observed that all through the epistles it is not so much the falsity as the irrelevance of the new teaching that is insisted on. The opponents of Timothy and Titus do not come before us, save perhaps in one particular to which we shall return, as openly denying any cardinal article of the Christian Creed. They are not represented, for instance, as are the heretics of the days of Ignatius, as denying the doctrine of the Incarnation. But the teaching with which they beguile the unwary is quite irrelevant. They are ἑτεροδιδάσκαλοι; their gospel is a 'different Gospel.' Their teachings are 'divers and strange' like those deprecated in another epistle of the Apostolic age, the Epistle to the Hebrews (Heb. xiii. 9). And so St Paul says in reference to them: "Foolish and ignorant questionings refuse" (2 Tim. ii. 23). "Shun foolish questionings...for they are unprofitable and vain" (Tit. iii. 9). The heretical teachers themselves are described as men who "strive about words to no profit" (2 Tim. ii. 14); and their vain talking and "profane babblings" are spoken of more than once (1 Tim. vi. 20; 2 Tim. ii. 16).

This irrelevance in speculation, however, is not merely foolish; it is positively mischievous. The history of religion presents many instances of the intimate connexion between vague and unmeaning theory and absurd or immoral practice. For the inevitable consequence of laying stress in religious matters on topics which have no proper significance in relation to life is that religion ceases to be a trustworthy guide to conduct. Mysticism encourages the ascetic habit in the best and purest souls whom it attracts, and so withdraws them from the discharge of common human duties. And when it has become the property of those whose passions are unruly, it furnishes a cloak for immorality and extravagance of every kind. In both directions St Paul saw the danger of the ἑτεροδιδασκαλία against which he warned Timothy and Titus; but the more immediate danger was that of undue asceticism. "The Spirit saith expressly," he writes, "that in later times some shall fall away from the faith, giving heed" to those who "forbid to marry and command to abstain from meats, which God created to be received with thanksgiving by them that believe and know the truth" (1 Tim. iv. 1—4). And again he declares that "in the last days grievous times will come"; for the result of this unreal religion will be the increase of teachers who "have the form of godliness, but have denied the power thereof" (2 Tim. iii. 1 ff.). "Of these are they that creep into houses, and take captive silly women laden with sins, led away by divers lusts, ever learning, and never able to come to the knowledge of the truth." Such grave irregularities are, as yet, no doubt, in the future; but nevertheless the Apostle is careful to warn Timothy about his own conduct in the presence of undue licence or undue asceticism. "Flee youthful lusts" (2 Tim. ii. 22): "Keep thyself pure" (1 Tim. v. 22); that is essential. But on the other hand do not give any sanction, by your practice to asceticism which may be injurious to health: "Be no longer a drinker of water, but use a little wine for thy stomach's sake, and thine often infirmities" (1 Tim. v. 23).

We have seen that the teaching against which the Pastorals give warning is irrelevant to religion and therefore likely to be mischievous in practice. But we must try to determine its character a little more closely. The heresy—for so we must call it—was essentially Jewish. So much is plainly implied and must be borne in mind. The men "whose mouth must be stopped" are "specially they of the circumcision" (Tit. i. 10). The fables to which no heed is to be given are "Jewish fables" (Tit. i. 14). The opponents against whom Timothy is to be on his guard "desire to be teachers of the law, though they understand neither what they say, nor whereof they confidently affirm" (1 Tim. i. 7). It is the "fightings about the law" that are pronounced in the Epistle to Titus to be "unprofitable and vain" (Tit. iii. 9). Thus, whatever the growth of the heresy may have been like, it had its roots in Judaism. We are not, of course, to confuse these apostles of novelty with the Judaizing opponents whom St Paul had to face in earlier years. There is nothing here of any insistence upon circumcision, or upon the perpetual obligations of the Mosaic law. That is now a thing of the past within the Christian Society. Christianity had won for itself a position independent of Judaism, though no doubt its independence would only be fully appreciated by its own adherents. To the eye of a stranger Christianity was still a Jewish sect. But it was not so counted by Christians themselves. Jewish thought would necessarily influence men brought up in the atmosphere of the synagogue and the temple, but the influence would hardly be consciously felt. And we find that the opposition which Timothy and Titus were to offer to the novel doctrines that were gaining popularity, was suggested not because the doctrines were Jewish, but because they were fabulous and unedifying. "I exhorted thee," writes St Paul to

Timothy, "to tarry at Ephesus,...that thou mightest charge certain men not to teach a different doctrine, neither to give heed to fables and endless genealogies, the which minister questionings rather than a dispensation of God which is in faith" (1 Tim. i. 1—3). So he bids Titus "shun foolish questionings and genealogies" (Tit. iii. 9).

What then are these "genealogies" which the Apostle finds so unfruitful? The answer that has been most commonly given to this question of late years has been found in the peculiar tenets of the Gnostics. It has been supposed that traces of a kind of Judaistic Gnosticism may be found in the Epistle to the Colossians, that it becomes more prominent in the Pastorals, and that we see it in full vigour in the Letters of Ignatius. And no opinion on the condition of parties in the early Church which has the authority of Bishop Lightfoot can be lightly treated, or discarded without the most careful examination. We shall thus have to scrutinise with attention the language of the Pastorals to determine whether it affords sufficient ground for our ascribing the term Gnostic to the frivolous teaching condemned by St Paul.

Of the beginnings of Gnosticism we know very little. We find it fully developed in various forms in the second century, as soon as the Church had become affected by Greek speculation; and there is no serious historical difficulty in the way of supposing it to have been current at Ephesus as early as the year 67. But of direct evidence we have little to produce. The term Gnostic is generally taken to include all those who boast a superior knowledge of spiritual things to that possessed by their neighbours; and the Gnostics of whom history tells us constructed elaborate theories as to the precise relations between God and His universe, as to the origin of evil, as to the various ranks and orders of created beings—theories which repel everyone who now examines them, inasmuch as one feels that they are quite unverifiable where they are not demonstrably unscientific or absurd. It is not necessary to explain how natural was such a development in the religion of Jesus when brought into contact with Greek philosophy; we go on to point out that, however true it is that such teaching was popular fifty years later, there is no certain trace of it in the Pastoral Epistles.

To begin with, it has been acutely pointed out by Weiss that language is used in the Epistle to Titus of the strange teachers which is quite inconsistent with the claims made by the Gnostics with whom history has made us familiar : "They confess that they know God" says St Paul—θεὸν ὁμολογοῦσιν εἰδέναι (Tit. i. 16). For, surely, ὁμολογοῦσιν would be a most inappropriate word to use of the claim to the exceptional and superlative knowledge of the Supreme put forward by Gnostic teachers ; their claim was more than a 'confession,' it was a boast of exclusive privilege. And when we turn to the phrases in the Pastoral Epistles which are supposed distinctively to indicate Gnostic doctrine, we find that they afford but an insecure basis for any such opinion, and that in every case a more natural explanation is suggested by the Jewish roots and affinities of the teaching under consideration. "Shun genealogies and strifes and fightings about the law," says St Paul (Tit. iii. 9), "for they are unprofitable." "Do not give heed to myths and endless gene-alogies which minister questionings" (1 Tim. i. 4). Now the close association in the former passage of the γενεαλογίαι with μαχαὶ νομικαί, 'fightings about the law,' should of itself teach us that here is no thought of long strings of emanations of æons or angels, such as Irenæus speaks of in later days, but some specu-lation intimately allied to Judaism. And Dr Hort[1] seems to have pointed out the true explanation. 'Myths and genealogies' occur in similar close connexion in Polybius (IX. 2. 1) ; and the historian seems to refer to the legendary Greek mythologies, and the old world stories about the pedigree and birth of heroes. So too Philo includes under τὸ γενεαλογικόν all the primitive history in the Pentateuch. And we know that legends had been multi-plied during the later periods of Hebrew history as to the patriarchs and the early heroes in a degree for which there is, perhaps, no parallel elsewhere. One branch of the Haggadah, or illustrative commentary on the Old Testament, was full of such legend; and traces of Jewish Haggadoth have been found by

[1] *Judaistic Christianity*, pp. 135 ff.

some in the canonical books themselves. In the curious production called the *Book of Jubilees* we have a conspicuous proof of the stress laid upon genealogies as the bases upon which legends might be reared[1]. Indeed the care with which family pedigrees were preserved is illustrated by the remarkable genealogies incorporated in two of the Gospels. There were, to be sure, special reasons why these should be counted of deep interest for Christians ; but the fact that genealogies were regarded as appropriate subjects for curious and respectful enquiry may be established from many other sources. When the Pastoral Letters, then, tell us that genealogies and strifes about the law and foolish questionings formed part of the stock in trade of the new teachers, we are not led to think of any specially Greek lines of speculation, but of Hebrew legend and casuistry.

Once more, the " oppositions of the knowledge falsely so called " (1 Tim. vi. 20) have been supposed to have reference to certain peculiar tenets of Gnosticism. And it is true that a Gnostic teacher, Marcion, nearly a century later published a book entitled ἀντιθέσεις, "Oppositions of the Old and New Testaments"; and equally true that the phrase ψευδώνυμος γνῶσις is used by the Fathers of the second and third centuries as having special applicability to the controversies in which they were themselves interested. But such coincidences are merely verbal. The fact that the orthodox of later times caught up a phrase of St Paul which might serve as a convenient missile to hurl at adversaries is a fact not so entirely without parallel in later days that it need cause us to delay long over its explanation. And in truth, the phrase would be quite inapplicable to Marcion, who (despite his general description as a Gnostic) did not claim the possession of γνῶσις in any marked degree. However, it is only here needful to point out that a quite natural explanation of the phrase ἀντιθέσεις τῆς ψευδωνύμου γνώσεως follows from the

---

[1] In the curious treatise concerning Jewish antiquities wrongly attributed to Philo (printed in *Mikropresbyticon*, Basle 1550, pp. 295 ff.), a good deal of space is devoted in like manner to an enumeration of the descendants of the antediluvian patriarchs. See *Jewish Quarterly Review* for January, 1898.

conception of the heretical teachers as casuistical doctors of the law, which has just been suggested. 'Antitheses'—oppositions—might well describe "the endless contrasts of decisions, founded on endless distinctions[1]," with which the casuistry of the scribes was concerned. And allusions may be traced in the Gospels themselves to this claim of the scribes to superior γνῶσις ; the lawyers, for instance, were reproached for having taken away the key of knowledge (τῆς γνώσεως, Luke xi. 52).

These are the main features of the heretical doctrine that have been brought forward as suggesting affinities with Gnosticism; but we have found a more natural as well as a more exact correspondence in the speculations of Jewish doctors, and this agrees well with the general description of the heretical myths as Jewish.

It has been urged indeed by Lightfoot and others that the earlier forms of Gnostic error were of Jewish origin; and that all Gnostics were accustomed to treat the Old Testament as a field for mystical speculation. They also took much the same view of the impurity of matter as is hinted at in the Pastorals. And there is no reason for denying that Gnostic doctrine, in the large sense, may have had its roots in teaching such as that described in the Pastorals. It may very possibly have been præ-Christian. But of Gnosticism, properly so called, the Gnosticism of the second century, which was closely allied with Docetic views as to the Person of Christ, there is no distinctive trace ; and thus to use the term 'Gnostic' in reference to the heretical teachers of Ephesus and Crete is somewhat misleading, as it imports into our documents the ideas of a later age. There is nothing whatever specifically Gnostic ; there is much that is best explained as a Jewish development. And although this is not the place to enter on an enquiry as to the heresies treated of in the Epistle to the Colossians, it is probable that the same may be said of them. The φιλοσοφία and vain deceit of which St Paul speaks (Col. ii. 8) is really Jewish speculation which has taken to itself a Greek name ; the angelology of which the

---

[1] *Judaistic Christianity*, pp. 140 ff.

Colossian Epistle tells is Hebrew rather than Greek; the in-junction "let no man judge you in meat and drink" (Col. ii. 16) is of Jewish reference. Here and also in the Pastorals we are dealing with a heretical form of Christianity which arose from contact with Hebrew thought; and when we call it Gnostic we are using a word that has already—whether rightly or wrongly—been appropriated to a different period and has different associations.

There remain to be considered some minor peculiarities of the heretical teachers, which may enable us to fix with greater precision their place in Jewish thought. We are, indeed, not now in Palestine, but in South-west Asia Minor; and it would be rash to assume that the divisions of the Jewish schools which are found in the neighbourhood of Jerusalem are also to be found among the Jews of the Dispersion; but Jews are and always have been so conservative in their habits of thought that such an assumption—though we need not make it—would be at least plausible.

i. The new doctrine seems to have been not only esoteric in character, but exclusive in tendency. All religion which em-phasises unduly subtle distinctions and dogmas only to be apprehended by a learned and cultivated minority tends to spiritual pride and contempt of less favoured individuals. And it is hardly too much to see in the emphatic and prominent directions given by St Paul to Timothy as to the Catholic range of Christian prayer a reference to this growing tendency to spiritual exclusiveness. "I exhort you to make supplications and prayers...for all men....This is good and acceptable in the sight of God our Saviour, who willeth that all men should be saved and come to the knowledge of the truth. For there is one God, one mediator also between God and men, himself man, Christ Jesus" (1 Tim. ii. 4, 5). In earlier epistles (Rom. i. 16, v. 18, x. 12; 2 Cor. v. 15, &c.) St Paul had emphasised the universality of salvation, but in an entirely different context. He formerly had to do with those who were fain to exaggerate the spiritual privilege of the Jew, who claimed for the children of Abraham a monopoly of God's grace. He now has to do with those who are in danger of divorcing the religious from the secular life, and counting the Divine promises as exclusively meant for a few favoured persons.

ii. The Apostle's forecast of trouble conveys a significant warning : "Some shall fall away from the faith, giving heed to seducing spirits and doctrines of devils" (1 Tim. iv. 1). "Evil men and impostors (γόητες) shall wax worse and worse, deceiving and being deceived " (2 Tim. iii. 13). We are not to confuse the predictions of future error with descriptions of that which was actually a present danger ; but nevertheless the germ of the future apostasy lay in the existing disorders. And so it is worth noting that the adherents of the new teaching are described by a name which literally means ' wizards ' (γόητες), those who practise mysterious or magical rites. This harmonises well with what we read in the *Acts* (xix. 19) and elsewhere of the practice of magical arts at Ephesus. Such superstition was no new thing there.

iii. And, lastly, we are given one specific instance of an error of which two at least of the heretical teachers were guilty. "Shun profane babblings," says the Apostle in his last letter, "for they will proceed further in ungodliness, and their word will eat as doth a gangrene : of whom is Hymenæus and Philetus : men who concerning the truth have erred, saying that the resurrection is past already" (2 Tim. ii. 16). Weiss, who is perhaps the most judicious of the commentators on the Pastoral Letters, here warns us that we must not take the perversions of individuals as direct evidence for the general character of the erroneous teaching. And the warning is salutary ; but still it can hardly be doubted that the errors into which Hymenæus and Philetus fell were the outcome of the general principles on which they based their speculations, and that therefore this denial of a resurrection may be counted, if not a necessary, yet a natural accompaniment of the heretical teaching which Timothy had to oppose.

We have then arrived at this point. The heretical teachers at Ephesus and Crete were marked by the following characteristics : (1) They laid much store by irrelevant and unprofitable speculation about the Mosaic law and the Hebrew history. (2) They held views as to the impurity of matter which had already led them to set too high a value on the ascetic life, and which would, in the future, lead to immorality of conduct. (3) The future developments of their tenets would be associated with magic and diabolical arts. (4) They were exclusive in their attitude to their fellow men, and had not fully realised the Universality of the Gospel as revealed in the Fact of the Incarnation. (5) Some of them denied the doctrine of the Resurrection, interpreting it in a spiritual sense of the new life of believers. To sum up, they were professing Christians, but they display Jewish affinities rather than Greek.

Is there any sect of Judaism in which the germ of similar peculiarities may be found? "Speaking of the heresy of the later Epistles," said Bishop Lightfoot[1], "with reference to its position in the Gnostic system, we may call it *Judaic Gnosticism.* Speaking of it with reference to its position as a phase of Jewish thought, we may call it *Essene Judaism.*" We have seen that the first description here given of the heresy prevalent at Ephesus is open to misconception ; we pass on to enumerate the facts which seem to shew that the second suggestion is far more likely to be instructive.

All the peculiarities which have been collected of the heretical teaching contemplated in the Pastorals, save one, are found among the tenets of the Essene brotherhood as described by Josephus and Philo. The Essenes were ascetic to an extraordinary degree[2]; they conceived of themselves as a kind of spiritual aristocracy ; they are said to have possessed an apocryphal literature, and to have practised occult science ; and they spoke of the immortality of the soul rather than of the Resurrection of the Body, here standing in sharp contrast to the more conspicuous sect of the Pharisees. The one point for which direct evidence cannot be adduced is that we do not know that the Essenes devoted any special attention to the Haggadoth or legendary literature of Judaism, though the hint that they possessed secret books is significant. But in any case this feature of Jewish belief, though no doubt more prominent

[1] *Biblical Essays,* p. 416.
[2] See Josephus, *Bell. Jud.* ii. 8. 2 ff. and *Antt.* xviii. 1.

among the learned doctors of the law, would more or less affect all Jewish sects, and there would be nothing in it foreign to the habits of thought of the Essene brotherhood.

We conclude therefore that the heresiarchs at Ephesus and Crete were Christians who were affected by Essene tendencies of thought and practice[1]. This conclusion has been derived from the internal evidence of the Pastoral Epistles, and it falls in with the date which we have assigned to them on other grounds. Were they of a later period we should expect to find the heretical tendencies afterwards called Gnostic much more strongly marked, and the heresies themselves more exactly defined.

CHAPTER V.

BISHOPS AND PRESBYTERS IN THE PRIMITIVE CHURCH.

An investigation of the date of the Pastoral Epistles cannot leave out of account the nature of the ecclesiastical organisation which they seem to contemplate. We must ask ourselves if the stage which the development of the Church's life has reached in them is compatible with their origin in the lifetime of St Paul. And thus we are constrained to attempt here a brief summary of the existing evidence as to the growth of the several orders of the Christian Ministry during the first century of the Church's life. Few questions have been more warmly debated than this, and

[1] There is an additional circumstance, which may be adduced to support this conclusion. Among the fragments of the literature of this period which have survived, not the least remarkable is the Fourth Book of the *Sibylline Oracles*, a curious collection of verses reciting the fortunes of the towns in S.W. Asia Minor, ascribed on all hands to a date about 10 years subsequent to the Fall of Jerusalem. This book—whether written by a Christian or not—has points of contact with Essenism which can hardly be due to chance. Here then we have independent evidence for the influence of Essene teaching about 80 A.D. in the very district which has been the subject of our enquiry. And it is certainly remarkable that the word used all through this poem for the elect or the faithful is a word which is characteristic in the N.T. of the Pastoral Epistles; they are called εὐσεβεῖς, their habit of mind εὐσέβεια.

controversy has run high as to the precise functions of Christian ἐπίσκοποι and πρεσβύτεροι in the Apostolic age. By some the terms are regarded as almost synonyms, and as used in the New Testament to designate the same persons and to describe the same duties ; by others it is held that, while the two terms indicate different functions, yet these functions were discharged by the same individuals[1]; by others, again, it has been argued that from the beginning the ἐπίσκοπος has been distinct from the πρεσβύτερος as regards his duties and his gifts. The decision at which we arrive on these disputed points will necessarily modify and colour our interpretation of several important passages of the Pastoral Epistles, and is inextricably involved in any discussion of their date.

Before beginning the investigation, it may be well to remind ourselves of one or two distinctions that may keep us from confusing the issues. And first, we must not assume without proof that the significance of the Episcopate in the continuous life of the Church is bound up with its monarchical or diocesan character. Such an assumption would be entirely without foundation. For centuries (for example) in the Celtic Church there was a bishop attached to each monastery in subordination to the abbot, possessed of no special temporal dignity or administrative authority, but distinguished from the presbyters among whom he lived solely by virtue of his consecration to the Episcopal office, and by the powers which that consecration was believed to impart. It has never been counted part of the *essentia* of a Christian bishop, that he should exercise any absolute supremacy over the presbyters among whom he is resident. The function of rule is a function which has been accorded to him by the almost universal consent of Christendom, but that his rule should be of a monarchical character or even that he should have a dominating influence in the counsels of the presbyterate is something that would not be easy to establish as an ordinance of the primitive Christian Church. That such functions have been granted to the Episcopate is a matter of history ; that it is highly beneficial

---

[1] Cp. Chrysostom *in Phil.* i. 1 οἱ πρεσβύτεροι τὸ παλαιὸν ἐκαλοῦντο ἐπίσκοποι καὶ διάκονοι τοῦ Χριστοῦ, καὶ οἱ ἐπίσκοποι πρεσβύτεροι.

that they should be exercised—that disobedience to them as an infringement of established order and wholesome discipline is in the highest degree reprehensible—all this may be true. But it does not settle the question as to whether or not these functions belonged to the Episcopate in its earliest days, any more than it nullifies the fact that they were not exercised to any large extent by the bishops of at least one ancient Church.

Secondly, it is to be borne in mind that there is nothing inherently repugnant to the idea of the Christian episcopate in the presence of several bishops at one time in a Christian community. The diocesan idea is one of early growth, it is true ; and it is not hard to see its obvious and many advantages. But again it is not part of the *essentia* of the Episcopate. The Episcopal χάρισμα might be conferred upon several men who happened to be living in one city if the conditions of life in the early Church rendered it desirable that more than one bishop should be available to perform the special duties attaching to the Episcopal office.

And, once more, there is little reason for the assumption often confidently made that the development of the episcopal dignity must have proceeded exactly at the same rate and by the same route in the many widely separated Churches of primitive Christendom. It is entirely a question of evidence. If the evidence teach us that a monarchical Episcopate was developed more slowly in the West than in the East, or that the relations of the bishop or bishops to the presbyters were not always quite the same in all centres of Christian life in the first century, we must be prepared to admit and to interpret it.

Our first enquiry must be, Were there persons called ἐπίσκοποι in the Church of the first century who exercised different functions from the πρεσβύτεροι ? And, secondly, if we are thus to differentiate the ἐπίσκοπος from the πρεσβύτερος, on what facts are we to found our distinction ? What was the original difference in function ?

Primâ facie it would appear that there was some important distinction between them, not only because of the different etymology of the terms, but because the distinction became so soon rooted in the Christian consciousness. When we find that so well instructed a writer as Irenaeus, writing in the last quarter of the second century, not only counts the threefold order of bishop, priest, and deacon as the sole rule for the Church, but seems unconscious that any other rule had ever existed in fact or was possible in theory, we are at once impressed with the antiquity of the offices which he thus regards.

It is well to work backwards in this enquiry, and to start where the evidence is full and indisputable. We begin, then, with Ignatius, whose martyrdom took place *cir.* 115 A.D. The language of his epistles is very remarkable.

"Submit yourselves to the bishop and the presbytery" is the constant burden of his exhortations to the Churches of Asia Minor (*Eph.* 2, *Magn.* 2, *Trall.* 2, 13, *Smyrn.* 8). "As the Lord did nothing without the Father, so neither do ye anything without the bishop and the presbyters" (*Magn.* 7). "Let all men respect the deacons as Jesus Christ, even as they should respect the bishop as being a type of the Father and the presbyters as the council of God and as the college of Apostles. Apart from these there is not even the name of a Church" (*Trall.* 3). "There is one altar, as there is one bishop, together with the presbytery and the deacons my fellow-servants" (*Phil.* 4). It has been pointed out by more than one critic, and the remark seems well founded, that the emphasis laid by Ignatius upon this submission to the ministry in its threefold order is an indication that such submission was not universally practised as a Christian duty when he wrote. If there were no symptoms of insubordination at Ephesus, at Tralles, or at Philadelphia it would not have been natural for him to have dwelt in his letter of farewell on such a point at such length. But although we may not infer from his correspondence that the threefold ministry was as firmly established in the Churches of Asia Minor in his day as it was everywhere in the days of Irenaeus, we must infer that it was recognised there as the existing, though perhaps not the necessarily existing, system of Church rule.

It is remarkable that in Ignatius' letter to the Church of

Rome allusion to the Episcopate is not at all so prominent; unlike the other letters it contains no directions to be obedient to the bishop and the presbytery. It recognises the episcopal office solely by the words "God hath vouchsafed that the bishop from Syria should be found in the West, having summoned him from the East" (*Rom.* 2) and "Remember in your prayers the Church which is in Syria, which hath God for its shepherd in my stead. Jesus Christ alone shall be its bishop—He and your love" (*Rom.* 9). It thus appears that the evidence which Ignatius gives as to the Episcopate in the West and its relation to the presbyterate is not of the same formal and definite character as that which he supplies for the East. It is true at the same time that he speaks elsewhere (*Eph.* 3) of bishops as being settled in the farthest parts of the earth.

Next it is to be observed that, from the allusions made by Ignatius to the Christian ministry in the churches of Asia Minor, it seems that the presbyters constitute a sort of college or council, and are not merely individual ministers working under the sole and direct control of the bishop. Their authority is recognised as well as his. They are indeed to submit to him in reverence, as he tells the Magnesians (§ 3), who seem to have had a young bishop; but it is plain that they have a collective authority resident in their own body, in addition to whatever personal authority they may have had from their ministerial office. "Do all things in concord, the bishop presiding after the likeness of God and the presbyters after the likeness of the council of the Apostles" (§ 6). "Do nothing without the bishop; but be obedient also to the presbytery," he says to the Trallians (§ 2). And the particulars of the bishop's duty as distinct from the duty of the presbyterate, seem to come out most clearly in his letter to Polycarp. "Have a care for union" (§ 1). "Be not dismayed by those that teach strange doctrine, but stand firm" (§ 3). "Neglect not the widows" (§ 4). These three characteristics we shall see in the sequel to be especially significant.

The next witnesses that are to be cited are both of Rome, viz. Hermas and Clement.

Hermas speaks of deacons (*Sim.* 9. xxvi.) who "exercised

their office ill," as persons who "plundered the livelihood of
widows and orphans, and made gain for themselves from the
ministrations which they had received to perform." Their function was evidently concerned with the temporal relief of the poor,
and they had to do with Church money. The bishops he
goes on to speak of in direct connexion with the deacons, and
describes them as "hospitable persons who gladly received
into their houses at all times the servants of God...without
ceasing they sheltered the needy and the widows in their mini-
stration" (*Sim.* 9. xxvii.). It is noteworthy that this relief of
widows, perhaps the administration as opposed to the distribution of alms, has already appeared in Ignatius as one of the prominent parts of the duty of the ἐπίσκοπος. In addition to these,
Hermas knows of a distinct class of persons entrusted with
duties on behalf of the Church, of a very serious character.
He speaks in one place (*Vis.* 3. v.) of "Apostles and bishops and
teachers and deacons who...exercised their office of bishop and
teacher and deacon in purity...some of them already fallen on sleep
and others still living." Leaving on one side the *Apostles*, who
only continued for one generation, we have in addition to *bishops*
and *deacons*, *teachers*. And we hear of them again (*Vis.* 3. ix.) :
"I say unto you that are rulers of the Church, and that occupy
the chief seats (τοῖς προηγουμένοις τῆς ἐκκλησίας καὶ τοῖς πρωτο-
καθεδρίταις),...be not ye like the sorcerers... How is it that ye
wish to instruct the elect of God while ye yourselves have no
instruction ?" The persons who instruct are then, for Hermas,
in a position of rule. Who are they? Hear him again. The
little book that is written by Hermas in *Vis.* 2. iv. is to be read to
the people of the city of Rome by himself and by "the presbyters
who preside over the Church" (τῶν πρεσβυτέρων τῶν προΐστα-
μένων τῆς ἐκκλησίας). One copy of the little book is to be sent
to Clement (the bishop of Rome at this time), and it is notable
that then come the words, "He is to send it to the foreign cities,
for this is his duty." The special function of the bishop in this
matter is that of communication with other Churches (as above
we have seen it to be the entertainment of strangers); the special
function of the presbyters is to teach, and they have also (as in

Ignatius) certain ruling powers, they preside over the Church. This is the sum of the evidence of Hermas.

It is not too much to say that neither the language of Ignatius nor of Hermas would lead us to infer that the offices of the ἐπίσκοπος and the πρεσβύτερος were identical. So far they seem clearly enough defined, though the evidence is too scanty to enable us to learn in what relation the bishop stood as regards ruling power to the council of the presbyterate, or whether he always stood in the same relation.

We now come to the letter of Clement of Rome[1], the evidence of which as to the position of the ἐπίσκοπος as compared with that of the πρεσβύτερος happens to be peculiarly hard to interpret. The first passage to be cited is from § 42.

"The Apostles received the Gospel for us from the Lord Jesus Christ; Jesus Christ was sent forth from God. So then Christ is from God, and the Apostles from Christ. Both therefore came of the will of God in the appointed order....Preaching everywhere in country and town, they appointed their first-fruits, when they had proved them by the Spirit, to be bishops and deacons unto them that should believe. And this they did in no new fashion; for indeed it had been written concerning bishops and deacons from very ancient times; for thus saith the Scripture in a certain place, *I will appoint their bishops in righteousness and their deacons in faith*" (Is. lx. 17). This passage shews at the least that Clement (and his correspondents, for he does not argue the point as if it were one that could be disputed) held that the institution of bishops and deacons in the Christian Church was of Apostolic origin. He then proceeds (§ 44): "And our Apostles knew...that there would be strife over the name of the

---

[1] This document does not, indeed, purport to come from any individual, but from "the Church of God which sojourneth in Rome to the Church of God which sojourneth in Corinth." The true inference to be derived from this mode of address, when we remember the universal and early ascription of the letter to Clement, is that he occupied a position in the Roman Church which justified him in speaking on her behalf in communications with another Christian community. And this position, as we should gather from Hermas, would naturally be that of bishop which the tradition of early ages assigned to him.

bishop's office. For this cause, therefore...they appointed the aforesaid persons [sc. bishops and deacons], and afterwards they gave a further injunction, that if these should fall asleep, other approved men should succeed to their service. These therefore who were appointed by them or afterward by other men of repute, with the consent of the whole Church," he goes on, in reference to the schism which was the occasion of his letter, "these men we consider to have been unjustly thrust out from their service (λειτουργία). For it will be no light sin in us, if we thrust out of the bishop's office those who have offered the gifts unblameably and holily." So far Clement's witness is clear enough. He objects to the irregular removal from the bishop's office at Corinth of some regularly-appointed men. And two things seem to be fairly inferred from his language :—(1) that there were several bishops in the Corinthian Church at the time, i.e. that the monarchical episcopate was not yet established there ; and (2) that a special function of the bishop was "to offer the gifts" (προσφέρειν τὰ δῶρα). That is, in all probability, the function of the persons here called ἐπίσκοποι was to offer the alms and other gifts (including the elements) at the Eucharistic celebration. Their service is a λειτουργία ; this function is performed by them in the name of the whole Church. The next sentence contains the *crux* of the passage. "Happy are those presbyters who have gone before, seeing that their departure was fruitful and ripe ; for they have no fear lest anyone should remove them from their appointed place. For we see that ye have displaced certain persons, though they were living honourably, from the service (λειτουργίας) which they had respected blamelessly." Are we to say, on the strength of this passage, that the terms πρεσβύτεροι and ἐπίσκοποι are used interchangeably by Clement ?

That is the inference adopted by Lightfoot and many other writers. But it does not seem to be by any means certain that this is involved in Clement's words. Before we examine them more closely we shall turn back to § 40 of the Epistle. Clement is there illustrating the importance of Church order by an appeal to the O.T. dispensation ; and he uses language which suggests that he had a threefold ministry in his mind. "Unto the high priest," he says, "his proper services (λειτουργίαι) have been given, and to the priests their proper place (τόπος) is assigned, and upon the Levites their proper ministrations (διακονίαι) are laid. The layman (ὁ λαϊκὸς ἄνθρωπος) is bound by the layman's ordinances." We may not press this passage so as to urge that it indicates a single bishop, as there was only a single high-priest under the Hebrew religion; but it certainly seems that the application of the term λειτουργία to the first-mentioned Church officer, and of the term διακονία to the third, fixes the sense of the analogy, and entitles us to see here Clement's recognition of a distinction between ἐπίσκοποι and πρεσβύτεροι. The function of the one is described as a λειτουργία; the office of the other as a τόπος.

What duties came within the presbyteral τόπος? That for Clement, as for Hermas, the duty of *rule* belongs to the presbyters seems plain from §§ 54, 57. They constitute the body to which the rebels are exhorted to submit, and with which they should be at peace. And forming, as they do, the supreme authority in matters of discipline we naturally look among them for the 'men of repute' by whom 'with the consent of the whole Church' lawful bishops are appointed (§ 44). To make these appointments is, in fact, an important part of their duty. It is thus plain why the schism which occasioned Clement's letter is described as a "sedition against the presbyters" (§ 47). Certain ἐπίσκοποι had been thrust out from their functions at the instigation of two or three agitators (§§ 1, 47). But this was an invasion of the presbyteral prerogative. The right of deposition cannot belong to a less authoritative body than that which has the right of appointment. And that such irregular proceedings should have been acquiesced in by any considerable number of the faithful would naturally be most grievous to the presbyters whose place (τόπος) had been usurped.

In the light of these considerations let us read again the concluding words of § 44. "Happy are those presbyters who have gone before...for they have no fear lest anyone should remove them from their appointed place (τόπος). For we see that *ye* (ὑμεῖς, with special emphasis) have displaced certain persons from their service (λειτουργία)." In other words, the deposition of ἐπίσκοποι from their λειτουργία by unscrupulous agitation, would be a grievous attack upon the authority of the πρεσβύτεροι, within whose τόπος such deposition would properly fall. The language is carefully chosen ; the τόπος of the presbyter is distinct from the λειτουργία of the bishop, and yet it is upon the confusion of these words that the identification of πρεσβυτέροι and ἐπίσκοποι depends.

If this interpretation of Clement's language be accurate, it shews us a plurality of ἐπίσκοποι at Corinth, appointed by the πρεσβύτεροι—still indeed to be counted πρεσβύτεροι from one point of view, but exercising *special* functions on behalf of the Christian congregation at large. And this institution of ἐπίσκοποι Clement traces to the act of the Apostles themselves, in providing for the regular succession of ministers in the Church.

The testimony of Hermas and Clement is, as we have seen, primarily testimony as to the organisation of the Church at Rome, although Clement gives important incidental information as to the Christian community at Corinth. The only other documents which could tell us anything about the primitive rulers of the Church at the seat of Empire are 1 *Peter* and the Epistle to the *Hebrews*, both of which seem to have been written from Italy ; and the evidence they afford as to the primitive ἐπίσκοποι is very scanty. The author of 1 *Peter* recognises the existence of such a title, but he does not apply it directly to the heads of the Christian society. The great Head of the Church is spoken of as a "bishop of souls" (ii. 25), but the exhortation in the letter is addressed to the *presbyters* of certain Asiatic Churches[1].

We pass now to the *Didache* or 'Teaching of the Twelve Apostles,' probably current in Palestine some time in the early decades

---

[1] The presbyters who "exercise oversight"=πρεσβύτεροι ἐπισκοποῦντες (v. 1, 2) is not the true reading. And the writer does not speak of himself as 'bishop,' but as a "fellow-presbyter." The Epistle to the Hebrews does not mention ἐπίσκοποι at all, but it speaks of those that have the rule in the Churches to which it was addressed, the ἡγούμενοι (xiii. 7, 17).

of the second century. We are now on Eastern, not Western soil. The first thing that strikes us on reading this little book is the great prominence of the *prophets* and *apostles* in the Christian communities. The distinction between the *itinerant* and the *local* ministry has now gained pretty general acceptance[1]. Christianity was first spread (as it often is at the present day in heathen countries) by itinerant preachers going from place to place, local Church officials being only appointed when there was a congregation for them to minister to. The apostles of the *Didache* are not, of course, the original Twelve ; they are simply *missionaries*, as the word *apostles* properly signifies. And the distinction between them and the prophets is not very clearly marked. But the significant passage in the *Didache* for our present purpose is § 15 : "Appoint for yourselves therefore bishops and deacons worthy of the Lord, men who are meek, and not lovers of money, and also true and approved ; for unto you they also perform the service (λειτουργοῦσι τὴν λειτουργίαν) of the prophets and teachers." Here we have a hint of the gradual assumption of the prophetical office by the permanent officials of the Church. Spiritual functions begin now to be provided for by a local ministry, as ordinary gifts begin to supersede extraordinary ones, though the period of transition may have been long in some places : indeed the prominence of Montanism at one time shews the unwillingness to admit that the prophetical office had become obsolete. And, again, as in the other documents we have examined, the bishop is the officer of worship, with duties in connexion with the Eucharistic office (§§ 12, 15). We notice here two other points. (1) The bishops are mentioned in the plural, though when the *Didache* recognises the possibility of a prophet settling down in one place for his life, it furnishes a valuable clue as to the way in which a monarchical episcopate could readily arise even in the very earliest times. (2) There is no mention of presbyters so called, nor indeed is there any hint of any permanent Church officials save ἐπίσκοποι and διάκονοι. But we must not build up an argument on negative evidence.

[1] Cp. Lightfoot, *Phil.* p. 194.

The *Didache* does not tell us of presbyters; it does tell us of bishops. That is all we have a right to say.

The *Didache* is far removed in time from the Epistle to the Philippians; and yet a very similar phenomenon there presents itself. The salutation at the beginning is "to the saints at Philippi, with the bishops and deacons." Neither in this Epistle nor in any of St Paul's earlier Epistles are presbyters mentioned by name; and yet it would be impossible to deny their existence. Indeed, when we remember that the bishop's office seems to have included the duty of representing the Church, as well in formal communications with other Churches as in the acts of Eucharistic worship, we find no difficulty in understanding why the bishops should be specially mentioned in St Paul's salutation. The mention of deacons follows as a corollary. Wherever deacons are mentioned in the sub-apostolic literature (with one exception[1]) they are mentioned in close connexion with and in subordination to the bishops[2]. They are Church officials acting under the ἐπίσκοποι, who supervise or oversee their labours. This at least is part of the significance of the term ἐπίσκοπος.

The evidence so far would give, as it seems, no good ground for identifying the ἐπίσκοπος with the πρεσβύτερος; the terms are of distinct meaning and are kept fairly distinct in usage, the bishop being more of an *official*, the presbyter more of a *pastor* in our modern sense—both apparently having certain judicial functions. But whether they were applied to distinct individuals in the earliest Christian age is a more difficult question.

[1] The single exception occurs in the letter of 'Polycarp to the Church of Philippi, written sixty years later than the letter of St Paul to the same Church. Polycarp (§ 5) bids the young men at Philippi submit themselves "to the presbyters and the deacons as to God and Christ," the bishop or bishops of the Philippian Church not being mentioned at all. At this late date, however, it is hardly matter for doubt that the monarchical episcopate was established at Philippi as it was at Smyrna, and therefore, whatever the ground of the omission, we cannot attribute it to the non-existence of the office as a separate institution.

[2] Of which we have still a trace in our own Church organisation, where the *archdeacon* is counted the *oculus episcopi*.

Let us then examine the witness of the *Acts.* That book
repeatedly recognises the existence of presbyters associated with
the Apostles at Jerusalem. They are mentioned many times,
the most important passages being perhaps xi. 30 (which takes
it for granted that they were an existing body in the Church of
Jerusalem at that early stage) and the account of the Apostolic
Council of Jerusalem (see xv. 2, 4, 6, 22; xvi. 4). They are
present at the reception of St Paul by St James (xxi. 18); it is
to them that the alms for the poor brethren in Judæa are sent
by the hands of Barnabas and Saul (xi. 30). Their prominence
at Jerusalem is easy to understand. The name 'presbyter' was
taken over, it is hardly to be doubted, from Judaism. Jewish
presbyters appear in the Acts (xxiii. 14, xxiv. 1) and in the
Gospels frequently, and we are familiar with the title in the O.T.
They seem in N.T. times to have been the officers—not of the
synagogue, but of the συνέδριον, the 'seat of the elders'; and
their functions were in part disciplinary[1]. Such duties would
be especially important in the earliest days of Christianity at
Jerusalem; before the Catholic faith had been finally dissociated
from Judaism it was natural that the old title for Church officials
should remain, and that the duties connected with the term
'presbyter' should be conspicuous. And we find that the
organisation of the presbyterate seemed so important even in
these first years that St Paul and Barnabas appointed presbyters
in every Church on the first great missionary journey to Asia
Minor (Acts xiv. 23). The organisation was afterwards extended
to Ephesus, where we meet with presbyters holding a position
of prominence, apparently in a sense the representatives of the
Christian community, in ch. xx.

So far the *Acts.* And so, too, in the Epistle of St James; the
only servants of the Church that are mentioned are the presbyters, who are spoken of in connexion with a special spiritual
function, in the passage which speaks of the anointing of the
sick (Jas. v. 14). It is a little surprising to find no mention
whatever of presbyters in St Paul's Epistles until we come to

---

[1] See Hatch, *Bampton Lectures*, pp. 57, 58.

the last group of all, the pastoral letters written to Timothy and Titus. But though the name is absent, the thing is present. They are the προϊστάμενοι, those who have the rule. "We beseech you," he says to the Thessalonians, "to know them that labour among you, and are over you in the Lord" (1 Thess. v. 12). This is an instructive passage, for it suggests that the duties of προϊστάμενοι were largely pastoral, or concerned with the cure of souls. So at least the context would suggest. And in fact a comparison of the lists of χαρίσματα and of the servants of the Church in *Rom.*, 1 *Cor.*, and *Eph.* will leave no doubt on our minds that the προϊστάμενοι of *Rom.* xii. 8 and the κυβερνήσεις of 1 *Cor.* xii. 28 are to be identified with the ποιμένες of *Eph.* iv. 11.

But what of the ἐπίσκοπος in the *Acts*? And have we any hint as to the origin of the term?

It seems probable, on the whole, that the title of this office was taken over from the organisation of the contemporary Greek societies[1]. It can hardly be accident that we find no mention in the N.T. documents (or indeed in any early writings) of ἐπίσκοποι at Jerusalem, while they appear at Ephesus, at Philippi, at Crete, where Greek influences were dominant. At the same time we must not leave out of sight the fact that the words ἐπίσκοπος, ἐπισκοπεῖν are common in the LXX. It is quite intelligible from this point of view how they might have gained an early place in Christian speech. Indeed in Acts i. 20, when the Apostleship vacant through Judas's death was under discussion, one of the passages in the O.T. which was appealed to was τὴν ἐπισκοπὴν αὐτοῦ λαβέτω ἕτερος. But although this LXX. usage must have familiarised the term itself to those who were entrusted with the organisation of the Church, that the usefulness and the duties of the office were partly—at least—suggested by the practice of the Greek societies and guilds with which they came in contact is a plausible hypothesis.

What, then, it will be said, was the position of St James at

---

[1] Dr Hatch brings out in his *Bampton Lectures* (p. 37) the great similarity between some of the duties of the ἐπίσκοπος, more especially those which were concerned with the administration of Church funds, and the duties of an officer called the ἐπιμελητής in the pagan and Jewish associations of the day. See on 1 Tim. iii. 5 below.

the Apostolic Council? Was he not the ἐπίσκοπος? He was president. He spoke in the name of the assembly and gave his sentence with authority (Acts xv. 13, 19). Are not these the functions of the bishop, and may he not therefore be counted the first bishop of Jerusalem? We should probably be nearest the truth if we said that he certainly was in a position strikingly like that of the monarchical ἐπίσκοπος of a later date, and that he distinctly indicates the beginnings of that dignity at Jerusalem ; but it would be an anachronism to call him an ἐπίσκοπος. He is not so called by St Luke. He exercises his important functions as an Apostle, or at least as "the Lord's brother"; and it does not seem that any other title of dignity would have been deemed natural. It is noteworthy that the later bishops of Jerusalem counted themselves as his successors ; but we must not import the term ἐπίσκοπος into the narrative at this point. We are not yet told of an ἐπίσκοπος or of ἐπίσκοποι at Jerusalem, though the presbyters are many times mentioned.

The most puzzling passage in the *Acts* which relates to the connexion between the *presbyters* and the *bishops* may be now considered. When St Paul was addressing the presbyters of the Church at Ephesus (Acts xx. 28) he said, "Take heed to yourselves and to all the flock, in the which the Holy Ghost hath made you bishops." This is one of the passages on which reliance is mainly placed to establish the interchangeability in the N.T. of the terms we are considering. And *primâ facie* it points that way. Speaking (apparently) to presbyters, St Paul calls them bishops. If on this ground, however, we are to identify the offices, as well as the persons entrusted with the offices at Ephesus, we shall have great difficulty in explaining the speedy divergence of meaning between the terms, and indeed the use of two terms at all.

But the inference is surely a somewhat precarious one. No one imagines that the speeches in the *Acts* are recorded in their integrity, with all the accuracy of a modern shorthand report. And if we suppose (as Irenaeus did[1]) that among the Ephesian

---

[1] "In Mileto enim convocatis *episcopis et presbyteris* qui erant ab Epheso" (Iren. *Haer.* III. 14).

presbyters present *some* were bishops, there is no difficulty in St Paul's language. An unrecorded gesture on the speaker's part may have made his meaning clear to his hearers. Is there any improbability in the hypothesis that the speaker turned and addressed (*v.* 28) emphatically those of the presbyters who held the episcopal office? Indeed the speech (Acts xx. 18—35) naturally falls into two divisions. (1) From *v.* 18 to *v.* 27 the Apostle addresses the presbyters : "You know (ὑμεῖς ἐπίστασθε) how faithfully I preached in public and private : you were witnesses of it." (2) But from *v.* 28 onward the topics are different. "Take heed to yourselves (cp. 1 Tim. iv. 16) : beware of heresy, remembering how I admonished you individually in reference to this : you yourselves know (αὐτοὶ γινώσκετε)"—as if the persons addressed had special means of knowing this—"that I did not accept maintenance from the Church." Now to guard the faith against the encroachments of heresy, and to administer the Church's alms, were duties specially appropriate to the ἐπίσκοποι, as we have seen above. The whole passage certainly establishes— and the fact is important—the presence of several bishops at Ephesus, as at Philippi ; but that all the presbyters who were there were necessarily ἐπίσκοποι is quite a different proposition, very unlikely in itself, not demanded by the context, and not supported by the history of the Church in the next generation.

We proceed to examine the testimony of the Pastoral Epistles. The qualifications and functions of a bishop in these letters (leaving out of account the moral qualifications, which were of course paramount) may be placed under these heads : (*a*) He is to be above suspicion in matters of money (1 Tim. iii. 3 ; Tit. i. 7). This recalls to us what we read in the *Didache*, and elsewhere. The bishop has at least some financial functions ; probably he was the administrator of the Church funds, the deacons being subordinate dispensers (1 Tim. iii. 8). But this is not the bishop's most important function. (*b*) His control goes further ; it extends to the preservation of the apostolic tradition. He is the guardian of discipline, the true ἐπιμελητής (1 Tim. iii. 5) ; "holding by the faithful word which is according to the doctrine, that he may be able both to exhort in the wholesome doctrine

and to convict the gainsayers" (Tit. i. 9). (c) He must be of
good repute, because he is the *persona ecclesiae* ; he represents
the Church to those without (1 Tim. iii. 2, 7 ; Titus i. 7). All
this is very like the later idea of the ἐπίσκοπος, and unlike the
later idea of the πρεσβύτερος, save in one point. The bishop of
the Pastorals is to be *apt to teach* (1 Tim. iii. 2). This is not a
function that appears prominently in the later writings ; such a
peculiarly pastoral duty becomes rather appropriated to the presbyters. It seems further from 1 Tim. v. 17 that all the presbyters of the Pastorals did *not* teach ; "those who rule well are
to be counted worthy of double honour, especially those who
labour in the word and in teaching." *Rule* is their normal duty,
but of those who rule some do not teach.

One passage in the Pastorals, indeed, suggests at first sight
the identity of the ἐπίσκοπος and the πρεσβύτερος. "Appoint
presbyters in every city...if any be blameless...for the bishop
must be blameless as the steward of God" (Tit. i. 5—7). It can
hardly however be matter of accident that the ἐπίσκοπος is thus
markedly spoken of in the singular, while the πρεσβύτεροι are
mentioned in the plural, and that the definite article τὸν ἐπίσκοπον is here used (see note *in loc.*). And, apart from this
consideration, we can understand the language used if we remember that the presbyterate was a very important office from the
beginning, not only in view of its spiritual functions, but in
respect of the powers of the presbyteral council. Thus (as in
Clement) it would naturally be the body which would decide upon
the person or persons to be appointed to the episcopate. At first,
and probably as long as they had the power, for human nature
was much the same then as now, the presbyters would nominate
one of their own body for this office. The ἐπίσκοποι would be
all πρεσβύτεροι, though not necessarily *vice versâ*. And thus
when St Paul bids Titus be careful about the persons to be
ordained presbyter, *for* the bishop must be blameless, he need
not imply more than this, that as the bishop would naturally be
chosen out of the presbyteral body, it was of the highest importance that each member of that body should be of good
character.

On a review of all the evidence it is not too much to say that the only passages which even *suggest* the interchangeability in the N.T. of the terms ἐπίσκοπος and πρεσβύτερος are Acts xx. 28 and Tit. i. 7. But they are susceptible of explanations which fall in with the supposition that the words represent distinct functions (which might, on occasion, be discharged by the same individual). And thus we do not regard these passages as inconsistent with the conclusions to which all the other evidence points. These conclusions are four in number. (1) The episcopate and presbyterate were distinct in origin and in function ; the difference of name points to a difference in duty, although no doubt many duties would be common to both, especially in primitive and half-organised communities. (2) The bishops were originally selected by the presbyteral council, and probably from their own body. (3) There were often several bishops in one place, the number being a matter non-essential. (4) A conspicuous part of the bishop's duty was the administration of worship—the λειτουργία in the largest sense ; he is above all things an *official*, the representative of his Church and the director of its discipline.

A larger question is, no doubt, involved as to the significance of the bishop's office in the continuous life of the Church, which it does not come within the scope of this *Introduction* to discuss. There does not seem, however, to be good ground for rejecting Clement's express statement that the Apostles appointed ἐπίσκοποι to provide for the perpetual succession of the Christian ministry. They took over the office of *presbyter* from the Jewish Church, and gave to it higher and more spiritual functions, the due discharge of which was provided for by the χάρισμα or grace conveyed in the act of ordination, as the Pastoral Epistles teach (1 Tim. iv. 14 ; 2 Tim. i. 6). And so they took over the office of ἐπίσκοπος from the Greek societies in which Christianity was growing ; and they gave to that office also higher and more spiritual functions. The Greek ἐπίσκοπος in a secular association was a representative and responsible official, without any necessarily religious duties. The Christian ἐπίσκοπος was also a representative and responsible official. His position in respect of Church funds, in respect of communication with other Churches, and in respect of the liturgical service of the Christian society, all mark him as representing the Church, as the *persona ecclesiae.* These were all duties that in the first Christian generation were performed by Apostles. And they, as Clement informs us—and there does not seem to be any other key to the sequel,—delegated these duties to the ἐπίσκοποι that were to come after them, with the right of continuing that succession for the future. As time went on it was this last function that became especially prominent and was counted the *essentia* of the episcopal office ; nor could we now, even if we wished, alter the conception. For whether or not the institution of the Christian episcopate in this sense was due to the direct command of our Lord Himself—a question which we have no means of answering from history—certain it is that it was due to the direct and formal action of the Apostles whom He sent.

The bearing of this discussion upon the date of the Pastoral Epistles may be thus summarised. The Pastorals shew us the episcopate in a somewhat early stage of its development. The bishop's office is not yet so distinguished from that of the presbyter that he does not take part in the instruction of the faithful. The bishop of the Pastorals must be "apt to teach " (1 Tim. iii. 2). Again, the monarchical episcopate of the days of Ignatius is not yet established. However we describe the office held by Timothy and Titus in their own persons—and that it included that of bishop seems tolerably certain—we could not infer from the instructions given to them that there must be only one bishop in each community, which very early became the common practice of the Church. And though the bishops of the Pastorals must not be greedy of money, there is no such formal assignment of the duties falling to them as administrators of Church alms as we should expect in a second century pastoral letter. They are to be "given to hospitality" (1 Tim. iii. 2); but their office as representatives of the Church in its external relations does not come into the prominence that it assumed at a later period. Some of these indications may be trivial, but taken together they do not permit us to date the Pastorals later than the first century. But if the Pastoral Letters are first century documents, there is no adequate reason forbidding us to acquiesce in their own claim, confirmed by the unbroken tradition of the Christian Church, that they were written by the hand of St Paul.

CHAPTER VI.

THE GREEK TEXT.

The principles have been already explained (p. v.) by which the Greek text of the several books of the New Testament, as printed in this series, is determined. The main authorities (exclusive of the Patristic citations) for the text of the Pastoral Epistles may be thus classified :

i. *Uncial Manuscripts.*

ℵ, the famous Codex Sinaiticus (saec. IV), now at St Petersburg, published in facsimile type by its discoverer Tischendorf, in 1862. It contains the Epistles without any lacuna. The symbol ℵ^c is used to indicate the corrections introduced by a scribe of the 7th century, ℵ* denoting the autograph of the original scribe.

A, Codex Alexandrinus (saec. V), at the British Museum, published in photographic facsimile by Sir E. M. Thompson. It contains the Epistles without any lacuna.

C, Codex Ephraemi (saec. V), the Paris palimpsest (*Bibl. nat.* 9), first edited by Tischendorf. The text of the Epistles is lacking from 1 Tim. i. 1—iii. 9 and from 1 Tim. v. 20—vi. 21.

D$_2$, Codex Claromontanus (saec. VI), a Graeco-Latin MS. at Paris (*Bibl. nat.* 107), first edited by Tischendorf (1852). D$_2$^{c} denotes the readings introduced by a ninth century corrector. The Latin text is represented by the symbol *d*; it follows the Old Latin version, with modifications.

E, Codex Sangermanensis (saec. IX), a Graeco-Latin MS. at St Petersburg. The Greek text is a mere transcript of D$_2$, and is not therefore cited in this edition, as not being an independent authority. The Latin text *e* (a corrected copy of *d*) has been printed (not very accurately) by Belsheim (Christiania, 1885). The MS. is defective from 1 Tim. i. 1—vi. 15.

F, Codex Augiensis (saec. IX), a Graeco-Latin MS. at Trinity College, Cambridge (B. xvii. 1), edited by Scrivener (1859). The Greek text is almost identical with that of G, and therefore we do not cite it, save at 1 Tim. v. 21, where alone, among the readings recorded in our critical apparatus, F and G disagree. Its Latin version (*f*) is, however, worthy of being cited; it presents the Vulgate text, altered in some places.

G, Codex Boernerianus (saec. IX), a Graeco-Latin MS. at Dresden, edited by Matthaei (1791). It once formed part of the same volume as Codex Sangallensis (Δ) of the Gospels, and was evidently written by an Irish scribe. Its Latin version (*g*) is based on the prae-Hieronymian translation, but has been modified a good deal.

H, Codex Coislinianus (saec. VI), whose fragments are dispersed in various Libraries. The portions of the Pastoral Epistles which survive (at Paris and Turin) comprise 1 Tim. i. 4—iii. 2, iii. 7—13, vi. 9—13 ; 2 Tim. i. 17—ii. 9 ; Tit. i. 1—3, 15—ii. 5, iii. 13—15. They were edited by Omont[1], and some additional leaves were read by J. A. Robinson[2].

I, Codex Petropolitanus (saec. V), at St Petersburg, whose fragments were edited by Tischendorf. Of the Pastoral Epistles it contains Titus i. 1—13 only.

K, Codex Mosquensis (saec. IX), at Moscow, edited by Matthaei (1782) ; complete for these Epp.

L, Codex Angelicus (saec. IX), at Rome, collated by Tischendorf and Tregelles ; complete for these Epp.

P, Codex Porphyrianus (saec. IX), at St Petersburg, collated by Tischendorf. It is illegible in parts between 1 Tim. vi. 7—12 and between 2 Tim. i. 2—5.

T^g, a fragment (saec. V?), at Paris (Egyptian Mus. Louvre 7332), edited by Zahn[3]; it only contains 1 Tim. iii. 15, 16, vi. 3.

[1] *Notices et extraits*, XXXIII. i. p. 141 (1889).
[2] *Euthaliana*, p. 63 (1895).
[3] *Forschungen, Suppl. Clem.* p. 277.

Ψ, an unpublished Codex (saec. IX ?), at Mount Athos. It is said to be complete.

Z, Codex Patiriensis (saec. V), at Rome (Vat. Gr. 2061); it contains, *inter alia*, 1 Tim. v. 6—vi. 45 ; 2 Tim. i. 1—ii. 25 ; Tit. iii. 13—15. Its text has not been published in its entirety.

The fact that B is lacking for these Epistles deprives us of a primary authority the loss of which is very serious. As in the Pauline Epistles generally, the type of text known as 'Western' (here represented by DG) does not present such wide divergences from the other types as it does in the Gospels and Acts ; but nevertheless the combination DG is interesting. אACLP often go together, and form a group which, in Westcott and Hort's nomenclature, would be described as 'Alexandrian': the later uncials KLP represent the type which they call 'Syrian.' The combination א^c H *arm* is frequent, and needs attention.

ii. *Minuscules.*

The minuscule manuscripts are very numerous, and only a few need be mentioned. Those numbered Paul. 1, 2, 4, 7 (all at Basle) have a historical interest from the fact that Erasmus used them for the *editio princeps* (1516), but they are not of the first rank. 17 (saec. IX), "the queen of cursives," is at Paris; 37 is the famous Leicester codex = Ev. 69 ; 67 (at Vienna, saec. XI) ; 73 (at Upsala, saec. XI) ; 137 (at Paris, saec. XIII), and 181 (at Florence, saec. XIII) are also of importance.

iii. *Versions.*

1. *Latin.* Of Latin, Versions *d, e, f, g* have been already mentioned.

We have also of the Old Latin the fragmentary Codex Frisingensis (*r*) of the 5th or 6th century, containing 1 Tim. i. 12—ii. 15 ; v. 18—vi. 13, edited by Ziegler (Marburg, 1876).

Evidence is also to be found in the citations of Tertullian, Cyprian, the Latin Irenaeus, Hilary, and the *Speculum* (*m*), which represents the Bible of the Spaniard Priscillian.

The Vulgate of the Pauline Epistles differs but little from the prae-Hieronymian Latin.

2. *Syriac.* Here we have (*a*) the Peshitto (saec. III ?); and

(*b*) the Harclean version (saec. VII), based on the older version of Philoxenus (saec. VI).

3. *Egyptian.* Of these versions we have (*a*) the Bohairic or the North Coptic, and (*b*) the Sahidic or the South Coptic, the language of Upper Egypt. The dates of these versions are as yet undetermined, but they are probably later than the second century.

4. *Armenian.* This version is generally regarded as of the fifth century.

Where the testimony of these witnesses is cited in the following pages, it has been derived from the eighth edition of Tischendorf's *Novum Testamentum Graece.*

ΠΡΟΣ ΤΙΜΟΘΕΟΝ Α΄

ΠΡΟΣ ΤΙΜΟΘΕΟΝ Β΄

ΠΡΟΣ ΤΙΤΟΝ

ΠΡΟΣ ΤΙΜΟΘΕΟΝ Α΄

1 ¹Παῦλος ἀπόστολος Χριστοῦ Ἰησοῦ κατ' ἐπιταγὴν θεοῦ σωτῆρος ἡμῶν καὶ Χριστοῦ Ἰησοῦ τῆς ἐλπίδος ἡμῶν ²Τιμοθέῳ γνησίῳ τέκνῳ ἐν πίστει. χάρις, ἔλεος, εἰρήνη ἀπὸ θεοῦ πατρὸς καὶ Χριστοῦ Ἰησοῦ τοῦ κυρίου ἡμῶν.

³Καθὼς παρεκάλεσά σε προσμεῖναι ἐν Ἐφέσῳ, πορευόμενος εἰς Μακεδονίαν, ἵνα παραγγείλῃς τισὶν μὴ ἑτεροδιδασκαλεῖν ⁴μηδὲ προσέχειν μύθοις καὶ γενεαλογίαις ἀπεράντοις, αἵτινες ἐκζητήσεις παρέχουσιν μᾶλλον ἢ οἰκονομίαν θεοῦ τὴν ἐν πίστει· ⁵τὸ δὲ τέλος τῆς παραγγελίας ἐστὶν ἀγάπη ἐκ καθαρᾶς καρδίας καὶ συνειδήσεως ἀγαθῆς καὶ πίστεως ἀνυποκρίτου, ⁶ὧν τινὲς ἀστοχήσαντες ἐξετράπησαν εἰς ματαιολογίαν, ⁷θέλοντες εἶναι νομοδιδάσκαλοι, μὴ νοοῦντες μήτε ἃ λέγουσιν μήτε περὶ τίνων διαβεβαιοῦνται. ⁸οἴδαμεν δὲ ὅτι καλὸς ὁ νόμος, ἐάν τις αὐτῷ νομίμως χρῆται, ⁹εἰδὼς τοῦτο, ὅτι δικαίῳ νόμος οὐ κεῖται, ἀνόμοις δὲ καὶ ἀνυποτάκτοις, ἀσεβέσι καὶ ἁμαρτωλοῖς, ἀνοσίοις καὶ βεβήλοις, πατρολῴαις καὶ μητρολῴαις, ἀνδροφόνοις, ¹⁰πόρνοις, ἀρσενοκοίταις, ἀνδραποδισταῖς, ψεύσταις, ἐπιόρκοις, καὶ εἴ τι ἕτερον τῇ ὑγιαινούσῃ διδασκαλίᾳ ἀντίκειται, ¹¹κατὰ τὸ εὐαγγέλιον τῆς δόξης τοῦ μακαρίου

θεοῦ, ὃ ἐπιστεύθην ἐγώ. ¹²χάριν ἔχω τῷ ἐνδυναμώ-
σαντί με Χριστῷ Ἰησοῦ τῷ κυρίῳ ἡμῶν, ὅτι πιστόν
με ἡγήσατο θέμενος εἰς διακονίαν, ¹³τὸ πρότερον ὄντα
βλάσφημον καὶ διώκτην καὶ ὑβριστήν· ἀλλὰ ἠλεήθην,
ὅτι ἀγνοῶν ἐποίησα ἐν ἀπιστίᾳ, ¹⁴ὑπερεπλεόνασεν δὲ ἡ
χάρις τοῦ κυρίου ἡμῶν μετὰ πίστεως καὶ ἀγάπης τῆς ἐν
Χριστῷ Ἰησοῦ. ¹⁵πιστὸς ὁ λόγος καὶ πάσης ἀποδοχῆς
ἄξιος, ὅτι Χριστὸς Ἰησοῦς ἦλθεν εἰς τὸν κόσμον ἁμαρτωλοὺς σῶσαι, ὧν πρῶτός εἰμι ἐγώ· ¹⁶ἀλλὰ διὰ τοῦτο
ἠλεήθην, ἵνα ἐν ἐμοὶ πρώτῳ ἐνδείξηται Ἰησοῦς Χριστὸς
τὴν ἅπασαν μακροθυμίαν, πρὸς ὑποτύπωσιν τῶν μελλόντων πιστεύειν ἐπ᾽ αὐτῷ εἰς ζωὴν αἰώνιον. ¹⁷τῷ δὲ
βασιλεῖ τῶν αἰώνων, ἀφθάρτῳ ἀοράτῳ μόνῳ θεῷ, τιμὴ
καὶ δόξα εἰς τοὺς αἰῶνας τῶν αἰώνων· ἀμήν.

¹⁸Ταύτην τὴν παραγγελίαν παρατίθεμαί σοι, τέκνον
Τιμόθεε, κατὰ τὰς προαγούσας ἐπὶ σὲ προφητείας, ἵνα
στρατεύσῃ ἐν αὐταῖς τὴν καλὴν στρατείαν, ¹⁹ἔχων
πίστιν καὶ ἀγαθὴν συνείδησιν, ἥν τινες ἀπωσάμενοι
περὶ τὴν πίστιν ἐναυάγησαν· ²⁰ὧν ἐστὶν Ὑμέναιος καὶ
Ἀλέξανδρος, οὓς παρέδωκα τῷ σατανᾷ, ἵνα παιδευθῶσιν
μὴ βλασφημεῖν.

2 ¹Παρακαλῶ οὖν πρῶτον πάντων ποιεῖσθαι δεήσεις, προσευχάς, ἐντεύξεις, εὐχαριστίας, ὑπὲρ πάντων
ἀνθρώπων, ²ὑπὲρ βασιλέων καὶ πάντων τῶν ἐν ὑπεροχῇ
ὄντων, ἵνα ἤρεμον καὶ ἡσύχιον βίον διάγωμεν ἐν πάσῃ
εὐσεβείᾳ καὶ σεμνότητι. ³τοῦτο καλὸν καὶ ἀπόδεκτον
ἐνώπιον τοῦ σωτῆρος ἡμῶν θεοῦ, ⁴ὃς πάντας ἀνθρώπους
θέλει σωθῆναι καὶ εἰς ἐπίγνωσιν ἀληθείας ἐλθεῖν. ⁵εἷς
γὰρ θεός, εἷς καὶ μεσίτης θεοῦ καὶ ἀνθρώπων, ἄνθρωπος
Χριστὸς Ἰησοῦς, ⁶ὁ δοὺς ἑαυτὸν ἀντίλυτρον ὑπὲρ πάντων, τὸ μαρτύριον καιροῖς ἰδίοις, ⁷εἰς ὃ ἐτέθην ἐγὼ κῆρυξ

καὶ ἀπόστολος, ἀλήθειαν λέγω, οὐ ψεύδομαι, διδάσκαλος ἐθνῶν ἐν πίστει καὶ ἀληθείᾳ.

⁸ Βούλομαι οὖν προσεύχεσθαι τοὺς ἄνδρας ἐν παντὶ τόπῳ, ἐπαίροντας ὁσίους χεῖρας χωρὶς ὀργῆς καὶ διαλογισμοῦ· ⁹ ὡσαύτως καὶ γυναῖκας ἐν καταστολῇ κοσμίῳ, μετὰ αἰδοῦς καὶ σωφροσύνης κοσμεῖν ἑαυτάς, μὴ ἐν πλέγμασιν καὶ χρυσῷ ἢ μαργαρίταις ἢ ἱματισμῷ πολυτελεῖ, ¹⁰ ἀλλ᾽ ὃ πρέπει γυναιξὶν ἐπαγγελλομέναις θεοσέβειαν, δι᾽ ἔργων ἀγαθῶν. ¹¹ Γυνὴ ἐν ἡσυχίᾳ μανθανέτω ἐν πάσῃ ὑποταγῇ· ¹² διδάσκειν δὲ γυναικὶ οὐκ ἐπιτρέπω, οὐδὲ αὐθεντεῖν ἀνδρός, ἀλλ᾽ εἶναι ἐν ἡσυχίᾳ. ¹³ Ἀδὰμ γὰρ πρῶτος ἐπλάσθη, εἶτα Εὔα. ¹⁴ καὶ Ἀδὰμ οὐκ ἠπατήθη, ἡ δὲ γυνὴ ἐξαπατηθεῖσα ἐν παραβάσει γέγονεν, ¹⁵ σωθήσεται δὲ διὰ τῆς τεκνογονίας, ἐὰν μείνωσιν ἐν πίστει καὶ ἀγάπῃ καὶ ἁγιασμῷ μετὰ σωφροσύνης.

3 ¹ Πιστὸς ὁ λόγος· εἴ τις ἐπισκοπῆς ὀρέγεται, καλοῦ ἔργου ἐπιθυμεῖ. ² δεῖ οὖν τὸν ἐπίσκοπον ἀνεπίλημπτον εἶναι, μιᾶς γυναικὸς ἄνδρα, νηφάλιον, σώφρονα, κόσμιον, φιλόξενον, διδακτικόν, ³ μὴ πάροινον, μὴ πλήκτην, ἀλλὰ ἐπιεικῆ, ἄμαχον, ἀφιλάργυρον, ⁴ τοῦ ἰδίου οἴκου καλῶς προϊστάμενον, τέκνα ἔχοντα ἐν ὑποταγῇ μετὰ πάσης σεμνότητος,—⁵ εἰ δέ τις τοῦ ἰδίου οἴκου προστῆναι οὐκ οἶδεν, πῶς ἐκκλησίας θεοῦ ἐπιμελήσεται;—⁶ μὴ νεόφυτον, ἵνα μὴ τυφωθεὶς εἰς κρίμα ἐμπέσῃ τοῦ διαβόλου. ⁷ δεῖ δὲ καὶ μαρτυρίαν καλὴν ἔχειν ἀπὸ τῶν ἔξωθεν, ἵνα μὴ εἰς ὀνειδισμὸν ἐμπέσῃ καὶ παγίδα τοῦ διαβόλου. ⁸ Διακόνους ὡσαύτως σεμνούς, μὴ διλόγους, μὴ οἴνῳ πολλῷ προσέχοντας, μὴ αἰσχροκερδεῖς, ⁹ ἔχοντας τὸ μυστήριον τῆς πίστεως ἐν καθαρᾷ συνειδήσει. ¹⁰ καὶ οὗτοι δὲ δοκιμαζέσθωσαν

πρῶτον, εἶτα διακονείτωσαν ἀνέγκλητοι ὄντες. ¹¹ γυναῖκας ὡσαύτως σεμνάς, μὴ διαβόλους, νηφαλίους, πιστὰς
ἐν πᾶσιν. ¹² διάκονοι ἔστωσαν μιᾶς γυναικὸς ἄνδρες,
τέκνων καλῶς προϊστάμενοι καὶ τῶν ἰδίων οἴκων. ¹³ οἱ
γὰρ καλῶς διακονήσαντες βαθμὸν ἑαυτοῖς καλὸν περιποιοῦνται καὶ πολλὴν παρρησίαν ἐν πίστει τῇ ἐν Χριστῷ
Ἰησοῦ.

¹⁴ Ταῦτά σοι γράφω ἐλπίζων ἐλθεῖν πρὸς σὲ τάχιον·
¹⁵ ἐὰν δὲ βραδύνω, ἵνα εἰδῇς πῶς δεῖ ἐν οἴκῳ θεοῦ ἀναστρέφεσθαι, ἥτις ἐστὶν ἐκκλησία θεοῦ ζῶντος, στῦλος
καὶ ἑδραίωμα τῆς ἀληθείας. ¹⁶ καὶ ὁμολογουμένως μέγα
ἐστὶν τὸ τῆς εὐσεβείας μυστήριον· ὃς ἐφανερώθη ἐν
σαρκί, ἐδικαιώθη ἐν πνεύματι, ὤφθη ἀγγέλοις, ἐκηρύχθη
ἐν ἔθνεσιν, ἐπιστεύθη ἐν κόσμῳ, ἀνελήμφθη ἐν δόξῃ.

4 ¹ Τὸ δὲ πνεῦμα ῥητῶς λέγει ὅτι ἐν ὑστέροις
καιροῖς ἀποστήσονταί τινες τῆς πίστεως, προσέχοντες
πνεύμασιν πλάνοις καὶ διδασκαλίαις δαιμονίων, ² ἐν
ὑποκρίσει ψευδολόγων, κεκαυστηριασμένων τὴν ἰδίαν
συνείδησιν, ³ κωλυόντων γαμεῖν, ἀπέχεσθαι βρωμάτων,
ἃ ὁ θεὸς ἔκτισεν εἰς μετάλημψιν μετὰ εὐχαριστίας τοῖς
πιστοῖς καὶ ἐπεγνωκόσι τὴν ἀλήθειαν. ⁴ ὅτι πᾶν κτίσμα
θεοῦ καλόν, καὶ οὐδὲν ἀπόβλητον μετὰ εὐχαριστίας
λαμβανόμενον· ⁵ ἁγιάζεται γὰρ διὰ λόγου θεοῦ καὶ
ἐντεύξεως.

⁶ Ταῦτα ὑποτιθέμενος τοῖς ἀδελφοῖς καλὸς ἔσῃ διάκονος Χριστοῦ Ἰησοῦ, ἐντρεφόμενος τοῖς λόγοις τῆς
πίστεως καὶ τῆς καλῆς διδασκαλίας ᾗ παρηκολούθηκας·
⁷ τοὺς δὲ βεβήλους καὶ γραώδεις μύθους παραιτοῦ.
γύμναζε δὲ σεαυτὸν πρὸς εὐσέβειαν. ⁸ ἡ γὰρ σωματικὴ
γυμνασία πρὸς ὀλίγον ἐστὶν ὠφέλιμος· ἡ δὲ εὐσέβεια
πρὸς πάντα ὠφέλιμός ἐστιν, ἐπαγγελίαν ἔχουσα ζωῆς

τῆς νῦν καὶ τῆς μελλούσης. ⁹ πιστὸς ὁ λόγος καὶ πάσης ἀποδοχῆς ἄξιος. ¹⁰ εἰς τοῦτο γὰρ κοπιῶμεν καὶ ἀγωνιζόμεθα, ὅτι ἠλπίκαμεν ἐπὶ θεῷ ζῶντι, ὅς ἐστιν σωτὴρ πάντων ἀνθρώπων, μάλιστα πιστῶν. ¹¹ Παράγγελλε ταῦτα καὶ δίδασκε. ¹² μηδείς σου τῆς νεότητος καταφρονείτω, ἀλλὰ τύπος γίνου τῶν πιστῶν, ἐν λόγῳ, ἐν ἀναστροφῇ, ἐν ἀγάπῃ, ἐν πίστει, ἐν ἁγνείᾳ. ¹³ ἕως ἔρχομαι πρόσεχε τῇ ἀναγνώσει, τῇ παρακλήσει, τῇ διδασκαλίᾳ. ¹⁴ μὴ ἀμέλει τοῦ ἐν σοὶ χαρίσματος, ὃ ἐδόθη σοι διὰ προφητείας μετὰ ἐπιθέσεως τῶν χειρῶν τοῦ πρεσβυτερίου. ¹⁵ ταῦτα μελέτα, ἐν τούτοις ἴσθι, ἵνα σου ἡ προκοπὴ φανερὰ ᾖ πᾶσιν. ¹⁶ ἔπεχε σεαυτῷ καὶ τῇ διδασκαλίᾳ, ἐπίμενε αὐτοῖς· τοῦτο γὰρ ποιῶν καὶ σεαυτὸν σώσεις καὶ τοὺς ἀκούοντάς σου.

5 ¹ Πρεσβυτέρῳ μὴ ἐπιπλήξῃς ἀλλὰ παρακάλει ὡς πατέρα, νεωτέρους ὡς ἀδελφούς, ² πρεσβυτέρας ὡς μητέρας, νεωτέρας ὡς ἀδελφὰς ἐν πάσῃ ἁγνείᾳ. ³ Χήρας τίμα τὰς ὄντως χήρας. ⁴ εἰ δέ τις χήρα τέκνα ἢ ἔκγονα ἔχει, μανθανέτωσαν πρῶτον τὸν ἴδιον οἶκον εὐσεβεῖν καὶ ἀμοιβὰς ἀποδιδόναι τοῖς προγόνοις· τοῦτο γάρ ἐστιν ἀπόδεκτον ἐνώπιον τοῦ θεοῦ. ⁵ ἡ δὲ ὄντως χήρα καὶ μεμονωμένη ἤλπικεν ἐπὶ τὸν θεὸν καὶ προσμένει ταῖς δεήσεσιν καὶ ταῖς προσευχαῖς νυκτὸς καὶ ἡμέρας· ⁶ ἡ δὲ σπαταλῶσα ζῶσα τέθνηκεν. ⁷ καὶ ταῦτα παράγγελλε ἵνα ἀνεπίλημπτοι ὦσιν. ⁸ εἰ δέ τις τῶν ἰδίων καὶ μάλιστα οἰκείων οὐ προνοεῖται, τὴν πίστιν ἤρνηται καὶ ἔστιν ἀπίστου χείρων.

⁹ Χήρα καταλεγέσθω μὴ ἔλαττον ἐτῶν ἑξήκοντα γεγονυῖα, ἑνὸς ἀνδρὸς γυνή, ¹⁰ ἐν ἔργοις καλοῖς μαρτυρουμένη, εἰ ἐτεκνοτρόφησεν, εἰ ἐξενοδόχησεν, εἰ ἁγίων πόδας ἔνιψεν, εἰ θλιβομένοις ἐπήρκεσεν, εἰ παντὶ ἔργῳ

ἀγαθῷ ἐπηκολούθησεν. ¹¹ νεωτέρας δὲ χήρας παραιτοῦ· ὅταν γὰρ καταστρηνιάσωσιν τοῦ Χριστοῦ, γαμεῖν θέλουσιν, ¹² ἔχουσαι κρίμα ὅτι τὴν πρώτην πίστιν ἠθέτησαν· ¹³ ἅμα δὲ καὶ ἀργαὶ μανθάνουσιν περιερχόμεναι τὰς οἰκίας, οὐ μόνον δὲ ἀργαὶ ἀλλὰ καὶ φλύαροι καὶ περίεργοι, λαλοῦσαι τὰ μὴ δέοντα. ¹⁴ βούλομαι οὖν νεωτέρας γαμεῖν, τεκνογονεῖν, οἰκοδεσποτεῖν, μηδεμίαν ἀφορμὴν διδόναι τῷ ἀντικειμένῳ λοιδορίας χάριν· ¹⁵ ἤδη γάρ τινες ἐξετράπησαν ὀπίσω τοῦ σατανᾶ. ¹⁶ εἴ τις πιστὴ ἔχει χήρας, ἐπαρκείσθω αὐταῖς, καὶ μὴ βαρείσθω ἡ ἐκκλησία, ἵνα ταῖς ὄντως χήραις ἐπαρκέσῃ.

¹⁷ Οἱ καλῶς προεστῶτες πρεσβύτεροι διπλῆς τιμῆς ἀξιούσθωσαν, μάλιστα οἱ κοπιῶντες ἐν λόγῳ καὶ διδασκαλίᾳ. ¹⁸ λέγει γὰρ ἡ γραφή, Βοῦν ἀλοῶντα οὐ φιμώσεις, καί, Ἄξιος ὁ ἐργάτης τοῦ μισθοῦ αὐτοῦ. ¹⁹ κατὰ πρεσβυτέρου κατηγορίαν μὴ παραδέχου, ἐκτὸς εἰ μὴ ἐπὶ δύο ἢ τριῶν μαρτύρων. ²⁰ Τοὺς ἁμαρτάνοντας ἐνώπιον πάντων ἔλεγχε, ἵνα καὶ οἱ λοιποὶ φόβον ἔχωσιν.

²¹ Διαμαρτύρομαι ἐνώπιον τοῦ θεοῦ καὶ Χριστοῦ Ἰησοῦ καὶ τῶν ἐκλεκτῶν ἀγγέλων ἵνα ταῦτα φυλάξῃς χωρὶς προκρίματος, μηδὲν ποιῶν κατὰ πρόσκλισιν. ²² Χεῖρας ταχέως μηδενὶ ἐπιτίθει, μηδὲ κοινώνει ἁμαρτίαις ἀλλοτρίαις. σεαυτὸν ἁγνὸν τήρει. ²³ μηκέτι ὑδροπότει, ἀλλὰ οἴνῳ ὀλίγῳ χρῶ διὰ τὸν στόμαχον καὶ τὰς πυκνάς σου ἀσθενείας. ²⁴ Τινῶν ἀνθρώπων αἱ ἁμαρτίαι πρόδηλοί εἰσιν προάγουσαι εἰς κρίσιν, τισὶν δὲ καὶ ἐπακολουθοῦσιν· ²⁵ ὡσαύτως καὶ τὰ ἔργα τὰ καλὰ πρόδηλα, καὶ τὰ ἄλλως ἔχοντα κρυβῆναι οὐ δύνανται.

6 ¹ Ὅσοι εἰσὶν ὑπὸ ζυγὸν δοῦλοι, τοὺς ἰδίους δεσπότας πάσης τιμῆς ἀξίους ἡγείσθωσαν, ἵνα μὴ τὸ

ὄνομα τοῦ θεοῦ καὶ ἡ διδασκαλία βλασφημῆται. ²οἱ
δὲ πιστοὺς ἔχοντες δεσπότας μὴ καταφρονείτωσαν, ὅτι
ἀδελφοί εἰσιν, ἀλλὰ μᾶλλον δουλευέτωσαν, ὅτι πιστοί
εἰσιν καὶ ἀγαπητοὶ οἱ τῆς εὐεργεσίας ἀντιλαμβανόμενοι.
Ταῦτα δίδασκε καὶ παρακάλει. ³εἴ τις ἑτεροδιδασκαλεῖ καὶ μὴ προσέρχεται ὑγιαίνουσιν λόγοις τοῖς τοῦ
κυρίου ἡμῶν Ἰησοῦ Χριστοῦ καὶ τῇ κατ᾽ εὐσέβειαν
διδασκαλίᾳ, ⁴τετύφωται, μηδὲν ἐπιστάμενος, ἀλλὰ νοσῶν
περὶ ζητήσεις καὶ λογομαχίας, ἐξ ὧν γίνεται φθόνος,
ἔρις, βλασφημίαι, ὑπόνοιαι πονηραί, ⁵διαπαρατριβαὶ
διεφθαρμένων ἀνθρώπων τὸν νοῦν καὶ ἀπεστερημένων
τῆς ἀληθείας, νομιζόντων πορισμὸν εἶναι τὴν εὐσέβειαν.
⁶ἔστιν δὲ πορισμὸς μέγας ἡ εὐσέβεια μετὰ αὐταρκείας.
⁷οὐδὲν γὰρ εἰσηνέγκαμεν εἰς τὸν κόσμον, ὅτι οὐδὲ
ἐξενεγκεῖν τι δυνάμεθα· ⁸ἔχοντες δὲ διατροφὰς καὶ
σκεπάσματα, τούτοις ἀρκεσθησόμεθα. ⁹οἱ δὲ βουλόμενοι πλουτεῖν ἐμπίπτουσιν εἰς πειρασμὸν καὶ παγίδα
καὶ ἐπιθυμίας πολλὰς ἀνοήτους καὶ βλαβεράς, αἵτινες
βυθίζουσιν τοὺς ἀνθρώπους εἰς ὄλεθρον καὶ ἀπώλειαν.
¹⁰ῥίζα γὰρ πάντων τῶν κακῶν ἐστὶν ἡ φιλαργυρία, ἧς
τινὲς ὀρεγόμενοι ἀπεπλανήθησαν ἀπὸ τῆς πίστεως καὶ
ἑαυτοὺς περιέπειραν ὀδύναις πολλαῖς.

¹¹Σὺ δέ, ὦ ἄνθρωπε θεοῦ, ταῦτα φεῦγε· δίωκε δὲ
δικαιοσύνην, εὐσέβειαν, πίστιν, ἀγάπην, ὑπομονήν,
πραϋπαθίαν. ¹²ἀγωνίζου τὸν καλὸν ἀγῶνα τῆς πίστεως,
ἐπιλαβοῦ τῆς αἰωνίου ζωῆς, εἰς ἣν ἐκλήθης καὶ ὡμολόγησας τὴν καλὴν ὁμολογίαν ἐνώπιον πολλῶν μαρτύρων.
¹³παραγγέλλω σοι ἐνώπιον τοῦ θεοῦ τοῦ ζωογονοῦντος
τὰ πάντα καὶ Χριστοῦ Ἰησοῦ τοῦ μαρτυρήσαντος ἐπὶ
Ποντίου Πειλάτου τὴν καλὴν ὁμολογίαν, ¹⁴τηρῆσαί
σε τὴν ἐντολὴν ἄσπιλον ἀνεπίλημπτον μέχρι τῆς

ἐπιφανείας τοῦ κυρίου ἡμῶν Ἰησοῦ Χριστοῦ, [15] ἣν καιροῖς ἰδίοις δείξει ὁ μακάριος καὶ μόνος δυνάστης, ὁ βασιλεὺς τῶν βασιλευόντων καὶ κύριος τῶν κυριευόντων, [16] ὁ μόνος ἔχων ἀθανασίαν, φῶς οἰκῶν ἀπρόσιτον, ὃν εἶδεν οὐδεὶς ἀνθρώπων οὐδὲ ἰδεῖν δύναται· ᾧ τιμὴ καὶ κράτος αἰώνιον, ἀμήν.

[17] Τοῖς πλουσίοις ἐν τῷ νῦν αἰῶνι παράγγελλε μὴ ὑψηλοφρονεῖν, μηδὲ ἠλπικέναι ἐπὶ πλούτου ἀδηλότητι, ἀλλ' ἐπὶ θεῷ τῷ παρέχοντι ἡμῖν πάντα πλουσίως εἰς ἀπόλαυσιν, [18] ἀγαθοεργεῖν, πλουτεῖν ἐν ἔργοις καλοῖς, εὐμεταδότους εἶναι, κοινωνικούς, [19] ἀποθησαυρίζοντας ἑαυτοῖς θεμέλιον καλὸν εἰς τὸ μέλλον, ἵνα ἐπιλάβωνται τῆς ὄντως ζωῆς.

[20] Ὦ Τιμόθεε, τὴν παραθήκην φύλαξον, ἐκτρεπόμενος τὰς βεβήλους κενοφωνίας καὶ ἀντιθέσεις τῆς ψευδωνύμου γνώσεως, [21] ἥν τινες ἐπαγγελλόμενοι περὶ τὴν πίστιν ἠστόχησαν.

Ἡ χάρις μεθ' ὑμῶν.

ΠΡΟΣ ΤΙΜΟΘΕΟΝ Β΄

1 ¹Παῦλος ἀπόστολος Χριστοῦ Ἰησοῦ διὰ θελήματος θεοῦ κατ᾽ ἐπαγγελίαν ζωῆς τῆς ἐν Χριστῷ Ἰησοῦ ²Τιμοθέῳ ἀγαπητῷ τέκνῳ. χάρις, ἔλεος, εἰρήνη ἀπὸ θεοῦ πατρὸς καὶ Χριστοῦ Ἰησοῦ τοῦ κυρίου ἡμῶν.

³Χάριν ἔχω τῷ θεῷ, ᾧ λατρεύω ἀπὸ προγόνων ἐν καθαρᾷ συνειδήσει, ὡς ἀδιάλειπτον ἔχω τὴν περὶ σοῦ μνείαν ἐν ταῖς δεήσεσίν μου νυκτὸς καὶ ἡμέρας, ⁴ἐπιποθῶν σε ἰδεῖν, μεμνημένος σου τῶν δακρύων ἵνα χαρᾶς πληρωθῶ, ⁵ὑπόμνησιν λαβὼν τῆς ἐν σοὶ ἀνυποκρίτου πίστεως, ἥτις ἐνῴκησεν πρῶτον ἐν τῇ μάμμῃ σου Λωΐδι καὶ τῇ μητρί σου Εὐνίκῃ, πέπεισμαι δὲ ὅτι καὶ ἐν σοί. ⁶Δι᾽ ἣν αἰτίαν ἀναμιμνήσκω σε ἀναζωπυρεῖν τὸ χάρισμα τοῦ θεοῦ, ὅ ἐστιν ἐν σοὶ διὰ τῆς ἐπιθέσεως τῶν χειρῶν μου. ⁷οὐ γὰρ ἔδωκεν ἡμῖν ὁ θεὸς πνεῦμα δειλίας, ἀλλὰ δυνάμεως καὶ ἀγάπης καὶ σωφρονισμοῦ. ⁸μὴ οὖν ἐπαισχυνθῇς τὸ μαρτύριον τοῦ κυρίου ἡμῶν μηδὲ ἐμὲ τὸν δέσμιον αὐτοῦ, ἀλλὰ συνκακοπάθησον τῷ εὐαγγελίῳ κατὰ δύναμιν θεοῦ, ⁹τοῦ σώσαντος ἡμᾶς καὶ καλέσαντος κλήσει ἁγίᾳ, οὐ κατὰ τὰ ἔργα ἡμῶν ἀλλὰ κατὰ ἰδίαν πρόθεσιν καὶ χάριν τὴν δοθεῖσαν ἡμῖν ἐν Χριστῷ Ἰησοῦ πρὸ χρόνων αἰωνίων, ¹⁰φανερωθεῖσαν δὲ νῦν διὰ τῆς ἐπιφανείας τοῦ σωτῆρος ἡμῶν Χριστοῦ Ἰησοῦ,

καταργήσαντος μὲν τὸν θάνατον, φωτίσαντος δὲ ζωὴν καὶ ἀφθαρσίαν διὰ τοῦ εὐαγγελίου, ¹¹ εἰς ὃ ἐτέθην ἐγὼ κῆρυξ καὶ ἀπόστολος καὶ διδάσκαλος ἐθνῶν· ¹² δι᾿ ἣν αἰτίαν καὶ ταῦτα πάσχω, ἀλλ᾿ οὐκ ἐπαισχύνομαι· οἶδα γὰρ ᾧ πεπίστευκα, καὶ πέπεισμαι ὅτι δυνατός ἐστιν τὴν παραθήκην μου φυλάξαι εἰς ἐκείνην τὴν ἡμέραν. ¹³ ὑποτύπωσιν ἔχε ὑγιαινόντων λόγων ὧν παρ᾿ ἐμοῦ ἤκουσας ἐν πίστει καὶ ἀγάπῃ τῇ ἐν Χριστῷ Ἰησοῦ· ¹⁴ τὴν καλὴν παραθήκην φύλαξον διὰ πνεύματος ἁγίου τοῦ ἐνοικοῦντος ἐν ἡμῖν.

¹⁵ Οἶδας τοῦτο, ὅτι ἀπεστράφησάν με πάντες οἱ ἐν τῇ Ἀσίᾳ, ὧν ἐστιν Φύγελος καὶ Ἑρμογένης. ¹⁶ δῴη ἔλεος ὁ κύριος τῷ Ὀνησιφόρου οἴκῳ, ὅτι πολλάκις με ἀνέψυξεν καὶ τὴν ἅλυσίν μου οὐκ ἐπαισχύνθη, ¹⁷ ἀλλὰ γενόμενος ἐν Ῥώμῃ σπουδαίως ἐζήτησέν με καὶ εὗρεν. ¹⁸ δῴη αὐτῷ ὁ κύριος εὑρεῖν ἔλεος παρὰ κυρίου ἐν ἐκείνῃ τῇ ἡμέρᾳ. καὶ ὅσα ἐν Ἐφέσῳ διηκόνησεν, βέλτιον σὺ γινώσκεις.

2 ¹ Σὺ οὖν, τέκνον μου, ἐνδυναμοῦ ἐν τῇ χάριτι τῇ ἐν Χριστῷ Ἰησοῦ, ² καὶ ἃ ἤκουσας παρ᾿ ἐμοῦ διὰ πολλῶν μαρτύρων, ταῦτα παράθου πιστοῖς ἀνθρώποις, οἵτινες ἱκανοὶ ἔσονται καὶ ἑτέρους διδάξαι. ³ συνκακοπάθησον ὡς καλὸς στρατιώτης Χριστοῦ Ἰησοῦ. ⁴ οὐδεὶς στρατευόμενος ἐμπλέκεται ταῖς τοῦ βίου πραγματίαις, ἵνα τῷ στρατολογήσαντι ἀρέσῃ. ⁵ ἐὰν δὲ καὶ ἀθλῇ τις, οὐ στεφανοῦται ἐὰν μὴ νομίμως ἀθλήσῃ. ⁶ τὸν κοπιῶντα γεωργὸν δεῖ πρῶτον τῶν καρπῶν μεταλαμβάνειν. ⁷ νόει ὃ λέγω· δώσει γάρ σοι ὁ κύριος σύνεσιν ἐν πᾶσιν. ⁸ Μνημόνευε Ἰησοῦν Χριστὸν ἐγηγερμένον ἐκ νεκρῶν, ἐκ σπέρματος Δαυείδ, κατὰ τὸ εὐαγγέλιόν μου, ⁹ ἐν ᾧ κακοπαθῶ μέχρι δεσμῶν ὡς κακοῦργος, ἀλλὰ ὁ λόγος

τοῦ θεοῦ οὐ δέδεται. ¹⁰ διὰ τοῦτο πάντα ὑπομένω διὰ τοὺς ἐκλεκτούς, ἵνα καὶ αὐτοὶ σωτηρίας τύχωσιν τῆς ἐν Χριστῷ Ἰησοῦ μετὰ δόξης αἰωνίου. ¹¹ Πιστὸς ὁ λόγος· εἰ γὰρ συναπεθάνομεν, καὶ συνζήσομεν· ¹² εἰ ὑπομένομεν, καὶ συνβασιλεύσομεν· εἰ ἀρνησόμεθα, κἀκεῖνος ἀρνήσεται ἡμᾶς· ¹³ εἰ ἀπιστοῦμεν, ἐκεῖνος πιστὸς μένει, ἀρνήσασθαι γὰρ ἑαυτὸν οὐ δύναται.

¹⁴ Ταῦτα ὑπομίμνησκε, διαμαρτυρόμενος ἐνώπιον τοῦ θεοῦ μὴ λογομαχεῖν, ἐπ᾽ οὐδὲν χρήσιμον, ἐπὶ καταστροφῇ τῶν ἀκουόντων. ¹⁵ σπούδασον σεαυτὸν δόκιμον παραστῆσαι τῷ θεῷ, ἐργάτην ἀνεπαίσχυντον, ὀρθοτομοῦντα τὸν λόγον τῆς ἀληθείας. ¹⁶ τὰς δὲ βεβήλους κενοφωνίας περιΐστασο· ἐπὶ πλεῖον γὰρ προκόψουσιν ἀσεβείας, ¹⁷ καὶ ὁ λόγος αὐτῶν ὡς γάγγραινα νομὴν ἕξει· ὧν ἐστὶν Ὑμέναιος καὶ Φιλητός, ¹⁸ οἵτινες περὶ τὴν ἀλήθειαν ἠστόχησαν, λέγοντες ἀνάστασιν ἤδη γεγονέναι, καὶ ἀνατρέπουσιν τήν τινων πίστιν. ¹⁹ ὁ μέντοι στερεὸς θεμέλιος τοῦ θεοῦ ἔστηκεν, ἔχων τὴν σφραγῖδα ταύτην· Ἔγνω κύριος τοὺς ὄντας αὐτοῦ, καί· Ἀποστήτω ἀπὸ ἀδικίας πᾶς ὁ ὀνομάζων τὸ ὄνομα κυρίου. ²⁰ ἐν μεγάλῃ δὲ οἰκίᾳ οὐκ ἔστιν μόνον σκεύη χρυσᾶ καὶ ἀργυρᾶ, ἀλλὰ καὶ ξύλινα καὶ ὀστράκινα, καὶ ἃ μὲν εἰς τιμὴν ἃ δὲ εἰς ἀτιμίαν· ²¹ ἐὰν οὖν τις ἐκκαθάρῃ ἑαυτὸν ἀπὸ τούτων, ἔσται σκεῦος εἰς τιμήν, ἡγιασμένον, εὔχρηστον τῷ δεσπότῃ, εἰς πᾶν ἔργον ἀγαθὸν ἡτοιμασμένον. ²² τὰς δὲ νεωτερικὰς ἐπιθυμίας φεῦγε, δίωκε δὲ δικαιοσύνην, πίστιν, ἀγάπην, εἰρήνην μετὰ τῶν ἐπικαλουμένων τὸν κύριον ἐκ καθαρᾶς καρδίας. ²³ τὰς δὲ μωρὰς καὶ ἀπαιδεύτους ζητήσεις παραιτοῦ, εἰδὼς ὅτι γεννῶσιν μάχας· ²⁴ δοῦλον δὲ κυρίου οὐ δεῖ μάχεσθαι ἀλλὰ ἤπιον εἶναι πρὸς πάντας, διδακτικόν, ἀνεξίκακον, ²⁵ ἐν πραΰτητι

παιδεύοντα τοὺς ἀντιδιατιθεμένους, μήποτε δῷη αὐτοῖς
ὁ θεὸς μετάνοιαν εἰς ἐπίγνωσιν ἀληθείας, ²⁶ καὶ ἀνανήψωσιν ἐκ τῆς τοῦ διαβόλου παγίδος, ἐζωγρημένοι ὑπ᾽
αὐτοῦ εἰς τὸ ἐκείνου θέλημα.

3 ¹ Τοῦτο δὲ γίνωσκε, ὅτι ἐν ἐσχάταις ἡμέραις ἐνστήσονται καιροὶ χαλεποί. ² ἔσονται γὰρ οἱ ἄνθρωποι
φίλαυτοι, φιλάργυροι, ἀλαζόνες, ὑπερήφανοι, βλάσφημοι, γονεῦσιν ἀπειθεῖς, ἀχάριστοι, ἀνόσιοι, ³ ἄστοργοι,
ἄσπονδοι, διάβολοι, ἀκρατεῖς, ἀνήμεροι, ἀφιλάγαθοι,
⁴ προδόται, προπετεῖς, τετυφωμένοι, φιλήδονοι μᾶλλον ἢ
φιλόθεοι, ⁵ ἔχοντες μόρφωσιν εὐσεβείας τὴν δὲ δύναμιν
αὐτῆς ἠρνημένοι· καὶ τούτους ἀποτρέπου. ⁶ ἐκ τούτων
γάρ εἰσιν οἱ ἐνδύνοντες εἰς τὰς οἰκίας καὶ αἰχμαλωτίζοντες
γυναικάρια σεσωρευμένα ἁμαρτίαις, ἀγόμενα ἐπιθυμίαις
ποικίλαις, ⁷ πάντοτε μανθάνοντα καὶ μηδέποτε εἰς ἐπίγνωσιν ἀληθείας ἐλθεῖν δυνάμενα. ⁸ ὃν τρόπον δὲ Ἰαννῆς
καὶ Ἰαμβρῆς ἀντέστησαν Μωϋσεῖ, οὕτως καὶ οὗτοι ἀνθίστανται τῇ ἀληθείᾳ, ἄνθρωποι κατεφθαρμένοι τὸν νοῦν,
ἀδόκιμοι περὶ τὴν πίστιν. ⁹ ἀλλ᾽ οὐ προκόψουσιν ἐπὶ
πλεῖον· ἡ γὰρ ἄνοια αὐτῶν ἔκδηλος ἔσται πᾶσιν, ὡς
καὶ ἡ ἐκείνων ἐγένετο. ¹⁰ Σὺ δὲ παρηκολούθησάς μου
τῇ διδασκαλίᾳ, τῇ ἀγωγῇ, τῇ προθέσει, τῇ πίστει, τῇ
μακροθυμίᾳ, τῇ ἀγάπῃ, τῇ ὑπομονῇ, ¹¹ τοῖς διωγμοῖς,
τοῖς παθήμασιν, οἷά μοι ἐγένετο ἐν Ἀντιοχείᾳ, ἐν
Ἰκονίῳ, ἐν Λύστροις· οἵους διωγμοὺς ὑπήνεγκα, καὶ
ἐκ πάντων με ἐρύσατο ὁ κύριος. ¹² καὶ πάντες δὲ οἱ
θέλοντες ζῆν εὐσεβῶς ἐν Χριστῷ Ἰησοῦ διωχθήσονται.
¹³ Πονηροὶ δὲ ἄνθρωποι καὶ γόητες προκόψουσιν ἐπὶ τὸ
χεῖρον, πλανῶντες καὶ πλανώμενοι. ¹⁴ σὺ δὲ μένε ἐν
οἷς ἔμαθες καὶ ἐπιστώθης, εἰδὼς παρὰ τίνων ἔμαθες,
¹⁵ καὶ ὅτι ἀπὸ βρέφους [τὰ] ἱερὰ γράμματα οἶδας τὰ

δυνάμενά σε σοφίσαι εἰς σωτηρίαν διὰ πίστεως τῆς ἐν Χριστῷ Ἰησοῦ. ¹⁶ πᾶσα γραφὴ θεόπνευστος καὶ ὠφέλιμος πρὸς διδασκαλίαν, πρὸς ἐλεγμόν, πρὸς ἐπανόρθωσιν, πρὸς παιδίαν τὴν ἐν δικαιοσύνῃ, ¹⁷ ἵνα ἄρτιος ᾖ ὁ τοῦ θεοῦ ἄνθρωπος, πρὸς πᾶν ἔργον ἀγαθὸν ἐξηρτισμένος.

4 ¹ Διαμαρτύρομαι ἐνώπιον τοῦ θεοῦ καὶ Χριστοῦ Ἰησοῦ τοῦ μέλλοντος κρίνειν ζῶντας καὶ νεκρούς, καὶ τὴν ἐπιφάνειαν αὐτοῦ καὶ τὴν βασιλείαν αὐτοῦ, ² κήρυξον τὸν λόγον, ἐπίστηθι εὐκαίρως ἀκαίρως, ἔλεγξον, ἐπιτίμησον, παρακάλεσον, ἐν πάσῃ μακροθυμίᾳ καὶ διδαχῇ. ³ ἔσται γὰρ καιρὸς ὅτε τῆς ὑγιαινούσης διδασκαλίας οὐκ ἀνέξονται, ἀλλὰ κατὰ τὰς ἰδίας ἐπιθυμίας ἑαυτοῖς ἐπισωρεύσουσιν διδασκάλους κνηθόμενοι τὴν ἀκοήν. ⁴ καὶ ἀπὸ μὲν τῆς ἀληθείας τὴν ἀκοὴν ἀποστρέψουσιν, ἐπὶ δὲ τοὺς μύθους ἐκτραπήσονται. ⁵ σὺ δὲ νῆφε ἐν πᾶσιν, κακοπάθησον, ἔργον ποίησον εὐαγγελιστοῦ, τὴν διακονίαν σου πληροφόρησον. ⁶ Ἐγὼ γὰρ ἤδη σπένδομαι, καὶ ὁ καιρὸς τῆς ἀναλύσεώς μου ἐφέστηκεν. ⁷ τὸν καλὸν ἀγῶνα ἠγώνισμαι, τὸν δρόμον τετέλεκα, τὴν πίστιν τετήρηκα· ⁸ λοιπὸν ἀπόκειταί μοι ὁ τῆς δικαιοσύνης στέφανος, ὃν ἀποδώσει μοι ὁ κύριος ἐν ἐκείνῃ τῇ ἡμέρᾳ, ὁ δίκαιος κριτής, οὐ μόνον δὲ ἐμοὶ ἀλλὰ καὶ πᾶσι τοῖς ἠγαπηκόσι τὴν ἐπιφάνειαν αὐτοῦ.

⁹ Σπούδασον ἐλθεῖν πρός με ταχέως. ¹⁰ Δημᾶς γάρ με ἐγκατέλιπεν ἀγαπήσας τὸν νῦν αἰῶνα, καὶ ἐπορεύθη εἰς Θεσσαλονίκην, Κρήσκης εἰς Γαλατίαν, Τίτος εἰς Δαλματίαν· ¹¹ Λουκᾶς ἐστιν μόνος μετ᾽ ἐμοῦ. Μάρκον ἀναλαβὼν ἄγε μετὰ σεαυτοῦ· ἔστιν γάρ μοι εὔχρηστος εἰς διακονίαν. ¹² Τυχικὸν δὲ ἀπέστειλα εἰς Ἔφεσον. ¹³ τὸν φελόνην, ὃν ἀπέλιπον ἐν Τρῳάδι παρὰ Κάρπῳ,

ἐρχόμενος φέρε, καὶ τὰ βιβλία, μάλιστα τὰς μεμβράνας. ¹⁴Ἀλέξανδρος ὁ χαλκεὺς πολλά μοι κακὰ ἐνεδείξατο· ἀποδώσει αὐτῷ ὁ κύριος κατὰ τὰ ἔργα αὐτοῦ. ¹⁵ὃν καὶ σὺ φυλάσσου· λίαν γὰρ ἀντέστη τοῖς ἡμετέροις λόγοις. ¹⁶ἐν τῇ πρώτῃ μου ἀπολογίᾳ οὐδείς μοι παρεγένετο, ἀλλὰ πάντες με ἐγκατέλιπον· μὴ αὐτοῖς λογισθείη· ¹⁷ὁ δὲ κύριός μοι παρέστη καὶ ἐνεδυνάμωσέν με, ἵνα δι᾽ ἐμοῦ τὸ κήρυγμα πληροφορηθῇ καὶ ἀκούσωσιν πάντα τὰ ἔθνη, καὶ ἐρύσθην ἐκ στόματος λέοντος. ¹⁸ῥύσεταί με ὁ κύριος ἀπὸ παντὸς ἔργου πονηροῦ καὶ σώσει εἰς τὴν βασιλείαν αὐτοῦ τὴν ἐπουράνιον· ᾧ ἡ δόξα εἰς τοὺς αἰῶνας τῶν αἰώνων, ἀμήν.

¹⁹Ἄσπασαι Πρίσκαν καὶ Ἀκύλαν καὶ τὸν Ὀνησιφόρου οἶκον. ²⁰Ἔραστος ἔμεινεν ἐν Κορίνθῳ, Τρόφιμον δὲ ἀπέλιπον ἐν Μιλήτῳ ἀσθενοῦντα. ²¹σπούδασον πρὸ χειμῶνος ἐλθεῖν. ἀσπάζεταί σε Εὔβουλος καὶ Πούδης καὶ Λίνος καὶ Κλαυδία καὶ οἱ ἀδελφοὶ πάντες.

²²Ὁ κύριος μετὰ τοῦ πνεύματός σου. ἡ χάρις μεθ᾽ ὑμῶν.

ΠΡΟΣ ΤΙΤΟΝ

1 ¹Παῦλος δοῦλος θεοῦ, ἀπόστολος δὲ Ἰησοῦ Χριστοῦ κατὰ πίστιν ἐκλεκτῶν θεοῦ καὶ ἐπίγνωσιν ἀληθείας τῆς κατ' εὐσέβειαν ²ἐπ' ἐλπίδι ζωῆς αἰωνίου, ἣν ἐπηγγείλατο ὁ ἀψευδὴς θεὸς πρὸ χρόνων αἰωνίων, ³ἐφανέρωσεν δὲ καιροῖς ἰδίοις τὸν λόγον αὐτοῦ ἐν κηρύγματι, ὃ ἐπιστεύθην ἐγὼ κατ' ἐπιταγὴν τοῦ σωτῆρος ἡμῶν θεοῦ, ⁴Τίτῳ γνησίῳ τέκνῳ κατὰ κοινὴν πίστιν. χάρις καὶ εἰρήνη ἀπὸ θεοῦ πατρὸς καὶ Χριστοῦ Ἰησοῦ τοῦ σωτῆρος ἡμῶν.

⁵Τούτου χάριν ἀπέλιπόν σε ἐν Κρήτῃ, ἵνα τὰ λείποντα ἐπιδιορθώσῃ καὶ καταστήσῃς κατὰ πόλιν πρεσβυτέρους, ὡς ἐγώ σοι διεταξάμην, ⁶εἴ τις ἐστὶν ἀνέγκλητος, μιᾶς γυναικὸς ἀνήρ, τέκνα ἔχων πιστά, μὴ ἐν κατηγορίᾳ ἀσωτίας ἢ ἀνυπότακτα. ⁷δεῖ γὰρ τὸν ἐπίσκοπον ἀνέγκλητον εἶναι ὡς θεοῦ οἰκονόμον, μὴ αὐθάδη, μὴ ὀργίλον, μὴ πάροινον, μὴ πλήκτην, μὴ αἰσχροκερδῆ, ⁸ἀλλὰ φιλόξενον, φιλάγαθον, σώφρονα, δίκαιον, ὅσιον, ἐγκρατῆ, ⁹ἀντεχόμενον τοῦ κατὰ τὴν διδαχὴν πιστοῦ λόγου, ἵνα δυνατὸς ᾖ καὶ παρακαλεῖν ἐν τῇ διδασκαλίᾳ τῇ ὑγιαινούσῃ καὶ τοὺς ἀντιλέγοντας ἐλέγχειν. ¹⁰Εἰσὶν γὰρ πολλοὶ ἀνυπότακτοι, ματαιολόγοι καὶ φρεναπάται, μάλιστα οἱ ἐκ τῆς περιτομῆς, ¹¹οὓς δεῖ ἐπιστομίζειν, οἵτινες ὅλους οἴκους ἀνατρέπουσιν

διδάσκοντες ἃ μὴ δεῖ αἰσχροῦ κέρδους χάριν. ¹²εἶπέν τις ἐξ αὐτῶν ἴδιος αὐτῶν προφήτης, Κρῆτες ἀεὶ ψεῦσται, κακὰ θηρία, γαστέρες ἀργαί. ¹³ἡ μαρτυρία αὕτη ἐστὶν ἀληθής· δι' ἣν αἰτίαν ἔλεγχε αὐτοὺς ἀποτόμως, ἵνα ὑγιαίνωσιν ἐν τῇ πίστει, ¹⁴μὴ προσέχοντες Ἰουδαϊκοῖς μύθοις καὶ ἐντολαῖς ἀνθρώπων ἀποστρεφομένων τὴν ἀλήθειαν. ¹⁵πάντα καθαρὰ τοῖς καθαροῖς· τοῖς δὲ μεμιαμμένοις καὶ ἀπίστοις οὐδὲν καθαρόν, ἀλλὰ μεμίανται αὐτῶν καὶ ὁ νοῦς καὶ ἡ συνείδησις. ¹⁶θεὸν ὁμολογοῦσιν εἰδέναι, τοῖς δὲ ἔργοις ἀρνοῦνται, βδελυκτοὶ ὄντες καὶ ἀπειθεῖς καὶ πρὸς πᾶν ἔργον ἀγαθὸν ἀδόκιμοι.

2 ¹Σὺ δὲ λάλει ἃ πρέπει τῇ ὑγιαινούσῃ διδασκαλίᾳ. ²πρεσβύτας νηφαλίους εἶναι, σεμνούς, σώφρονας, ὑγιαίνοντας τῇ πίστει, τῇ ἀγάπῃ, τῇ ὑπομονῇ· ³πρεσβύτιδας ὡσαύτως ἐν καταστήματι ἱεροπρεπεῖς, μὴ διαβόλους, μὴ οἴνῳ πολλῷ δεδουλωμένας, καλοδιδασκάλους, ⁴ἵνα σωφρονίζουσιν τὰς νέας φιλάνδρους εἶναι, φιλοτέκνους, ⁵σώφρονας, ἁγνάς, οἰκουργούς, ἀγαθάς, ὑποτασσομένας τοῖς ἰδίοις ἀνδράσιν, ἵνα μὴ ὁ λόγος τοῦ θεοῦ βλασφημῆται. ⁶Τοὺς νεωτέρους ὡσαύτως παρακάλει σωφρονεῖν, ⁷περὶ πάντα σεαυτὸν παρεχόμενος τύπον καλῶν ἔργων, ἐν τῇ διδασκαλίᾳ ἀφθορίαν, σεμνότητα, ⁸λόγον ὑγιῆ ἀκατάγνωστον, ἵνα ὁ ἐξ ἐναντίας ἐντραπῇ μηδὲν ἔχων λέγειν περὶ ἡμῶν φαῦλον. ⁹Δούλους ἰδίοις δεσπόταις ὑποτάσσεσθαι, ἐν πᾶσιν εὐαρέστους εἶναι, μὴ ἀντιλέγοντας, ¹⁰μὴ νοσφιζομένους, ἀλλὰ πᾶσαν πίστιν ἐνδεικνυμένους ἀγαθήν, ἵνα τὴν διδασκαλίαν τὴν τοῦ σωτῆρος ἡμῶν θεοῦ κοσμῶσιν ἐν πᾶσιν.

¹¹Ἐπεφάνη γὰρ ἡ χάρις τοῦ θεοῦ σωτήριος πᾶσιν ἀνθρώποις, ¹²παιδεύουσα ἡμᾶς, ἵνα ἀρνησάμενοι τὴν ἀσέβειαν καὶ τὰς κοσμικὰς ἐπιθυμίας σωφρόνως καὶ

δικαίως καὶ εὐσεβῶς ζήσωμεν ἐν τῷ νῦν αἰῶνι, ¹³ προσδεχόμενοι τὴν μακαρίαν ἐλπίδα καὶ ἐπιφάνειαν τῆς
δόξης τοῦ μεγάλου θεοῦ καὶ σωτῆρος ἡμῶν Χριστοῦ
Ἰησοῦ, ¹⁴ ὃς ἔδωκεν ἑαυτὸν ὑπὲρ ἡμῶν ἵνα λυτρώσηται
ἡμᾶς ἀπὸ πάσης ἀνομίας καὶ καθαρίσῃ ἑαυτῷ λαὸν
περιούσιον, ζηλωτὴν καλῶν ἔργων.
¹⁵ Ταῦτα λάλει καὶ παρακάλει καὶ ἔλεγχε μετὰ
πάσης ἐπιταγῆς· μηδείς σου περιφρονείτω.
3 ¹ Ὑπομίμνησκε αὐτοὺς ἀρχαῖς ἐξουσίαις ὑποτάσσεσθαι, πειθαρχεῖν, πρὸς πᾶν ἔργον ἀγαθὸν ἑτοίμους
εἶναι, ² μηδένα βλασφημεῖν, ἀμάχους εἶναι, ἐπιεικεῖς,
πᾶσαν ἐνδεικνυμένους πραΰτητα πρὸς πάντας ἀνθρώπους. ³ ἦμεν γάρ ποτε καὶ ἡμεῖς ἀνόητοι, ἀπειθεῖς,
πλανώμενοι, δουλεύοντες ἐπιθυμίαις καὶ ἡδοναῖς ποικίλαις, ἐν κακίᾳ καὶ φθόνῳ διάγοντες, στυγητοί, μισοῦντες
ἀλλήλους· ⁴ ὅτε δὲ ἡ χρηστότης καὶ ἡ φιλανθρωπία
ἐπεφάνη τοῦ σωτῆρος ἡμῶν θεοῦ, ⁵ οὐκ ἐξ ἔργων τῶν ἐν
δικαιοσύνῃ ἃ ἐποιήσαμεν ἡμεῖς, ἀλλὰ κατὰ τὸ αὐτοῦ
ἔλεος ἔσωσεν ἡμᾶς διὰ λουτροῦ παλινγενεσίας καὶ
ἀνακαινώσεως πνεύματος ἁγίου, ⁶ οὗ ἐξέχεεν ἐφ᾽ ἡμᾶς
πλουσίως διὰ Ἰησοῦ Χριστοῦ τοῦ σωτῆρος ἡμῶν, ⁷ ἵνα
δικαιωθέντες τῇ ἐκείνου χάριτι κληρονόμοι γενηθῶμεν
κατ᾽ ἐλπίδα ζωῆς αἰωνίου. ⁸ πιστὸς ὁ λόγος, καὶ περὶ
τούτων βούλομαί σε διαβεβαιοῦσθαι, ἵνα φροντίζωσιν
καλῶν ἔργων προΐστασθαι οἱ πεπιστευκότες θεῷ. ταῦτά
ἐστιν καλὰ καὶ ὠφέλιμα τοῖς ἀνθρώποις· ⁹ μωρὰς δὲ
ζητήσεις καὶ γενεαλογίας καὶ ἔρεις καὶ μάχας νομικὰς
περιίστασο· εἰσὶν γὰρ ἀνωφελεῖς καὶ μάταιοι. ¹⁰ αἱρετικὸν ἄνθρωπον μετὰ μίαν καὶ δευτέραν νουθεσίαν
παραιτοῦ, ¹¹ εἰδὼς ὅτι ἐξέστραπται ὁ τοιοῦτος καὶ
ἁμαρτάνει ὢν αὐτοκατάκριτος.

¹²Ὅταν πέμψω Ἀρτεμᾶν πρὸς σὲ ἢ Τυχικόν, σπούδασον ἐλθεῖν πρός με εἰς Νικόπολιν· ἐκεῖ γὰρ κέκρικα παραχειμάσαι. ¹³Ζηνᾶν τὸν νομικὸν καὶ Ἀπολλὼ σπουδαίως πρόπεμψον, ἵνα μηδὲν αὐτοῖς λείπῃ. ¹⁴μανθανέτωσαν δὲ καὶ οἱ ἡμέτεροι καλῶν ἔργων προΐστασθαι εἰς τὰς ἀναγκαίας χρείας, ἵνα μὴ ὦσιν ἄκαρποι.

¹⁵Ἀσπάζονταί σε οἱ μετ᾽ ἐμοῦ πάντες. ἄσπασαι τοὺς φιλοῦντας ἡμᾶς ἐν πίστει.

Ἡ χάρις μετὰ πάντων ὑμῶν.

NOTES

ANALYSIS OF FIRST EPISTLE TO TIMOTHY.

Introductory. Salutation (i. 1—2).
Repetition of charge already given to Timothy (i. 3—20).

I. Practical directions about Public Worship.
   i. It is to include prayers for all men (ii. 1—8).
   ii. Women are not to lead the devotions of the congregation (ii. 9—15).

II. Qualifications of officials of the Church.
   i. Bishops (iii. 1—7).
   ii. Deacons (iii. 8—13) and Deaconesses (iii. 11).

The aim of all the foregoing instructions is :—
ἵνα εἰδῇς πῶς δεῖ ἐν οἴκῳ θεοῦ ἀναστρέφεσθαι (iii. 15).
A quotation from an early hymn (iii. 16).

III. The dangers of the future (iv. 1—5).
Timothy's duty, in respect of :—
   i. The false asceticism (iv. 6—10).
   ii. His personal conduct (iv. 11—16).

IV. The status in the Church of:
   i. Its older members (v. 1, 2).
   ii. Widows in respect of
      (a) Their maintenance (v. 3—8).
      (b) Their organisation in an order (v. 9—16).
   iii. Presbyters (v. 17—25).
   iv. Slaves (vi. 1, 2).

Renewed warnings against false doctrine (vi. 3—5) and in especial against the vanity and the perils of wealth (vi. 6—11).

Epilogue. i. Personal encouragement to Timothy (vi. 11—16).
   ii. Charge to the rich Christians at Ephesus (vi. 17—19).
   iii. Timothy's responsibility as guardian of the faith (vi. 20).

Benediction (vi. 21).

CHAPTER I.

1. ἀπόστολος Χριστοῦ Ἰησοῦ. So ℵD₂GP d f g; but Ἰησοῦ Χριστοῦ AKL. St Paul's use as to the order of words in these introductory formulae varies. In *Rom.* (?), 1 *Cor.* (?), *Gal.*, *Tit.*, he adopts the order Ἰησ. Χρ., whereas in 2 *Cor.*, *Eph.*, *Phil.*, *Col.*, 2 *Tim.* he has Χρ. Ἰησ. as ~~here~~.

Before the second Χριστοῦ Ἰησοῦ ℵD₂ᶜKL prefix κυρίου; *om* AD₂*GP d f g.

2. πατρός. So ℵ*AD₂*G d f g; πατρὸς ἡμῶν ℵᶜD₂ᶜKLP.

4. ἐκζητήσεις. So ℵA and some cursives; D₂GHKLP have ζητήσεις. The compound form, as occurring nowhere again in N.T. or LXX., would readily be corrected into ζητήσεις. Cp. vi. 4; 2 Tim. ii. 23; Tit. iii. 9.

οἰκονομίαν. So ℵAGHKLP the Bohairic and Armenian versions. The rec. text has οἰκοδομίαν with D₂ᶜ; this is the source of the Western reading οἰκοδομήν, found in D₂*; d f g m have *aedificationem* with which the Peshito agrees.

9. πατρολῴαις καὶ μητρολῴαις. This is the spelling of the best MSS.; the rec. text, following the majority of the cursives, has πατραλῴαις, μητραλῴαις.

12. Before χάριν, the rec. text with D₂KL inserts καί, which would be quite in accordance with Pauline usage; it is, however, omitted by ℵAGP f g.

ℵ* and some cursives have ἐνδυναμοῦντι (as in Phil. iv. 13); but ℵᶜAD₂GKLP support ἐνδυναμώσαντι.

13. τὸν πρότερον is the 'received' reading, with D₂ᶜKL; ℵAD₂*GP &c. have τὸ πρ.

16. Ἰησοῦς Χριστός. So ℵKLP with the Syriac and Egyptian versions; Westcott and Hort follow AD₂ and the Latin Versions in reading Χριστὸς Ἰησοῦς (which occurs six times in the preceding verses of the chapter) giving Ἰησ. Χρ. a place in their margin.

ἅπασαν with ℵAG &c. is preferable to πᾶσαν of D₂KLP and the rec. text. At the same time it is noteworthy that ἅπας only occurs once elsewhere in the Pauline Epistles (Eph. vi. 13), πᾶς being the usual form.

17. μόνῳ θεῷ. So ℵ*AD₂*G and nearly all versions. ℵᶜD₂ᵇᶜKLP and the Peshito add σοφῷ after μόνῳ; but this (the reading of rec. text) is probably a corruption introduced from Rom. xvi. 27. See Jude 25 for a similar variation.

18. στρατεύσῃ. So ℵ*D₂*; but στρατεύῃ (the reading of the rec. text) is supported by ℵᶜAD₂ᶜGKLP &c., and is preferred by Westcott and Hort.

1, 2. SALUTATION.

1. The ordinary form of salutation in a private letter of the period would be simply: Παῦλος Τιμοθέῳ χαίρειν. But St Paul's Epistles differ from ordinary letters in two respects: (*a*) they were written with a direct religious purpose, (*b*) they are semi-official in character, not merely the communications of a private friend, but the instructions of one entrusted with authority. Hence (*a*) for the brief χαίρειν (which is the form of salutation in the Ep. of St James alone among N.T. Epistles; cp. Acts xv. 23) is substituted χάρις καὶ εἰρήνη in eleven of the Pauline Epistles (as in St John's greeting to the Seven Churches, Rev. i. 4), the fuller χάρις, ἔλεος, εἰρήνη being used in the remaining two (1 and 2 Tim.), both forms having a deep religious significance: (*b*) the apostolic office of St Paul is explicitly mentioned at the outset in nine out of his thirteen Epistles, the remaining four being letters written in conjunction with others (1 and 2 Thess., Phil., and Philemon), and (with the exception of Philemon) having their official character indicated in other ways. It would seem from *v.* 3 in this Epistle that St Paul's authority had been challenged at Ephesus, and hence his claim to the title of ἀπόστολος is here especially in place.

κατ' ἐπιταγὴν θεοῦ κ.τ.λ. The more frequent form with St Paul is διὰ θελήματος θεοῦ (1 Cor. i. 1; 2 Cor. i. 1; Eph. i. 1; Col. i. 1; 2 Tim. i. 1), and some see in the alteration of phrase an intention to lay especial stress here on the apostolic office of St Paul as given him by Divine *command*. But it is hardly safe to find so much significance in the change. The central thought is one which was ever present to St Paul, viz. that the Apostolic ministry with which he was entrusted was a direct commission from God and not from men. κατ' ἐπιταγήν is thoroughly Pauline; cp. Rom. xvi. 26; 1 Cor. vii. 6; Tit. i. 3.

θεοῦ σωτῆρος ἡμῶν. The title σωτήρ is not applied to God the Father by St Paul outside the Pastoral Epistles (see 1 Tim. ii. 3, iv. 10; Tit. i. 3, ii. 10, iii. 4, but cp. 1 Cor. i. 21 for the same thought), and the only other instances in the N.T. of this usage are Luke i. 47 and Jude 25. But the title was familiar to the Hebrew religion and often occurs in the LXX.; see Ps. xxiv. 5, lxi. 7; Isa. xii. 2; Wisd. xvi. 7; Bar. iv. 22; 3 Macc. vii. 16. We have it also in Philo (*de migr. Abr.* 5, *de Vita cont.* 11), and in the *Sibylline Oracles* (iii. 35). St Paul, who in his earlier letters uses σωτήρ of Christ, generally reverts in these latest letters to the old Jewish thought that the ultimate source and fount of salvation is the Eternal Father, a thought which the Gospel explained and enriched; but cp. Tit. ii. 14, for σωτήρ applied to Christ.

The article is omitted before σωτῆρος, as the title has become almost like a proper name. See on Tit. i. 13.

καὶ Χριστοῦ Ἰησοῦ τῆς ἐλπίδος ἡμῶν, i.e. the ground of our hope, Him on whom our hopes are fixed. Cp. Col. i. 27 Χριστὸς ἐν ὑμῖν, ἡ ἐλπὶς τῆς δόξης. See also for the σωτήρ as the ἐλπίς Ps. lxiv. 6; Ecclus. xxxi. 15. The phrase Ἰησοῦ Χριστοῦ τῆς ἐλπίδος ἡμῶν is used afterwards by Ignatius (*Magn.* 11 and *Trall.* inscr.).

2. Τιμοθέῳ γνησίῳ τέκνῳ ἐν πίστει. *To Timothy, true child in faith.* Timothy (see Acts xvi. 1—3) might fitly be so described; ἐν πίστει expresses the sphere of the relationship between him and St Paul (see Titus iii. 15). The older man was to him, as we say, a 'father in God.' Cp. the parallel phrase in Tit. i. 4 γνησίῳ τέκνῳ κατὰ κοινὴν πίστιν and 1 Cor. iv. 17. Timothy was thus a recognised representative of his spiritual father. The young men among the Therapeutae (Philo *de Vit. cont.* 9) are described in like manner as ministering to their elders καθάπερ υἱοὶ γνήσιοι.

χάρις, ἔλεος, εἰρήνη. As has been already said, this full formula of salutation is used by St Paul only here and in 2 Tim. i. 2 (ἔλεος is spurious in Tit. i. 4); it is found again in the N.T. letters only in 2 John 3. Lightfoot (note on 1 Thess. i. 1) finds "in the additional touch of tenderness communicated by ἔλεος in these later Epistles a sense of the growing evils which threatened the Church."[1] But we have εἰρήνη ἐπ᾽ αὐτοὺς καὶ ἔλεος in Gal. vi. 16; and, again, ἔλεος ὑμῖν καὶ εἰρήνη καὶ ἀγάπη πληθυνθείη in Jude 2. The combination of ἔλεος and εἰρήνη occurs also in Tobit vii. 12 (‭‬): and that of χάρις καὶ ἔλεος in Wis. iii. 9, iv. 15. Even *grace* will not give *peace* to man, unless *mercy* accompany it; for man needs pardon for the past no less than strength for the future. And so the combination of the Greek with the Hebrew salutation, of χάρις with εἰρήνη (first suggested, perhaps, by the form of the priestly blessing in Num. vi. 24), was not doctrinally exact or complete, if it was intended to convey the idea of the best Christian blessing, without the addition of ἔλεος. As persecution came on the Church, we find Ignatius (*Smyrn.* 12) adding yet another word, ὑπομονή, as a grace needful for the Christian. See on this subject Hort on 1 Pet. i. 2.

ἀπὸ θεοῦ πατρὸς καὶ Χρ. Ἰησοῦ τοῦ κυρίου ἡμῶν. Christ is coupled with the Father as the source of blessing in the salutation in all of St Paul's letters, with the exception of Colossians, where we have the shorter form χάρις ὑμῖν καὶ εἰρήνη ἀπὸ θεοῦ πατρὸς ἡμῶν. It is through Christ that the blessings of the Father come upon the Church.

3—11. REPETITION OF CHARGE ALREADY GIVEN TO TIMOTHY.

3. καθὼς παρεκάλεσά σε. There is no apodosis here; the sentence is unfinished, and grammatically incoherent. The writer meant to add words like οὕτω καὶ νῦν παρακαλῶ or οὕτω ποίει, but he was carried away by the rapid flow of his thought (see note on *v.* 18). Thus the A.V. adds at the end of *v.* 4 "*so do,*" in italics. This is quite in St Paul's manner (cp. Gal. ii. 6), and would be beyond the art of a forger to produce.

παρεκάλεσα, *I exhorted,* is perhaps a shade less strong than the parallel διεταξάμην, *I charged,* of Tit. i. 5; see on 1 Tim. iv. 13.

προσμεῖναι. *To abide.* προσμένειν is not used by Paul outside 1 Timothy; cp. Acts xviii. 18.

---

[1] It is worth remarking that in *vv.* 13, 16 St Paul twice draws attention to the ἔλεος which was so conspicuously shewn to himself.

πορευόμενος εἰς Μακεδονίαν. *When I was going into Macedonia.*
For the necessity of remanding this visit to a time outside the period
covered by the *Acts*, see *Introd.* p. xxiv. ff.

ἵνα παραγγείλῃς τισίν. *That thou mightest charge certain men.*
Classical Greek would require the optative mood after the past tense
παρεκάλεσα: but in the N.T. the use of ἵνα with the optative is seldom
found. παραγγελία is a regular term for 'an order' passed along the
line (παρά); see *v.* 5. The purpose of Timothy's continued residence
in Ephesus was that he might check the progress of heretical doctrine.
The false teachers are not named (their names were no doubt known
to Timothy), but they are described vaguely as τινές: this is St Paul's
usual way of referring to opponents (cp. *v.* 19 and 1 Cor. iv. 18, 2 Cor.
iii. 1, Gal. i. 7).

μὴ ἑτεροδιδασκαλεῖν. *Not to teach other* [sc. incongruous] *doctrine.*
The word ἑτεροδιδασκαλεῖν only occurs in the Greek Bible here and at
vi. 3. The element ἑτερο- points to irrelevance and incongruity of
teaching (see *Introd.* p. xlvi.), as in 2 Cor. xi. 4, Gal. i. 6 εὐαγγέλιον
ἕτερον; it is equivalent, in fact, to ἕτερα διδάσκειν, 'to be a teacher of
ἕτερα.' In our own Ordinal both priests and bishops are instructed
that it is their duty to drive away not only "erroneous" but "strange"
doctrine. So the false teachers are to be warned not 'to play at
deviations' from the faith. ἑτεροδιδασκαλεῖν is used by Ignatius
(*Polyc.* 3); similar verbal forms are νομοδιδάσκαλος (1 Tim. i. 7), καλοδιδάσκαλος (Tit. ii. 3), ψευδοδιδάσκαλος (2 Pet. ii. 1), κακοδιδασκαλεῖν
([2 Clem.] 10), ἐθελοδιδάσκαλος (Hermas *Sim.* ix. 22. 2), λαθροδιδασκα-
λεῖν (Iren. *Haer.* iii. 4. 2).

4. μηδὲ προσέχειν. *Not to give heed*, cp. especially Tit. i. 14.
The word is not used by St Paul outside the Pastorals, but is found in
other N.T. writers and is common in the LXX.

μύθοις καὶ γενεαλογίαις ἀπεράντοις. *To myths and endless genealogies.* The reference of these words, and the nature of the heretical
teaching which is deprecated, have already been discussed in the
Introduction (chap. iv.). The *myths* and *genealogies* were of Jewish
origin, and related to the heroes and patriarchs of early Hebrew
history; such legendary matter was foreign to the Gospel, and study
of it would distract from the essential doctrines of the Christian faith,
The word μῦθος (see 1 Tim. iv. 7; 2 Tim. iv. 4; Tit. i. 14) only
occurs once in the N.T. outside the Pastorals, viz. in 2 Pet. i. 16, and
once in the LXX. (Ecclus. xx. 19); γενεαλογία is only found in the Greek
Bible here and at Tit. iii. 9, but we have γενεαλογεῖσθαι in 1 Chr. v. 1;
ἀπέραντος, *interminable*, occurs twice in the LXX., but only here in
N.T. The connexion between μῦθοι and γενεαλογίαι is illustrated by
the rule of interpretation laid down by Cornutus, one of the later
Stoics: δεῖ δὲ μὴ συγχεῖν τοὺς μύθους...μηδ' εἴ τι προσεπλάσθη ταῖς κατ'
αὐτοὺς παραδιδομέναις γενεαλογίαις ὑπὸ τῶν μὴ συνέντων κ.τ.λ. (see
Zeller's *Stoics &c.* p. 356).

ἀπέραντος means *endless* and so 'tiresome.' There is no limit
(πέρας) to this sort of speculation, and nothing comes of it,

αἵτινες. *Inasmuch as they*=quippe quae; cp. Tit. i. 11.

ἐκζητήσεις παρέχουσι. *Minister questionings.* In like manner in Tit. iii. 9 the γενεαλογίαι are preceded by μωρὰς ζητήσεις. These questionings, according to the view which has been taken above of the heresies in the thought of the writer, were not so much concerned with abstract speculations (like the Gnostic enquiries about the origin of evil) as with legend and casuistry. Dr Hort suggested[1] that as *myths and genealogies* would include the Haggadoth or legendary developments of Hebrew history, so the *questionings* would embrace the problems of the Halacha, the other great province of Jewish teaching. This may have been the case, but it seems more natural in this context to understand by the ἐκζητήσεις something like the *Quaestiones in Genesin* of Philo. The vanity and unprofitableness of such enquiries may well have been present to the mind of St Paul.

μᾶλλον ἢ οἰκονομίαν θεοῦ τὴν ἐν πίστει. *Rather than the dispensation of God which is in faith.* οἰκονομία may mean either (*a*) the office of an οἰκονόμος, or (*b*), as here, the system by which he orders his household. Here the Church is the οἰκία, its members οἰκεῖοι, the plan on which God the great οἰκονόμος distributes His blessings, the οἰκονομία. So the word is often used by early writers of the Incarnation, as being the heart and kernel of the οἰκονομία. Cp. Aristides *Apol.* xv. καὶ τελέσας τὴν θαυμαστὴν αὐτοῦ οἰκονομίαν διὰ σταυροῦ θανάτου ἐγεύσατο ἑκουσίᾳ βουλῇ κατ' οἰκονομίαν μεγάλην. The heretical myths would do far more to encourage idle enquiries about matters of no importance than to promote that Divine dispensation whose sphere is faith, and not antiquarian curiosity. See the critical note, and, for St Paul's use of οἰκονομία, cp. Col. i. 25; Eph. i. 10, iii. 2, 9. Lightfoot (*Revision of N.T.* p. 184) called attention to the curious fact that in the English Bible of 1611 the word θεοῦ was left untranslated by inadvertence, the rendering there found being "edifying (reading οἰκοδομίαν) which is in faith"; in 1638 the mistake was discovered, and 'godly' was inserted after the earlier English versions.

5. τὸ δὲ τέλος. *But* (sc. in contrast with the irrelevant teaching of the ἑτεροδιδάσκαλοι) *the aim*, or final cause: cp. Rom. x. 4.

τῆς παραγγελίας. *Of the charge.* The reference is not to the Mosaic law, but to the whole of the practical teaching bound up with the Gospel; the word is suggested by παραγγείλῃς of *v.* 3 (where see note). This is the charge with which Timothy was entrusted (*v.* 18).

ἐστὶν ἀγάπη. *Is love*, sc. to men, not to God, which is not here in question. On the other hand, the fanciful ζητήσεις of the false teachers bred strife (2 Tim. ii. 23). As "love is the fulfilling of the Law" (Rom. xiii. 10), so it is the aim and purpose of the Gospel ethics, as the greatest Christian grace (1 Cor. xiii. 13). The word ἀγάπη has been described as "foreign to profane Greek" and as an ecclesiastical word, first appearing in literature in the LXX. But we find it in Egyptian Greek, in a letter, e.g., of the second century B.C.;

---

[1] *Judaistic Christianity*, p. 137.

and it is probable that the LXX. only took over and consecrated to high uses a word already current in the popular speech of Greek Egypt[1].

ἐκ καθαρᾶς καρδίας κ.τ.λ. The source of this ἀγάπη is threefold:— (i.) *a pure heart*, for which the Psalmist prayed (Ps. li. 6); cp. Matt. v. 8. καρδία stands in Scripture for the moral affections and emotions, the pathological, as contrasted with the intellectual, element of the moral faculty. Where this is corrupted (as was the case with the false teachers at Ephesus, vi. 5), the springs of moral action and spiritual insight (Matt. xv. 8) are poisoned, cp. 2 Tim. ii. 22;—(ii.) *a good conscience*. The συνείδησις represents the self sitting in judgement on self; it stands for the self-conscious and rational element in the man. Emphasis is specially laid on a good conscience in the Pastorals, e.g. *v.* 19, iii. 9, 2 Tim. i. 3; in sharp contrast with one who has a good conscience, the false teachers are κεκαυστηριασμένοι τὴν ἰδίαν συνείδησιν (iv. 2); cp. 1 Pet. iii. 16; Heb. xiii. 18[2];—(iii.) *faith unfeigned*. This brings in a reference to God, as the source and spring of love. Love is indeed for man the outward and appropriate manifestation of faith; cp. πίστις δι' ἀγάπης ἐνεργουμένη (Gal. v. 6). The juxtaposition of *a good conscience* and *faith* is significant; all through the Pastorals the intimate connexion of the two, the close relation between creed and life, is a prominent thought (see on Tit. i. 15). Again, we find this test of *faith unfeigned* lacking in the false teachers; they are ἀδόκιμοι περὶ τὴν πίστιν (2 Tim. iii. 8). The word ἀνυπόκριτος is applied to *faith* here and at 2 Tim. i. 5; it is applied to *love*, Rom. xii. 9; 2 Cor. vi. 6.

6. ὧν, sc. the three above-mentioned sources of ἀγάπη. ὧν is apparently governed by ἀστοχήσαντες, not by ἐξετράπησαν.

τινές. Note the usual vague reference to the false teachers.

ἀστοχήσαντες. *Having missed (their aim)*. ἀστοχεῖν is only used here and at vi. 21, 2 Tim. ii. 18 in N.T. (cp. Ecclus. vii. 19, viii. 9), and, in each case, of the failure of the ἑτεροδιδάσκαλοι; they may have meant well, but through want of sound method they failed to reach their goal.

ἐξετράπησαν. *Have swerved aside*, as from the straight path. Being once in the right way, they did not keep to it. ἐκτρέπεσθαι occurs four times in the Pastorals, but not again in St Paul; cp. Amos v. 8 and Hebr. xii. 13.

εἰς ματαιολογίαν. *To vain talking.* This was a special characteristic of the false teachers, who busied themselves unduly with vain and irrelevant questions; they are called ματαιολόγοι in the parallel passage Tit. i. 10. The abstract word ματαιολογία does not occur again in the Greek Bible.

---

[1] See Deissmann, *Bibelstudien*, p. 81.
[2] The necessity of a 'pure conscience,' if prayer is to be acceptable and effective, is frequently alluded to in the early liturgies, and also by Clement of Rome. See, for references, Lightfoot *Clement* I. 389 *n.* Cp. also the strong expression [2 Clem.] § 16 προσευχὴ δὲ ἐκ καλῆς συνειδήσεως ἐκ θανάτου ῥύεται.

ματαιολογία, *vaniloquium*, has in many ages and countries, and not only at Ephesus in the days of Timothy, proved the bane of theology. The subtleties of the Talmud are not worse than the absurdities of speculation to be found in so great a book as the *Summa Theologica* of St Thomas Aquinas.

7. θέλοντες εἶναι νομοδιδάσκαλοι. *Desiring to be* (i.e. almost *claiming* to be) *teachers of the law*, sc. of the Mosaic law. The false teaching had its roots in Judaism, and the intention of its exponents was good; they failed in their aims for the reasons now to be explained.

μὴ νοοῦντες μήτε ἃ λέγουσιν κ.τ.λ. *Understanding neither what they say, nor the subjects concerning which they make confident assertions.* Their ματαιολογία was, in many instances, devoid of meaning (μὴ νοοῦντες κ.τ.λ.); and they did not understand the principles underlying the Mosaic law which they professed to expound (μήτε περὶ τίνων κ.τ.λ.). Cp. 2 Tim. ii. 7 νόει ὃ λέγω. διαβεβαιοῦσθαι is found in the Greek Bible only here and at Tit. iii. 8 περὶ τούτων βούλομαί σε διαβεβαιοῦσθαι; it signifies positive affirmation and entire confidence on the part of the speaker.

8—11.   DIGRESSION TO AVOID MISUNDERSTANDING OF WHAT HAS BEEN JUST SAID.

8. οἴδαμεν δὲ κ.τ.λ. *But we know that the law is good, if a man use it lawfully.* For οἴδαμεν δέ cp. Rom. ii. 2, iii. 19, viii. 28 and οἴδαμεν ὅτι πάντες γνῶσιν ἔχομεν (1 Cor. viii. 1) 'we grant that &c.': the phrase introduces a *concession.* St Paul hastens on to explain that a true νομοδιδάσκαλος is a valuable minister of godliness; it is only the irrelevances and trivialities of these would-be teachers of the law that he deprecates. The law (sc. the Mosaic law) is good, if it be used for the purposes for which law (not only the law of Moses, but law in general) is intended, viz. to restrain ‚evil-doing; but not, if it be used as a peg on which to hang unverifiable speculation, or as a system of casuistry by which either asceticism, on the one hand, or licence, on the other, may be defended. He does not here take into account the function of law in developing a consciousness of sin which he elsewhere expounds (e.g. Rom. v. 20); the primary subject of law, in his thought, is not the righteous man, but the sinner, as he proceeds to explain.

καλὸς ὁ νόμος. The adj. καλός (also used of law at Rom. vii. 16) is used with unusual frequency in the Pastorals,' occurring 24 times, as against 16 occurrences in the other letters of St Paul. It expresses the 'beauty of holiness' in a fashion which no single English word can reproduce. To a Greek the union between 'goodness' and ' beauty' was almost inseparable in thought, and the best translation for καλός is, often, simply 'good.' But it has a shade of meaning which ἀγαθός has not, inasmuch as it directs attention to the outward and visible beauty of that which is 'good,' whilst ἀγαθός does not suggest anything beyond the intrinsic quality. See on ch. ii. 10 below.

νομίμως. The paronomasia or word-play is quite in St Paul's manner; law is good, if it be used *lawfully*, i.e. suitably to the purposes which law is intended to serve. The adverb νομίμως only occurs elsewhere in the Greek Bible at 2 Tim. ii. 5; 4 Macc. vi. 18.

9. **εἰδὼς τοῦτο.** This refers to the foregoing τις; the view which must be taken of the law by the teacher who would use it lawfully is now expounded.

δικαίῳ νόμος οὐ κεῖται. *The law* (sc. the Mosaic law, in particular, although the proposition is true of law in general) *is not laid down* (enacted) *for a righteous man* (δίκαιος being here used in its largest sense). κεῖμαι is the passive of τίθημι. τίθημι νόμον 'I enact a law,' sc. for other people; but κεῖται νόμος, 'the law is enacted,' and so is binding. It is quite in accordance with St Paul's usage to omit the article before νόμος when it signifies the Mosaic law; there are many examples in the Epistles to the Romans (e.g. ii. 25) and the Galatians (ii. 19).

ἀνόμοις δὲ καὶ ἀνυποτάκτοις. *But for the lawless and unruly,* a general description of those who will not submit to the restraints of law, viewed as an ordinance of *man.* We have the epithet ἀνυπότακτος again in Tit. i. 6, 10, and (in the sense of 'not subject to') in Heb. ii. 8; it is not found in the LXX., nor elsewhere in the N.T., but ὑποτάσσειν is a common Pauline word.

ἀσεβέσι καὶ ἀμαρτωλοῖς. *The ungodly and sinners,* a general description of those who will not obey the law, viewed now as an ordinance of *God.* ἀσεβής is the man without inward reverence, ἁμαρτωλός the man who defies God by outward act. The two epithets are conjoined again 1 Pet. iv. 18 (a quotation of Prov. xi. 31) and Jude 15.

These lawless ones are now more exactly described, the order of the Decalogue being followed, and the extremest form of the violation of the Commandment being specified in each case.

ἀνοσίοις καὶ βεβήλοις. *The unholy and profane.* Such is the temper which lies at the root of the sin of perjury, explicitly forbidden in the Third Commandment. ἀνόσιος is a LXX. word, only occurring again in N.T. at 2 Tim. iii. 2; βέβηλος is also a LXX. word, but not found in St Paul outside the Pastorals. βέβηλος conveys the idea of *secularity* (see esp. Lev. x. 10; Heb. xii. 16), and strictly means what may be 'walked on' (βα-), and so is outside the shrine.

πατρολῴαις καὶ μητρολῴαις. *Smiters of fathers and smiters of mothers.* These words do not occur again in the Bible, but are common in Greek literature; the rendering of A.V. and R.V. 'murderers of fathers' is, no doubt, legitimate, but it is not the sin of *murder,* but of *dishonouring parents,* which is here uppermost in the writer's thought, and the wider translation is justified by the usage of the words elsewhere. For this extreme and outrageous violation of the Fifth Commandment the punishment of death was provided in the Mosaic law (Ex. xxi. 15).

ἀνδροφόνοις. *Manslayers.* The word only occurs in the Greek Bible elsewhere at 2 Macc. ix. 28. Murder is, in itself, the worst and most explicit manifestation of human *hate*, forbidden in the Sixth Commandment.

10. πόρνοις, ἀρσενοκοίταις. *Fornicators, sodomites* ; the most repulsive forms of the violation of the Seventh Commandment. Cp. 1 Cor. vi. 9.

ἀνδραποδισταῖς. *Men-stealers.* A man's most precious possession is *himself*, and the worst form of thieving (condemned in the Eighth Commandment) is that practised by slave-dealers, whose booty is not *things*, but *persons.* Thus Philo (*de Spec. Leg.* IV. 4) has a section περὶ ἀνδραποδιστῶν, whom he explains to be the worst kind of thieves. This crime, again, was punishable with death according to the Pentateuchal Code (Exod. xxi. 16; Deut. xxiv. 7), though the word ἀνδραποδιστής is not found elsewhere in the Greek Bible.

ψεύσταις, ἐπιόρκοις. *Liars, perjurers.* To suppress the truth is a form of 'false witness,' but the worst form is a false charge made on oath. ἐπίορκος is not found again in the N.T.; but cp. Matt. v. 33.

καὶ εἴ τι ἕτερον κ.τ.λ. Only those sins have been enumerated of which human law can take cognisance, and so violations of the Tenth Commandment are not specified in this dreadful catalogue. The concluding phrase is very like Rom. xiii. 9 καὶ εἴ τις ἑτέρα ἐντολή κ.τ.λ., and is quite in St Paul's manner.

τῇ ὑγιαινούσῃ διδασκαλίᾳ. *To sound doctrine.* This remarkable metaphor, according to which the true doctrine is *wholesome*, and the false, *diseased*, is repeated again and again in the Pastoral Epistles. We have ὑγιαίνουσα διδασκαλία here; 2 Tim. iv. 3; Tit. i. 9, ii. 1; ὑγιαίνοντες λόγοι vi. 3; 2 Tim. i. 13; ὑγιαίνειν τῇ πίστει 2 Tim. i. 13; Tit. ii. 2; λόγος ὑγιής Tit. ii. 8; and in 2 Tim. ii. 17 the false λόγος is compared to a γάγγραινα. It has been suggested that this medical phraseology may be due to the influence of St Luke the physician. Again, it might be urged that such language only continues the metaphor by which in earlier letters of St Paul the Christian Society is compared to a body. When the Body of Christ is in a sound condition, the expression of its belief will be healthy; and if it be diseased, the false doctrine will be like a gangrene eating into its vitals. But in truth the comparison of the soundness of the moral and spiritual judgement to the health of the body is not so far-fetched or so novel as to need elaborate explanation. In Greek literature it is common. Clement of Alexandria, commenting on ch. vi. 3 (*Strom.* I. 8), quotes in illustration a line of Euripides (*Phoen.* 473) in which the ἄδικος λόγος is said to be νοσῶν ἐν αὑτῷ. Plato, in a famous passage (*Republ.* IV. 18), explains ἀρετὴ μὲν ἄρα, ὡς ἔοικεν, ὑγίειά τέ τις ἂν εἴη καὶ κάλλος καὶ εὐεξία ψυχῆς, κακία δὲ νόσος τε καὶ αἶσχος καὶ ἀσθένεια. (Cp. also Plutarch *Vir. mor.* 2.) And so in the LXX. of Prov. xxxi. 8 (xxiv. 76) we have κρῖνε πάντας ὑγιῶς, as parallel to κρῖνε δικαίως. But we perhaps come nearest to the metaphor as used in the Pastorals in the Stoic idea that the πάθη were diseases, which the wise man should

eradicate by every means in his power.   So in Philo we have the very
phrase of St Paul anticipated: ἔτι τῶν παθῶν καὶ νοσημάτων παρευημε-
ρούντων **τοὺς ὑγιαίνοντας λόγους** (*de Abrah.* 38), i.e. ' the passions and
diseases prevailing over the sound λόγοι.'   And with this well accords
the language of the Collect for St Luke's Day, where we pray that "by
the wholesome medicines of the doctrine delivered by him, all the
diseases of our souls may be healed."

The word διδασκαλία is used with peculiar frequency in the
Pastorals, occurring 13 times in the sense of *doctrine*, as in Eph. iv.
14; Col. ii. 22. (Cp. Matt. xv. 9.)   It is found twice (1 Tim. iv. 13,
where see note, and v. 17) in the sense of *instruction* or *art of teaching*,
as in Rom. xii. 7, xv. 4.   It was natural that, in the development of
the Church's life, the word for *teaching* should gradually come to be
used for the *content of the teaching*, the doctrine taught.   See note on
iv. 13.

11.   κατὰ τὸ εὐαγγέλιον κ.τ.λ.   This seems to be in connexion with
the 'sound doctrine' of which the Apostle has just spoken; viz. *if
there be anything else opposed to the sound doctrine, according to the
gospel of the glory* &c.

τὸ εὐαγγέλιον τῆς δόξης τοῦ μακαρίου θεοῦ.   Cp. the expression τὸ
εὐαγγέλιον τῆς δόξης τοῦ Χριστοῦ in 2 Cor. iv. 4.   In both cases δόξης is
the genitive of *contents*; the import or substance of the good tidings
preached is 'the glory of God,' which is described in Rom. v. 2 as the
object of the Christian's hope (cp. also Tit. ii. 13).   δόξα is in these
passages used for a glorious revelation of God, as in Acts vii. 2; and
the meaning of the whole phrase is that, according to the Gospel of
the glorious revelation vouchsafed in Jesus Christ, justification comes
not through the law.   The use of the law is negative, to restrain and
punish evildoers; but obedience to it has of itself no justifying efficacy.   Cp. Rom. iii. 20.

τοῦ μακαρίου θεοῦ.   This and vi. 15 are the only two passages either
in O.T. or N.T. where μακάριος is applied to God.   God is not only
εὐλογητός, the Object of His creatures' blessing, but μακάριος, having
in Himself the fulness of bliss (cp. Tit. ii. 13).   So in Homer and
Hesiod the gods are called μάκαρες θεοί, and the epithet is frequently
used by Philo.

ὃ ἐπιστεύθην ἐγώ.   This is characteristically Pauline; cp. Rom. iii.
2; 1 Cor. ix. 17; Gal. ii. 7; 1 Thess. ii. 4; Tit. i. 3.

12—17.   PARENTHETIC DOXOLOGY.

These verses are a digression, quite in the manner of St Paul,
suggested by the thought of the Divine mercy vouchsafed to him
personally.   Cf. 1 Cor. xv. 9; Eph. iii. 8.

12.   χάριν ἔχω.   This formula of thankfulness (instead of the more
usual εὐχαριστῶ with which St Paul begins nearly all his letters)
occurs again 2 Tim. i. 3.   Cp. Luke xvii. 9 and Heb. xii. 28.

τῷ ἐνδυναμώσαντι. *To Him that hath enabled me*; a favourite expression with Paul in reference to the grace of Christ. In the Ephesian letter he bids his correspondents ἐνδυναμοῦσθε ἐν κυρίῳ (Eph. vi. 10); he charges Timothy ἐνδυναμοῦ ἐν τῇ χάριτι τῇ ἐν Χρ. Ἰησοῦ (2 Tim. ii. 1); of himself he says ὁ κύριος...ἐνεδυνάμωσέ με (2 Tim. iv. 17), and (a close parallel to the present passage) πάντα ἰσχύω ἐν τῷ ἐνδυναμοῦντί με (Phil. iv. 13). In the beginning of his ministry it was said Σαῦλος δὲ μᾶλλον ἐνεδυναμοῦτο (Acts ix. 22); and the spiritual δύναμις, needed for the due discharge of the apostolic office, was never lacking throughout his course. The aorist participle here suggests a direct reference to the early days of his preaching (see *v.* 13), but we must not limit the reference to these. A study of the verb in the various contexts in which it is found is instructive. Of all the faithful may the words be used, ἐδυναμώθησαν ἀπὸ ἀσθενείας (Heb. xi. 34); none can more fully realise their truth than those upon whom the burden and responsibility of the pastoral office have been imposed.

ὅτι. *That*, not *because*. The sentence expresses the *reason* of his thankfulness.

πιστόν. The word occurs eleven times in this Epistle. Here it means 'trustworthy,' as at 1 Cor. iv. 2; Heb. xi. 11. See on i. 15 and iv. 3 below.

ἡγήσατο. This is a common Pauline word. Cp. 1 Thess. v. 13; 2 Cor. ix. 5; Phil. ii. 3, 25 &c.

θέμενος. *Appointing* me (note the tense); the word is used of the Divine purpose (as in 1 Thess. v. 9) and so is not equivalent to 'putting me,' cp. 1 Tim. ii. 7; 2 Tim. i. 11.

διακονίαν. The word διακονίαν is used here, not specially of the function discharged by a διάκονος, but in the general sense of 'ministry.' St Paul frequently speaks of his apostolic office as a διακονία and of himself as a διάκονος. Compare, e.g., Rom. xi. 13 τὴν διακονίαν μου δοξάζω, also 2 Cor. v. 18, vi. 3; and, again, Col. i. 23 τοῦ εὐαγγελίου...οὗ ἐγενόμην ἐγὼ Παῦλος διάκονος, and 1 Cor. iii. 5; 2 Cor. iii. 6; Eph. iii. 7 &c. διακονία, in short, originally meant service of any sort; it is applied in Acts i. 17, 25 to the service of apostleship, and is continually used throughout the Pauline Epistles in a wide and general sense. By the second century the words διακονία, διάκονος were generally restricted to the third order of the Christian ministry, and the beginnings of this specialisation of meaning may be traced in the N.T. Cp. e.g. Rom. xvi. 1; Phil. i. 1; 1 Tim. iii. 8, 12 (where see notes). Thus the use of this word here to denote the apostolic office is in favour of an early date for the Epistle. No writer of the second century (by which time the distinction of orders was fully recognised) would have used a term then significant of the lowest grade in the ministry for St Paul's ministerial work; cp. 2 Tim. iv. 5.

13. τὸ πρότερον ὄντα. *Although I was aforetime.* Cp. Gal. iv. 13 for the significance of τὸ πρότερον.

βλάσφημον καὶ διώκτην καὶ ὑβριστήν. The βλάσφημος displays his hostility to the truth chiefly in *words* (see Acts xxvi. 11); the διώκτης, in *deeds* (see Gal. i. 13, where St Paul refers to his zeal as a persecutor). The term ὑβριστής only occurs once again in N.T., viz. Rom. i. 30; it conveys the idea of violence and outrage (see Acts viii. 3). It is a stronger word than either of the other two.

ἀλλὰ ἠλεήθην, ὅτι κ.τ.λ. *Howbeit I obtained mercy because*, &c. See Acts iii. 17, and our Lord's prayer for His executioners, Luke xxiii. 34.

14. ὑπερεπλεόνασεν. A rare word, not found elsewhere in N.T. or in the LXX.; it occurs in the *Psalms of Solomon*, v. 19, and in Hermas, *Mand.* v. 2. St Paul shews a marked inclination in all four groups of his letters for verbs compounded with ὑπέρ, e.g. ὑπεραυξάνω (2 Thess. i. 3); ὑπερβαίνω (1 Thess. iv. 6); ὑπερεκτείνω (2 Cor. x. 14), ὑπερεντυγχάνω (Rom. viii. 26); ὑπερνικάω (Rom. viii. 37); ὑπερυψόω (Phil. ii. 9); ὑπερφρονέω (Rom. xii. 3); all of which are ἅπαξ λεγόμενα in the N.T. Compare with the present passage ὑπερεπερίσσευσεν ἡ χάρις (Rom. v. 20).

The simple title ὁ κύριος ἡμῶν, without the addition of Ἰησοῦς Χριστός either before or after, is only used by St Paul here and at 2 Tim. i. 8; cp. Heb. vii. 14.

μετὰ πίστεως κ.τ.λ. Faith and love are the characteristic concomitants of the grace of our Lord. The best gifts of the grace which is from Christ are faith in Him, and love which, centred in Him, necessarily embraces all the members of that human family whose brotherhood is revealed in the Fact of the Incarnation. There is an intimate connexion between them; ἀγάπη μετὰ πίστεως is part of St Paul's benediction at the close of the Ephesian letter (Eph. vi. 23); the breastplate 'πίστεως καὶ ἀγάπης' is part of the Christian panoply (1 Thess. v. 8); it is indeed through 'love' that 'faith' manifests itself most plainly; cp. Gal. v. 6, πίστις δι᾽ ἀγάπης ἐνεργουμένη. See on 1 Tim. i. 5 and Tit. ii. 2.

15. πιστὸς ὁ λόγος. This remarkable formula is peculiar to the Pastorals. Here and in iv. 9 the words καὶ πάσης ἀποδοχῆς ἄξιος are added; in iii. 1, 2 Tim. ii. 11, and Tit. iii. 8 we have the simple form πιστὸς ὁ λόγος. In iii. 1 it introduces a saying which may well have become proverbial at this stage of the Church's development, *If a man seeketh the office of a bishop, he desireth a good work.* In 2 Tim. ii. 11 the words which follow probably formed part of an early Christian hymn (εἰ γὰρ συναπεθάνομεν, καὶ συνζήσομεν κ.τ.λ.). In the three remaining cases it refers to some important statement of doctrine tersely and generally expressed (as here and in iv. 8, 9), or with more detail (as in Tit. iii. 8). πιστός is used in the sense of *trustworthy* (see below on iv. 3); and a 'faithful saying' in the Pastorals indicates a maxim (whether of doctrine or practice) on which full reliance may be placed. There is nothing in the N.T. quite analogous to the phrase. We have πιστὸς ὁ θεός (1 Cor. i. 9, x. 13; 2 Cor. i. 18), πιστὸς ὁ καλῶν (1 Thess. v. 24), but these do not help us much. A more instructive parallel is afforded by οὗτοι οἱ λόγοι πιστοὶ καὶ ἀληθινοί εἰσιν of Rev. xxi. 5, xxii. 6. The usual Latin rendering of πιστός in the phrase πιστὸς ὁ λόγος is *fidelis*; but at this verse r has *humanus*, a reading also adopted by Augustine in one place. See crit. note on iii. 1.

πάσης ἀποδοχῆς ἄξιος. ἀποδοχή only occurs again in the Greek Bible at iv. 9. It had come to mean *approbation* in late Greek; cp. Philo (*de Praem. et Poen.* 2) where the man who is ἀποδοχῆς ἄξιος is contrasted with the ὑπαίτιος. Cp. also an inscription found at Ephesus[1]:

> Τίτου Αἰλίου
> Πρίσκου ἀνδρὸς δοκιμωτάτου καὶ
> πάσης τιμῆς καὶ ἀποδοχῆς ἀξίου.

The rendering *acceptation* gives the nearest sense here; cp. Acts ii. 41, οἱ μὲν οὖν ἀποδεξάμενοι τὸν λόγον αὐτοῦ ἐβαπτίσθησαν.

We thus translate: *worthy of all* (universal) *acceptation*. As always in such constructions in St Paul, πᾶς is used *extensively*, not *intensively*, and the phrase is equivalent to 'acceptation by everyone,' or as we have it in our office of Holy Communion (where this verse is one of the Comfortable Words) "worthy of all men to be received."

Χρ. Ἰη. ἦλθεν εἰς τὸν κόσμον. The phrase is, with this exception, only found in the Fourth Gospel (see John i. 9, xii. 46, xvi. 28), and is not characteristically Pauline; it here occurs in a doctrinal formula so familiar and undisputed among Christians as to take rank as a 'faithful saying.' Indirectly the expression involves, as has been often pointed out, the pre-existence or προύπαρξις of the Redeemer; but the prominent thought in the 'saying' is simply that Redemption was part of the purpose of the Incarnation. The 'coming into the world' is the assumption of human nature by the Eternal Word. It is worth observing that throughout this Epistle the name of our Lord is Χριστὸς Ἰησοῦς, not Ἰησοῦς Χριστός. It is God's Anointed who is man's Saviour.

ἁμαρτωλοὺς σῶσαι. Parallels from the Gospels readily suggest themselves; St Luke v. 32 is the nearest in form. The statement is quite general.

ὧν πρῶτός εἰμι ἐγώ. "Non quia prior peccavit, sed quia plus peccavit" (Aug. *Serm.* 299); πρῶτος here applies not to time, but to degree; Paul is 'chief,' not 'first' of sinners. The phrase may seem extravagant, and indeed would hardly have commended itself to a forger; but it is quite in conformity with St Paul's way of speaking of himself and his conversion. Cp. 1 Cor. xv. 9 and Eph. iii. 8, where the expressions "the least of the Apostles," "less than the least of all saints," are used by him. Such language is not to be described as mere rhetoric; it is too often found in the writings of the most saintly and most sincere to permit of any such explanation. For instance, Ignatius again and again speaks of himself as 'the last' (ἔσχατος) of

[1] See *Classical Review* I. 1, p. 4.

the Christians at Antioch, among whom he is not worthy to be reckoned (*Ephes.* 21; *Magn.* 14, &c.). The Confessions of St Augustine, the autobiography of Bunyan, the letters of Dr Pusey, furnish other notable illustrations. The truth is that in proportion as a man fixes his ideal high, in proportion as he appreciates the possibilities of what St Paul calls 'life in Christ,' in that proportion will his actual progress in the spiritual life appear poor and unworthy of the grace with which he has been endowed. It is noteworthy that the Apostle does not say 'of whom I *was* chief,' but 'I *am*,' by the present tense marking the abiding sense of personal sinfulness.

16. ἀλλὰ διὰ τοῦτο ἠλεήθην, ἵνα κ.τ.λ. '*Howbeit for this cause I obtained mercy,* viz., *that* &c.' διὰ τοῦτο emphasises the following ἵνα, as in 2 Cor. xiii. 10.

ἐν ἐμοὶ πρώτῳ, *in me as chief*; this is the rendering of the Revisers, and certainly brings out the connexion with ὧν πρῶτός εἰμι ἐγώ of the preceding verse better than A.V. "first." As Bengel puts it: 'Incomparabile exemplum Pauli, sive peccatum sive misericordiam spectes.' This is borne out by the words which follow, *that in me as chief Jesus Christ might shew forth* ('display,' 'give a signal instance of') *the entire range of His long-suffering.* ἅπας (see critical note) is stronger than the more usual πᾶς, and is deliberately used by St Paul here. A close parallel is found in Eph. ii. 7, ἵνα ἐνδείξηται ἐν τοῖς αἰῶσιν τοῖς ἐπερχομένοις τὸ ὑπερβάλλον πλοῦτος τῆς χάριτος αὐτοῦ ἐν χρηστότητι ἐφ' ἡμᾶς ἐν Χρ. Ἰη.

μακροθυμίαν. This is a late Greek word, of frequent occurrence in N.T. and LXX., but rarely elsewhere (it is found e.g. in Plutarch). In 2 Tim. iii. 10 and iv. 2 (and generally in St Paul) it is applied to the *longsuffering* which becomes a Christian apostle; here, as in Rom. ii. 4, ix. 22; 1 Pet. iii. 20, it is used of God.

πρὸς ὑποτύπωσιν κ.τ.λ. ὑποτύπωσις does not occur in the Greek Bible save here and in 2 Tim. i. 13. It is, literally, an 'outline sketch,' and so a 'pattern' or 'ensample'; and the meaning is that the purpose of the manifestation of the Divine longsuffering to St Paul was that he might furnish a type or *ensample of them which should hereafter believe.* A somewhat similar expression is found in 2 Pet. ii. 6, ὑπόδειγμα μελλόντων ἀσεβεῖν τεθεικώς, where it is applied to the Cities of the Plain, which were, as we say in common speech, 'made an example of' for their abominations.

πιστεύειν ἐπ' αὐτῷ εἰς ζωὴν αἰώνιον. Faith in Christ has as its consequent eternal life. For πιστ. ἐπ' αὐτῷ, cp. Is. xxviii. 16 (quoted in Rom. ix. 33 and x. 11) πᾶς ὁ πιστεύων ἐπ' αὐτῷ οὐ καταισχυνθήσεται.

17. We have here a characteristic breaking out into a doxology. A complete list of the Apostolic doxologies has been drawn out by Dr Westcott (*Additional Note* on Heb. xiii. 21)[1], and will repay careful study. In the three doxologies of the Pastoral Epistles (1 Tim. i. 17, vi. 16, and 2 Tim. iv. 18) we may perhaps observe a greater

---

[1] See also Chase, *Lord's Prayer in the Early Church*, p. 168 ff.

tendency to dwell on the absolute Eternity, Power, Unity of the God-head, than in the expressions of thanksgiving in the earlier letters; but the main features are the same in all. In only one instance, 1 Pet. iv. 11, is the verb expressed, ᾧ ἐστὶν ἡ δόξα καὶ τὸ κράτος; and it seems probable that in every instance ἐστίν rather than ἔστω should be understood. So the verb in the doxology at the end of the Lord's Prayer (Matt. vi. 13) is in the indicative mood. A doxology is not a prayer or an aspiration; it is a reverent and thankful statement of the Divine glory.

τῷ δὲ βασιλεῖ τῶν αἰώνων. This exact phrase occurs elsewhere in the Greek Bible only in Tobit xiii. 6, 10, and in Rev. xv. 3 (where the received text has τῶν ἁγίων); but it naturally flows from the language of Ps. cxlv. 13, ἡ βασιλεία σου βασιλεία πάντων τῶν αἰώνων. Cp. Exod. xv. 18 (where Philo read βασιλεύων τῶν αἰώνων, *De Mundo*, 7), Ecclus. xxxvi. 19, and Bk of Enoch ix. 4, where one of the texts has βασιλεὺς τῶν αἰώνων. See also *Book of Jubilees*, xxv. 15; xxxi. 13. The cor-responding expression οἱ βασιλεῖαι τοῦ αἰῶνος τούτου, which occurs in Ignatius (*Rom.* 6), brings the meaning out well. There is no reference to the *aeons* of Gnostic heresy; αἰών in the singular means an 'age,' a certain limit of time, and so ὁ αἰὼν οὗτος is 'this present age.' But in the plural, when we sum up these 'ages' or 'world periods,' we arrive at the idea of eternity; and 'the King who rules over the ages' is 'the King eternal.' So too εἰς τὸν αἰῶνα = 'to the end of this present age'; but εἰς τοὺς αἰῶνας = 'for ever.'

ἀφθάρτῳ ἀοράτῳ μόνῳ. All three adjectives qualify θεῷ, not the preceding βασιλεῖ τῶν αἰώνων. ἄφθαρτος θεός is a combination only found again in Rom. i. 23; but ἄφθαρτος is a regular epithet of Deity in Philo (e.g. *Quod deus immut.* 6). For ἀόρατος we may compare Rom. i. 20; Col. i. 15, and Heb. xi. 27. With both expressions cp. ὁ μόνος ἔχων ἀθανασίαν...ὃν εἶδεν οὐδεὶς ἀνθρώπων of vi. 16.

μόνῳ θεῷ. Bengel calls this a 'magnifica lectio' (see critical note). Cp. John xvii. 3, τὸν μόνον ἀληθινὸν θεόν, Rom. xvi. 27 and ch. vi. 15. Compare also Philo's μὰ τὸν ἀληθῆ μόνον θεόν (*Leg. All.* ii. 17) and ἡ θεοῦ μόνου θεραπεία (*De Prof.* 7).

τιμὴ καὶ δόξα. This combination in a doxology occurs again only in Rev. v. 13. Cp. Rev. iv. 9 and Rom. ii. 7, 10.

εἰς τοὺς αἰῶνας τῶν αἰώνων· ἀμήν. Perhaps this phrase implies that the form of doxology in this verse had become stereotyped by liturgical use. At all events this is a common ending. See Heb. xiii. 21; 1 Pet. iv. 11, v. 11; Rev. vii. 12: cp. Psalms *passim*.

18, 19. THE CHARGE TO TIMOTHY REITERATED.

18. ταύτην τὴν παραγγελίαν. If the interval of 15 verses were not so long, it would be natural to take this as the apodosis of καθὼς παρεκάλεσά σε of *v.* 3, but it seems better to suppose (see note *in loc.*) that the protasis there is never complemented, and that the sentence (quite in St Paul's manner) breaks off unfinished. Chrysostom and many commentators explain ταύτην τὴν παραγγελίαν by what follows, ἵνα στρατεύσῃ, &c.; but this is not so much the *matter* as the *motive* of the charge. The reference is rather to the παραγγελία of *v.* 5, the main subject of the Epistle; and this is confirmed by the close similarity of verses 6 and 19.

παρατίθεμαί σοι. The same word is used in 2 Tim. ii. 2; Timothy in his turn is to 'commit' to faithful men that which he has received; cp. 1 Tim. vi. 20; 2 Tim. i. 12, 14.

κατὰ τὰς προαγούσας ἐπὶ σὲ προφητείας. This committal of trust is *according to the prophecies directed to thee previously.* We have the phrase προαγούσης ἐντολῆς, 'a foregoing commandment' in Heb. vii. 18; but here ἐπὶ σέ requires the sense 'leading up to' (cp. Ezek. xiii. 16). What the prophecies spoken of were it is impossible to determine with confidence. Hort (*Christian Ecclesia*, p. 181 ff.) put forward the hypothesis that St Paul's action in the circumcision of Timothy at Lystra (Acts xvi. 3), and his choice of the young convert as an associate in the work of the Gospel, were prompted by prophetic voices which then *led the way* to Timothy. But, when we compare the language of iv. 14, in which the χάρισμα given to Timothy, διὰ προφητείας μετὰ ἐπιθέσεως τῶν χειρῶν τοῦ πρεσβυτερίου, is mentioned, it seems more probable that in both this verse and iv. 14 the reference is to prophecies uttered at the ordination of Timothy. Cp. Clem. Alex. *Quis Dives*, § 42, ἕνα τέ τινα κληρώσων τῶν ὑπὸ τοῦ πνεύματος σημαινομένων. Thus the plural προφητείας would be explained by the number of the 'prophets' present. The description in Acts xiii. 2 of the ordination of S. Paul himself helps us in some measure to realise such a scene.

ἵνα στρατεύσῃ κ.τ.λ. *That in* (the strength of) *them* (sc. the prophecies spoken over him) *thou mayest war the good warfare.* This is the purpose which St Paul has in view in recalling to Timothy the words of hope and promise used at his ordination. στρατεία is 'militia,' a campaign, and is not to be confounded with μάχη, which is but a single battle. The ὅπλα of this στρατεία are spoken of, 2 Cor. x. 4. The idea, however, is quite distinct from that in vi. 12, ἀγωνίζου τὸν καλὸν ἀγῶνα (cp. also 2 Tim. iv. 7), where see the note. Cp. 4 Macc. ix. 23, where the exclamation is recorded of one of the martyr-brethren, ἱερὰν καὶ εὐγενῆ στρατείαν στρατεύσασθε περὶ τῆς εὐσεβείας.

19. **ἔχων πίστιν καὶ ἀγαθὴν συνείδησιν.** Cp. *v.* 5, where *faith* and a '*good conscience*' are named as sources of that *love* which is the τέλος τῆς παραγγελίας.

ἥν τινες ἀπωσάμενοι. *Which* [sc. the good conscience] *some having thrust from them.* The verb is expressive of a wilful and violent act. For τινες see on *v.* 3 above.

περὶ τὴν πίστιν ἐναυάγησαν. *Have made shipwreck in the matter of the faith.* ναυαγεῖν only occurs in the N.T. here and in 2 Cor. xi. 25; and so far may be called a 'Pauline' word, but it is not uncommon in late Greek.

ἡ πίστις here (though the presence of the article would not by itself determine this) is to be taken *objectively*, as equivalent to 'the Christian faith,' not *subjectively*, of the faith of individuals. The words πιστός, πίστις have an interesting history, which cannot be here discussed at length[1]; but a few references must be given. πίστις, which in Philo is used quite vaguely of belief and trust in God, became to the early Christians gradually equivalent to faith in Christ as the supreme revelation of God. This faith grew by degrees in clearness and distinctness, until it embraced the Incarnation, the Atonement, and all the great dogmas of the Gospel; from this the transition was easy to the word being used objectively to signify the *content*, as it were, of a Christian's belief, to signify, in short, the Christian Creed, the Gospel. Among the more conspicuous instances of this use of the word in the N.T. outside the Pastorals may be noted Acts vi. 7, xiii. 8, xvi. 5; Gal. i. 23, iii. 23; Phil. i. 27. In the Pastorals, which give us a more developed form of Christianity, we find as is natural a proportionately larger number of examples of this usage; and out of 33 occurrences of πίστις in these Epistles the *objective* sense seems to be required in 1 Tim. i. 19, iv. 1, 6, v. 8, vi. 10, 21; 2 Tim. iii. 8, iv. 7; Tit. i. 13. See notes *in loc.* in each case.

20. EXAMPLES OF 'SHIPWRECKS OF FAITH.'

20. Ὑμέναιος. This is doubtless the same Hymenæus who is mentioned as a heretical teacher in 2 Tim. ii. 17.

Ἀλέξανδρος. An Alexander is mentioned three times in connexion with Ephesus: (i.) here; (ii.) an Alexander was put forward as their spokesman by the Jews on the occasion of the uproar excited by the silversmiths at Ephesus (Acts xix. 33); (iii.) 'Alexander the coppersmith' (2 Tim. iv. 14) who 'did much evil' to St Paul. The designation ὁ χαλκεύς suggests that there were at all events two men of the same name; and this appears again from the consideration that (i.) was a heretical Christian, while (ii.) was a Jew (Acts xix. 34). ὁ χαλκεύς might be either; but there are no sufficient data to determine the question.

παρέδωκα τῷ σατανᾷ. In 1 Cor. v. 5 St Paul directs the Corinthian Church in the case of a certain notorious sinner, παραδοῦναι τὸν τοιοῦτον τῷ σατανᾷ εἰς ὄλεθρον τῆς σαρκός, ἵνα τὸ πνεῦμα σωθῇ κ.τ.λ.; and the formula *to deliver to Satan* has plainly the same significance there as here. It is certainly a *disciplinary* or *remedial* and not a merely *punitive* penalty in both cases (cp. Job ii.·6, where a similar expression is used of Job's sufferings, εἶπεν δὲ ὁ κύριος τῷ διαβόλῳ Ἰδοὺ παραδίδωμί σοι αὐτόν), and it was a penalty within the power of the Church to inflict. The aorist παρέδωκα here seems to indicate that St Paul's action, whatever it was, took place at Ephesus at a definite time; and this marks its official character. It seems then best to suppose that the 'delivering over to Satan' was a spiritual penalty, like excommunication, the strong phrase resting on the principle that the kingdoms of Christ and of Satan are mutually exclusive (see

---

[1] See Lightfoot, *Galatians,* p. 154 ff., and Hort, 1 *Peter,* p. 81 ff.

Acts xxvi. 18; Col. i. 13), and that this was accompanied by the supernatural infliction of bodily sickness, which it was believed would follow the authoritative sentence. The cases of Ananias and Sapphira (Acts v. 1—11) and of Elymas (Acts xiii. 11) witness to the power granted to the Apostles of calling down supernatural punishments on evil-doers in exceptional circumstances.

ἵνα παιδευθῶσιν. This is the purpose of the sentence, *that they may be disciplined* &c., either by supernatural penalties (ὄλεθρον τῆς σαρκός, 1 Cor. v. 5) or by the mere fact of exclusion from the Christian society and consequent loss of privilege.

CHAPTER II.

3. Rec. text with אᶜD₂GKLP, and all (except the Egyptian) versions add γὰρ after τοῦτο. It is omitted by א*A and was apparently introduced solely to emphasise the connexion between v. 2 and v. 3.

7. Rec. text with א*D₂ᶜKL adds ἐν Χριστῷ after λέγω; this is plainly a gloss introduced from Rom. ix. 1, and is omitted by אᶜAD₂*GP and all early versions.

8. διαλογισμοῦ. So א*AD₂KLP d f m and the received text; the plural διαλογισμῶν (used everywhere else in N.T. except Luke ix. 46, 47) is supported by אᶜGg and the Syriac versions, and is preferred by Westcott and Hort, who put διαλογισμοῦ in their margin.

9. Rec. text is ὡσαύτως καὶ τὰς γυναῖκας. τάς (added in D₂ᵇᶜKL) and most cursives) is omitted by אAD₂*GP. καί is found in אᶜD₂GKL and all the versions, but א*AP omit it. Westcott and Hort read ὡσαύτως γυναῖκας.

κοσμίῳ. So the bulk of authorities; but κοσμίως is found in אᶜD₂*G and is given a place in Westcott and Hort's margin.

χρυσῷ. So rec. text with אD₂KL. AGP have χρυσίῳ.

12. διδάσκειν δὲ γυναικί. γυναικὶ δὲ διδάσκειν is the order in KL and most cursives; text אAD₂GP.

14. ἐξαπατηθεῖσα. So א*AD₂*GP. Rec. text has ἀπατηθεῖσα, following אᶜD₂ᵇᶜKL and most cursives; this is obviously a correction of the text suggested by the simple verb ἠπατήθη, in the first clause of the verse.

Chap. II. 1—8. I. Practical directions about public worship.

i. Prayer is to be made for all men.

1. οὖν. As in 2 Tim. ii. 1, so here, οὖν marks the transition from the general charge to the particular injunctions.

πρῶτον πάντων. The expression does not occur again in N.T.; it does not merely denote the order of time, but the order of dignity. The directions which follow relate to public prayer and the conduct of

public devotions; and of these the most important is that which
emphasises the Catholic nature of Christian worship. The opening
sentence of the Prayer for the Church Militant is taken from this
verse, viz., "Almighty and everliving God, who by Thy holy Apostle
hast taught us to make prayers, and supplications, and to give thanks,
for all men," and such intercessions for those in authority in Church
and State are found in the primitive liturgy in the *Apostolic Constitutions.* In these latest Epistles of St Paul we seem to have a more
developed form of common worship than is found in earlier letters.

ποιεῖσθαι is middle voice, as the order of words shews, not passive:
'I exhort (you) to make &c.' Cp. Luke v. 33, οἱ μαθηταὶ Ἰωάνου...δεήσεις
ποιοῦνται, and Phil. i. 4, μετὰ χαρᾶς τὴν δέησιν ποιούμενος. ποιεῖσθαι is
often used with a noun to express by way of periphrasis what would
be more simply stated by a verb, e.g. Luke xiii. 22, πορείαν ποιούμενος.

δεήσεις, προσευχάς, ἐντεύξεις, εὐχαριστίας. The four words are not
to be too sharply distinguished, inasmuch as they point to different
moods of the suppliant rather than to the different forms into which
public prayer may be cast. δέησις expresses the sense of *need* (what
we require, δεῖ), and is a less comprehensive term than προσευχή; the
former being equivalent to 'supplication' (*imploratio*), and the latter
to 'prayer' in general (*oratio*). προσευχή is always used in a religious
sense of prayers addressed to God, and in this differs from the other
three terms, which are all used of human intercourse as well. ἔντευξις
is the regular word for a 'petition' to a superior, e.g. to the emperor,
as in Just. *Apol.* i. 1, in the Petrie Papyri *passim,* and in inscriptions.
In 2 Macc. iv. 8, the only place where it occurs in the Greek Bible
outside the Pastorals, it has a reference to a conference between Jason
and Antiochus. It is used of a petition to God here and in ch. iv. 5;
and also in Philo (*Quod det. pot.* § 25, ἐντεύξεις καὶ ἐκβοήσεις), and in
Hermas (*Mand.* x. 3). Probably the leading idea in the word is that
of boldness of access, of confidence. Though the substantive is not
employed elsewhere by St Paul, ἐντυγχάνειν, 'to entreat,' is Pauline;
see e.g. Rom. viii. 27. The translation 'intercessions' in A.V. and
R.V. is misleading, as it suggests a limitation of the meaning to
petition *for others,* which is not involved. ('Intercession,' however, in
the English of the A.V. had a wider sense, as may be seen from Jer.
xxvii. 18, xxxvi. 25.) εὐχαριστία is not yet confined to the special
ecclesiastical significance which it was soon to have; in this context it
is simply that 'thanksgiving' which is the complement of all true
prayer (cp. Phil. iv. 6, ἐν παντὶ τῇ προσευχῇ καὶ τῇ δεήσει μετ' εὐχαριστίας). Augustine, who interprets it here of the Eucharist, under-
stands by the three preceding terms the liturgical prayers before the
consecration, at the consecration, and at the blessing of the congregation, respectively (*Ep.* cxlix. (lix.) 16). This is an anachronism. To
sum up, then, we may (1) with Origen, regard the four words as
arranged in an ascending scale: the needy suppliant (δέησις) as he
goes on is led to ask for larger blessings (προσευχή), and then becoming bold he presents his ἔντευξις, which being granted, his devotion
issues in thanksgiving. Or (2) we may more simply take the words

in two contrasted pairs, δέησις being related to προσευχή as the particular to the general (see Eph. vi. 18), and ἔντευξις to εὐχαριστία as petition to thanksgiving.

ὑπὲρ πάντων ἀνθρώπων. This is the key-note of Catholic worship, perhaps emphasised here in reference to the growing exclusiveness of the heretical sects. But it is an element of worship which always needs emphasis in times of stress and difficulty, as it is then very often neglected. Cp. Eph. vi. 18.

2. ὑπὲρ βασιλέων, '*for kings*'; not 'for *the* kings,' as Baur interpreted, finding here a reason for placing the Epistle in the time of the Antonines, when two emperors shared the throne. The practice, commendable at all times and not without parallel in Jewish history (see Ezra vi. 10 and Josephus, *B. J.* ii. 17. 2), was especially important for Christians to observe in early days, when their attitude to the state religion exposed them to the suspicion of disloyalty, and is frequently insisted on by the early Apologists (e.g. Tert. *Apol.* 30, 31). Prayers for rulers are a conspicuous feature in the early liturgies. Cp. also Rom. xiii. 1; 1 Pet. ii. 13, and Tit. iii. 1. Polycarp (§ 12) repeats the injunction, apparently with reference to this passage. It will be remembered that Nero was the reigning emperor when St Paul wrote these words, which adds to the impressiveness of the injunction.

καὶ πάντων τῶν ἐν ὑπεροχῇ ὄντων, *all in authority*; for the phrase cp. 2 Macc. iii. 11, ἀνδρὸς ἐν ὑπεροχῇ κειμένου, and see 1 Pet. ii. 13. The Latin versions render *qui in sublimitate sunt*.

ἵνα κ.τ.λ. expresses the leading thought in State prayers. The idea is clearly brought out in our Prayer for the Church Militant:…"our Queen, that under her we may be godly and quietly governed."

The distinction drawn by commentators between ἤρεμος and ἡσύχιος, that the former refers to freedom from trouble *without*, and the latter from trouble *within*, is hardly to be pressed. For the latter word cp. Plato's ἡσύχιος ὁ σώφρων βίος (*Charm.* 160 B).

The word εὐσέβεια calls for special notice as being one of a group of words occurring in St Paul's writings for the first time in the Pastoral Epistles, and there used repeatedly. In these letters εὐσέβεια occurs 11 times, εὐσεβεῖν once, and εὐσεβῶς twice, the only other instances in the N.T. of these terms being 4 in 2 Peter and 2 in Acts; we have also εὐσεβής in Acts x. 2, 7, xxii. 12, and 2 Pet. ii. 9. These words are all found in the LXX., with greater frequency in the later books; and, indeed, are common in Greek literature, both early and late (e.g. in Philo and Josephus). That they were within St Paul's sphere of knowledge is thus assured; and, as a matter of fact, he has the corresponding forms ἀσέβεια and ἀσεβής in *Romans*. But why he should not have used them before and yet should use them so often in these latest letters is among the unsolved problems of the phraseology of the Pastorals, although corresponding literary phenomena have been often observed (see *Introd.* p. xxxviii.). It is worth remarking that this group of words is similarly prominent in Book IV. of the *Sibylline Oracles* (*cir.* 80 A.D.), as designating the elect of God. εὐσέβεια is a more general word than θεοσέβεια (see ii. 10) and is almost equivalent to the Latin *pietas*, due esteem of superiors, whether human or Divine, while θεοσέβεια is restricted to God as its object. However in the N.T. εὐσέβεια always has reference to God; and in the present passage this is well brought out by the juxtaposition of σεμνότης; σεμνότης manifests itself by our demeanour in human society, εὐσέβεια by the fulfilment of duty to God. In the later days of Athanasius εὐσέβεια had almost come to be equivalent to *orthodoxy*; and Arius, writing to Eusebius, plays upon this, ending his letter with the words ἀληθῶς εὐσέβιε.

σεμνότης is also peculiar to these letters (see iii. 4 and Tit. ii. 7); *gravity* best conveys the meaning, an intense conviction of the seriousness of life, and the difficulty of realising the Christian ideal (see note on Tit. i. 7). One of the resolutions set down in Dr Pusey's penitential rule was "to pray daily for σεμνότης[1]"; and the underlying idea is one that must not be left out of sight. Bishop Butler's comment on the passage, though he takes no account of the context, is itself a signal example of such σεμνότης: "It is impossible," he says (*Sermons on Public Occasions*, v.), "to describe the general end which Providence has appointed us to aim at in our passage through the present world in more expressive words than these very plain ones of the Apostle....To lead *a quiet and peaceful life* &c. is the whole that we have any reason to be concerned for. To this the constitution of our nature carries us; and our external condition is adapted to it."

3, 4. REASONS FOR THE FOREGOING DIRECTION TO PRAY FOR ALL MEN.

3. τοῦτο καλὸν καὶ κ.τ.λ. *This is good and acceptable in the sight of God our Saviour.* The γάρ of the received text is unnecessary and is insufficiently supported (see crit. note): τοῦτο refers back to *v.* 1, *v.* 2 being of the nature of a parenthesis. It is a question whether both καλόν and ἀπόδεκτον, or only the latter word, are to be taken with ἐνώπιον τοῦ σωτῆρος ἡμῶν θεοῦ. The passage usually cited as in point is 2 Cor. viii. 21: προνοοῦμεν γὰρ καλὰ οὐ μόνον ἐνώπιον Κυρίου, ἀλλὰ καὶ ἐνώπιον ἀνθρώπων. And there is no doubt that καλόν in the present passage *might* in like manner be taken with the following ἐνώπιον. But it seems simpler to take καλόν by itself, as marking the intrinsic excellence of such prayers as those in question, the Apostle going on to add that they are specially acceptable in the sight of God, the Universal Saviour.

ἀπόδεκτος is found in the Greek Bible only here and in v. 4; cp. εὐπρόσδεκτος of Rom. xv. 16. See note on ἀποδοχή (i. 15).

For the phrase *God our Saviour*, see the note on i. 1; here the expression has peculiar point and force, and is further defined by the words which follow.

4. ὃς πάντας κ.τ.λ. *whose will it is* &c. ὅς is equivalent to *quippe qui*, and introduces a clause explanatory of what has preceded. θέλει, not βούλεται, is the word used; not a single Divine volition, but the

[1] Liddon's *Life of Pusey*, III. 105.

general purpose of God, antecedent to man's use of His grace, is here in the Apostle's thought. Whatever be the ultimate issue in fact, the Divine intention is that *all* men shall be saved. That this Divine intention may be thwarted by man's misuse of his free will, is part of the great mystery of evil, unexplained and inexplicable; but that its bounty is not confined to particular races or individuals but takes in the whole race of man, is of the very essence of the Gospel. Cp. Matt. v. 45; Tit. ii. 11. It is possible that certain forms of Gnostic heresy, which held that certain classes of men, the uninitiated and unspiritual, are incapable of salvation, are here aimed at; but the introduction of the statement of the breadth of the Gospel is sufficiently explained by the context. See, however, *Introd.* p. liii.

καὶ εἰς ἐπίγνωσιν ἀληθείας ἐλθεῖν. This is inseparably connected with σωθῆναι; *the Life* is only reached through *the Truth*, Who is also *the Way.* Cp. αὕτη ἐστὶν ἡ αἰώνιος ζωή, ἵνα γινώσκωσίν σε τὸν μόνον ἀληθινὸν θεόν κ.τ.λ. (John xvii. 3). ἐπίγνωσις is a thoroughly Pauline word. (See Eph. i. 17; Phil. i. 9; Col. i. 9.) The phrase ἐπίγνωσις ἀληθείας occurs thrice again in the Pastorals (2 Tim. ii. 25, iii. 7; Tit. i. 1; cp. Heb. xi. 26, and Philo *Quod omn. prob.* 11), and is significant of that aspect of the Gospel, which naturally comes into prominence, when its mutilation or perversion has begun to lead souls astray into heresy.

5—7. FURTHER REASONS FOR THE DOCTRINE THAT ALL MEN COME WITHIN THE SCOPE OF GOD'S SAVING PURPOSE.

These are threefold, (i.) the Unity of God, (ii.) the Incarnation, and (iii.) the Atonement of Christ. To take them in order:

(i.) **5. εἰς γὰρ θεός,** *for God is one.* This is connected immediately with *v.* 4, and only indirectly with *v.* 1. The Unity of God was indeed the centre of the Hebrew religion, but the inference here derived from it was not self-evident to the mind of the Jew. To him Jehovah was the God of the chosen people, and the exclusion of Gentiles from His grace and bounty did not present itself as strange or inconsistent with the character of the Supreme. But when it is analysed the conception of the Unity of God is seen to carry with it the truth that the Supreme stands in the same ultimate relation to all His creatures, and that His Divine purposes of love and mercy must embrace all mankind. So St Paul explains in Rom. iii. 30 that God is the God of Gentile as well as Jew, εἴπερ εἷς ὁ θεός, ὃς δικαιώσει περιτομὴν ἐκ πίστεως καὶ ἀκροβυστίαν διὰ τῆς πίστεως; cp. also Rom. x. 12.

(ii.) *There is also one mediator between God and men, Himself man, Christ Jesus.* As there is only one God, so there is only one Way to God: "No man cometh unto the Father, but by Me" (John xiv. 6). Christ is the only Mediator (the mediation of saints or angels is quite unscriptural), and He has, in becoming man, taken up all human nature into Himself. In Him all men are summed up, and so He is the representative, not of this or that man only, but of all mankind. Thus, again, *all* men in Him "shall be made alive"; the saving graces of the Risen Lord are placed within the reach of all. This

is clearly brought out in the words ἄνθρωπος Χρ. ᾿Ιη. at the end of
the clause. Christ is not *a* man, but *man* in the widest sense.

The title μεσίτης must not be overlooked. In Gal. iii. 19 it is used
of Moses (as in the *Assumptio Moysis,* i. 14, iii. 12, and in Philo, *Vit. Mos.*
iii. 19) ; but frequently in Hebrews of our Lord. In the latter Epistle
it is always found in conjunction with διαθήκη. In the present case
it is used more simply than in either of the other Epp. where it
occurs, and indicates that as there is only *one* mediator or go-between
between God and man, so the way of mediation must be alike open to
all. This is brought out forcibly by the addition of the word ἄνθρωπος
(without the article) at the end, which involves in itself, as has been
shewn, the universal bounty of the Incarnation. It is possible that
there was here present to St Paul's mind the contrast between Moses
the μεσίτης for the Jews only, and the *Mediator of a new covenant*
(Heb. ix. 15), whose mediation was for all mankind, Jew and Gentile
alike.

(iii.) 6. The third doctrinal reason for the salvability of all men,
is the universal purpose of the Atonement : ὁ δοὺς ἑαυτὸν ἀντίλυτρον
ὑπὲρ **πάντων.** Jesus Christ gave Himself a ransom on behalf of all,
and hence we may conclude that it is God's will that all should be
saved. The phraseology requires careful attention. ὁ δοὺς ἑαυτόν, He
gave *Himself,* not merely His *Death.* Cp. Gal. i. 4, ii. 20; Eph. v. 2;
Tit. ii. 14, &c., and δοῦναι τὴν ψυχὴν αὐτοῦ λύτρον ἀντὶ πολλῶν (Matt.
xx. 28 ‖ Mark x. 45). ἀντίλυτρον is a word occurring only here, though
the full meaning of it is contained in the passage last cited from the
Gospels; the doctrinal bearing of the preposition is by no means to
be lost sight of. The usual language of the N.T. is, that Christ died
ὑπὲρ ἡμῶν, i.e. *on our behalf*; but at Matt. xx. 28 the prep. ἀντί is
used. Here we have the compound ἀντίλυτρον preceding ὑπὲρ πάντων,
which suggests that both the elements represented by ἀντί *instead of,*
and ὑπέρ *on behalf of,* must enter into any Scriptural theory of the
Atonement. Cp. 4 Macc. vi. 29.

τὸ μαρτύριον καιροῖς ἰδίοις. *The testimony in its own seasons.*
These words are parenthetical, and in apposition to all that has gone
before. τὸ μαρτύριον is equivalent to τὸ μαρτυρούμενον, the thing which
is testified to, the purport of the Church's witness. The great subject
of the testimony to be borne by the Church from age to age is the
Universality of Redemption through the One Mediator. The antecedent
is not merely ὁ δοὺς...πάντων, but the whole of verses 4, 5, 6. This
witness was not of a character which could have been borne by the
Jewish Church; it was reserved for the dispensation of the Gospel,
καιροῖς ἰδίοις.

The formula καιροῖς ἰδίοις occurs twice again in the Pastoral Epistles,
at 1 Tim. vi. 15 and Tit. i. 3, in the former of which passages the
reference of ἰδίοις is clearly defined by the context to God, the subject
of the sentence in each case. Here (as at Tit. i. 3) it is simply *in due
seasons* as in Gal. vi. 9, καιρῷ γὰρ ἰδίῳ κ.τ.λ., and the outlook is to the
future of the Church.

7. **εἰς ὅ.** sc. μαρτύριον.

ἐτέθην. The Apostle's ministry was not self-chosen. Cp. ch. i. 12, θέμενος εἰς διακονίαν; the entire clause is repeated 2 Tim. i. 11, εἰς ὃ ἐτέθην ἐγὼ κῆρυξ καὶ ἀπόστολος καὶ διδάσκαλος. The emphatic ἐγώ should not be overlooked. κῆρυξ is only found in the N.T. in these two passages and in 2 Pet. ii. 5, where it is used of Noah. But κηρύσ-σειν is a common Pauline word; see e.g. for the collocation of κῆρυξ and ἀπόστολος, Rom. x. 15: πῶς κηρύξωσιν ἐὰν μὴ ἀποσταλῶσιν; As κῆρυξ expresses his work, so ἀπόστολος (here used in the higher sense of the word) expresses his Divine mission.

The parenthetical ἀλήθειαν λέγω, οὐ ψεύδομαι (cp. Rom. ix. 1 and critical note) may be taken to refer either to what precedes or to what follows. If the former, it would be a strong assertion of his apostoli-cal authority, perhaps introduced with a view to false teachers at Ephesus who denied it. But it is far better to take it as introducing his claim to be διδάσκαλος ἐθνῶν, *doctor gentium*, the mention of which is especially in place here, as he is insisting on the Universality of the Gospel message. See esp. Rom. xi. 13; Gal. ii. 7—9, for his assertion of this great claim.

ἐν πίστει καὶ ἀληθείᾳ. There can be little doubt that ἀλήθεια is here to be explained in connexion with the ἀλήθεια of v. 4, to the knowledge of which it is God's will that all men should come. That is to say, ἀλήθεια does not directly refer to the spirit of the teacher, but to the content of his lesson; it is the λόγος ἀληθείας (2 Cor. vi. 7) which he preaches. And this objective sense of ἀλήθεια makes it natural to take πίστις in the same way; it does not refer to the Apostle's confidence, or to the subjective conditions of his ministry, but to *the faith* which he commends to his hearers. See note on i. 19 above.

8—15.   ii.   FURTHER DIRECTIONS AS TO THE DEMEANOUR AT PUBLIC WORSHIP OF (*a*) MEN, (*b*) WOMEN.

8.   (*a*) THE DUTY OF MEN.

8. βούλομαι οὖν. βούλομαι is more specific than θέλω, and conveys here the idea of an authoritative desire; cp. v. 14; οὖν resumes the general subject, after the quasi-digression of vv. 3—7.

τοὺς ἄνδρας. *the men*, in antithesis to *the women*, for whom separate instructions follow in v. 9. The men are to lead the worship of the faithful; the women are to be silent.

ἐν παντὶ τόπῳ. This makes the directions general, *in every region*, i.e. where the Gospel is known; cp. 1 Cor. i. 2; 2 Cor. ii. 14; 1 Thess. i. 8. St Paul is only speaking of public prayers, not of private devotion; but he lays down as his first rule that men shall lead the worship of the congregation wherever Christians are assembled. Observe the connexion is προσεύχεσθαι ἐν παντὶ τόπῳ, not ἐν παντὶ τόπῳ ἐπαίροντας κ.τ.λ. The thought that prayer may be offered in any and every place, as at every time (1 Thess. v. 17), is not relevant to the context here.

ἐπαίροντας ὁσίους χεῖρας. To pray with uplifted and outspread hands was the Jewish habit. See Pss. cxli. 2, cxliii. 6; Lam. iii. 41; 1 Kings viii. 22 ; 2 Macc. xiv. 34, and (an interesting parallel) Philo, *de Hum.* 2, τὰς καθαρὰς...χεῖρας εἰς οὐρανὸν ἀνατείνας; cp. *de vita Cont.* §§ 8, 11. It was also the posture adopted in blessing (Lev. ix. 22; Luke xxiv. 50). The practice seems to have been followed in the early Christian Church. Cp. Clem. Rom. 29, προσέλθωμεν αὐτῷ ἐν ὁσιότητι ψυχῆς, ἁγνὰς καὶ ἀμιάντους χεῖρας αἴροντες πρὸς αὐτόν. See also Clem. Alex. *Strom.* VII. 7, and Tert. *Apol.* 30; *de Orat.* 11. The posture of the *orantes* depicted in the Catacombs is one of standing with uplifted and outstretched arms.

As the attitude of body is described, so is the state of mind. The hands must be *holy*, i.e. the life must be without reproach; compare for this phrase Ps. xxiii. 4 and James iv. 8. Observe that we have ὁσίους χεῖρας, not ὁσίας, as we should naturally expect. But adjectives in -ιος are not infrequently used as if they were of two terminations only; cp. Luke ii. 13.

χωρὶς ὀργῆς καὶ διαλογισμοῦ, *without wrath and disputation.* Either would mar the charity which prays for all men. "Anger," says Jeremy Taylor, "is a perfect alienation of the mind from prayer." χωρὶς ὀργῆς is the reflexion of that clause in the Lord's Prayer "as we forgive them that trespass against us"; to be able to recite it with sincerity is to have advanced far indeed in the Christian life. And again, χωρὶς διαλογισμοῦ, *without disputation*; in our prayers we leave our differences behind us, and in the awe of the Divine presence we realise in some measure how poor a thing is theological controversy.

διαλογισμοῦ (see critical note) is probably the true reading. διαλογισμός might mean 'doubting' (see Luke xxiv. 38), but this would seem foreign to the context here; the general N.T. sense (see e.g. Rom. xiv. 1; Phil. ii. 14) is 'disputation.'

9—15. (*b*) THE CONDUCT OF WOMEN IN THE CHRISTIAN ASSEMBLY.

9. ὡσαύτως κ.τ.λ. We must understand βούλομαι. Some commentators take the words down to σωφροσύνης as referring to the demeanour of women at public prayer, προσεύχεσθαι being supplied: "I wish likewise that women pray in modest apparel with shamefastness and sobriety," κοσμεῖν ἑαυτάς going with what follows. Such directions would be *similar* to the rule laid down in 1 Cor. xi. 13, that women should be veiled at the assemblies of the faithful, when prayer is being offered. But this would be a very unnatural arrangement of the words; and the position of κοσμεῖν especially would be awkward. It is better to suppose that St Paul, beginning his sentence with ὡσαύτως as if he were going to add directions about the public devotions of women, goes off in a different direction and supplies principles for their general deportment and dress. This is quite in his manner. We take κοσμεῖν ἑαυτάς, then, as co-ordinated with προσεύχεσθαι of *v.* 8.

The introductory ὡσαύτως occurs with peculiar frequency in the

Pastorals (see iii. 8, 11, v. 25; Tit. ii. 3, 6); it is only used twice elsewhere by St Paul (Rom. viii. 26; 1 Cor. xi. 25).

καταστολῇ. A word only found in the Greek Bible here and in Isa. lxi. 3. It means *dress*; κατάστημα of Tit. ii. 3 is a more general word, equivalent to 'demeanour' or 'deportment.'

μετὰ αἰδοῦς καὶ σωφροσύνης. *With shamefastness and sobriety.* This, the rendering of both A.V. and R.V., is as near to the Greek as we can go in English. The Greek words have a long history behind them, and have no exact equivalents in modern speech. Both together well describe the discretion and modesty of Christian womanhood.

αἰδώς is almost = *verecundia*; it is a nobler word than αἰσχύνη, inasmuch as it implies (1) a *moral* repugnance to what is base and unseemly, and (2) *self-respect*, as well as restraint imposed on oneself from a sense of what is due to others; neither (1) nor (2) enters into αἰσχύνη. Thus αἰδώς here signifies that modesty which shrinks from overstepping the limits of womanly reserve. Wiclif's felicitous rendering *shamefastness* has been retained in nearly all the English versions, although both etymology and meaning have been obscured by the corrupt spelling 'shame-facedness'; *shamefastness* is really that which is established and held fast by an honourable shame[1]. αἰδώς is a common term in philosophical writers, but in the LXX. it is found only 3 Macc. i. 19, iv. 5; it does not occur elsewhere in the N.T.

σωφροσύνη is a word of much wider meaning. It was one of the four cardinal virtues in the Platonic philosophy, the others being φρόνησις, δικαιοσύνη, and ἀνδρεία (cp. Philo, *Leg. Alleg.* i. 19). Primarily it signifies (as in Aristotle) a command over bodily passions, a state of perfect self-mastery in respect of appetite. It marked the attitude towards pleasure of the man with a well-balanced mind, and was equally opposed to asceticism and to over-indulgence. *Sobriety* is perhaps its nearest equivalent in English, but this fails to do justice to the high place which the idea of 'moderation' occupied in the Greek mind. The old etymology given by Chrysostom, σωφροσύνη λέγεται ἀπὸ τοῦ σώας τὰς φρένας ἔχειν, shews how intimately it was connected with the sense of self-control.

The word does not occur in the older books of the LXX., for there is nothing corresponding to it in Hebrew moral systems. To the Hebrews ethics had always a religious basis, the revealed will of God supplied an objective standard of right and wrong; and thus the self-regarding aspect of Greek philosophy had no place in their thoughts. And for a somewhat similar reason—though qualifications would here be necessary—it can never occupy as high a place in Christian ethics as it did in Greek[2]. See note on φίλαυτος, 2 Tim. iii. 2.

But, in the later books of the LXX., as soon, indeed, as Hebraism came into contact with Hellenism, the word σωφροσύνη and its cognates make their appearance. Thus we have σωφρόνως in Wisd.

---

[1] See Trench, *Synonyms of N.T.*, xx. (First Series).
[2] And this is true, despite the fact that σωφροσύνη has a much wider sphere in modern Christendom than it ever had in Greece, and is really conceived of as a nobler virtue. Cp. Green, *Prolegomena to Ethics*, p. 289 ff.

ix. 11, and σωφροσύνη in Wisd. viii. 7 and 2 Macc. iv. 37, both σώφρων and σωφροσύνη occurring repeatedly in 4 Macc., where (i. 31) σωφροσύνη is defined as ἐπικράτεια τῶν ἐπιθυμιῶν (see further on Tit. i. 8). In St Paul's writings this group of words is applied to sobriety and self-command of mind as well as of body. Thus 2 Cor. v. 13 σωφρονεῖν is used (as in Mark v. 15 ‖ Luke viii. 35) of being *sane in mind*; and in Rom. xii. 3 it is contrasted with ὑπερφρονεῖν; cp. Acts xxvi. 25 (in a speech of St Paul), ἀληθείας καὶ σωφροσύνης ῥήματα. In the Pastorals the words occur with peculiar frequency. We have σωφροσύνη here and ii. 15; σώφρων, iii. 2, Tit. i. 8, ii. 2, 5; σωφρονεῖν, Tit. ii. 6; σωφρονίζειν, Tit. ii. 4; σωφρονισμός, 2 Tim. i. 7; and σωφρόνως, Tit. ii. 12. The writer's marked preference for this group of words is indeed one of the unsolved problems of the vocabulary of the Pastoral Epistles. See *Introd.* p. xxxvii.

ἐν πλέγμασιν, *with plaitings*; this finds its explanation in the ἐμπλοκῆς τριχῶν of 1 Pet. iii. 3, a passage strictly parallel to this in its warnings against excessive finery. There is probably no literary connexion between these two passages, similar as they are; they both breathe the same spirit, inasmuch as they deal with the same topic from the same point of view.

10. The adornment is to be δι' ἔργων ἀγαθῶν. This is certainly the true construction; ὃ πρέπει...θεοσέβειαν is parenthetical. The stress laid on 'good works' all through the Pastoral Epistles is very remarkable; no other Epistles of St Paul lay at all the same emphasis on right living, as the index to right belief. It is possible that the particular forms of heresy with which the Churches of Ephesus and Crete were threatened rendered it necessary to expose the vanity of theological speculations without ethical background, and the impossibility of treating creed apart from life. Thus the heretics of Tit. i. 16 while they 'confess that they know God' yet 'deny Him by their works'; they are πρὸς πᾶν ἔργον ἀγαθὸν ἀδόκιμοι. As here the best adornment of womanhood is found δι' ἔργων ἀγαθῶν, so the test of a widow to be placed on the Church's list is εἰ παντὶ ἔργῳ ἀγαθῷ ἐπηκολούθησεν (1 Tim. v. 10). The phrase, *prepared* (or 'equipped') *for every good work* occurs three times (2 Tim. ii. 21, iii. 17; Tit. iii. 1).

There is nothing, of course, in all this inconsistent with St Paul's previous teaching. Similar expressions occur, though with less frequency, in his earlier Epistles. ἵνα περισσεύητε εἰς πᾶν ἔργον ἀγαθόν was his hope for the Corinthians (2 Cor. ix. 8); ὑπομονὴ ἔργου ἀγαθοῦ is the spirit which shall be rewarded hereafter (Rom. ii. 7); he prays for the Colossians that they may be fruitful ἐν παντὶ ἔργῳ ἀγαθῷ (Col. i. 10); and in another Epistle he explains that these ἔργα ἀγαθά are prepared of God that we should walk in them (Eph. ii. 10). And in the Pastoral Epistles themselves there are passages which bring out the complementary truth, that it is not by works that we are saved, with all the clearness and distinctness of the Epistle to the Romans. Thus in 2 Tim. i. 9 Paul speaks of God who saved us οὐ κατὰ τὰ ἔργα ἡμῶν ἀλλὰ κατὰ ἰδίαν πρόθεσιν; and again in Tit. iii. 5 οὐκ ἐξ

ἔργων τῶν ἐν δικαιοσύνῃ ἃ ἐποιήσαμεν ἡμεῖς ἀλλὰ κατὰ τὸ αὐτοῦ ἔλεος
ἔσωσεν ἡμᾶς κ.τ.λ.

We have not yet, however, exhausted the references in the Pastorals
to 'good works.' In eight other passages ἔργα καλά are spoken of,
a phrase similar to though not identical with ἔργα ἀγαθά, and specially
noteworthy because it is not found in any of the other letters of St Paul.

Something has already been said (see on i. 8) of the distinction
between ἀγαθός and καλός, and the usage of the phrase καλὰ ἔργα
in the Gospels (Matt. v. 16; Mark xiv. 6; John x. 32), in the Ep. to
the Hebrews (x. 24), and the First Ep. of St Peter (ii. 12) corroborates
the distinction there suggested. So in the Pastoral Epistles the
phrase καλὰ ἔργα is used in reference to good works which are seen of
men and which illustrate the beauty of the Christian life. If not
πρόδηλα, *notoriously evident*, at all events they cannot remain always
hidden (1 Tim. v. 25). The true riches are those of ἔργα καλά (1 Tim.
vi. 18); if a man desires a bishopric he desires a καλὸν ἔργον (1 Tim.
iii. 1); God's chosen are a λαὸς περιούσιος, ζηλωτὴς καλῶν ἔργων (Tit.
ii. 14); Titus is to be a τύπος καλῶν ἔργων (Tit. ii. 7); and he is to
bid the people under his care καλῶν ἔργων προΐστασθαι (Tit. iii. 8, 14).

It would, however, be unsafe to press the distinction between ἔργα
καλά and ἔργα ἀγαθά in the Pastorals. The two phrases seem to be
used interchangeably in 1 Tim. v. 9, 10, and it is not impossible that
they are renderings of an Aramaic phrase which had come into use.
To speak of ἔργα καλά or of ἔργα ἀγαθά is quite foreign to Greek ethics.

ὃ πρέπει κ.τ.λ. Cp. Eph. v. 3 καθὼς πρέπει ἁγίοις.

ἐπαγγελλομέναις θεοσέβειαν. I.e. *professing religion*. ἐπαγγέλλεσθαι in N.T. generally means 'to promise'; but the meaning *to
profess*, necessary for the sense here, is quite legitimate and is ex-
emplified by the lexicons; cp. vi. 21. θεοσέβεια is a LXX. and classical
word, occurring here only in N.T. It is used in a quasi-technical
sense for 'the religious life'; and θεοσεβής has something of the same
ambiguity as our word 'religious,' which, rightly applicable to all
God-fearing persons, is yet sometimes confined to members of a con-
ventual or monastic order. The A.V. and R.V. make no distinction
between θεοσέβεια and εὐσέβεια, rendering both words *godliness*. See
on ii. 2 above.

Some Latin authorities (*r* and Cyprian) render θεοσέβειαν curiously by
castitatem, and *am* has *pudicitiam*, but the usual Latin rendering is
pietatem.

11. γυνὴ ἐν ἡσυχίᾳ μανθανέτω. We should observe the close
parallelism in thought between these directions and those laid down
in 1 Cor. xiv. 34, 35: αἱ γυναῖκες ἐν ταῖς ἐκκλησίαις σιγάτωσαν, οὐ γὰρ
ἐπιτρέπεται αὐταῖς λαλεῖν· ἀλλὰ ὑποτασσέσθωσαν, καθὼς καὶ ὁ νόμος
λέγει. εἰ δέ τι μανθάνειν θέλουσιν, ἐν οἴκῳ τοὺς ἰδίους ἄνδρας ἐπερωτά-
τωσαν, αἰσχρὸν γάρ ἐστιν γυναικὶ λαλεῖν ἐν ἐκκλησίᾳ.

Women are to be learners ἐν πάσῃ ὑποταγῇ. This is not, of course,
primarily in reference to their general attitude to men, but only to
their behaviour at public worship. The reason assigned, however, in
vv. 13, 14 gives the direction a wider bearing. Cp. 1 Pet. iii. 5.

The 'subjection of women' is a topic freely debated at the present day; and, although it has been argued that St Paul is basing his rules on the position assigned to the sex in the society of his time, rather than laying down precepts of universal and permanent obligation, there can be no doubt that the distinction which he makes between the respective duties of men and women lies deep down in the facts of human nature as originally constituted. See on Tit. ii. 5. With ἐν πάσῃ ὑποταγῇ may be compared πάσης ἀποδοχῆς ἄξιος (i. 15) and ἐν πάσῃ εὐσεβείᾳ (ii. 2) and μετὰ πάσης σεμνότητος of iii. 4.

12.   διδάσκειν δὲ γυναικὶ οὐκ ἐπιτρέπω. A woman is to *learn*; she is not permitted to *teach* in the public assembly of Christians. The renewal of the prohibition at the Fourth Council of Carthage in 398 seems to shew, as Ellicott observes, that a neglect of this Apostolic ordinance had crept into the African Church. Women were, however, expressly permitted to teach others of their own sex; and we have not to go outside the Pastoral Epistles for a recognition of the value of their private teaching of the young. See 2 Tim. iii. 14; and Tit. ii. 3, where it is recommended that the πρεσβύτιδες should be καλοδιδάσκαλοι.

The construction οὐ...οὐδέ, which occurs in this verse, is thoroughly Pauline; see Rom. ii. 28, ix. 7, 16.

αὐθεντεῖν. This is a ἅπ. λεγ. in the Greek Bible, although we have αὐθέντης and αὐθεντία in Wisd. xii. 6 and 3 Macc. ii. 29. The αὐθέντης is the perpetrator of a crime, as distinguished from an accomplice, and the word was especially applied to a murderer. From this it came to mean one who does anything with his own hand,—'the responsible person,' and so 'a ruler'; and thence we have the verb in the sense 'to lord it over.'

ἐν ἡσυχίᾳ. The repetition of this word at the end of the sentence is emphatic. It is a favourite word with St Paul, in reference to the Christian life. See, e.g., ch. ii. 2 and 2 Thess. iii. 12.

13, 14.   FROM THE HISTORY OF HUMAN ORIGINS TWO REASONS ARE ASSIGNED FOR THE PROHIBITION TO WOMEN TO TEACH AND EXERCISE AUTHORITY OVER MEN.

(i.)   The first of these is derived from the *order of creation*.

13.   Ἀδὰμ γὰρ πρῶτος ἐπλάσθη, εἶτα Εὔα. There is a somewhat similar argument in 1 Cor. xi. 9, which see. That Adam was created first implies a certain superiority; such at least seems to be the Apostle's thought.

The word πλάσσειν is specifically used for the creation of man; see e.g. Gen. ii. 7; the usual rendering of the Latins for ἐπλάσθη is *formatus est*, but *am* has *figuratus*.

(ii.)   The second reason is based on the history of the Fall; the woman was deceived, not the man, and this suggests that she will be an unfit guide. 'From a woman was the beginning of sin' said the Son of Sirach (Ecclus. xxv. 24). *Facilius decepta, facilius decipit,* as Bengel tersely puts it.

14. Ἀδὰμ οὐκ ἠπατήθη. What Adam did, he did of his own choice and with open eyes.

On the other hand Eve was entirely deceived, ἐξαπατηθεῖσα. (See crit. note.)   Compare Gen. iii. 13 ὁ ὄφις ἠπάτησέν με.   The compound verb ἐξαπατάω is a common Pauline word (see Rom. vii. 11; 1 Cor. iii. 18).   And so, Eve *being beguiled hath fallen into transgression.* The perfect tense, γέγονε, is used in preference to the aorist, as the case of Eve has permanent application; cp. Gal. iv. 23.   Note that the construction γίγνεσθαι ἐν (1 Cor. ii. 3; 2 Cor. iii. 7) is Pauline.   The term παράβασις is here used in its strict sense of a transgression of law (Rom. iv. 15; Gal. iii. 19).

At this point the writer passes from Eve, the mother and prototype of the sex, to womankind generally.

15. σωθήσεται κ.τ.λ.   The connexion of thought is as follows. The woman fell into transgression, and the judgement pronounced on her for all time was ἐν λύπαις τέξῃ τέκνα (Gen. iii. 16): the fulfilment of her proper duty shall be accompanied with pain.   But yet shall she be safely brought through her τεκνογονία, if she abide in faith and love &c.   That which may be her curse may also be her highest blessing if she use it aright.   St Paul has been deprecating the assumption by woman of duties, such as that of public teaching, which have not been assigned to her in the Providence of God; he ends with a word of encouragement to her if she confine herself to her own sphere; σωθήσεται *she shall be saved* not only in her body, but in the highest sense of all[1].

The construction σωθήσεται διά has a strict parallel in 1 Cor. iii. 15: αὐτὸς δὲ σωθήσεται, οὕτως δὲ ὡς διὰ πυρός. τεκνογονία is not the meritorious cause of woman's salvation; it is the sphere, being her natural duty, in which she may hope to find it.   The emphasis laid in these Epistles on good works, especially on the performance of the common duties of life, has already been remarked (see on *v.* 10 above).

Two other interpretations have been proposed: (1) that of Chrysostom, who regards τεκνογονία as identical here with τεκνοτροφία, the Christian education of children, and supposes an implied τέκνα to be the subject of μείνωσιν.   But τεκνογονία cannot be thus explained; τεκνογονεῖν is used in this very Epistle (v. 14) in its ordinary sense of bearing children.   And further such an interpretation does not harmonise with the context.   (2) Many modern commentators lay stress on the article τῆς and interpret διὰ τῆς τεκνογονίας as *through the Child-Bearing*, sc. of the Blessed Virgin, the τεκνογονία in the Apostle's mind being the Saviour's Birth, foreshadowed in Gen. iii. 16.   But it is impossible to suppose that St Paul would have spoken of the Nativity of Christ as ἡ τεκνογονία without any further explanation. The interpretation must be counted among those pious and ingenious flights of fancy, which so often mislead the commentator on Holy

---

[1] The cases of man and woman are exactly parallel.   For man there is pronounced the doom of labour (Gen. iii. 17); yet labour is discipline through which he may win his way to God. 'Laborare est orare.'   For woman it is ordained, 'In sorrow she shall bring forth' (Gen. iii. 16).   Yet by it and by the duties involved, she is trained for the kingdom of Heaven.

Scripture. The Latin versions give the sense correctly, *per filiorum generationem.*

μείνωσιν. The promise is given to *woman* (ἡ γυνή); its fulfilment is for such *women* as *continue in faith,* &c. Hence the plural, and likewise the aorist, specifying to these what was given generally. The thought of the whole passage may be illustrated by 1 Cor. vii. 20: ἕκαστος ἐν τῇ κλήσει ᾗ ἐκλήθη ἐν ταύτῃ **μενέτω.**

ἐν πίστει καὶ ἀγάπῃ καὶ ἁγιασμῷ. Faith and love will issue in holiness. Cp. ch. i. 14.

μετὰ σωφροσύνης. σωφροσύνη has already been spoken of as a grace specially to be commended to Christian women. See on *v.* 9 above.

CHAPTER III.

1. For πιστός D₂* has ἀνθρώπινος, following its Latin version *humanus,* which is also read by m; g has *humanus vel fidelis.* See on i. 15.

2. The best MSS. (אAD₂GH) have ἀνεπίλημπτον (which should also be read in v. 7 and vi. 14); the received spelling ἀνεπίληπτον has the support of KL and most cursives.

3. Rec. text after πλήκτην inserts μὴ αἰσχροκερδῆ (from Tit. i. 7) with 37 and many other cursives; *om.* all uncials and versions.

7. Rec. text after δεῖ δὲ inserts αὐτόν with D₂KLP and Latin Vss.; *om.* אAGH.

8. א* and 3 cursives omit σεμνούς here, but it is unquestionably part of the primitive text.

14. **πρὸς σὲ.** These words omitted by G (but represented in f g) and the Armenian version are placed by Westcott and Hort in square brackets.

τάχιον. This, the reading of rec. text, is supported by אD₂ᶜGKL and most cursives; Westcott and Hort and the Revisers read ἐν τάχει with ACD₂*P.

15. After δεῖ, some Western authorities (followed by the Latin Vulgate) insert σε; but its insertion is due to a misconception of the meaning. See note *in loc.*

16. The important variants in this verse require close attention. θεός of the rec. text is found in CᶜD₂ᶜKLP and the vast majority of cursives; but it has no support from the versions, and the earliest fathers who have it, viz. Didymus of Alexandria and Gregory of Nyssa, date from the latter part of the fourth century. On the other hand ὅς is read in אA*C*G 17. 73. 181, and the Egyptian versions, and is witnessed to by Origen (probably) and by Epiphanius, Theodore and Cyril of Alexandria (certainly). And again, the Western reading ὅ, found in D₂*fg, the Vulgate and the Latin fathers generally, is a manifest corruption of ὅς, introduced because of the preceding τὸ μυστήριον. The Syriac versions have a relative pronoun, but it is not certain whether it is meant to render ὅς or ὅ, as in Syriac there is no neuter. Thus, on the whole, external authority is overwhelmingly on the side of ὅς. The variant θεός would readily arise from the true reading, as confusion of Θ͞Ϲ and Ο͞Ϲ would be easy; the similarity, indeed, being so great that the reading of A has long been matter of controversy. That it witnesses to ὅς and not to θεός is, however, the opinion of most of the experts who have recently inspected the manuscript, although competent persons who had access to it a hundred years ago, when it was in better condition, believed it to read θεός. For a full discussion of all the evidence, reference should be made to Tischendorf *in loc.* or to Westcott and Hort's note (*Notes on Select Readings*, p. 133) or to Scrivener's *Introduction*, II. 390.

II. Qualifications of the Officials of the Church.

1—7. i. Bishops.

Having spoken of the conduct of public worship, the Apostle proceeds to expound the qualifications requisite for those who hold office in the Church, the ἐπίσκοποι (*vv.* 1—7) and the διάκονοι (*vv.* 8—13). The significance of these terms, as used in the Pastoral Epistles, has been dealt with in the *Introduction*, chap. v. It seems clear that they are used here in an official sense, and further, from the manner in which the qualifications of the ἐπίσκοποι and διάκονοι are discussed, that the instructions relate to officials whose existence in the Church is well established and of considerable standing.

1. πιστὸς ὁ λόγος. This formula (see on i. 15) has been referred (e.g. by Chrysostom) to the words which precede, but it seems better to take it with the terse sentence which follows, viz.: *If any man aspires to the episcopate, he desires a noble work.* On the force of καλός see on i. 8, ii. 10 above; it is, however, the word ἔργον upon which stress is laid, not the dignity or the honour of the episcopate, but its proper duties (*negotium* not *otium*). There is nothing in the maxim inconsistent with the spirit expressed by *Nolo episcopari*; unwillingness to undertake so heavy a burden may coexist with a full sense of the gravity and importance of the episcopal function. It is to be borne in mind that at this stage of the Church's existence, the duties of the ἐπίσκοπος would be rather hazardous than honourable in the sight of men; and a maxim like this might well have arisen from the unwillingness of Christian converts to be raised to so conspicuous a position as that which the official representatives of the Church would necessarily occupy.

ὀρέγεται. Outside 1 Tim. the word is only found in the Greek Bible in Heb. xi. 16; but it is common in profane authors. It conveys no bad sense of 'grasping,' and is a true *vox media*. *Aspires to* gives its proper force.

2. δεῖ οὖν. *Therefore is it necessary &c.* The ἔργον is καλόν, and demands *therefore* men of high moral character no less than of ability in affairs. *Bonum negotium bonis committendum* says Bengel.

τὸν ἐπίσκοπον. Stress is perhaps not to be laid on the singular number (see *Introd.* p. lxxii.), since it may be used generically. Yet it is remarkable that both here and at Tit. i. 7 the singular is found, while the διάκονοι are mentioned (*v.* 8) in the plural[1]. And the presence of the definite article, which is so sparingly used in the Pastorals, seems to be significant.

ἀνεπίλημπτον. The bishop must be *without reproach*. This is a classical word, not found outside this Epistle (cp. v. 7, vi. 14) in N.T. or LXX.; it is stronger than ἄμεμπτος or ἀνέγκλητος, for it implies not only that the man is of good report, but that he deserves it: μὴ παρέχων κατηγορίας ἀφορμήν is the Scholiast's comment on the word, Thuc. v. 17. "The rule that a *defectus bonae famae* is a canonical impediment to Ordination is based upon this, although the Apostolic language is in reality more exacting....The *si quis* before Ordination, and the confirmation before Episcopal Consecration, at the present day, are designed to secure what this word prescribes." (Liddon *in loc.*)

The qualifications now given are not, it will be observed, descriptive of the actual functions of Church officers; they have reference to spiritual and moral, not to official, requirements, and are not to be regarded as exhaustive. The list of a bishop's qualifications in *vv.* 2—7 should be compared with that in the parallel passage Titus i. 6—9. There are some differences, although on the whole there is a marked similarity. Here e.g. we have κόσμιον, ἐπιεικῆ, ἄμαχον (but see Tit. iii. 2), μὴ νεόφυτον, and δεῖ μαρτυρίαν καλὴν ἔχειν ἀπὸ τῶν ἔξωθεν, which are not found in Titus; while μὴ αὐθάδη, μὴ ὀργίλον, φιλάγαθον, δίκαιον, ὅσιον, ἐγκρατῆ, ἀντεχόμενον τοῦ κατὰ τὴν διδαχὴν πιστοῦ λόγου of the later Epistle have no place here. It is not necessary to invent a theory (such as that each list was drawn up in view of the needs of the local Church) to account for these differences. They are neither more nor greater than might be expected in two letters written during the same period by the same man to two friends under somewhat similar circumstances. Neither list, as has been said, can be regarded as exhaustive.

μιᾶς γυναικὸς ἄνδρα. The sense is fixed by the parallel clause in ch. v. 9 (see note) ἑνὸς ἀνδρὸς γυνή which cannot possibly mean anything but a woman who has not re-married after the death or divorce of her husband. It excludes from ecclesiastical position those who have been married more than once. For ordinary Christians second marriages are not forbidden: see esp. Rom. vii. 3; 1 Cor. vii. 9 and 39; and 1 Tim. v. 14. But they are forbidden to the ἐπίσκοπος, to the διάκονοι (*v.* 12), and to the χῆραι who are put on the Church's list, inasmuch as it is all important that they should be ἀνεπίλημπτοι[2]. For these persons is prescribed περὶ τὸν ἕνα γάμον σεμνότης (Clem. Alex. *Strom.* III. 1). Clement (*l.c.*) goes on to explain that second marriages,

---

[1] Yet the same thing occurs in v. 1, 2 where πρεσβυτέρῳ is singular and νεωτέρους plural, but there we find no definite article.

[2] Under the Pentateuchal law, the regulations about marriage were in like manner stricter for the priests than for the people; the priest was forbidden to marry a widow or a divorced woman (Lev. xxi. 14).

though not forbidden by the law, are a breaking in upon the Christian
ideal of faithful union between one man and one woman. But, whatever truth there be in this view (see Matt. xix. 4; Eph. v. 32) it is not
expressed here by St Paul, whose injunction μιᾶς γυναικὸς ἄνδρα is
directly suggested by the statement that the bishop is to be ἀνεπίλημπτος. The point is that he must not lay himself open to charges like
that of ἀκρατεία.

How far such a prohibition is binding in the present condition of
the world and of the Church is another question. It must be remembered that St Paul is not enumerating here the *essential* characteristics
of a bishop; he is dwelling upon certain moral and personal qualities
which, in the Church of that day, it was desirable that he should
possess. And it has been argued with considerable force that regulations of this sort cannot be regarded as of universal and permanent
obligation, for circumstances may so change as to render them unwise
or unnecessary. The Roman, the Greek, and the Anglican Com-
munions have, as a matter of history, all departed from the letter of
this rule; the Roman in forbidding the marriage of the clergy in
general; the Greek in requiring celibacy of bishops; and the Anglican
in permitting their re-marriage. The sense of the Church plainly is
that this regulation, at least, may be modified by circumstances. See
below on διδακτικός.

Other interpretations of these disputed words are (*a*) that they
forbid polygamy. But, although polygamy is said to have been not
unknown among the Jews of the Apostolic age (Joseph. *Antt.* XVII. 12;
Just. Mart. *Trypho* 134), it was quite an exceptional thing; and it
was never countenanced by Christians. Polygamy would not have
been lawful for *any* Christian convert, whether from Judaism or from
heathendom; and therefore the special prohibition in the case of a
bishop would have been without point. Such an interpretation is
indeed absolutely excluded by the parallel clause ἑνὸς ἀνδρὸς γυνή of
ch. v. 9. (*b*) That they forbid any deviation from the ordinary laws of
Christian purity of life. But this is not a satisfactory or precise
interpretation of the words. (*c*) That the ἐπίσκοπος *must* be a married
man, not a celibate. This would not only be inconsistent with 1 Cor.
vii. 17, but does not represent the force of μιᾶς, the emphatic word
in the sentence. No explanation is adequate save that which lies on
the surface, viz. the ἐπίσκοπος must be married only once, if at all.

νηφάλιον. The word does not occur in the Greek Bible outside
the Pastoral Epp.; but νήφειν is a Pauline word (see 1 Thess. v. 6
&c.). Primarily having reference to sobriety in the case of wine, it
has here the more extended sense of *temperate*.

σώφρονα. See on ii. 9 above. σώφρων is a word of higher meaning
and wider use than νηφάλιος. Compare the juxtaposition in 1 Pet. iv.
7: σωφρονήσατε οὖν καὶ νήψατε.

κόσμιον, *orderly*. This expresses the outward manifestation of the
spirit of σωφροσύνη. The 'wise man' of the Stoics was to be κόσμιος
(Stob. II. 240); and the idea is also found, though in an absurd and
exaggerated form, in Aristotle's description of the μεγαλόψυχος: καὶ

κίνησις δὲ βραδεῖα τοῦ μεγαλοψύχου δοκεῖ εἶναι, καὶ φωνὴ βαρεῖα, καὶ λέξις στάσιμος· οὐ γὰρ σπευστικὸς ὁ περὶ ὀλίγα σπουδάζων κ.τ.λ. (*Nic. Eth.* IV. iii. 34). The ἐπίσκοπος, at least, must be *vir compositus et ordinatus* (Seneca, *de vita beata* 8).

φιλόξενον. The duty of hospitality was especially incumbent on the ἐπίσκοπος as the *persona ecclesiae*; but it is also recommended to widows (ch. v. 10), and to all Christians (Rom. xii. 13; Heb. xiii. 2; 1 Pet. iv. 9; 3 John 5). The duty was of even greater moment in the Apostolic age than now; a Christian e.g. might readily find cause of offence in the meat set before him in any heathen household (see 1 Cor. x. 28 &c.), and it was therefore specially incumbent on Christians to minister hospitality to their brethren.

διδακτικόν. So 2 Tim. ii. 24 and Tit. i. 9, where this qualification is more fully expressed. Cp. also Eph. iv. 11. This was, perhaps, not part of the formal duty of the ἐπίσκοπος (see *Introd.* p. lxxii.); it was a desirable qualification in view of the special circumstances of Ephesus and Crete. That it should be mentioned at all as pertaining to the ἐπίσκοπος is an argument in favour of the comparatively early date of the Pastoral Epistles.

3. μὴ πάροινον. πάροινος expresses more than φίλοινος or than the μὴ οἴνῳ πολλῷ προσέχοντας of *v.* 8; it means a man *given over to wine*. It is generally rendered *quarrelsome over wine* (cp. Isa. xli. 12), a *brawler*, but there does not seem sufficient reason for importing this into it, as the idea is brought out in the next mentioned attribute.

μὴ πλήκτην, *no striker*; this vice is a common outcome of παροινία. πάροινος and πλήκτης are to be taken in their literal sense, and not in any refined meaning. The absence of such vices would not now be regarded as necessary to mention in a list of episcopal qualifications; but each age has its own special sins to guard against. A *Regula solitariorum* founded on the Benedictine Rule has a quaint comment on the words, which shews how necessary such an injunction remained many generations after St Paul's day. "*Non percussorem,*...sed non ita dictum est ut si discipulum habuerit, et facultas permiserit, non pie uerberetur,*" with a reference to Prov. xxiii. 13[1].

ἐπιεικῆ. *Forbearing* perhaps best expresses this word; in the N.T. it is found outside the Pastorals in Phil. iv. 5 only. Cp. 2 Cor. x. 1. Aristotle devotes a chapter (*Nic. Eth.* v. 10) to the ἐπιεικής, the 'equitable' man, who does not press for the last farthing of his legal rights. We are not to emphasise ἀλλά, so as to point any sharp contrast between πάροινος and ἐπιεικής, although no doubt they indicate very different characters. Cp. Tit. iii. 2.

ἄμαχον, *not contentious*; in the Greek Bible only found in Pastorals, as also πάροινος and πλήκτης.

ἀφιλάργυρον. This word is only found here and in Heb. xiii. 5 (φιλαργυρία is denounced again in ch. vi. 10). It is replaced in Tit. i. 7 by μὴ αἰσχροκερδῆ, which has thence got into the received text in this verse. See on *v.* 8 and the note on φιλαργυρία (1 Tim. vi. 10).

[1] Migne, *P.L.* CIII. 598.

4. ἰδίου. Repeated again in *v.* 5, in contrast to θεοῦ.

καλῶς. A characteristic word of the Pastorals (see on i. 8, ii. 10 above).

προϊστάμενον. We find this verb applied to the officers of the Church also in Rom. xii. 8; 1 Thess. v. 12, and to πρεσβύτεροι in ch. v. 17 (see *Introd.* p. lxix.).

τέκνα κ.τ.λ. The parallel clause in Titus i. 6 is: τέκνα ἔχων πιστά, μὴ ἐν κατηγορίᾳ ἀσωτίας ἢ ἀνυπότακτα.

ἔχοντα. This is to be taken in subordination to προϊστάμενον: *having his children in subjection.* For ἐν ὑποταγῇ see ii. 11. This verse, like *v.* 2, certainly seems to contemplate as the normal, and not merely a permissible, state of things that the ἐπίσκοπος should be a married man whose wife has borne him children.

μετὰ πάσης σεμνότητος. For the form of the phrase see note on ii. 11. Both the order of the words and the natural sense lead us to connect this clause with ἔχοντα, rather than with τὰ τέκνα. σεμνότης (see note on ii. 2) is hardly a grace of childhood ; we approve it in the προϊστάμενος, but its presence in those over whom his rule is exercised does not afford any convincing proof of his fitness for rule; see on Tit. i. 7.

5. The verse is parenthetical, and the argument is *a minori ad maius.* Tacitus has almost the same idea: "A se suisque orsus primum domum suam coercuit (sc. Agricola) quod plerisque haud minus arduum est quam provinciam regere" (*Agr.* 19). The conception of the ἐπίσκοπος as the οἰκονόμος, and of the Church as οἶκος θεοῦ, the *familia* or *household* of which the Master is God, is touched on by St Paul in 1 Cor. iv. 1; Gal. vi. 10; Eph. iii. 9; and has its roots in the O.T. (Cp. Num. xii. 7 and Hosea viii. 1.) Ability to rule is here represented as an indispensable qualification for the due discharge of the office of an ἐπίσκοπος. See below on *v.* 15.

πῶς ἐπιμελήσεται. We find πῶς followed by a future of moral capacity, as here, in 1 Cor. xiv. 7, 9, 16. The verb ἐπιμελεῖσθαι occurs elsewhere in the N.T. only in Luke x. 34, 35; the presidents of the Essene communities were called ἐπιμεληταί (Josephus *B. J.* II. 8. 6). The ἐκκλησία in question is the local Christian community over which the ἐπίσκοπος is placed. See on *v.* 12 and on *v.* 15.

6. μὴ νεόφυτον. *Not a recent convert.* The word (in the N.T. only found here) is used in the LXX. of newly planted trees (Ps. cxliv. 12), and thus is used by St Paul (cp. 1 Cor. iii. 6) of one who has been recently baptized. Christianity was long enough established at Ephesus to make such a rule practicable ; and, in itself, it is highly reasonable. In Tit. i. 6 this condition is omitted; it might have been inconvenient, as the Church there was of recent foundation. The ordination of recent converts from heathenism is forbidden in *Can. Apost.* 80.

τυφωθείς. *Beclouded*, sc. with pride at his elevation. τῦφος is *smoke* or *steam*, and the underlying idea is the bewildering and confusing effect of self-conceit. τυφοῦσθαι only occurs in the Greek Bible here, vi. 4 and 2 Tim. iii. 4; but it is common in Greek literature.

εἰς κρίμα κ.τ.λ. The difficulty in this clause is resident in the words τοῦ διαβόλου. We observe, first, that the general structure of the sentence is parallel to the final clause of *v.* 7; and hence that τοῦ διαβόλου should be taken similarly in both cases. It must, therefore, in *v.* 6, as in *v.* 7, be a *gen. subjecti*, not a *gen. objecti*; it is the κρίμα passed by the διάβολος, not the κρίμα pronounced on him (as in *v.* 7 the παγίς is laid by him and not for him), that is here in question. Who then is ὁ διάβολος? It means *the devil* in 2 Tim. ii. 26, as in Eph. iv. 27 and vi. 11, these being the only places where the word is found in St Paul's writings with the definite article prefixed. But διάβολος, without the article, occurs three times in the Pastoral Epistles (ch. iii. 11; 2 Tim. iii. 3 and Tit. ii. 3) in the sense of *slanderer* or *accuser*; and we have Ἀμὰν ὁ διάβολος in Esther viii. 1 (cp. vii. 4). It seems therefore, despite the *general* usage of the N.T. according to which ὁ διάβολος = *the devil*, legitimate to take it here as equivalent to *the accuser*. This rendering alone preserves the parallelism of clauses in *vv.* 6 and 7, and alone gives sequence to the thought of the writer. *The accuser* or *slanderer* is one of those people, to be found in every community, whose delight is to find fault with the demeanour and conduct of anyone professing a strict rule of life; that such opponents were known in the Apostolic Churches, the language of the Epistles repeatedly indicates. If the words be thus taken, there is no allusion to the fall of the devil through pride, or to the judgement passed on him (Jude 6); and we translate: *no novice, lest being puffed up he fall into the judgement passed by the slanderer.* The phrase ἐμπίπτειν εἰς occurs again ch. vi. 9.

7. δὲ καί. The καί serves to connect this with *v.* 6; *but* he must *also* &c.

μαρτυρίαν. Not μαρτύριον as in ii. 6; there the reference is to the witness to the truth of facts and doctrines, here to the character of persons.

ἀπὸ τῶν ἔξωθεν. οἱ ἔξω is St Paul's regular description (1 Cor. v. 12; Col. iv. 5; 1 Thess. iv. 12) for those who are not Christians and so οἰκεῖοι τῆς πίστεως (Gal. vi. 10). Far from being a new convert, it is desirable that a bishop should be a Christian of standing and repute among his heathen neighbours.

εἰς ὀνειδισμὸν κ.τ.λ. Again, the important words are τοῦ διαβόλου, which are evidently here *gen. subjecti*, not *gen. objecti*. The context of παγὶς τοῦ διαβόλου in 2 Tim. ii. 26 determines τοῦ δ. to refer *there* to *the devil*; but here as plainly the context requires us to take it in the more general sense of *the slanderer* or *accuser*. Verses 6 and 7 refer to the reputation of the ἐπίσκοπος, an important matter, for he must be ἀνεπίλημπτος (*v.* 2), and not to the snares set for him by Satan. We thus take both ὀνειδισμός and παγίς with τοῦ διαβόλου, and translate ...*the reproaches and snares prepared by slanderers.* An ὀνειδισμός from οἱ ἔξω is a thought familiar to St Paul: cp. Rom. xv. 3 (Ps. lxix. 9) οἱ ὀνειδισμοὶ τῶν ὀνειδιζόντων σὲ ἐπέπεσαν ἐπ' ἐμέ, and also Rom. xi. 9 (Ps. lxix. 22).

A comparison of the qualifications of ἐπίσκοποι enumerated above with the characteristics of the Stoic σοφός (Diog. Laert. vii. 116 ff.) is interesting. We cannot think it impossible that the Apostle was acquainted with the latter list, which was one of the commonplaces of Stoic teaching of the day. And, although there are wide divergences, as might be anticipated, between the teaching of Zeno and of St Paul (cp. for instance the Stoic thesis that the σοφός should be *pitiless* (§ 123)), yet the coincidences are striking. The ἐπίσκοπος is to be a married man and his family is spoken of as an object of his affection (*vv.* 2, 4, 5); so too with the σοφός (§§ 120, 121). The ἐπίσκοπος is not to be a novice ἵνα μὴ τυφωθείς &c. (*v.* 6); the σοφός is to be ἄτυφος. The ἐπίσκοπος is not to be πάροινος (*v.* 3) and yet Timothy is advised (*v.* 23) to use wine in moderation; for the σοφός it is prescribed καὶ οἰνωθήσεσθαι μέν, οὐ μεθυσθήσεσθαι δέ (§ 118). Two attributes of the ἐπίσκοπος are given in the order σώφρονα, κόσμιον (*v.* 2); in connexion with the virtues of the σοφός it is said τῇ δὲ σωφροσύνῃ [ἕπεται] κοσμιότης (§ 126). And lastly the instructions to Timothy about bodily exercise (iv. 8) recall the practice of the σοφός in the same matter: τὴν ἄσκησιν ἀποδέξεται ὑπὲρ τῆς τοῦ σώματος ὑπομονῆς (§ 123).

8, 9. ii. DEACONS.

8. διακόνους. The plural number is, perhaps, significant, in contrast to τὸν ἐπίσκοπον of *v.* 2. See on διάκονοι *Introd.* p. lxvii.

ὡσαύτως. *In like manner*; the δεῖ εἶναι of the preceding verses is, of course, to be supplied.

σεμνούς. See note on ii. 2.

μὴ διλόγους. This word is only found here in the Greek Bible; διλογεῖν, διλογία occur in Xenophon in the sense of *repetition*, and thus δίλογοι here may be equivalent to (*a*) *talebearers.* But (*b*) the meaning is probably akin to that of δίγλωσσος (Prov. xi. 13; Ecclus. v. 9), viz. *double-tongued. Ad alios alia loquentes* is Bengel's paraphrase, excellent as usual. Such a habit would be fatal to the usefulness of an official whose duties would necessarily bring him into close and frequent association with all classes. Polycarp (§ 5) notes that the deacons are not to be δίλογοι, an obvious reminiscence of this passage.

προσέχοντας. St Paul only uses this verb in the Pastorals (but cp. Acts xx. 28); *addicted to* gives the sense here. Again, the appropriateness of such a caution is plain, when the house-to-house visitation entailed by the office of the διάκονος is remembered.

μὴ αἰσχροκερδεῖς. *Not greedy of base gains*, as at Tit. i. 7, 11; cp. also 1 Pet. v. 2. The reference is plainly to the illicit disposal of Church funds, a temptation which would specially press upon those concerned with the distribution of alms. See also on Tit. i. 11.

9. ἔχοντας. *Holding*, as contrasted with *teaching*, which did not come within the province of the διάκονος.

τὸ μυστήριον τῆς πίστεως. The genitive might be either (*a*) *appositional*, descriptive of the substance of the μυστήριον, *the Mystery of the Faith*, or (*b*) *subjective*, 'the mystery on which faith rests and which it has embraced.' Either would give good sense, but the analogy of τὸ μυστήριον τῆς εὐσεβείας in *v*. 16 and of τὸ μυστήριον τῆς ἀνομίας in 2 Thess. ii. 7 suggest that the subjective sense is preferable here. The other meaning would be, however, quite admissible and is favoured by the presence of the definite article. See note on i. 19.

μυστήριον is a secret, concealed from the mass of mankind, but revealed to the initiated; and the Christian μυστήριον is thus (Matt. xiii. 11; Eph. i. 9; Rom. xvi. 25) the secret of salvation in Christ revealed to the faithful through the Divine Spirit. Cp. iii. 16.

ἐν καθαρᾷ συνειδήσει. Cp. i. 5, 19 and the notes thereon, and note the close connexion all through this Epistle between a good conscience and a sound faith; it is hard to divorce creed from life.

It will be observed that the qualification given in this verse is one which is required of all Christians, and not only of διάκονοι. As in the case of ἐπίσκοποι (see note on *v*. 2), the writer is not giving a complete list of the specific duties and qualities of the deacons, but suggesting certain conditions to which it was indispensable that candidates for the diaconate should conform. And it is instructive that this spiritual qualification of faith and a good conscience is explicitly mentioned in the case of the lower rather than the higher order of the ministry of service.

10. καὶ...δέ. *And...also*; i.e. the διάκονοι no less than the ἐπίσκοποι.

δοκιμαζέσθωσαν πρῶτον. *Let them first be proved.* This does not refer to any formal examination of the candidates for the diaconate, either by Timothy or by the officers of the Church, so much as to the general verdict of the community concerning their life and conversation. The qualities enumerated in *vv*. 8, 9 are such as would be patent to observation. So Clem. Rom. (§ 42) has δοκιμάσαντες τῷ πνεύματι and (§ 44) διαδέξωνται ἕτεροι δεδοκιμασμένοι ἄνδρες.

εἶτα διακονείτωσαν ἀνέγκλητοι ὄντες. *Then let them serve as deacons, if no charge is brought against them.*

11.   PARENTHETIC:—DEACONESSES.

11. γυναῖκας ὡσαύτως κ.τ.λ. It is difficult to determine who the 'women' are, who are thus brought into the middle of the paragraph which deals with the qualifications of deacons. Excluding impossible interpretations, they must be either (*a*) the *wives of the deacons* or (*b*) the *deaconesses* of the Church. If the former we should have expected τὰς γυναῖκας αὐτῶν, if the latter, τὰς διακόνους; the Greek is quite as ambiguous as the R.V. 'women.' That there were deaconesses in the early Church, we know; the case of Phœbe (Rom. xvi. 25) is familiar, and Pliny (*Ep*. x. 97) has mention of "duabus ancillis

quae ministrae dicebantur." A century later than Pliny we find
elaborate rules as to the female diaconate laid down in the *Apostolic
Constitutions*[1]. The ancient interpreters took this view of the passage,
and it has been urged by many modern commentators that interpretation (*a*) is excluded by the absence of any corresponding regulation
as to the wives of the ἐπίσκοποι, as well as by the silence of the
writer concerning any domestic duties of the women in question.
An argument *e silentio* is, no doubt, always precarious; and, further,
it is to be remembered that a deacon's wife would of necessity share
his work which was largely occupied with the sick and needy, and it
is thus intelligible that it would be necessary to have an eye to her
character in the selection of her husband for the diaconate; whereas
the wife of an ἐπίσκοπος is in no way partner of his responsibilities,
and should not be permitted to meddle in the administration of the
Church. The absence of any regulations for the bishops' wives might
be thus accounted for. But on the whole interpretation (*b*) seems to
be more consonant with the usages of Christian antiquity, as well as
with the general structure of the chapter before us, and with the fact
that historically the deacons always chose their own wives without
any reference to the judgement of the Church. We therefore translate
(with Lightfoot[2]) γυναῖκας, *deaconesses*, and find here the earliest
regulations as to the διακονίσσαι who in succeeding ages played an
important part in the Church's life[3].

σεμνάς. See above on ii. 2; this corresponds, of course, to σεμνούς
of *v.* 8.

μὴ διαβόλους. See note on iii. 6; the phrase corresponds to μὴ
διλόγους of *v.* 8.

νηφαλίους. See note on iii. 2; the word is here used in its primary
sense of *sober*, and balances μὴ οἴνῳ πολλῷ προσέχοντας of *v.* 8.

πιστὰς ἐν πᾶσιν. *Faithful in all things.* A general statement,
but perhaps laid down here with special reference to the virtue of
trustworthiness, which, in matters of money, was peculiarly demanded
of the διάκονος, whether man or woman. See note on μὴ αἰσχροκερδεῖς
of *v.* 8.

12, 13. THE QUALIFICATIONS OF DEACONS (*continued*).

12. The injunctions of this verse are identical with those laid down
before in the case of ἐπίσκοποι; see the notes on *vv.* 2, 3. If a man's
family is disorderly, it constitutes a *presumption* that there has been
something amiss in the methods by which he has governed and
ordered his household. It will be remembered that in our Ordinal

---

[1] The first six books of the *Apost. Const.* embody an *Apostolic Didascalia*
(now only extant in Syriac and Latin) which is probably of the third century.
The regulations therein given for Deacons and Deaconesses are in some respects
less elaborate and more primitive than those laid down in the corresponding
(third) book of the *Apost. Const.*, and are very similar to those given in the
Pastoral Epistles.
[2] *On a Fresh Revision of the New Testament*, p. 114.
[3] See on the general question, Cecilia Robinson, *The Ministry of Deaconesses.*

stress is laid on the due ordering of the family and the home; and
candidates for the orders of deacon and priest engage 'to frame and
fashion their own lives and *the lives of* [*their*] *families*, according to
the doctrine of Christ.'

13. The meaning of βαθμὸν καλόν is the key to this verse. βαθμός
(ἅπ. λεγ. in the N.T.) means primarily a 'step,' and it has been
interpreted often of (*a*) a step in the ministry, the *gradus presbyte-
ratus*; the meaning of the verse being, then, that those who have served
the office of deacon well are rewarded by being raised to the presbyterate
(or the episcopate). But this is not in harmony with the context,
and savours of a later period than that of the Epistle. The regular
promotion of deacons was, apparently, not known in the Apostolic or
sub-Apostolic age. But (*b*) βαθμός may well mean 'standing' or
'position'; and thus the passage speaks of the 'vantage-ground' in
respect of the Christian community which will be gained by a deacon
who has honourably discharged his duties. The reputation he has
acquired may become the means of further and wider usefulness.
Another interpretation (*c*) is that of 'a good standing' in respect,
not of men, but of God, the reference being to the spiritual growth
of the διάκονοι; in this view, ἀποθησαυρίζοντας ἑαυτοῖς θεμέλιον καλὸν
εἰς τὸ μέλλον of vi. 19 would be a close parallel. But such an interpretation robs γάρ of its force, and ignores the connexion it implies
between verses 12 and 13. Bearing in mind the point of the injunction that the διάκονοι should be μιᾶς γυναικὸς ἄνδρες, viz. that they
should be without reproach in the eyes of the Christian community,
we see that a transition to any comment on their spiritual progress
here or their final destiny hereafter would be out of place, while an
observation in reference to their good repute among the faithful
would be entirely apposite. On these grounds we decide in favour of
(*b*); the 'good standing' acquired by the διάκονος is his position of
greater trust among those to whom he ministers, in itself a great
reward, because of the larger opportunities which it gives.

περιποιοῦνται, *acquire.* The verb περιποιεῖσθαι does not appear
elsewhere in St Paul's Epistles; but cp. Acts xx. 28 and 1 Thess. v.
9 &c. The translation of the A.V., *purchase*, has come to suggest an
idea of traffic which the word does not contain.

πολλὴν παρρησίαν. In accordance with the view taken above of
βαθμὸν καλόν, this phrase finds a parallel in 2 Cor. vii. 4; the 'boldness' acquired by the καλῶς διακονήσαντες is boldness in respect of
men, not in respect of God. This latter is a familiar N.T. idea (e.g.
1 John iii. 21), but is not here prominent.

ἐν πίστει τῇ ἐν Χρ. 'I. This is the sphere in which the παρρησία
is exhibited, and the source from which it ultimately springs. Cp.
Col. i. 4.

14, 15. THE AIM OF ALL THE FOREGOING INSTRUCTIONS.

14. ταῦτα, i.e. the foregoing instructions about public worship,
and about the officers of the Church, contained in chaps. ii. and iii.;
cp. ταύτην τὴν παραγγελίαν at the close of ch. i.

γράφω. The present is used rather than the epistolary aorist; cp. 1 Cor. iv. 14; Gal. i. 20 &c.

πρὸς σέ. These words are enclosed in square brackets by Westcott and Hort; but they are well attested (see crit. note) and are quite in Paul's manner. Cp. Rom. i. 10, 13; 2 Cor. i. 15.

τάχιον, *more speedily*, sc. than you might suppose from the fact that I am writing to you. The force of the comparative should not be overlooked; cp. Heb. xiii. 23. The reading ἐν τάχει (see crit. note) is probably an explanatory gloss.

15. πῶς δεῖ ἐν οἴκῳ θεοῦ ἀναστρέφεσθαι, *how men ought to behave themselves in God's household.* This is the general subject of chaps. ii. and iii.; and the insertion of σε after δεῖ (see crit. note), or the limitation of the words to Timothy (*how thou oughtest to behave thyself* &c.), is quite misleading. On οἶκος θεοῦ see note on *v.* 5 above; cp. also 2 Tim. ii. 20. No stress can be laid on the absence of the definite article, which is used but sparingly throughout the Pastorals.

ἥτις, *quippe quae*, explanatory of οἶκος θεοῦ.

ἐκκλησία θεοῦ ζῶντος. The term ἐκκλησία, representing the קָהָל of the O.T., has, like its Hebrew original, a double meaning, sometimes being used for the local Christian congregation, sometimes in the larger sense of the new Israel in covenant relation with God. Thus *God's household which indeed is the Ecclesia of the living God* is the assembly of the faithful, baptized into the Threefold Name. ἡ ἐκκλησία τοῦ θεοῦ is a frequent expression of St Paul's (cp. 1 Cor. x. 32; Acts xx. 28 &c.).

We have the phrase *the living God* again in ch. iv. 10; cp. Deut. v. 26; 2 Cor. iii. 3, vi. 16 &c. It may perhaps point a contrast with the idols of the heathen, such as Artemis of Ephesus; but (more probably) it emphasises the continuous providence of God in the guidance of His Church: He is not to be conceived of merely as the Supreme Being, but as the Heavenly Master Whose care is over all His family.

στῦλος καὶ ἑδραίωμα τῆς ἀλ., *a pillar and stay of the Truth.* Here, the absence of the definite article seems to be deliberate. The Church is not *the* pillar of the Truth, for the Truth has other supports in conscience and in Scripture; but the Church, and every local branch of the Church, is *a* pillar and stay of the Truth. Without such external aids, such permanent witness, the Truth itself might be endangered. And such a conception of the Church justifies the minuteness of the injunctions that have been given in chaps. ii. and iii.; whatever contributes to the dignity of the Church's worship and to the worthiness of the Church's ministers, in so far is a strengthening of the majesty of the Truth[1].

---

[1] The expression στῦλος καὶ ἑδραίωμα τῆς ἀληθείας has been referred by some, not to the Church, but to Timothy himself, on the grounds that στῦλος is generally applied to *persons* in the N.T. (Gal. ii. 9; Rev. iii. 12), and that the Letter of the Churches of Lyons and Vienne (Eus. *H.E.* v. 1. 6) speaks of the martyr Attalus as στῦλος καὶ ἑδραίωμα, with an evident reminiscence of this passage. But if στῦλος καὶ ἑδρ. κ.τ.λ. here referred to Timothy, we should certainly expect

ἑδραίωμα is not found elsewhere in the Greek Bible, but St Paul has ἑδραῖος several times (1 Cor. vii. 37, xv. 58; Col. i. 23). It seems to mean *bulwark* or *stay* (Vulg. *firmamentum*) rather than *ground* or *foundation*, the sense usually assigned to it here.

16. THE SUBSTANCE OF THE FAITH.

16. καὶ ὁμολογουμένως μέγα... *And confessedly great* &c.: ὁμολο-γουμένως (ἅπ. λεγ. in N.T.) is to be taken with μέγα. Compare τὸ μυστήριον τοῦτο μέγα ἐστίν of Eph. v. 32, in both cases μέγα referring to the *importance*, not to the *obscurity*, of the μυστήριον. μυστήριον does not necessarily carry with it the idea of *mysteriousness*, in the modern sense of unintelligibility; it simply means a *secret*, into which some have been initiated (see on *v.* 9).

τὸ τῆς εὐσεβείας μυστήριον. τῆς εὐσεβείας, like τῆς πίστεως in *v.* 9, is a possessive genitive: *the mystery of piety*, i.e. the mystery which piety embraces, and on which it feeds. This mystery or secret is not an abstract doctrine; it is the Person of Christ Himself. Cp. Col. i. 27 τὸ πλοῦτος τῆς δόξης τοῦ μυστηρίου τούτου ἐν τοῖς ἔθνεσιν, ὅ ἐστιν Χριστὸς ἐν ὑμῖν, ἡ ἐλπὶς τῆς δόξης; and see the note on εὐσέβεια at ii. 2.

ὃς ἐφανερώθη κ.τ.λ. The critical note gives a summary of the evidence as to the reading, once much disputed, but now hardly doubtful. It seems probable from the parallelism of the clauses and from the rhythmical arrangement that the words ὃς ἐφανερώθη... ἀνελήμφθη ἐν δόξῃ are a quotation from an early hymn on the Incarnation. Writing to the Churches of Asia Minor, St Paul speaks of Christian hymns (Eph. v. 19; Col. iii. 16); and it has even been thought that Eph. v. 14 is a fragment of one. At all events the familiar witness of Pliny (*Ep.* x. 97) is explicit; he reports that the Christians of Bithynia were wont "carmen Christo quasi Deo dicere secum invicem"; a description applying well enough to the verse before us, which was probably meant for antiphonal singing. If, then, it be the case that we are here dealing not with St Paul's own words, but with an apposite quotation introduced by him, the abruptness of ὅς at once disappears. It is the relative to an antecedent not ex-pressed in the quotation, but impossible to mistake.

The clauses fall into three contrasted pairs:

(i.) *The revelation and its proofs.*

(a) **ἐφανερώθη ἐν σαρκί.** We need not assume any polemical reference to Gnosticism or Docetism, though there are very early traces of these false opinions (see 1 John iv. 2, 3); a statement of the Incarnation is not necessarily controversial, and the tone of this fragment is one of triumphant thankfulness rather than of argument. Cp. John i. 4; Phil. ii. 6; 1 John i. 2. The verb φανερόω is common in St Paul's writings (see Rom. iii. 21; 2 Tim. i. 10), as well as in

accusatives, and further the full phrase is far stronger than στῦλος by itself, too strong, indeed, to be used of any single individual. The expression, as used of Attalus, is a *quotation* and a somewhat loosely applied quotation; its occurrence in the Letter of the Churches of Lyons and Vienne cannot be taken as ruling the *interpretation* of the verse before us.

St John, and it is to be observed that when used in the passive it implies the Pre-existence of the Person Who is the subject of the sentence. Thus, whether ὅς or θεός be read, the word ἐφανερώθη involves the superhuman nature of Him Who was *manifested in the flesh.* The nearest parallel *in form* in St Paul is Rom. viii. 3 ἐν ὁμοιώματι σαρκὸς ἁμαρτίας.

(b) **ἐδικαιώθη ἐν πνεύματι,** *justified in the spirit.* δικαιόω is not, of course, used here in the technical sense familiar in St Paul's Epistles, but in its ordinary signification, as in Matt. xi. 19; Luke vii. 35; Rom. iii. 4 (Ps. li. 6). πνεύματι is in contrast to σαρκί (cf. 1 Pet. iii. 18 θανατωθεὶς μὲν σαρκί, ζωοποιηθεὶς δὲ πνεύματι); πνεῦμα signifies the higher principle of spiritual life, as distinguished at once from σάρξ, the flesh, and ψυχή, the physical life. The phrase, then, states that, as Christ was manifested in human flesh, so in His spiritual activities, words and works, He was proved to be what He claimed to be, Son of God no less than Son of man; His Personal claims were vindicated. So in Rom. i. 3 we have: ὁρισθέντος υἱοῦ θεοῦ ἐν δυνάμει κατὰ πνεῦμα ἁγιωσύνης ἐξ ἀναστάσεως νεκρῶν, where πνεῦμα is to be taken, as here, of the human spirit of the Redeemer.

(ii.) *Its extent and mode.*

ὤφθη ἀγγέλοις, ἐκηρύχθη ἐν ἔθνεσιν. The antithesis between ἄγγελοι and ἔθνη is emphatic. The revelation to *angels*, the rational creatures *nearest* to God, is of a different character from the revelation to the Gentiles, the *heathen* world (as opposed to Israel), and so *farthest* from God. A revelation which embraces these two extreme classes will take in all rational creation; the blessings of the Incarnation stretch beyond the sphere of human life. The revelation to Gentiles is *mediate*, by preaching, and it was this with which St Paul was specially entrusted (Eph. iii. 8; cp. Rom. xvi. 26); the revelation to the higher orders of created intelligences is *immediate*, by vision (ὤφθη; cp. 1 Cor. xv. 6, 8). We are not to think here of any special manifestation to angels during the Lord's earthly life, such as are recorded at Matt. iv. 11 and at Luke xxii. 43; but of the fuller knowledge of Christ's Person which was opened out to the heavenly host by the Incarnation. Such things angels "desire to look into" (1 Pet. i. 12); and St Paul declares (Eph. iii. 10) that the preaching to the Gentiles was "to the intent that now unto the principalities and the powers in the heavenly places might be made known through the Church the manifold wisdom of God, according to the eternal purpose which He purposed in Christ Jesus our Lord." Cp. also 1 Cor. iv. 9 θέατρον ἐγενήθημεν τῷ κόσμῳ καὶ ἀγγέλοις καὶ ἀνθρώποις.

(iii.) *Its consummation on earth and in heaven.*

(a) **ἐπιστεύθη ἐν κόσμῳ.** κόσμος has no evil sense here; it is the *world* which God loved (John iii. 16). The prayer of the Lord was ἵνα ὁ κόσμος πιστεύῃ ὅτι σύ με ἀπέστειλας. This is the consummation on earth of His Redemptive Work; from the heavenly side it is

(b) **ἀνελήμφθη ἐν δόξῃ.** This is the distinctive word used of the Ascension in Mark xvi. 19, and in Acts i. 2. *He was received up* [and is now] *in glory*; ἐν δόξῃ expresses the permanent condition of His being. Cp. 1 Pet. i. 11. Thus the sequence all through the verse is from the Incarnation to the Ascension, though it is a logical sequence rather than a historical one.

CHAPTER IV.

2. κεκαυστηριασμένων. This is the spelling of the best MSS. (אAL); κεκαυτηριασμένων, the spelling of the *text. rec.*, is found in CD₂GKP &c.

3. ἀπέχεσθαι. On account of the difficulty of construction, Dr Hort suggested that this word might have been a primitive corruption of ἢ ἅπτεσθαι or καὶ γεύεσθαι; but see note *in loc.* Bentley had previously conjectured that κελευόντων had dropped out before ἀπέχεσθαι.

μετάλημψιν. So אAD₂*G; μετάληψιν, the received spelling, is found in CD₂°KLP.

6. Rec. text has Ἰησοῦ Χριστοῦ with D₂° and cursives; but Χρ. Ἰησοῦ is found in אACD₂*GKLP &c. See critical note on i. 16.

παρηκολούθηκας. So nearly all authorities; but Westcott and Hort, on the authority of CG, give a place in their margin to παρηκολούθησας, the true reading in 2 Tim. iii. 10 (which see).

10. Rec. text inserts καὶ before κοπιῶμεν with GKL; *om.* אACD₂P and Vss.

ἀγωνιζόμεθα. So א*ACGK; ὀνειδιζόμεθα is read by א°D₂LP and Vss. It is possible that ἀγωνιζόμεθα may be a correction suggested by Col. i. 29; and Westcott and Hort give ὀνειδιζόμεθα a place in their margin.

ἠλπίκαμεν. So nearly all MSS.; but Westcott and Hort give a place in their margin to the aorist ἠλπίσαμεν, which is found in D₂* 17. See note *in loc.*

12. Rec. text inserts ἐν πνεύματι before ἐν πίστει with KLP (arising, probably, from an original misreading of πίστει or possibly from a reminiscence of ἐν ἀγάπῃ πνεύματι in 1 Cor. iv. 21; cp. Col. i. 8 and 2 Cor. vi. 6; *om.* אACD₂G and Vss.

15. Rec. text inserts ἐν before πᾶσιν with D₂°KLP (a mistaken explanatory gloss), *om.* אACD₂*G and Vss.

III. The dangers of the future. 1—6.

1. The Church is *a pillar and ground of the Truth*, and yet even in her bosom error arises. This is the force of the adversative δέ in iv. 1; it refers back to iii. 15. Despite the privileges and graces of the Church, '*the Spirit expressly* (ῥητῶς) *says that in later times some shall fall away from the faith*,' τῆς πίστεως being here *objective.* See note on i. 19. The meaning of ῥητῶς λέγει is a question. It is possible that St Paul had in his mind some now forgotten prophecy of an 'Apocryphal' book like the *Sibylline Oracles* or the *Book of Enoch*; but it seems better to refer the phrase to some forecast of the Christian prophets, whose words were overruled by a power not their own, for *prophecy* was a gift of the Holy Spirit. Cp. Acts xx. 23, xxi. 11.

ἐν ὑστέροις καιροῖς, i.e. in times future to the speaker (as opposed to προτέροις; cp. 1 Chr. xxix. 29), not 'the *last* times,' which would require ἐσχάτοις. See 2 Tim. iii. 1; 2 Pet. iii. 3; Jude 18.

ἀποστήσονται signifies a more complete apostasy than ἀστοχεῖν τῆς π. (i. 6) or ναναγεῖν περὶ τὴν π. (i. 19). For the word cp. Luke viii. 13; Heb. iii. 12 and 2 Thess. ii. 3 ἡ ἀποστασία.

προσέχοντες κ.τ.λ. *Giving heed to seducing spirits and to doctrines of devils.* St Paul had an ever present sense of the power and the activity of evil spirits (Eph. vi. 12, &c.). They are the *ultimate*, the false teachers of the next verse being the *proximate*, cause of the errors about to appear in the Church. The πνεῦμα τῆς πλάνης (1 John iv. 6) is ever opposed to the πνεῦμα τῆς ἀληθείας.

διδασκαλίαις δαιμονίων. *Gen. subj.*, 'the doctrines *taught* by devils'; cp. σοφία δαιμονιώδης (Jas. iii. 15). There is a false as well as a true διδασκαλία. See on διδασκαλία at i. 10.

2. ἐν ὑποκρίσει ψευδολόγων. *Through the hypocrisy of men that speak lies.* ψευδολόγων (only here in Greek Bible) is not to be taken (see punctuation of A.V.) with δαιμονίων; these 'speakers of lies' are the instruments through which the demoniac powers exercise their influence.

κεκαυστηριασμένων τὴν ἰδίαν συνείδησιν. *Branded in their own conscience.* καυστηριάζεσθαι does not occur elsewhere in the Greek Bible, but we have καυστηρία in 4 Macc. xv. 22 ; and in Hippocrates καυστηριάζειν is 'to cauterize.' The A.V. translates "seared as with a hot iron"; thus the thought would be of the ἀναλγησία, the lack of moral sensitiveness, apparent in the ψευδολόγοι. But the metaphor more probably has reference to the *penal branding* of criminals. This brand-mark of sin is not indeed visible to the world; but it is known to the man himself. Here is the force of ἰδίαν; these hypocrites, with their outward show of holiness and of extreme asceticism, *dum alios tamen urgent* (Bengel), have the brand of sin on their own consciences. Contrast with this τὰ στίγματα τοῦ Ἰησοῦ of Gal. vi. 17 and the emphasis laid on a 'good' conscience all through the Pastorals; see on i. 5. Cp. also Tit. iii. 11 and the note thereon.

3. κωλυόντων γαμεῖν, ἀπέχεσθαι βρωμάτων. See critical note. If the text is not corrupt, the construction is a little awkward, although the sense is plain, and we must suppose some word like διδασκόντων or κελευόντων to precede ἀπέχεσθαι: *forbidding to marry* and commanding *to abstain from meats*. There is a similar ellipse in Lucian *Charon* § 2 κωλύσει ἐνεργεῖν καὶ [sc. ποιήσει] ζημιοῦν.

The false asceticism is two-fold, (*a*) in respect of marriage, (*b*) in respect of food. It is viewed not as present, but as future, and as the

practical consequence of the apostasy foretold in *v.* 1. The germ of
it, however, was already in being. Among the Essenes ὑπεροψία
γάμου (Joseph. *B. J.* ii. 8. 2) was not unknown, and the Therapeutae
described by Philo (*de vit. Cont.* 4) practised abstinence from food.
The former error, in itself foreign to Jewish ideas, does not receive
here formal refutation from the Apostle, probably because it
had not yet appeared in the Christian communities; but the latter
had already been recognised in more directions than one. The Colossian heresy (Col. ii. 16) laid stress on precise regulations as to food;
and Rom. xiv. shews that to such questions a quite undue importance
was attached. This is not surprising, when the minuteness of the
Levitical law on these points is borne in mind. But the refutation
of the error is plain and decisive. These 'meats' are the creation of
God (not of the Demiurge, as a later Gnosticism, with its dualistic
view of the impurity of matter, taught), and were created *that they
might be received* (εἰς μετάλημψιν) *with thanksgiving.*

μετάλημψις (not elsewhere in Greek Bible) is, of course, not to be
confused with ἀπόλαυσις (vi. 17); it is the *use*, not necessarily the
enjoyment, of the Divine gifts which is the final purpose of creation.

μετὰ εὐχαριστίας. Thanksgiving is to accompany the use of the
gifts of creation, as it is to accompany all requests for future benefit
(Phil. iv. 6). Cp. εἰ ἐγὼ χάριτι μετέχω, τί βλασφημοῦμαι ὑπὲρ οὗ ἐγὼ
εὐχαριστῶ; (1 Cor. x. 30).

τοῖς πιστοῖς καὶ ἐπεγνωκόσι τὴν ἀλήθειαν. *By them that believe
and know the truth,* i.e. in contrast to the unbelieving Jews or to the
'weak brethren' (Rom. xiv. 21), the half-instructed Christians, who
had not yet arrived at ἐπίγνωσις ἀληθείας (see on ch. ii. 4 above).
The absence of the article before ἐπεγνωκόσι shews that the πιστ. καὶ
ἐπεγν. τὴν ἀλ. are to be taken as constituting a single class of persons,
the 'faithful.'

The word πιστός is here used in the active sense, common in later
Greek but rare in the N.T. and nowhere found in the LXX., of
believing. We have it again used thus *vv.* 10, 12, v. 16, vi. 2, and
Tit. i. 6; but the older sense 'faithful' or 'trustworthy' is more
frequent. See on i. 19 above.

4, 5.   RESTATEMENT AND FURTHER JUSTIFICATION OF THE PRECEDING
PRINCIPLE.

4. ὅτι. This is not to be taken specially in connexion with
ἀλήθειαν, but with the whole of the preceding statement—*because.*

πᾶν κτίσμα θεοῦ καλόν. *Every creature of God is good.* See Gen.
i. 31; Ecclus. xxxix. 33, and (although the thought is here slightly
different) Rom. xiv. 14; cp. also Acts x. 15.

κτίσμα does not occur elsewhere in St Paul's writings (although
frequent in LXX.); he generally has κτίσις. Possibly the word is here
used of set purpose, to mark with emphasis the handiwork of the
Creator.

καλόν. A favourite word in the Pastorals (see on i. 8 above); it signifies absolute worth, the thought here being quite different from Tit. i. 15, viz. *for the pure all things are pure*, sc. for their use. See note *in loc.*

οὐδὲν ἀπόβλητον μετὰ εὐχαριστίας λαμβανόμενον. *Nothing is to be rejected if it be received with thanksgiving.* This is a distinct idea from that of the *objective* goodness of God's gifts. The words have striking verbal similarity to Homer's: οὔ τοι ἀπόβλητ' ἐστὶ θεῶν ἐρικυδέα δῶρα (*Il.* III. 65). ἀπόβλητος is not found elsewhere in N.T. or LXX. Note that the all important condition μετὰ εὐχαριστίας λαμβ. is repeated from *v.* 3; cp. 2 Cor. iv. 15.

5. ἁγιάζεται γὰρ κ.τ.λ. Not only is πᾶν κτίσμα objectively good (καλόν), but it is also, despite the Fall and its consequences (Rom. viii. 20), good in relation to man, provided it be received μετὰ εὐχαριστίας; *then* ἁγιάζεται, *it is sanctified*, each time that it is used. The present tense shews that it is no single Divine act which is here in the mind of the writer, but a continued and recurring sanctification. εὐχαριστία is used in its most general sense; but the view of life here presented may be described as *sacramental*.

διὰ λόγου θεοῦ καὶ ἐντεύξεως. What is the meaning of λόγος θεοῦ here? The tense of ἁγιάζεται (see above) shews that it cannot be referred (*a*) to the Incarnate Word, as the Creative Agent (John i. 3), or (*b*) to the Divine voice of creation (Gen. i. 31; cp. Acts x. 15). The general sense of the clause undoubtedly is that meat becomes sanctified for man's use by devout, thankful, and prayerful reception (see above on ii. 1 for ἔντευξις); and thus the Apostle seems to have had in his mind the pious practice of 'grace before meat.' Hence the point to be determined is the meaning of λόγος θεοῦ, if λόγ. θεοῦ καὶ ἔντ. is a description of such εὐχαί. Now the commonest and most general meaning of λόγος θεοῦ in the N.T. is the Divine message spoken or delivered under the guidance of the Divine Spirit (see Additional Note at end of chapter iv.), but no such general meaning will fit the context here. It is true that St Paul (Col. iii. 16) follows up the exhortation εὐχάριστοι γίνεσθε by adding ὁ λόγος τοῦ χριστοῦ ἐνοικείτω ἐν ὑμῖν πλουσίως...διδάσκοντες καὶ νουθετοῦντες ἑαυτοὺς ψαλμοῖς, ὕμνοις κ.τ.λ.; and it has been urged that in like manner in the present passage the εὐχαριστία, which is the condition of right use of God's gifts, is the outcome of the indwelling λόγος θεοῦ, which is then understood (*c*) of the Divine utterance through the mouth of the person who offers his grace before meat. But, though λόγ. θ. καὶ ἔντ. constitute *one* conception, yet the connecting καὶ *distinguishes* λόγ. θ. from ἔντευξις; λόγ. θ. seems to mark some special feature which differentiates *this* ἔντευξις from prayer in general. And this special feature in the earliest Christian age (as is still the case) was the employment in the 'grace' of phrases from Holy Scripture. An interesting form from the Apostolical Constitutions (vii. 49) runs as follows:

εὐλογητὸς εἶ κύριε ὁ τρέφων με ἐκ νεότητός μου, ὁ διδοὺς τροφὴν πάσῃ σαρκί· πλήρωσον χαρᾶς καὶ εὐφροσύνης τὰς καρδίας ἡμῶν, ἵνα πάντοτε πᾶσαν αὐτάρκειαν ἔχοντες, περισσεύωμεν εἰς πᾶν ἔργον ἀγαθὸν ἐν Χριστῷ

'Ιησοῦ τῷ κυρίῳ ἡμῶν, δι' οὗ σοὶ δόξα τιμὴ καὶ κράτος εἰς τοὺς αἰῶνας, ἀμήν, which is packed with Scriptural phrases[1]. The words of the Psalter (e.g. Ps. cxlv. 15, 16) have often been used for this pious purpose. Hence we conclude (*d*) that λόγος θεοῦ in the verse before us refers to the words of the O.T. which were commonly embodied (by the Jews as well as by the early Christians) in the εὐχαὶ ἐπ' ἀρίστῳ or prayers before meat: *for it is sanctified through the Word of God and prayer.*

6—10. i. TIMOTHY'S DUTY IN RESPECT OF THE FALSE ASCETICISM.

6. ταῦτα ὑποτιθέμενος κ.τ.λ. *In setting these things* (sc. the principles laid down in *vv.* 4, 5) *before the brethren.* ὑποτίθεσθαι (cp. Rom. xvi. 4) does not carry with it the idea of *reminding* or *advising*, but simply of *expounding*.

διάκονος. Here used in its most general sense of *minister.* See above on διακονίαν (i. 12), and cp. 2 Tim. iv. 5; 2 Cor. xi. 23 &c.

Χριστοῦ Ἰησοῦ. This places the duty of Timothy in respect of false asceticism on a very high level; he is to expound the principles of *vv.* 4, 5 as *a good minister of Christ Jesus.*

ἐντρεφόμενος. The word does not occur elsewhere in the Greek Bible, but its meaning is not doubtful, *being nurtured*, the present participle indicating a *continual* nourishment and training. Cp. 2 Tim. iii. 14.

τοῖς λόγοις τῆς πίστεως. The A.V. renders *in the words of faith*, which seemingly means *the words in which faith expresses itself* (cp. 1 Cor. ii. 4 σοφίας λόγοι). The R.V. (more correctly) lays stress on the article, *in the words of the faith*, understanding πίστις objectively of the Christian creed, rather than *subjectively* of the belief of individuals (see note on i. 19). τῆς πίστεως in any case must be taken in close connexion with καὶ τῆς καλῆς διδασκαλίας; and *the words of the faith and the good doctrine* have reference to formal doctrinal statements in which Timothy had been instructed and to which he could continually appeal. It is natural to think at once of the 'Faithful Sayings' of the Pastoral Epistles (see above on i. 15).

ᾗ παρηκολούθηκας. *Which thou hast followed*, sc. until now. The A.V. "whereunto thou hast attained " does not give the sense accurately. Compare 2 Tim. iii. 10 σὺ δὲ παρηκολούθησάς μου τῇ διδασκαλίᾳ.

7. τοὺς δὲ βεβήλους καὶ γραώδεις μύθους παραιτοῦ. *But eschew profane and old wives' fables.* παραιτεῖσθαι, 'to refuse,' 'to have nothing to do with,' does not occur in St Paul outside the Pastorals (1 Tim. v. 11; 2 Tim. ii. 23; Tit. iii. 10), but is found in St Luke (xiv. 18; Acts xxv. 11) and in Heb. xii. 25 &c., as well as in the LXX.

---

[1] Cp. Tertullian (*Apol.* xxxix.), speaking of the ἀγάπαι, "Non prius discumbitur, quam oratio ad deum praegustetur......post aquam manualem et lumina, ut quisque de scripturis sanctis vel de proprio ingenio potest, provocatur in medium deo canere......aeque oratio convivium dirimit." This refers to the exhortation given in connexion with the prayer before and after the common meal, and not necessarily to the prayer itself.

The def. art. τούς suggests that current and familiar myths are in the writer's mind; he is not speaking now of the ascetic extravagances of the future, but of the trivial and foolish teachings with which Timothy was in contact at Ephesus. For μύθους see above on i. 4, and for βεβήλους on i. 9.

γραώδεις, 'anile.' The word does not occur elsewhere in the Greek Bible, but is found in Strabo and other writers. It is quite unnecessary and far-fetched to see here, with Baur, a reference to the Valentinian story of Sophia Achamoth (Iren. *Haer.* I. 4. 5).

γύμναζε δὲ σεαυτὸν πρὸς εὐσέβειαν. *But* (in contrast to any such false asceticism as that foreshadowed in *v.* 3) *discipline thyself unto godliness.* πρός is used of the *aim* and *motive* of the discipline; cp. 1 Cor. vii. 35. See note on iii. 7.

8. ἡ γὰρ σωμ. γυμν. κ.τ.λ. *For the discipline of the body is profitable for a little, but godliness is profitable for all things.* We should not understand either γύμναζε or γυμνασία of gymnastic training for the games or athletic exercise, although the words are so taken by Chrysostom and others; any such idea is foreign to the context. In contrast with the extravagant asceticism which St Paul fears in the future, the true γυμνασία or discipline of the body (*a*) is only to be practised in moderation; it is profitable πρὸς ὀλίγον (*ad modicum*, not as in Jas. iv. 14 *for a little time*); and (*b*) is undertaken, not because of false views of the impurity of matter, but as a means to an end, πρὸς εὐσέβειαν. Cp. 1 Cor. ix. 27. This εὐσέβεια is *profitable* (ὠφέλιμος does not occur in the Greek Bible outside the Pastorals, but St Paul has ὠφέλεια and ὠφελεῖν) *for all things*. See note on ii. 2.

ἐπαγγελίαν ἔχουσα κ.τ.λ. *Inasmuch as it has* (the causal use of the participle) *promise of the life which now is, and of that which is to come.* Observe that here is no guarantee of the worldly prosperity of the εὐσεβής (as in Ps. i. 3 and often in the O.T.); ζωή is the higher principle of life, in contrast with βίος which takes account of the man's environment; cp. Luke xii. 15 οὐκ ἐν τῷ περισσεύειν τινὶ ἡ ζωὴ αὐτοῦ ἐστιν ἐκ τῶν ὑπαρχόντων αὐτῷ and 2 Tim. i. 1. See Heb. ix. 15.

9. πιστὸς ὁ λόγος καὶ πάσ. ἀπ. ἄξ. See above on i. 15. It is not certain what the reference is. This formula refers without doubt to what *follows* in i. 15, and equally without doubt to what *precedes* in Tit. iii. 8. Hence its reference in any given instance must be determined by the context. On the whole it seems more natural here to understand it of the saying at the close of *v.* 8 about the blessings of εὐσέβεια. Verse 10 does not read like a familiar or proverbial saying, and the γάρ after εἰς τοῦτο seems to be explanatory. (Yet compare 2 Tim. ii. 11.)

10. εἰς τοῦτο γὰρ κ.τ.λ. The whole verse is explanatory of the motive and the aim of the γυμνασία or discipline of the body, as of all earthly struggle.

κοπιῶμεν. κόπος means 'wearying fatigue,' and κοπιάω ordinarily means 'to be weary of.' The word carries special allusion here to the training for athletic contests, a sense which it frequently bears, as

e.g. at Phil. ii. 16. It is used in Rom. xvi. 6, 12; 1 Cor. xv. 10; Gal.
iv. 11 of the daily work of an Apostle. The reading ἀγωνιζόμεθα (see crit.
note) is better supported than ὀνειδιζόμεθα of the received text; cp.
Col. i. 29 εἰς ὃ καὶ κοπιῶ ἀγωνιζόμενος, and also [2 Clem.] § 7 οὐ πάντες
στεφανοῦνται, εἰ μὴ οἱ πολλὰ κοπιάσαντες καὶ καλῶς ἀγωνισάμενοι.

ἠλπίκαμεν. The perfect marks the continued ἐλπίς of the believer;
we have set our hope. Cp. vi. 17 where ἐλπίζειν is again followed by
ἐπί, with the dative, the preposition marking the ground of the
hope (cp. Rom. xv. 12). See Hort on 1 Pet. i. 13. For θεῷ ζῶντι see
on iii. 15.

σωτὴρ πάντων ἀνθρώπων. See note on i. 1; the phrase is found in
Wisd. xvi. 7, διὰ σέ, τὸν πάντων σωτῆρα.

μάλιστα πιστῶν. μάλιστα is used just as at Gal. vi. 10; Phil.
iv. 22, i.e. *especially.* There is, then, a special sense in which God
is the Saviour *of those who believe*, as distinct from *all men*; it is
only *in those who believe* that the Divine intention that *all men should
be saved* (ii. 4) can be completely fulfilled. For the same thoughts
stated in the reverse order, see 1 John ii. 2.

11—16.   ii.   TIMOTHY'S DUTY IN RESPECT OF HIS PERSONAL CONDUCT.

11.   παράγγελλε ταῦτα. *These things command*; sc. the mode and
measure of bodily discipline which has been under discussion. The
recurrence is noteworthy of the somewhat vague ταῦτα (iii. 14, iv. 6,
15, v. 7, vi. 3) as the counterpart to the trivial teachings which are
repudiated.

καὶ δίδασκε. *And teach*; i.e. the doctrine on which the practical
rules of discipline depend. δίδασκε refers to the *theory* of conduct,
παράγγελλε to *practice.*

12.   μηδείς σου τῆς νεότητος καταφρονείτω. This is advice to
Timothy, not a command to the members of the Church at Ephesus,
though no doubt they would take note of it. σου depends on νεότητος
and is not directly governed by καταφρ.: *let no man despise thy youth.*
νεότης (a word not occurring again in St Paul's Epistles, though
found in his speech before Agrippa in Acts xxvi. 4) is a relative term.
Timothy must have been about 30 years of age at this time (cp. again
2 Tim. ii. 22), and was thus young in comparison with St Paul and
in respect of the duties which were incumbent on him, though not by
any means a boy or immature[1]. See further in *Introduction* p. xliii.,

---

[1] The term νεότης is common in the LXX. The phrase 'wife of thy youth'
(ἐκ νεότητός σου, Prov. v. 18; Mal. ii. 14) shews that it is not restricted to the
period of childhood (cp. Lam. iii. 27). "Polybius (XVII. 12. 5) speaks of Flaminius
as νέος κομιδῆ, 'very young,' because, as he explains, 'he was not more than
30 years old,' and he uses this same expression of Hiero (I. 8. 3), who seems to
have been then close upon 35, and of Philopoemen (II. 67. 5), who was then over
30......So likewise Galen in one passage (*Op.* XIII. p. 599) describes himself as
νέος τὴν ἡλικίαν when he was entering upon his 29th year, and in another
(*Op.* XIX. p. 15) as νέος ὢν ἔτι, though he was in his 34th year at the time"
(Lightfoot, *Ignatius*, I. 448). In Xen. *Mem.* I. 2. 35, Charicles says, μηδὲ σὺ
διαλέγου νεωτέροις τριάκοντα ἐτῶν in answer to Socrates' demand ὁρίσατέ μοι
μέχρι πόσων ἐτῶν δεῖ νομίζειν νέους εἶναι τοὺς ἀνθρώπους, which shews that νέος

and for the reverence due to young bishops cp. Ignatius *Magnes.* 3 and *Apost. Const.* ii. 1. In an earlier Epistle St Paul had expressed similar anxiety that Timothy should be treated with respect: ἐὰν δὲ ἔλθῃ Τιμόθεος...μή τις οὖν αὐτὸν ἐξουθενήσῃ (1 Cor. xvi. 11). Cp. the advice to Titus (ii. 15) μηδείς σου περιφρονείτω.

ἀλλὰ τύπος γίνου τῶν πιστῶν. *But be a pattern of the believers,* not merely an example *to* them but a model *for* them. So Titus is counselled περὶ πάντα σεαυτὸν παρεχόμενος τύπον καλῶν ἔργων (Tit. ii. 7). St Paul refers more than once to the duty which was incumbent on himself to be a τύπος to his converts (Phil. iii. 17; 2 Thess. iii. 9).

ἐν λόγῳ, ἐν ἀν. κ.τ.λ. The order should be noted. Timothy is to be a τύπος τῶν πιστῶν (1) in outward conduct, in speech and act, *in word and in manner of life.* Compare Rom. xv. 18 λόγῳ καὶ ἔργῳ and Col. iii. 17, and for ἀναστροφή *conversation,* a favourite word of St Paul, cp. Gal. i. 13; Eph. iv. 22. He is also to be a τύπος (2) in inward disposition, ἐν ἀγάπῃ, ἐν πίστει, ἐν ἁγνείᾳ, *in love, in faith, in purity,* graces which may be said to cover respectively our duty to *man,* to *God,* and to *ourselves* (cp. Tit. ii. 12). The classical substantive ἁγνεία only occurs again in the N.T. in ch. v. 2 (it is a false reading in Gal. v. 23); but we have ἁγνός in v. 22 of this Epistle, and ἐν ἁγνότητι (the later Greek word) in 2 Cor. vi. 6, references which seem to define its meaning here. It signifies *purity* of life and motive, and not merely *chastity,* which is only one outward manifestation of the Christian grace of ἁγνεία. It is interesting to note that in the prayer before the Benediction in our Form of Consecration of Bishops, where the words of this verse are reproduced, for ἐν ἁγνείᾳ we have the double rendering "in chastity and in purity," indicating this larger meaning of ἁγνεία.

ἐν πνεύματι of the rec. text is an interpolation (see crit. note).

13. ἕως ἔρχομαι. Possibly the present tense implies a more confident expectation than would be suggested by ἕως ἂν ἔλθω; cp. iii. 14 ἐλπίζων ἐλθεῖν πρὸς σὲ τάχιον.

πρόσεχε, *give heed;* see note on the word at iii. 8.

τῇ ἀναγνώσει, τῇ παρακλήσει, τῇ διδασκαλίᾳ. These are the three main departments of the public duties of a pastor. (*a*) ἀνάγνωσις, *reading,* is not the *private* study of Scripture (Chrys.), but the *public* reading of the O.T. in the congregation, a custom taken over from the synagogue (Luke iv. 16; Acts xv. 21; 2 Cor. iii. 14). The Apostolic letters were also read in the Christian assemblies in the Apostolic age (Col. iv. 16; 1 Thess. v. 27); and by the time of Justin Martyr's *Apology* (i. 67) portions of O.T. and N.T. Scripture alike were read aloud by the ἀναγνώστης at the Sunday Service. (*b*) The ἀνάγνωσις τοῦ νόμου was accustomed to be followed by the παράκλησις or *exhortation* (Acts xiii. 15), corresponding to a modern sermon. παράκλησις

was an elastic word, but that a reasonable limit to fix was 30 years. St Paul is called νεανίας at the time of Stephen's martyrdom (Acts vii. 58), when he must have been about 30 years old. This was probably also the limit of *adulescentia* among the Romans; it is often said that it lasted until 40, but for this there is not good evidence.

is the regular word in Philo for an 'appeal' to the individual to rise
to the higher life of philosophy. (c) διδασκαλία. This word in the
Pastorals generally means 'doctrine,' but here it is used in the sense
of *teaching*. (See note on i. 10.) It is closely connected with παράκλησις, as the *appeal* to the heart and conscience ultimately rests
on the *instruction* provided for the intellect. Both come within the
pastor's province. Cp. Rom. xii. 7 εἴτε ὁ διδάσκων ἐν τῇ διδασκαλίᾳ,
εἴτε ὁ παρακαλῶν ἐν τῇ παρακλήσει, and vi. 2 below ταῦτα δίδασκε καὶ
παρακάλει.

14. μὴ ἀμέλει τοῦ ἐν σοὶ χαρίσματος, *neglect not the gift that is in
thee.* ἀμελεῖν is not found elsewhere in St Paul, but it is a LXX. word
(cp. Heb. ii. 3); χάρισμα, on the other hand, is characteristically
Pauline, occurring 16 times in his Epistles and only once elsewhere
in N.T. (1 Pet. iv. 10). This *gift* is not a charm which is supposed to
act of itself, without the cooperation of its possessor; it may be
neglected and needs to be kindled into a flame (see 2 Tim. i. 6). To
neglect God's gifts, whether of nature or of grace, is a sin.

ὃ ἐδόθη σοι, i.e. by God; cp. 1 Cor. xii. 4 for such spiritual gifts.

διὰ προφητείας. πρ. is here without doubt the *gen. sing.*, although
some have taken it as *acc. pl.*; διά expresses the medium or vehicle
through which the gift came, as μετά in the next clause marks the
attestation of its bestowal.

The whole passage must be taken in close connexion with i. 18
κατὰ τὰς προαγούσας ἐπὶ σὲ προφητείας (see the note thereon), and with
2 Tim. i. 6 δι' ἣν αἰτίαν ἀναμιμνήσκω σε ἀναζωπυρεῖν τὸ χάρισμα τοῦ
θεοῦ, ὅ ἐστιν ἐν σοὶ διὰ τῆς ἐπιθέσεως τῶν χειρῶν μου. The allusion of
all three passages seems to be to the same event. Hort argues
(*Christian Ecclesia*, p. 184 ff.) that this was the 'laying of hands' on
Timothy by the presbyters (see Acts xiv. 23) at Lystra during the
early days of his discipleship. But more probably the event in question
was the ordination or 'consecration' of Timothy by St Paul, in the
presence and with the ratification of the Ephesian College of presbyters.
For this office Timothy had been marked out by the προφῆται whose
utterances would be regarded as giving the Divine sanction (i. 18);
the spiritual χάρισμα for his new spiritual work was bestowed on him
(a) διὰ προφητείας, which has reference either to the προφητεῖαι of i. 18
or to the words of prayer used by a προφήτης on this solemn occasion,
and (b) διὰ τῆς ἐπιθέσεως τῶν χειρῶν μου, by the imposition of St Paul's
hands (2 Tim. i. 6). This act was accompanied (μετά) by the imposition of the hands of the presbyters who were present; but the difference of preposition indicates clearly that their action had a different
significance from that of the Apostle. The custom of our own ordinal
that 'the Bishop *with* the priests present' shall lay their hands upon
the ordinands is derived from this passage. Prayer and imposition of
hands as the instruments of ordination have been already mentioned in
the *Acts*, in vi. 6 of the Appointment of the Seven, and in xiii. 1—3 of
the ordination of Barnabas and Saul. The custom of χειροθεσία, as the
outward sign of the transmission of a spiritual grace, was taken over

from Judaism: it is said e.g. of Joshua (Deut. xxxiv. 9) ἐνεπλήσθη πνεύματος συνέσεως, ἐπέθηκεν γὰρ Μωυσῆς τὰς χεῖρας αὐτοῦ ἐπ᾽ αὐτόν. Liddon points out in his note on this verse that when in Num. viii. 10 the Israelites are said to have 'laid their hands' on the Levites, the χειροθεσία merely signified their recognition of the separateness of the Levites, just as in the passage before us the χειροθεσία of the College of presbyters did no more than *attest* the authoritative χειροθεσία of the Apostle.

τοῦ πρεσβυτερίου. The word is used in Luke xxii. 66, Acts xxii. 5 of the Sanhedrin; it is here used for the first time of the confraternity of presbyters, a sense in which it frequently appears in Ignatius.

15. ταῦτα μελέτα. μελετάω only occurs once again in N.T. (Acts iv. 25) and then in a quotation from the LXX. (Ps. ii. 1). It may mean either (a) *meditate, ponder,* as in that passage, or (b) *practise,* the latter being the prevailing meaning of the word. But (a) here seems more suitable to the context, *ponder these things,* sc. the injunctions of vv. 12, 13, 14.

ἐν τούτοις ἴσθι. Cp. Horace "omnis in hoc sum"; and "totus in illis."

προκοπή, *progress,* whether in the Christian life or (more especially) in fitness for his office. The word only occurs in N.T. here and in Phil. i. 12, 25, but is found in LXX.; cp. 2 Tim. ii. 16, iii. 9, 13 where the verb προκόπτειν is used of progress in the direction of evil.

φανερὰ ᾖ πᾶσιν. Cp. Matt. v. 16.

16. ἔπεχε σεαυτῷ, *take heed to thyself.* ἐπέχειν is used in a somewhat similar way in Acts iii. 5. The warning is put impressively by Bishop Butler in a fragment found among his papers:—"Be more afraid of thyself than of the world."

καὶ τῇ διδασκαλίᾳ, *and to thy teaching*; not 'to the doctrine,' sc. of the Apostles. It was his own presentation of truth, of which he was to be heedful.

ἐπίμενε αὐτοῖς, *continue in them.* In what? If the punctuation of the text be followed αὐτοῖς must refer to σεαυτῷ καὶ τῇ διδασκαλίᾳ, a somewhat harsh construction. But perhaps we should rather connect it with what follows, in which case we may take αὐτοῖς as having reference to the ταῦτα of v. 15 and indeed to all the preceding injunctions.

τοῦτο γὰρ ποιῶν κ.τ.λ. *In doing this thou shalt save both thyself and them that hear thee.* σώζειν is to be taken in its highest sense; the faithful pastor must save himself in saving others.

τοὺς ἀκούοντάς σου. ἀκούειν τινός is not found elsewhere in St Paul's Epistles, but it is frequent in Luke. Compare Acts xxii. 7 (in a speech of Paul's) ἤκουσα φωνῆς with Acts ix. 4 (the direct narrative) ἤκουσεν φωνήν.

ADDITIONAL NOTE.

The 'Word of God' in the New Testament.

The growth in meaning of the phrase ὁ λόγος τοῦ θεοῦ is worthy of fuller investigation than it can receive here; but it may be useful to tabulate the instances (38 in all) of its occurrence in the N.T.

In the corresponding O.T. phrase 'the Word of the Lord,' ὁ λόγος τοῦ κυρίου (1 Chr. xvii. 3 &c.), the prominent idea is (*a*) the word which *came from God* (*gen. subjecti*) rather than the word which *tells of God* (*gen. objecti*); and in the N.T. also this is the primary sense, which, however, passed gradually, as the phrase became familiar, into the sense of the *whole revealed message of God to the world* (as distinguished from ῥῆμα θεοῦ, a special utterance for a special purpose, e.g. Luke iii. 2; Eph. vi. 17; Heb. vi. 5). It is thus (*b*) a synonym for *the Gospel*, preached by Christ and His Apostles, which may, again, be conceived of as (*c*) embodied in the *Person of Christ* Himself. From another point of view God's message to the world may be regarded as (*d*) recorded for man's guidance in the Scriptures of the O.T. In each case the word, whether *the Word spoken*, the *Word Incarnate*, or the *Word written*, is God's word (ὁ λόγος τοῦ θεοῦ).

(*a*) John x. 35 εἰ ἐκείνους εἶπεν θεοὺς πρὸς οὓς ὁ λόγος τοῦ θεοῦ ἐγένετο κ.τ.λ.

1 John ii. 14 καὶ ὁ λόγος [τοῦ θεοῦ] ἐν ὑμῖν μένει.

1 Pet. i. 23 ἀναγεγεννημένοι...διὰ λόγου ζῶντος θεοῦ καὶ μένοντος.

2 Pet. iii. 5 γῆ ἐξ ὕδατος καὶ δι' ὕδατος συνεστῶσα τῷ τοῦ θεοῦ λόγῳ.

The three latter passages might be differently classified, but it is convenient to place them here, as in each case it is the *source* rather than the *content* of ὁ λόγος on which emphasis is laid.

(*b*) *The Word spoken.* i. St Luke's writings. In this sense the phrase is a favourite one with Luke, who uses it four times in the Gospel and twelve times in the Acts, viz.:

Luke v. 1 [The multitude came] ἀκούειν τὸν λόγον τοῦ θεοῦ.

Luke viii. 11 ὁ σπόρος ἐστὶν ὁ λόγος τοῦ θεοῦ.

Luke viii. 21 οὗτοι εἰσιν οἱ τὸν λόγον τοῦ θεοῦ ἀκούοντες καὶ ποιοῦντες.

Luke xi. 28 μακάριοι οἱ ἀκούοντες τὸν λόγον τοῦ θεοῦ καὶ φυλάσσοντες.

Acts iv. 31 ἐλάλουν τὸν λόγον τοῦ θεοῦ μετὰ παρρησίας.

Acts vi. 2 καταλείψαντας τὸν λόγον τοῦ θεοῦ διακονεῖν τραπέζαις.

Acts vi. 7 ὁ λόγος τοῦ θεοῦ ηὔξανεν.

Acts viii. 14 δέδεκται ἡ Σαμαρία τὸν λόγον τοῦ θεοῦ.

Acts xi. 1 τὰ ἔθνη ἐδέξαντο τὸν λόγον τοῦ θεοῦ.

Acts xii. 24 ὁ δὲ λόγος τοῦ θεοῦ [*al.* κυρίου] ηὔξανεν καὶ ἐπληθύνετο.

Acts xiii. 5 κατήγγελλον τὸν λόγον τοῦ θεοῦ.

Acts xiii. 7 ἐπεζήτησεν ἀκοῦσαι τὸν λόγον τοῦ θεοῦ.

Acts xiii. 44 ἡ πόλις συνήχθη ἀκοῦσαι τὸν λόγον τοῦ θεοῦ [*al.* κυρίου].

Acts xiii. 46 ...λαληθῆναι τὸν λόγον τοῦ θεοῦ.

Acts xvii. 13 κατηγγέλη...ὁ λόγος τοῦ θεοῦ.

Acts xviii. 11 διδάσκων...τὸν λόγον τοῦ θεοῦ.

In some of these passages the phrase has almost come to be a synonym for the Gospel.

ii.   The Epistles of St Paul.

In one passage, Rom. ix. 6 οὐχ οἷον δὲ ὅτι ἐκπέπτωκεν ὁ λόγος τοῦ θεοῦ, the phrase is almost equivalent to the *declared purpose* of God, a sense approximating to (*a*); but he generally uses it in sense (*b*) as a synonym for the Gospel preached, viz. :

1 Cor. xiv. 36 ἢ ἀφ᾽ ὑμῶν ὁ λόγος τοῦ θεοῦ ἐξῆλθεν, ἢ εἰς ὑμᾶς μόνους κατήντησεν ;

2 Cor. ii. 17 οὐ γάρ ἐσμεν ὡς οἱ πολλοὶ καπηλεύοντες τὸν λόγον τοῦ θεοῦ.

2 Cor. iv. 2 μηδὲ δολοῦντες τὸν λόγον τοῦ θεοῦ.

Col. i. 25 πληρῶσαι τὸν λόγον τοῦ θεοῦ, τὸ μυστήριον τὸ ἀποκεκρυμμένον κ.τ.λ.

1 Thess. ii. 13 ἐδέξασθε οὐ λόγον ἀνθρώπων ἀλλὰ καθὼς ἀληθῶς ἐστὶν λόγον θεοῦ.

2 Tim. ii. 9 ὁ λόγος τοῦ θεοῦ οὐ δέδεται.

Tit. ii. 5 ἵνα μὴ ὁ λόγος τοῦ θεοῦ βλασφημῆται.

iii.   The Apocalypse.

Here in four instances out of five, it stands for the Gospel and is coupled with *the testimony of Jesus*, viz.:

Rev. i. 2 ὃς ἐμαρτύρησεν τὸν λόγον τοῦ θεοῦ καὶ τὴν μαρτυρίαν Ἰησοῦ Χριστοῦ.

Rev. i. 9 διὰ τὸν λόγον τοῦ θεοῦ καὶ τὴν μαρτυρίαν Ἰησοῦ.

Rev. vi. 9 διὰ τὸν λόγον τοῦ θεοῦ καὶ διὰ τὴν μαρτυρίαν ἣν εἶχον.

Rev. xx. 4 διὰ τὴν μαρτυρίαν Ἰησοῦ καὶ διὰ τὸν λόγον τοῦ θεοῦ.

iv.   The Epistle to the Hebrews.

Heb. xiii. 7 οἵτινες ἐλάλησαν ὑμῖν τὸν λόγον τοῦ θεοῦ.   This is sense (*b*). Heb. iv. 12 ζῶν γὰρ ὁ λόγος τοῦ θεοῦ καὶ ἐνεργής κ.τ.λ.   This notable statement seems to mark the transition from (*b*) to (*c*), from the Revelation of God to the Logos, who was Himself the Revealer.

(*c*)   *The Word Incarnate.*   This sense of the personal, Incarnate, Logos we have explicitly once, viz.:

Rev. xix. 13 κέκληται τὸ ὄνομα αὐτοῦ, ὁ Λόγος τοῦ θεοῦ.

This is the sense of λόγος brought out prominently in the Prologue to St John's Gospel (i. 1—3).

(*d*)   *The Word Written.*   From a consideration of the passages quoted above it appears that ὁ λόγος τοῦ θεοῦ generally stands in the N.T. for the Divine message revealed to men, indirectly by the prophets of the O.T. and the Apostles of the N.T., and directly by Christ Himself.   This message is recorded, in part, in the pages of the O.T., and it is thus plain that in a certain sense the title 'the word of God' is applicable to the revelation of the Divine counsels therein contained. The revelation recorded in the O.T. would unquestionably have been regarded by a Jew as truly ὁ λόγος τοῦ θεοῦ.   So Philo speaking of the βίβλος γενέσεως of Gen. ii. 4 adds βιβλίον δὲ εἴρηκε τὸν τοῦ θεοῦ λόγον (*Leg. all.* i. 8, cp. *Leg. all.* ii. 26).   We may be sure that no Apostle would have excluded Scripture from the agencies to which the title might be given.   And there are two or three passages in the N.T. where the title seems to be actually so applied, viz.

Matt. xv. 6 ἠκυρώσατε τὸν λόγον [*al.* νόμον] τοῦ θεοῦ διὰ τὴν παράδοσιν ὑμῶν.

Mark vii. 13 ἀκυροῦντες τὸν λόγον τοῦ θεοῦ τῇ παραδόσει ὑμῶν ᾗ παρεδώκατε.

In the second of these parallel passages (at least) there is no doubt about the true reading; and it is hard to doubt that the contrast between the canonical Scripture of the O.T. and the unauthorised comments and additions of the scribes is the point of emphasis.

The other passage coming under this head has been already commented on, viz.

1 Tim. iv. 5 ἁγιάζεται γὰρ διὰ λόγου θεοῦ καὶ ἐντεύξεως. In this verse it is difficult to explain the context on any hypothesis save that λόγος θεοῦ is here used of the Scriptures of the O.T.

The result of this investigation tends to confirm the legitimacy of the title 'the Word of God' as commonly applied to Holy Scripture. It seems to have the authority of the N.T. (Matt. xv. 6 ‖ Mark vii. 13 and 1 Tim. iv. 5). It is nevertheless remarkable that the title is but rarely so applied in early Christian literature. Clement of Rome comes near it when he introduces an O.T. quotation (as he does twice, §§ 13, 56) with the phrase φησὶν ὁ ἅγιος λόγος. But Origen is the earliest writer in whom I have succeeded in finding the full title ὁ λόγος τοῦ θεοῦ applied to Scripture. After quoting Jer. iv. 5, 6 he goes on: εἰς ἀτείχιστον πόλιν οὐ βούλεται ἡμᾶς εἰσελθεῖν ὁ λόγος τοῦ θεοῦ (Hom. v. *in Jerem.* § 16; cp. also *Hom.* xiii. *in Exod.*). The phrase is frequent by the time we get to Chrysostom, and Augustine has it also (*in Ps.* cviii. 1, cxxix. 1). But this is not the place to trace its history further. It has been thought desirable to state fully the usage of the N.T., as it is interesting in itself and important in its bearing on the interpretation of 1 Tim. iv. 5.

CHAPTER V.

4. Rec. text inserts καλὸν καὶ (from ch. ii. 3) before ἀπόδεκτον with some cursives and versions; *om.* ℵACD₂GKLP.

5. Rec. text (and Tregelles) insert τὸν before θεὸν with ℵᶜAD₂KL (cp. 1 Pet. iii. 5); *om.* ℵ*CGP, followed by Tischendorf (cp. ch. iv. 10). Lachmann and Westcott and Hort place it in square brackets. For θεὸν ℵ*D₂* have κύριον, and it is possible that, after all, ἐπὶ κύριον may be the true reading. See note *in loc.*

8. Rec. text has τῶν before οἰκείων with CD₂ᵇᶜKLP (repeated from τῶν ἰδίων); *om.* ℵD₂*G.

προνοεῖται. So ℵ*D₂*GK. The received text (which Westcott and Hort here prefer, relegating προνοεῖται to the margin) has προνοεῖ with ℵᶜACD₂ᶜLP &c. See 2 Cor. viii. 21 where there is a similar conflict of authorities, some having the middle and some the active voice of the verb.

11. **καταστρηνιάσωσιν.** So (rightly) the text. rec. with ℵCD₂KL; καταστρηνιάσουσιν is found in AGP. The indicative with ὅταν would, no doubt, be possible; but the weight of MS. evidence is against it here.

15. ἐξετράπησάν τινες is the order in AFG g; txt אCD₂KLP d f &c.

16. ἐπαρκείσθω. So אAG ; ἐπαρκείτω CD₂KLP. It is not easy to decide whether the active or the middle form is to be preferred.

Rec. text has πιστὸς ἤ before πιστὴ with D₂KL, the majority of the cursives, the Syriac versions and good Greek patristic authorities; *om.* אACGP and the Bohairic version. There are Latin authorities on both sides, and it is possible that the disputed words may have been omitted through a copyist's inadvertence; but yet the weight of evidence is against them.

18. ACP f follow the order of the LXX. οὐ φιμώσεις βοῦν ἀλοῶντα (as in 1 Cor. ix. 9); but the order in the text is supported by אD₂GKL d g.

19. Some Latin MSS. known to Jerome seem to have omitted the words ἐκτὸς...μαρτύρων; and it is possible that we have a trace of this in Cyprian *Test.* iii. 76; but the variant is only a curiosity of criticism.

21. Χριστοῦ ᾿Ιησοῦ. So אAD₂*G, the Latin and the Egyptian Vss. ; rec. text has κυρίου ᾿Ιησοῦ Χριστοῦ with D₂ᶜKLPF and the Syriac.

πρόσκλισιν. This spelling is supported by אGK and the Latin versions ; AD₂LP have πρόσκλησιν which gives no tolerable sense and might readily have arisen through itacistic interchange of ι and η. See note *in loc.*

23. Rec. text has σου after στόμαχον with D₂ᶜGKL and most versions; *om.* אAD₂*P.

25. Rec. text has τὰ καλὰ ἔργα with KL; txt follows אAD₂GP. Also rec. after πρόδηλα adds ἔστι with KL (D₂GP add εἰσι); *om.* אA. At the end of the verse rec. text has δύναται with אGKL, but the reading δύνανται is found in AD₂P 17 and some other cursives, and is adopted by recent editors. The use of a *plural* verb after a neuter plural subject (which is never found in Attic Greek) is very common in the N.T., and it is the ordinary rule in Modern Greek.

IV. THE STATUS IN THE CHURCH OF VARIOUS CLASSES OF PERSONS.
i. 1, 2. ELDER MEN AND WOMEN.

1. πρεσβύτερος here means *any elder man* (cp. John viii. 9 and πρεσβύτας, Tit. ii. 2), as is plain from the context; there is no idea of ecclesiastical office. The LXX. use both πρεσβύτερος and πρεσβύτης as renderings of זָקֵן, the former being generally employed where an 'elder' in an official sense is meant. But, like πρεσβύτης, it often means no more than 'an old man,' as here. The injunction is the necessary complement of iv. 12, and is perhaps suggested by the thought of Timothy's νεότης.

ἐπιπλήξῃς. This is ἅπ. λεγ. in the Greek Bible (ἐπίπληξις is found in 2 Macc. vii. 33 only), though common in classical writers. It is stronger than ἐπιτιμᾶν (2 Tim. iv. 2), the usual N.T. word, and signifies *to rebuke severely.* Field cites from Hierocles (Stob. *Flor.* T. LXXIX. 53) a good parallel for this injunction. κἂν εἴ τί που γένοιντο παραμαρτάνοντες...ἐπανορθωτέον μέν, ἀλλ' οὐ μετ' ἐπιπλήξεως, μὰ Δία, καθάπερ ἔθος πρὸς τοὺς ἐλάττονας ἢ ἴσους ποιεῖν, ἀλλ' ὡς μετὰ παρακλήσεως. That is, ἐπίπληξις is *rebuke* addressed to one's juniors; παράκλησις is *entreaty* addressed to one's equals.

ἀλλὰ παρακάλει ὡς πατέρα, *but exhort him as a father*; παρακαλεῖν being used (as always in the Pastorals) in the sense of grave exhortation.

νεωτέρους ὡς ἀδελφούς. We must understand παρακάλει or some such verb before νεωτέρους. Timothy is to address his counsels to the younger men *as brothers*; he was himself, comparatively speaking, 'young' (see on iv. 12 above), and the form of his exhortations must be in accordance with this. It will be observed that there is no corresponding caution given to Titus (see Tit. ii. 6), of whose age we are not told anything; the inference that he was an older man than Timothy, though somewhat precarious, is nevertheless plausible.

2. πρεσβυτέρας ὡς μητέρας κ.τ.λ. *The elder women as mothers, the younger as sisters, in all purity.* ἐν πάσῃ ἁγνείᾳ (see on iv. 12) has special reference to the νεωτέρας. Ellicott appositely quotes Jerome's prudent advice (*Epist.* lii. 5): 'omnes puellas et virgines Christi aut aequaliter ignora aut aequaliter dilige.' Cp. the corresponding passage in the Ep. to Titus (ii. 4), where the discipline of the younger women is to be delegated to the elders of their own sex; here the thought is not so much of the training and directing of the νεωτέραι as of Timothy's personal relations to them.

ii. 3—16. THE STATUS OF WIDOWS.

3—8. (a) CONCERNING THEIR MAINTENANCE.

3. χήρας τίμα κ.τ.λ. *Honour as widows those that are widows indeed.*

ἡ ὄντως χήρα is a *bona fide* widow, i.e. one who is alone in the world without husband or grown-up children to support her. This is apparent from the next verse. The force of τίμα has been disputed; but although τιμᾶν does not as a rule carry the idea of material support, it does not exclude it (cp. διπλῆς τιμῆς in *v.* 17 and St Matthew xv. 5 ff.), and it is plain that to an ὄντως χήρα due honour and respect would necessarily involve such assistance. In the earliest days of the Church the support of widows was counted a Christian duty, as the narrative of Acts vi. 1 ff. shews. Cp. Ignat. *Polyc.* 4 χῆραι μὴ ἀμελείσθωσαν.

4. This verse is parenthetical. If a widow has children or grandchildren, pious care for her needs is *their* duty.

The nominative to μανθανέτωσαν has been understood variously by commentators; e.g. the Vulgate has *discat* and Chrysostom makes χῆραι the subject, 'If any widows have offspring, their first duty is to their own households.' But this introduces an idea foreign to the context and does not afford a good sense for ἀμοιβὰς ἀποδιδόναι τοῖς προγόνοις; also εὐσεβεῖν is more appropriate of children than of parents. We therefore take τέκνα ἢ ἔκγονα as the subject of μανθα-νέτωσαν.

ἔκγονα is not found elsewhere in the N.T., nor is ἀμοιβή; but ἔκγονος occurs often in the LXX. (cp. Ecclus. xl. 15) and ἀμοιβή is a common word (though not in LXX. yet in Aq.). πρόγονοι is only found in N.T. here and at 2 Tim. i. 3, but we have it in Ecclus. viii. 5; 2 Macc. viii. 19, xi. 25, in its usual sense of *dead* ancestors. Plato, however (*Laws* XI. 931 E), applies it, as here, to *living* parents: it is perhaps used by the writer in this verse to balance ἔκγονα. The A.V. *nephews* now conveys a wrong meaning for ἔκγονα, but in 1611 the word *nephew* signified *grandchild*.

πρῶτον. Respect to parents is the *first* duty of children; if it is in their power they are bound further to *requite* them (ἀμοιβὰς ἀποδ.) for their care.

τὸν ἴδιον οἶκον εὐσεβεῖν, to *shew piety towards their own household*. The peculiar obligation of the duty is marked by the use of ἴδιον; the support of widowed parents should not be left to the charity of the Church where the children are old enough to undertake the responsibility. See on 2 Tim. i. 5.

For ἀπόδεκτος see on ii. 3.

5. We now come to the characteristics of the true widow. Bereft of her natural supporters, she has fixed her hopes on God, who is her strength, and is given to continual prayer. Liddon aptly quotes Jerome (*ad Ageruch.* exxiii. 6) "quibus Deus spes est et omne opus oratio."

μεμονωμένη is explanatory of the preceding ἡ ὄντως χήρα: μονοῦσθαι is ἅπ. λεγ. in N.T., but is a common Greek word.

ἤλπικεν ἐπὶ τὸν θεόν. Cp. 1 Pet. iii. 5 αἱ ἅγιαι γυναῖκες αἱ ἐλπίζουσαι εἰς θεόν, and 2 Cor. i. 10 εἰς ὃν ἠλπίκαμεν ὅτι καὶ ἔτι ῥύσεται. ἐπί (like εἰς) with the acc. expresses the direction *towards* which hope looks; ἐπί with the dat. (as at iv. 10) indicates the ground of hope and points to that *in* which hope rests. The reading κύριον (adopted by Weiss) may be right (see crit. note), but more probably it has replaced θεόν through a reminiscence of Ps. iv. 6 ἐλπίσατε ἐπὶ Κύριον, or some similar passage.

προσμένει, *abides in.* The πρός seems to intensify the sense; cp. τῇ προσευχῇ προσκαρτεροῦντες (Rom. xii. 12). The compound verb is only used by St Paul here and at i. 3; it occurs in Jud. iii. 25; Wisd. iii. 9.

ταῖς δεήσεσιν καὶ ταῖς προσευχαῖς. See on ii. 1.

νυκτὸς καὶ ἡμέρας. This is *always* the order in St Paul (not ἡμ. καὶ νυκτ.); cp. 1 Thess. ii. 9, iii. 10; 2 Tim. i. 3. The whole clause recalls the description of the widow Anna (Luke ii. 37) νηστείαις καὶ δεήσεσιν λατρεύουσα νύκτα καὶ ἡμέραν.

6. ἡ δὲ σπαταλῶσα κ.τ.λ., *but she* (i.e. the widow) *that liveth riotously is dead while she liveth.* σπαταλᾶν only occurs in N.T. here

and at Jas. v. 5; cp. Ezek. xvi. 49 (where it is used of one of the sins
of Sodom and her daughters) and Ecclus. xxi. 15.

The conception of spiritual death, of death in life, is frequent in
St Paul; see Rom. vii. 10, 24; Eph. iv. 18, and cp. Rev. iii. 1 where it
is said of the Church of Sardis...ὅτι ζῇς καὶ νεκρὸς εἶ.

7. καὶ ταῦτα παράγγελλε. καί carries us back to a former injunction at iv. 11; ταῦτα must refer to some counsel or warning about
widows (and not about widows and their children), for plainly those
who are to be ἀνεπίλημπτοι (on which word see iii. 2) are the χῆραι
alone. Hence the things in question (ταῦτα) would seem to be contained in vv. 5, 6 which describe respectively the marks of 'the widow
indeed' and of her who through her dissipated life has forfeited all
claim to the title, which otherwise would naturally belong to her. It
will be a duty for Timothy to reiterate these, ἵνα ἀνεπίλημπτοι ὦσιν.

8. εἰ δέ τις κ.τ.λ. A formal enunciation of the principle of which
the duty set forth in v. 4 is an illustration; τις stands for any of the
τέκνα ἢ ἔκγονα there spoken of, who are here also the subject of the
sentence.

τῶν ἰδίων καὶ μάλιστα οἰκείων. ἴδιοι are relatives; οἰκεῖοι those near
relatives who form part of the family. The latter have peculiar
claims to the regard of a Christian man.

τὴν πίστιν ἤρνηται κ.τ.λ. If any one neglect this plain duty he has
(a) practically denied the Christian faith, considered as a rule of life
(see Matt. xv. 5), and (b) is, thus, worse than an unbeliever, for even
heathen recognise duty to parents as of primary obligation. ἄπιστος
is used here, as in 1 Cor. vii. 15, of a heathen, one who has not the
faith. That this natural duty was emphasised by prae-Christian
teachers hardly needs proof; cp. Anaxim. *apud* Stob. LXXIX. 37 τί γάρ
ἐστι δικαιότερον ἢ τοὺς γενέσεως καὶ παιδείας αἰτίους ὄντας ἀντευεργετεῖν;
It is worthy of notice, however, that "the Essenes were not permitted
to give relief to their relatives without leave from their ἐπίτροποι,
though they might freely do so to others in need; see Joseph. *Bell.
Jud.* II. 8. 6" (Ellicott).

The words χείρων and ἀρνεῖσθαι, which occur in this verse, are not
found in St Paul outside the Pastorals; but they are LXX. words and
quite common elsewhere.

9, 10. (*b*) WIDOWS AS AN ORGANISED BODY IN THE CHURCH.

9. We read in the Gospels of the ministry of women (Luke viii. 3;
Matt. xxvii. 55), and also in the Acts (ix. 36). In Rom. xvi. 1
Phoebe, a διάκονος of the Church at Corinth, is mentioned. When we
come to the Pastoral Epistles, we find that χῆραι are an organised
body, of whose names a register is kept; and in the verses before us
(*vv.* 9 ff.) their qualifications are enumerated. *Let no one be enrolled
as a widow who is less than sixty years of age* &c. χήρα is to be taken
as predicate, not as subject; and καταλέγειν (ἅπ. λεγ. in N.T.) means
'to place on a list.' Now it is plain that χήρα here cannot stand
simply for the desolate and destitute widow, whose maintenance has

been the subject of the preceding verses; for the Church would not limit her charity to the needy by strict conditions like those of *vv.* 9, 10. Again these χῆραι can hardly be the same as διακόνισσαι, for the limit of age would be unreasonable in the case of *all* active workers (although it is true that the Theodosian Code (xvi. 2. 27) at a later period speaks of *sixty* as the age for a deaconess). They are here πρεσβύτιδες rather than διακόνισσαι. And thus we conclude that we have in this verse the earliest notice of the *ordo viduarum*, which is often mentioned in sub-Apostolic and early patristic literature. They had a claim to maintenance, and in return were entrusted with certain duties, such as the care of orphans, and were expected to be diligent in intercessory prayer. For instance, Polycarp (*Phil.* 4) after speaking of priests and deacons, goes on to widows..."an altar of God," because from their age and comparative leisure they were supposed to give special attention to prayer. A form of prayer for the use of 'widows' is found in the *Apostolical Constitutions* (iii. 13). A notice of them in Lucian (*de morte Peregrini* 12) in connexion with orphans suggests that they were in his time quite an established institution. The order was at first restricted to αἱ ὄντως χῆραι, but after a time virgins and even young virgins seem to have been admitted, a practice which Tertullian deprecates. Ignatius (*Smyrn.* 13) speaks of τὰς παρθένους τὰς λεγόμενας χήρας; but this may only mean that from the purity of their lives the enrolled widows might be counted virgins. In any case at this early stage of the Church's life only αἱ ὄντως χῆραι, desolate widows, were admissible into the order, and the conditions of admission are before us—first, they must be at least sixty years old, and secondly, they must be *univirae*.

ἑνὸς ἀνδρὸς γυνή. Polyandry was condemned alike by heathen and Jew, and such a reference is here out of the question. The expression plainly means a widow, who has not remarried after her husband's death, or divorce. Even in Roman society *nuptiae secundae* were looked on with disfavour, and a *univira* was highly esteemed. To have married only once was an indication of ἐγκράτεια, and so is required by the Apostle of ecclesiastical persons, women as well as men (see iii. 2 and notes), who should be 'above suspicion.' See Luke ii. 36. Tertullian's words *ad Uxor.* i. 7 explain the passage well: "Praescriptio apostoli declarat...cum viduam adlegi in ordinationem nisi univiram non concedit." Cp. also *Const. Apost.* vi. 17, and the passage from Philo *de Profugis* quoted below on Tit. ii. 5.

10. A widow to be placed on the Church's list must be ἐν ἔργοις καλοῖς μαρτυρουμένη, *well reported of in the matter of good works.* The emphasis laid on ἔργα καλά in the Pastoral Epistles has been already remarked (see on ii. 10 above): of the good works which would espe cially come within the widow's province a few are enumerated.

εἰ ἐτεκνοτρόφησεν, *if she hath brought up children,* whether her own or the children of others. χῆραι are frequently mentioned in connexion with orphans of the Church (e.g. Hermas *Mand.* 8 and Lucian *de morte Peregr.* 12); but it would be quite as unreasonable to *confine* the reference to these, as to *exclude* it, and so to forbid a barren widow a place on the list. τεκνοτροφέω occurs only here in the Greek Bible.

εἰ ἐξενοδόχησεν, *if* (sc. at any time) *she hath used hospitality to strangers.* The *word* ξενοδοχέω is not found again in N.T. or LXX.; but cp. Matt. xxv. 35 ξένος ἤμην καὶ συνηγάγετέ με. Like the 'bishop' (iii. 2, on which see note) the 'widow' will be φιλόξενος, although from her circumstances it may be on a more humble scale. This qualification, however, suggests (what is reasonable in itself) that the widow who is placed on the Church's list need not necessarily be destitute of worldly wealth or dependent for her maintenance on the Church's alms.

εἰ ἁγίων πόδας ἔνιψεν, *if she hath washed the saints' feet.* This was a not unfamiliar feature of Eastern hospitality; it was a service of humility (1 Sam. xxv. 41), as of love (Luke vii. 38), and was commended to the Apostles by the Lord Himself (John xiii. 14). But this last command does not seem to have been understood literally by those to whom it was addressed; and so in the case of the Church's widows it was the spirit of their hospitality, rather than any such detail, which would enter into consideration. Note ἁγίων; this humility of service is only due to fellow Christians, who are the most welcome guests of all.

εἰ θλιβομένοις ἐπήρκεσεν, *if she hath relieved the afflicted,* whether "in mind, body or estate." ἐπαρκέω is only found in N.T. here and at *v.* 16; but it occurs in 1 Macc. viii. 26, xi. 35 and is a common Greek word.

εἰ παντὶ ἔργῳ ἀγαθῷ ἐπηκολούθησεν, *if she hath followed every good work.* See on ii. 10 above. The A.V. and R.V. have "diligently followed"; but ἐπί seems here (as in 1 Pet. ii. 21) to mark *direction* rather than *intensity,* the pursuit of good works whether initiated by others or by oneself.

(c) 11—16. YOUNG WIDOWS.

11. νεωτέρας δὲ κ.τ.λ., *but younger widows refuse,* sc. to put on the roll of χῆραι. νεωτέρας is used generally, as in *v.* 2, and not merely of set reference to the age limit of 60: for the force of παραιτοῦ see on iv. 7. These young widows are not, of course, ineligible for relief; but they are to be refused admission to the *ordo viduarum,* and that for two reasons: (*a*) from the risk to which they are exposed of unfaithfulness to religious engagements (*vv.* 11, 12), and (*b*) because of the danger for them in the duties of the ecclesiastical χήρα (*v.* 13).

ὅταν γὰρ καταστρηνιάσωσιν τοῦ Χριστοῦ κ.τ.λ., *for when they have come to wax wanton against Christ, they desire to marry.* ὅταν with the aor. subj. (see crit. note and 1 Cor. xv. 24, 27; Tit. iii. 12 &c.) has reference to a particular, but undetermined, point of time. καταστρηνιᾶν is not found elsewhere; it may have been formed by St Paul on the analogy of κατακαυχᾶσθαί τινος (Rom. xi. 18) to direct attention to the yoke which imposes the restraint. The simple verb στρηνιᾶν 'to wax wanton' occurs in Rev. xviii. 7, 9; the metaphor is that of a young animal trying to free itself from the yoke, and becoming restive through its fulness of life.

τοῦ Χριστοῦ. Christ is the Heavenly Bridegroom, against whom the desire of remarriage (lawful in ordinary cases in the absence of religious engagements, 1 Cor. viii. 39) is an unfaithfulness; even the *wish* to marry another is to be false to the συνθήκη with Christ, which they made when they undertook the widow's office as ἑνὸς ἀνδρὸς γυναῖκες.

12. ἔχουσαι κρίμα, *having judgement*; i.e. they are self-condemned, ἔχουσαι being almost equivalent to ἑαυταῖς παρέχουσαι. Cp. *v.* 20 and Rom. xiii. 2.

ὅτι τὴν πρώτην πίστιν ἠθέτησαν, *because they have made void their first faith*, sc. with the heavenly Bridegroom. πίστις is not Christian faith, but the pledge which they undertook on being enrolled in the χηρικόν (cp. Rev. ii. 4). There is no thought, of course, of the pledge of faithfulness to the *first* husband; he is not in question. πρώτην is used, as commonly in N.T. Greek, for προτέραν (e.g. Acts i. 1).

13. ἅμα δὲ καί, introducing the second reason for the exclusion of young women from the order of 'widows.'

ἀργαὶ μανθάνουσιν κ.τ.λ. The translation is doubtful. We may construe (a) *being idle, they pick up information*, as they go about from house to house &c.; or, 'in idleness, they are always learning,' but nothing comes of it. This would be comparable to the γυναικάρια ...πάντοτε μανθάνοντα of 2 Tim. iii. 6, 7. But (i.) this is to take μανθάνειν in a somewhat forced way, and (ii.) the antithesis in the next clause is spoilt, οὐ μόνον δὲ ἀργαὶ ἀλλὰ καὶ κ.τ. λ. It is better to render with the A.V. and R.V., (b) *they learn to be idle, going about from house to house*, sc. in the discharge of their allotted ministrations. Their want of sobriety and steadiness may lead them to use their opportunities of usefulness as an excuse for idleness and gossip. This construction of μανθάνειν is not without parallel, although unusual; e.g. Field cites Chrys. ix. 259 B εἰ ἰατρὸς μέλλοις μανθάνειν.

ἀργός is not found in St Paul save here and at Tit. i. 12 (in a quotation), but it is a LXX. word.

οὐ μόνον δὲ...ἀλλὰ καί.... This is a regular Pauline construction; cf. 2 Cor. vii. 7.

φλύαροι, *garrulous, tattlers*. We have φλυαρεῖν in 3 John 10, but φλύαρος (once in LXX. at 4 Macc. v. 10) does not occur elsewhere in the N.T.

περίεργοι, *busybodies*. Cf. 2 Thess. iii. 11 μηδὲν ἐργαζομένους ἀλλὰ περιεργαζομένους. For περίεργος (which is not a LXX. word, and is not used elsewhere in St Paul) cp. Acts xix. 19.

λαλοῦσαι τὰ μὴ δέοντα, *speaking things which they ought not*. That is, they are likely to make mischief, carrying from house to house private matters which have come to their knowledge in the course of their official visits.

14. βούλομαι οὖν, *I desire therefore*: more definite than θέλω, as expressive of a special exertion of will. See on ii. 8. The οὖν refers to both the reasons assigned (*vv.* 11—13) for the unfitness of young widows for the *ordo viduarum*.

νεωτέρας γαμεῖν, *that the younger* widows *marry*. The context suggests that it is especially young *widows* that are in the thought of the writer; but no doubt the advice would apply to young women in general, as the A.V. seems to take it. γαμεῖν may be used either of first or of second marriages; cp. 1 Cor. vii. 9.

τεκνογονεῖν, οἰκοδεσποτεῖν, *bear children, rule their household.* Neither of these words is found again in the Greek Bible, but we have τεκνογονία in ii. 15 and οἰκοδεσπότης in the Gospels. The right ordering of the household is a very important duty in the view of the writer; cp. iii. 4, 12.

μηδεμίαν ἀφορμὴν διδόναι, *give no occasion*; cp. 2 Cor. v. 12.

τῷ ἀντικειμένῳ, *to the adversary*, sc. not Satan, but human adversaries (ἀντικείμενοι, of whom there are all too many, 1 Cor. xvi. 9; Phil. i. 28; cp. Tit. ii. 8) who are very ready to find fault. Cp. iii. 6.

λοιδορίας χάριν, *for reviling*; cp. Tit. ii. 5. λοιδορία does not occur again in St Paul, but it is a LXX. word; cp. 1 Pet. iii. 9. We have λοιδορεῖν 1 Cor. iv. 12, and λοίδορος 1 Cor. v. 11, vi. 10.

15. ἤδη γάρ τινες ἐξετράπησαν ὀπίσω τοῦ σατανᾶ, *for already some are turned aside after Satan.* To support his advice (βούλομαι κ.τ.λ.) St Paul adduces the weighty argument of past experience (γάρ). Some ecclesiastical widows have already proved unfaithful to their pledges to the heavenly Bridegroom and have followed the seducer, Satan. It has been argued that this indicates that the *ordo viduarum* had been in existence for a considerable time, and that thus the date of the Epistle must be postponed to a period subsequent to St Paul's labours; but (*a*) it must be remembered that the experience to which appeal is made is not necessarily confined to the Church at Ephesus, but extends over all the Christian communities known to St Paul, and (*b*) ἤδη, 'already,' seems to indicate that the order had *not* been long established, for disorders had arisen before they might naturally have been expected.

ἐξετράπησαν, i.e. swerved from the path of virtue. See note on i. 5.

ὀπίσω τοῦ σατανᾶ. Cp. Acts xx. 30 (in the speech of St Paul to the Ephesian elders) ἀποσπᾶν τοὺς μαθητὰς ὀπίσω ἑαυτῶν.

16. εἴ τις πιστὴ κ.τ.λ. This may be either (*a*) a repetition of the injunction of *vv.* 4, 8, the duty being now described as incumbent on *all* relatives, and not merely on children and grandchildren; or (*b*) a direction as to the maintenance of those younger widows who do not remarry and who are, in virtue of their age (*vv.* 11—13), ineligible for admission to the χηρικὸν τάγμα. It appears from the context that (*b*) is more probable; but in any case there is a difficulty in πιστή. There seems no reason why *female* relatives should be mentioned to the exclusion of *male*; and yet (see critical note) the evidence for the omission of πιστὸς ἤ is too weighty to be set aside.

ἐπαρκείσθω. See critical note, and for the word see on *v.* 10.

βαρείσθω. The classical form is βαρύνειν. Cp. 2 Cor. i. 8, v. 4; 1 Thess. ii. 9 &c.

iii. **17—25.** THE DIGNITY AND THE DISCIPLINE OF THE PRESBYTERATE.

17. The πρεσβύτεροι here are not the *elder men* (as in *v.* 1), but the Church officials who bear that honourable name. Their duties and their relation to the ἐπίσκοποι have already been discussed in the *Introduction*, chap. **v.**, and it is unnecessary to repeat what was there said.

οἱ καλῶς προεστῶτες κ.τ.λ. The emphasis is on καλῶς: the presbyters who preside *well* are to be *counted worthy of double honour*. There is no distinction suggested between two classes of presbyters, some who rule and some who do not rule; *rule* is the normal duty of the πρεσβύτεροι in the society where they are placed. Thus in 1 Thess. **v.** 12 they are called προϊστάμενοι and a similar injunction to the Church is given: εἰδέναι τοὺς **κοπιῶντας** ἐν ὑμῖν καὶ **προϊσταμένους** ὑμῶν ἐν κυρίῳ κ.τ.λ.

διπλῆς τιμῆς. 'Honour to whom honour is due' is St Paul's general principle (Rom. xiii. 7), and this τιμή may include material support; cp. τίμα in *v.* 3 above, and our use of *honorarium* for a fee. The connecting link between *vv.* 3—16 and *vv.* 17—25 is in this word τιμή. The maintenance of the various classes of a new society is always a matter for most anxious consideration; St Paul first deals with the case of the *widows,* and then by a natural transition proceeds to mention the provision to be made for the *presbyters.* He is thus led on to discuss their dignity and their discipline. *Double honour,* i.e. *ample* provision, must be ensured for them; διπλῆ is not to be taken as equivalent to 'double of the sum paid to widows,' or in any similar way, but without any definite numerical reference. Cp. *Apost. Const.* ii. 28.

μάλιστα οἱ κοπιῶντες κ.τ.λ. The primary function of presbyters is to bear rule in the society, but those who, in addition, *labour in the word and in teaching* are especially to be honoured at this stage of the Church's life. Teaching fell more and more to the πρεσβύτεροι as the office of the Evangelist ceased. But even in Cyprian (*Epist.* xxix.) *presbyteri doctores* are mentioned, which indicates that there were some presbyters in his day who did not belong to the class of teachers.

ἐν λόγῳ καὶ διδασκαλίᾳ, *in the word and in teaching.* λόγος is the Divine Word which the presbyters, as good pastors, are to deliver to the souls of their flock; διδασκαλία is the instruction, addressed to the reason rather than to the heart, with which their message is to be accompanied. Cp. Barnabas § 19 διὰ λόγου κοπιῶν.

18. **λέγει γὰρ ἡ γραφή.** This is the ordinary Pauline formula of citation from the O.T.; see Rom. iv. 3, xi. 2; Gal. iv. 30.

βοῦν ἀλοῶντα οὐ φιμώσεις. *Thou shalt not muzzle the ox when he treadeth out the corn,* a citation of Deut. xxv. 4, applied in a somewhat similar way by St Paul at 1 Cor. ix. 9. Not the letter of the law only, but the broad moral principle behind it is here appealed to by the Apostle.

καί, Ἄξιος ὁ ἐργάτης τοῦ μισθοῦ αὐτοῦ. This maxim occurs nowhere in the O.T., although the principle involved is often enunciated,
e.g. at Lev. xix. 13; Deut. xxiv. 14. It *does* occur verbally in Luke x.
7 (cp. Matt. x. 10), in the report of our Lord's charge to the Seventy
whom He sent forth; and it has been sometimes thought (*a*) that the
writer of this Epistle here appeals to St Luke's Gospel as ἡ γραφή.
But, even if we place the Epistle outside St Paul's lifetime, we cannot
bring it down to a date late enough to permit us to think of the author
citing the Synoptic Gospels as Scripture, in the same breath with the
O.T. (*b*) It has been suggested, again, that St Paul here quotes a
well-known saying of the Lord which would for him have all the
authority of ἡ γραφή. But true as this may be, we can hardly con-
ceive of him as introducing such a saying by the formula λέγει γὰρ ἡ
γραφή, γραφή being reserved by him for the Sacred Canon of the O.T.
And therefore (*c*) we conclude that this opening formula only applies
to the quotation from Deuteronomy, and that the words ἄξιος ὁ ἐργάτης
τοῦ μισθοῦ αὐτοῦ are added by the writer by way of explanation and
confirmation. It may well be that this was a familiar proverb,
appealed to here by St Paul as it was appealed to by the Lord in the
passage quoted from St Luke. We have, for instance, in Euripides
(*Rhes.* 191) a similar thought: πονοῦντα δ᾽ ἄξιον μισθὸν φέρεσθαι: and
again in Phocylides *Fr.* 17 μισθὸν μοχθήσαντι δίδου. Such an obvious
principle of natural justice may well have taken a proverbial form.
St Paul, in short, first quotes from Deut. xxv. 4, and then adds *And*
[*as you know*] *the labourer is worthy of his hire.*

19. κατὰ πρεσβυτέρου κατηγορίαν κ.τ.λ. *Against a presbyter receive
not an accusation except &c.* κατηγορία and παραδέχομαι are not found
in St Paul's writings outside the Pastorals, but they are common
words, although the former does not happen to occur in the LXX.
We have κατήγορος, κατηγορεῖν frequently in the Greek Bible (e.g. Rom.
ii. 15).

ἐκτὸς εἰ μή. We have this pleonastic form of negation at 1 Cor. xiv.
5, xv. 2; it is fairly common in late writers such as Plutarch[1].

ἐπὶ δύο ἢ τριῶν μαρτύρων. Words taken in substance from Deut. xix.
15; cp. Deut. xvii. 6. The general principle is appealed to by St Paul
in 2 Cor. xiii. 1, by our Lord in John viii. 17, and also in Heb. x. 28.
The force of ἐπὶ is hardly doubtful. The analogy of 2 Cor. xiii. 1
confirms the translation of the R.V. *at the mouth of,* which is the
meaning of the precept in its original place in Deut. xix. 15 ἐπὶ
στόματος δύο μαρτύρων κ.τ.λ. And we adopt this rendering, although
στόματος is omitted in the verse before us, and although ἐπὶ with the
gen. (as in 1 Cor. vi. 1) gives a good sense, *in the presence of, coram.*
The precept is here interesting, as marking the beginnings of presbyteral discipline. Timothy is directed, in order to avoid any slightest
injustice, to follow the precedents of the old law in his supervision of
the Church at Ephesus. Two witnesses at least must give evidence
if charges against a presbyter are to be entertained.

---

[1] See Deissmann, *Bibelstudien,* p. 115, who points out that ἐκτὸς εἰ μή is
found in an inscription of Mopsuestia in Cilicia.

20. τοὺς ἁμαρτάνοντας. Those found sinning, sc. the presbyters, with whose discipline the whole section is taken up. So also ἐνώπιον πάντων does not mean that the whole congregation is to be assembled when a presbyter receives rebuke, but that the sentence shall be delivered in the presence of all his *co-presbyters.* The case is quite different from such a case as that contemplated in Matt. xviii. 15; for Timothy will act, not as a private individual, but as the representative of the Church and the official guardian of its discipline.

ἵνα καὶ οἱ λοιποὶ φόβον ἔχωσιν, *that the rest also* (sc. the other presbyters) *may have fear*; cp. Deut. xiii. 11. The sentence is delivered *in public* for the sake of those who hear it.

21. διαμαρτύρομαι ἐνώπιον τοῦ θεοῦ. We have this formula again in 2 Tim. ii. 14, iv. 1; the only other place in St Paul where the compound διαμαρτύρεσθαι occurs is 1 Thess. iv. 6. διά has an intensive force: *I solemnly charge thee.*

τοῦ θεοῦ καὶ Χρ. Ἰησοῦ. It is plain that here, as in 2 Tim. iv. 1, Granville Sharp's canon as to the non-repetition of the definite article does not hold; for it cannot be doubted that Θεός the Eternal Father is invoked as distinct from Χρ. Ἰησοῦς, the Judge of all judges (John v. 27; Acts xvii. 31, and 2 Cor. v. 10). But, as has been observed, such quasi-official words as Χριστός are often used without the article, like proper names.

τῶν ἐκλεκτῶν ἀγγέλων. The commentators cite the apposite parallel from Josephus (*B. J.* II. 16. 4): μαρτύρομαι δ᾽ ἐγὼ μὲν ὑμῶν τὰ ἅγια, καὶ τοὺς ἱεροὺς ἀγγέλους τοῦ θεοῦ. The force of ἐκλεκτῶν has been variously explained. It is quite unnecessary to bring in the idea of (*a*) *guardian* angels of particular churches, as e.g. at Rev. ii. 1. Nor (*b*) can we suppose that ἐκλεκτῶν is introduced to distinguish the angels who are in the thought of the writer from the *fallen* spirits of evil (2 Pet. ii. 4; Jude 6); ἄγγελος without any qualifying epithet is consistently used throughout the N.T. for the *holy* angels, and the addition of ἐκλεκτῶν for the purpose of such a distinction would be in this context otiose and gratuitous. It seems better (*c*) to regard ἐκλεκτῶν as a natural and fitting epithet of angels who are the *chosen* ministers of God, and who watch with tender interest over the affairs of men (1 Cor. iv. 9; 1 Tim. iii. 16).

ἵνα ταῦτα φυλάξῃς, *that thou observe these things*, sc. the precepts about the trial of presbyters in *vv.* 19, 20.

χωρὶς προκρίματος, μηδὲν ποιῶν κ.τ.λ. πρόκριμα and πρόσκλισις are both ἅπ. λεγ. in the Greek Bible; the former is strictly a *vox media*, but is here used to express preconceived judgement against the accused or *prejudice*, as πρόσκλισις indicates undue *partiality* towards either side. The solemnity of the adjuration with which the verse opens marks the importance which the writer attaches to the jurisdiction that Timothy is to exercise being fulfilled with an open mind and without respect of persons.

22. The thought of πρόσκλισις or partiality in his dealings with the Ephesian presbyters on Timothy's part suggests the warning χεῖρας

ταχέως μηδενὶ ἐπιτίθει. (a) Some modern commentators and a few of the
Latin fathers understand this of the *reconciling of penitent presbyters*
who have fallen into sin. Such reconciliation was doubtless attended
with χειροθεσία in later ages (see e.g. Cyprian *Ep.* 74, Eus. *H. E.* VII.
2), but there is no evidence that it was an accustomed usage in
Apostolic times, nor is χειροθεσία or any similar phrase used in such
a context elsewhere in the N.T. It is better, then, (b) with the early
Greek commentators (e.g. Chrysostom) to interpret the injunction as
prohibiting hasty ordinations. ἐπίθεσις τῶν χειρῶν is used of the act
of ordination in ch. iv. 14; 2 Tim. i. 6, as well as at Acts vi. 6, xiii.
3; in Acts viii. 17, 18, 19 of imparting a special χάρισμα, and in Heb.
vi. 2 quite vaguely (though probably of Confirmation). It will be
remembered that the Church has sanctioned the interpretation of
the words which refers them to ordination, by embodying them in the
Ember Collect. The precept is thus in accordance with the rule
about deacons (iii. 10) οὗτοι δὲ δοκιμαζέσθωσαν πρῶτον. ταχέως is
expressive of undue haste, which is much to be deprecated.

μηδὲ κοινώνει ἁμαρτίαις ἀλλοτρίαις, *neither be partaker of other
men's sins,* sc. by ordaining unworthy persons. κοινωνεῖν with the
dative of the thing shared in is common in the N.T., e.g. Rom. xv.
27; ἁμαρτίαις recalls and is suggested by ἁμαρτάνοντας of *v.* 20. The
sequence of thought is easy : Do not lightly entertain accusations
against a presbyter (*v.* 19); Do not spare rebuke if he fall into sinful
habits (*v.* 20); Be not partial (*v.* 21); Do not admit him to the presbyterate without due enquiry (*v.* 22ᵃ); If you do, you accept responsibility for his sins, which, in a manner, you have made your own
(*v.* 22ᵇ). And this last grave thought leads on to the personal warning
σεαυτὸν ἁγνὸν τήρει, *keep thyself pure,* sc. pure in the first instance
as not being κοινωνός of another man's sins, and in a more general
reference as well. See for ἁγνός note on iv. 14 : with σεαυτὸν τήρει cp.
2 Cor. xi. 9.

23.   ἁγνεία does not refer only to bodily purity and discipline; it is
rather concerned with purity of intention and singleness of life.
This may however be misapprehended, and to avoid any mistaken
inference from σεαυτὸν ἁγνὸν τήρει in the direction of undue asceticism
the Apostle parenthetically adds *Be no longer a water-drinker, but use
a little wine &c.*

ὑδροποτεῖν (only here in the N.T., but a common word) is not equivalent to ὕδωρ πίνειν; it means to drink water *habitually,* to be a 'total
abstainer' from wine (cp. Dan. i. 12 LXX.). This it appears Timothy
had been (for such is the force of μηκέτι; cp. Rom. vi. 6; 2 Cor. v. 15),
possibly under Essene influences (see Philo *de Vit. cont.* 4), but more
probably by way of protest against the sin of drunkenness, which the
injunctions in iii. 3, 8 suggest was a crying evil at Ephesus, if the
ἐπίσκοποι themselves needed to be warned against it. We have other
warnings of a like nature at Rom. xiii. 13 ; Gal. v. 21; Tit. ii. 3;
1 Pet. iv. 3. But what is commended to Timothy is *temperance* in
the use of wine, not *total abstinence* from it: οἴνῳ ὀλίγῳ χρῶ, in contrast with οἴνῳ πολλῷ deprecated in iii. 8.

διὰ τὸν στόμαχον. στόμαχος does not occur again in the Greek Bible, but is, of course, a common word. Wetstein aptly cites Libanius *Epist.* 1578, πέπτωκε καὶ ἡμῖν ὁ στόμαχος ταῖς συνεχέσιν ὑδροποσίαις; cp. Pliny *Hist. Nat.* xxiii. 22.

καὶ τὰς πυκνάς σου ἀσθενείας, *and thine oft infirmities.* St Paul uses ἀσθενεία of his own bodily infirmity at Gal. iv. 13 ; πυκνός does not occur again in his letters, but cp. Luke v. 33; Acts xxiv. 26; 2 Macc. viii. 8. Timothy is here described as a man of weak health, for whom the ascetic life would be dangerous and unwise.

It is obvious to remark how improbable it is that such a precept as this, and introduced thus parenthetically, should occur in a forged letter. Like 2 Tim. iv. 13 it is a little touch of humanity which is a powerful argument for the genuineness of the Epistle in which it is found.

The duty of careful enquiry into the character of ordinands. V. 23 was parenthetical, and the general subject is now resumed: character is difficult to judge, therefore do not (*a*) hastily accept (*v.* 24) or (*b*) hastily refuse (*v.* 25).

24. To avoid a falsely favourable estimate, remember that while some men's sins are notoriously evident (πρόδηλοι) and *lead the way* to judgement (i.e. they go before like heralds, as it were), the sins of other men are hidden and *follow* the perpetrators (i.e. their sin will find men out at last, but it does not always proclaim the impending judgement beforehand). The practical inference is that one in Timothy's position dare not rest satisfied with formal negative evidence as to the character of those upon whom he *lays hands*; 'nothing to their discredit' is not a sufficient guarantee, unless careful and detailed enquiry has been made.

πρόδηλος only occurs again in N.T. at Heb. vii. 14, and in LXX. at Judith viii. 29 ; 2 Macc. iii. 17, xiv. 39.

25. ὡσαύτως κ.τ.λ. *So also* (and this is the second maxim to be remembered in the diagnosis of character) while *some* kinds of *good works are notoriously evident,* there are also good works which, though not conspicuous, cannot remain hidden, if full investigation is made. This maxim will prohibit hasty rejection or condemnation of any man, on the plea that his good works are not apparent at the first glance, for καλὰ ἔργα are not always done in public, though they cannot be concealed from a careful scrutiny.

τὰ ἄλλως ἔχοντα, *those that are otherwise,* sc. those that are not πρόδηλα, as explained above.

CHAPTER VI.

3. Tischendorf is almost alone among critical editors in his adoption of προσέχεται the reading of אᵃ* (formerly conjectured by Bentley) for the better attested προσέρχεται.

4. ἔρις. So אAKP, Egyptian and Peshito Syriac Vss; but D₂GL the Latins and the Harclean Syriac support ἔρεις. D₂* also has φθόνοι for φθόνος, which suggests that the singular has in both cases been corrected into the plural in conformity with βλασφημίαι &c. which follow.

5. παραδιατριβαὶ of the received text is only found in some cursives ; διαπαρατριβαὶ is read by אAD₂GLP &c. Compounds of δια-παρα are rare, which may account for the variant as a correction of the primitive reading. See note *in loc.*

εὐσέβειαν. After this the rec. text adds ἀφίστασο ἀπὸ τῶν τοιούτων with D₂ᶜKLP and Syriac Vss ; *om.* אAD₂*G, Latin and Egyptian Vss. See note *in loc.*

7. The reading in the text is that of א*AG 17 r, but (see note) is not without intrinsic difficulty. Before ὅτι אᶜD₂ᵇᶜKLP and most cursives insert δῆλον, while D₂* m insert ἀληθές. Both additions have patristic support, but there can be little doubt that they are corrections of the primitive text. Hort suggested that ὅτι is only an accidental repetition of the last two letters of κόσμον, ΟΝ being read as ΟΤΙ.

8. **διατροφάς.** So אAL f; but διατροφήν is supported by D₂GKP d g m and is given a place in Westcott and Hort's margin.

9. **παγίδα.** D₂G and the Old Latin Vss add τοῦ διαβόλου from iii. 7. Cp. 2 Tim. ii. 26.

11. Rec. text has τοῦ before θεοῦ with אᶜD₂GKLP, and this is adopted by Tregelles and given a place in Westcott and Hort's margin. The article is omitted by א*A 17 and by Tischendorf and Lachmann. See on verse 13.

πραϋπαθίαν. So א*AGP; πραότητα, the more usual word, is read by D₂KLאᶜ.

12. After ἤν the rec. text inserts καί, but it is omitted by all the uncials.

13. Tischendorf follows א*G and some Latin authorities in omitting σοι; ins. אᶜAD₂KLP &c.
Before θεοῦ AD₂GKLP insert τοῦ, but Tischendorf following א rejects the article.
Rec. text has ζωοποιοῦντος with אKL; but ζωογονοῦντος is the reading of AD₂GP 17.

Χριστοῦ Ἰησοῦ. So AD₂KLP d and Harclean Syriac; Ἰησοῦ Χρ. is read in אG f g, the Peshito Syriac and Egyptian versions. See critical note on i. 16.

17. Tischendorf follows א in reading ὑψηλὰ φρονεῖν, which is also placed in Westcott and Hort's margin (cp. Rom. xi. 20). ὑψηλοφρονεῖν is read by AD₂EGKLP.

ἐπὶ θεῷ. (i.) For ἐπὶ (found in אAD₂*GP) the rec. text has ἐν supported by D₂ᶜKL. (ii.) The rec. text, with AD₂ᶜEKLP, inserts τῷ before θεῷ; the article is omitted by אD₂*G. (iii.) The rec. text with D₂EKL adds τῷ ζῶντι after θεῷ; this is omitted by אAGP &c., and was apparently introduced from ch. iv. 10.

πάντα πλουσίως. This is the uncial order; the rec. text has πλουσίως πάντα following cursive authority.

19. ὄντως. So אAD₂*E*GH; but rec. text has αἰωνίου with D₂ᶜKLP. See verse 12.

20. παραθήκην. So all the uncials: the rec. text has παρακαταθήκην with many cursives.

κενοφωνίας. So אAD₂EKLP &c.; G has καινοφωνίας, by itacism, which the Latin Versions support, *vocum novitates.*

21. μεθ' ὑμῶν. So אAGP; μετὰ σοῦ is the reading of rec. text, following D₂EKL &c. Cp. 2 Tim. iv. 22 and Tit. iii. 15.

אᶜD₂ᵇᶜEKLP &c. add ἀμήν; this is absent from א*AD₂*G &c.

The subscription printed in the rec. text, viz. Πρὸς Τιμόθεον πρώτη ἐγράφη ἀπὸ Λαοδικείας, ἥτις ἐστὶ μητρόπολις Φρυγίας τῆς Πακατιανῆς, is found in KL and elsewhere; א 17 have simply πρὸς Τιμόθεον ᾱ; D₂E add ἐπληρώθη; A 120 &c. have πρὸς τιμοθ. ᾱ ἐγράφη ἀπὸ Λαοδικείας· P has πρ. τιμόθ. ᾱ ἐγράφη ἀπὸ νικοπόλεως, and there are other variants. See *Introd.* p. xxxii.

---

iv. 1, 2. DUTY OF SLAVES TO THEIR MASTERS, WHETHER HEATHEN OR CHRISTIAN.

1. ὅσοι κ.τ.λ. The construction is thoroughly Pauline; cp. Rom. ii. 12; Gal. iii. 10, &c.

ὑπὸ ζυγὸν δοῦλοι, *under the yoke as slaves,* as the order of the words shews.

τοὺς ἰδίους δεσπότας, *their several masters.* But ἴδιος may be used without special emphasis, as in iii. 4, v. 4 and the parallel passage Tit. ii. 9; cp. Eph. v. 22 αἱ γυναῖκες τοῖς ἰδίοις ἀνδράσιν κ.τ.λ. The LXX. sometimes (especially in the later books) render the possessive pronoun by ἴδιος, and in late Greek the word is used for ἑαυτοῦ, ἑαυτῶν.

St Paul has δεσπότης in the Pastoral Epistles only (2 Tim. ii. 21; Tit. ii. 9); elsewhere in similar contexts he has κύριος (Eph. vi. 5; Col. iii. 22, iv. 1). δεσπότης (common in the LXX.; cp. 1 Pet. ii. 18) is perhaps the harsher word, but Philo (*Quis rer. div. haer.* 6) says that it is synonymous with κύριος, although he suggests a distinction between them, based on a false etymology.

πάσης τιμῆς ἀξίους. The τιμή of *widows* (v. 3) and of *presbyters* (v. 17) has been enforced; we now come to the τιμή due to heathen masters from Christian slaves. Christianity taught that in Christ there was "neither bond nor free," and gradually, through this teaching, the evils of slavery became mitigated and removed; but the Apostles and their successors were ever careful (see the various passages cited above and Ep. to Philemon *passim*) to preach to slaves the duty of obedience to their masters, in the existing condition of society. Unlike the Therapeutae and the Essenes who are said to have encouraged insubordination, as a practical corollary from the doctrine of the brotherhood of man, the Christian Church avoided any teaching which might seem to countenance a *bellum servile,* with its frightful consequences. Slaves were to commend their religion by the performance of their duty in their humble station. See on Tit. ii. 5.

ἵνα μὴ τὸ ὄνομα κ.τ.λ., *that the Name of God and the doctrine be not blasphemed.* For slaves to have refused obedience would have brought immediate discredit on the Christian Faith, as subversive of the foundations of heathen society. St Paul quotes in Rom. ii. 24 the words of Isa. lii. 5 τὸ ὄνομα τοῦ θεοῦ δι᾽ ὑμᾶς βλασφημεῖται ἐν τοῖς ἔθνεσιν (cp. 2 Sam. xii. 14; Ezek. xxxvi. 23), which are also in his mind here. Cp. [2 Clem.] § 13 for a like use of the phrase.

2. The exceptional case of *Christian* masters is next dealt with.

οἱ δὲ πιστοὺς κ.τ.λ., *let those who have believers as their masters not despise them, because they are brethren.* Equal membership in the Kingdom of Christ is not to be a pretext for the neglect of social duty to superiors.

ἀλλὰ μᾶλλον δουλ., *but let them serve them the rather.* μᾶλλον is emphatic (cp. Rom. xiv. 13; Eph. v. 4); heathen masters have their claim to service, but Christian masters have an additional claim in that they are πιστοὶ καὶ ἀγαπητοί, linked with their slaves by common faith and love.

πιστοί εἰσιν καὶ ἀγ. κ.τ.λ. πιστοὶ καὶ ἀγαπητοί must be the predicate of the sentence, which determines that οἱ τῆς εὐεργεσίας ἀντιλαμβανόμενοι, the subject, must be a description of the *masters* who have already been called πιστούς at the beginning of the verse. ἀντιλαμβάνεσθαι only occurs twice elsewhere in the N.T., viz. Luke i. 54 (in a quotation from the LXX. where it is frequent) and Acts xx. 35 (in a speech of St Paul); in both these instances it is equivalent to *succurrere,* a meaning which is not applicable here. In late Greek, however, it sometimes means 'to be sensible of,' *percipere,* of anything which acts upon the senses (cp. Porphyr. *de Abstin.* i. 46 μήτε ἐσθίων πλειόνων ἡδονῶν ἀντιλήψεται); and so may be rendered here (with all the versions) 'to partake of.' εὐεργεσία is (*a*) not the Benefit of Redemption; that is not here in question. And as (*b*) the *masters* are the subject of the sentence, it can have no reference to the benefits which they may *confer* upon their slaves. It remains therefore that we take it (*c*) as the benefit which the masters *receive* from the heartiness of their slaves' obedience. Alford cites an apposite passage from Seneca (*de benef.* III. 21), in which the question *an beneficium dare servus domino possit* is answered in the affirmative, and where the definition is given *quidquid est quod servilis officii formulam excedit, quod non ex imperio sed ex voluntate praestatur, beneficium est.* We therefore translate the words before us, *because they that are partakers* [sc. the masters] *of the benefit* [the improved quality of the service] *are faithful and beloved.* The A.V. is here incorrect.

ταῦτα δίδασκε καὶ παρακάλει. See on iv. 11. The only question is as to the reference of ταῦτα. It *may* refer to what *follows,* but the usage of it in similar contexts throughout the Epistle (iii. 14, iv. 6, 11, 15) makes it more probable that it refers to what precedes, viz. the directions just given about the demeanour of slaves.

3—5. Renewed warnings against false teachers.

3. εἴ τις ἑτεροδιδασκαλεῖ κ.τ.λ., *if any man teach other* [sc. in-consistent] *doctrine* &c.   For ἑτεροδιδασκαλεῖν see on i. 3, the only other place where the word is found; it is here used in contrast to διδάσκε of the preceding verse, and probably the feature of the false teaching which is, for the moment, in the writer's mind, is its *world-liness*. He has just declared that slaves are not to make their Christianity a pretext for seeking social advancement; and he proceeds to give a warning against the heretical teachers who, by their example, would encourage the idea that *godliness is a way of gain*.

μὴ προσέρχεται, *assenteth not* (see crit. note).   In the N.T. as a rule εἰ with the indicative (supposed reality) takes οὐ, where classical Greek would have μή (cp. iii. 5, v. 8); here however the more correct literary form εἰ...μή is found. (See Blass, *Grammar of N. T. Greek*, § 75, 3.) προσέρχεσθαι is not used elsewhere by St Paul, and in all the other passages where it occurs in the N.T., it is used of the *approach* of the body, and not of the *assent* of the mind; the latter sense is, however, quite legitimate and not uncommon in later Greek. Cp. Ecclus. i. 28; Acts x. 28 and the term προσήλυτος, as marking the transition from the original to the derivative meaning.

ὑγιαίνουσιν λόγοις, *wholesome words* ; see on i. 10.

τοῖς τοῦ κυρίου ἡμῶν 'Ι. Χ., *those of our Lord Jesus Christ.* This is a *gen. originis*.   There is no reference to actual words of the Lord, but to the fact that He (and not man) is the *source* of the sound doctrine, of which His words furnish the *standard*.

καὶ τῇ κατ' εὐσέβειαν διδασκαλίᾳ. The *test* of the διδασκαλία is its conformity with that εὐσέβεια (see on ii. 2), without which it is im-possible to appreciate the moral distinctions so vital in all sound theology; cp. Tit. i. 1.

In *v.* 3 the ἑτεροδιδασκαλία is described as discrepant both from the standards and appropriate test of the true doctrine; its practical results are now brought forward, a picture of the false teacher himself being first drawn.

4. τετύφωται, *he is beclouded* ; see on iii. 6.   The Vulgate rendering is *superbus est*, and the older Latin versions have *inflatus est*, but this is to change the metaphor.

μηδὲν ἐπιστάμενος, *knowing nothing*; compare the similar words at i. 7. ἐπίστασθαι is not found again in the Pauline Epp.; but cp. Acts xx. 18, xxii. 19, xxiv. 10, xxvi. 26.

ἀλλὰ νοσῶν περὶ κ.τ.λ., *but doting about* &c. νοσεῖν is ἅπ. λεγ. in the N.T., but it is a common LXX. word; when followed by περί with the acc., it suggests the idea of morbid movement round a central point. For the metaphor of sickness and health as applied to the spiritual state see note on i. 10.   The heretical teachers are regarded more as 'ill-conditioned,' than as teaching falsehood.

ζητήσεις καὶ λογομαχίας, *questionings and disputes of words* ; com-pare i. 4—6. λογομαχία does not occur elsewhere in the Greek Bible (we have λογομαχεῖν in 2 Tim. ii. 14); it is a late Greek word, and seems to mean here not 'a dispute *about* words,' but 'a dispute in which words are the weapons,' and so is almost equivalent to *controversy*. The fruits of such controversy are now enumerated.

φθόνος, ἔρις, *envy, strife.* These are also associated by St Paul at Rom. i. 29; Gal. v. 21 (see crit. note).

βλασφημίαι, *evil speakings*, sc. not against God, but (as at Eph. iv. 31; Col. iii. 8) against one another.

ὑπόνοιαι πονηραί. We have ὑπόνοια πονηρά also in Ecclus. iii. 24; ὑπόνοια does not occur, save in these two places, in the Greek Bible; it is a *surmise*, or evil *suspicion*.

5. διαπαρατριβαί, *incessant wranglings*; the first of two prepositions in a composite word governs the meaning, and thus διά is emphatic, signifying the persistency and obstinacy of the disputes: παρατριβή is *friction.* διαπαρατ. is ἅπ. λεγ. in the Greek Bible. The usual Latin rendering is *conflictationes* or *conflictiones*, but r preserves the curious form *perconfricationes*, 'perpetual frictions.'

διεφθαρμένων ἀνθρ. τὸν νοῦν, *of men depraved in mind*; νοῦς is the moral reason, furnishing the intellectual element of conscience. When this is corrupted, the eye of the soul is darkened and cannot catch the Divine light. Cp. 2 Tim. iii. 8 ἄνθρωποι κατεφθαρμένοι τὸν νοῦν, and Eph. iv. 17.

καὶ ἀπεστερημένων τῆς ἀληθείας, *and bereft of* (not only 'destitute of') *the truth.* The expression is even stronger than that used of the false teachers in Tit. i. 14: ἀνθρώπων ἀποστρεφομένων τὴν ἀλήθειαν: cp. 1 Tim. i. 19. St Paul has ἀποστερεῖσθαι again in 1 Cor. vi. 7, 8.

νομιζόντων πορισμὸν εἶναι τὴν εὐσέβειαν, *supposing that godliness is a way of gain.* The A.V. "supposing that gain is godliness" is undoubtedly wrong, as is shewn by the order of the words and the position of the article. For a like construction with νομίζω cp. 1 Cor. vii. 26. πορισμός, 'a gainful trade,' is found in the N.T. only in this passage; and in LXX. at Wisd. xiii. 19, xiv. 2. This characteristic of the false teachers is alluded to again, Tit. i. 11; Seneca, in like manner, speaks of some "qui philosophiam velut aliquod artificium venale didicerunt" (*Ep.* 108).

The words at the end of this verse in the Received Text, ἀφίστασο ἀπὸ τῶν τοιούτων, are insufficiently supported (see crit. note); they were probably added by a copyist who did not understand the construction of the clause, having failed to observe that the apodosis begins at τετύφωται (v. 4).

6—10. THE VANITY AND THE PERILS OF WEALTH.

6. ἔστιν δὲ κ.τ.λ. *But*, &c. emphatic: εὐσέβεια is not a gainful trade, but for all that there is a sense in which *godliness with contentment is great gain*, not only for the next world, but also for this. Compare iv. 8, where εὐσέβεια has been declared to be πρὸς πάντα ὠφέλιμος, ἐπαγγελίαν ἔχουσα ζωῆς τῆς νῦν καὶ τῆς μελλούσης. That riches are not essential to true well-being was a commonplace of pre-Christian philosophy, which laid great emphasis on αὐτάρκεια or the 'self-sufficiency' of the wise man. Thus Cicero (*Paradox.* 6) has the aphorism: "contentum vero suis rebus esse maximae sunt certissimae divitiae." In the LXX. the same thought is expressed in the Sapiential books: e.g. σύνταξον δέ μοι τὰ δέοντα καὶ τὰ αὐτάρκη (Prov. xxx. 8), and ζωὴ αὐτάρκους ἐργάτου γλυκανθήσεται (Ecclus. xl. 18). Comp. Prov. xv. 16 and *Ps. Solomon.* v. 18, 20. St Paul's words go deeper, inasmuch as they lay stress on εὐσέβεια as a chief condition of happiness, and recognise the proper place of αὐτάρκεια, as *contentment* not *self-sufficiency*. αὐτάρκεια occurs only once again in N.T., in 2 Cor. ix. 8, and there is equivalent to *sufficiency*; but the true parallel to the present passage is Phil. iv. 11 ἔμαθον ἐν οἷς εἰμὶ **αὐτάρκης** εἶναι.

7.   οὐδὲν γὰρ κ.τ.λ. *For we brought nothing into the world, neither can we carry anything out.* The construction (see crit. note) is difficult. If we read (as manuscript authority requires) ὅτι οὐδὲ ἐξενεγκεῖν, the meaning of ὅτι has been variously explained. (*a*) It has been taken as equivalent to *quia*, 'because.' The general sense then would be that the *reason why* we brought nothing into the world is because we can carry nothing out of it. But this seems an unnatural and far-fetched sentiment, and we cannot accept such a rendering, if any other will fit the words. (*b*) The copyists who inserted δῆλον seem to have thought that there was an *ellipse* of δῆλον or some word like it. It is, however, hardly admissible to assume such an ellipse, unless it can be illustrated by a clear example. 1 John iii. 20 has been adduced, but (see Westcott *in loc.*) can be better explained otherwise. Field adduces an example from Chrysostom, but it is not conclusive. (*c*) It remains then to take ὅτι as *resumptive* : *we brought nothing into the world;* I say, *that neither can we carry anything out*; a somewhat irregular construction, but not impossible. The words (familiar to us from their place in the Burial Service) may be illustrated from writers of widely different schools. Comp. e.g. Job i. 21; Eccl. v. 15; Hor. *Odes* II. 14. 21; Propert. IV. 4. 13; Seneca (*Ep.* 102) "excutit natura redeuntem sicut intrantem. Non licet plus auferre quam intuleris"; and (a close parallel in words as well as in thought) Philo *de Sacrif.* 6 τὸν μηδὲν εἰς κόσμον, ἀλλὰ μηδὲ σαυτὸν εἰσενηνοχότα; γυμνὸς μὲν γάρ, θαυμάσιε, ἦλθες, γυμνὸς πάλιν ἀπίῃς.

8.   ἔχοντες δὲ κ.τ.λ. *But if we have food and raiment we shall be therewith content.*

διατροφή is only found in the Greek Bible elsewhere at 1 Macc. vi. 49, where it is in the singular. σκέπασμα does not occur again in LXX. or N.T.; etymologically it might include *shelter* as well as *clothing* (as Philo explains, *de Praem.* 17, σκέπης δὲ διττὸν εἶδος), but this would be to bring in an inappropriate idea here. *Food and raiment* are the two indispensable conditions of life, although the true ζωή is 'more' than even these (Matt. vi. 25). Josephus describes the Essenes (*B. J.* II. 8. 5) as ζωσαμένοι σκεπάσμασι λινοῖς; and also uses the word σκεπάσματα unmistakably in the sense of clothing, in *Ant.* xv. 9. 2.

ἀρκεσθησόμεθα is not imperatival, but future, with a slightly authoritative sense. Cp. Heb. xiii. 5 ἀρκούμενοι τοῖς παροῦσιν, and Clem. Rom. (§ ii.) τοῖς ἐφοδίοις τοῦ θεοῦ ἀρκούμενοι.

9. οἱ δὲ βουλόμενοι πλουτεῖν κ.τ.λ. *But*, on the other hand, *they who desire* (who are minded, a more definite word than θέλοντες) *to be rich* &c. It is not the mere *possession* of wealth, but the *desire* to be rich, the *grasping* after riches as the supposed end of life, whose ill results are now described.

ἐμπίπτουσιν εἰς πειρασμὸν κ.τ.λ., *fall into a temptation and a snare.* Again we have a close parallel in the words of Seneca: "Dum divitias consequi volumus in mala multa incidimus" (*Ep.* 87).

καὶ ἐπιθυμίας πολλὰς κ.τ.λ., *and many foolish and hurtful lusts.* βλαβερός is only found again in the Greek Bible at Prov. x. 26.

αἵτινες, *which indeed,* cp. iii. 15.

βυθίζουσιν τοὺς ἀνθρώπους, *drown men,* sc. mankind in general, as the article τοὺς indicates. βυθίζειν only occurs again in Greek Bible at 2 Macc. xii. 4 and Luke v. 7.

εἰς ὄλεθρον καὶ ἀπώλειαν, *in destruction and perdition.* The two words are not to be very sharply distinguished. ἀπώλεια=*utter loss* is the regular word for the soul's perdition, e.g. Phil. i. 28, iii. 19; but ὄλεθρος is also used in this sense, e.g. 1 Thess. v. 3; 2 Thess. i. 9, though also for "the destruction of the flesh" only (1 Cor. v. 5).

10. ῥίζα γὰρ πάντων τῶν κακῶν ἐστιν ἡ φιλαργυρία. *For the love of money is the root of all evils,* an emphatic, rhetorical, statement. To lay stress, as the Revised Version has done, on the absence of the article before ῥίζα, seems unnecessary, and the resultant translation "a root of all kinds of evil," though no doubt giving us a more scientifically exact maxim than the A.V. presents, is far less forcible. Quite as strong statements had been made about this vice before St Paul's day. Comp. Apollodorus *Frag.*

ἀλλὰ σχεδόν τι τὸ κεφάλαιον τῶν κακῶν
εἴρηκας· ἐν φιλαργυρίᾳ γὰρ πάντ' ἔνι,

or Diog. Laert. vi. 50 τὴν φιλαργυρίαν εἶπε μητρόπολιν πάντων τῶν κακῶν. Or again, Ammian. Marcell. xxxi. 4 *aviditas materia omnium malorum.*

τῶν κακῶν refers, of course, to *moral* not *physical* evils; to *sins* whether of *omission* or *commission.*

φιλαργυρία, defined by the Stoics as ὑπόληψις τοῦ τὸ ἀργύριον καλὸν εἶναι (Diog. vii. 111), is a *passive* vice, as contrasted with the *active* grasping of πλεονεξία, which indeed has a much wider range. The latter might co-exist with prodigal expenditure; not so φιλαργυρία, which is the miser's sin, the *auri sacra fames* of Virgil (*Aen.* iii. 56). Thus the older Latin rendering *avaritia* gives the sense better than the Vulgate *cupiditas.* The word only occurs again in the Greek Bible in 4 Macc. i. 26, ii. 15; but we have the adjective φιλάργυρος in 2 Tim. iii. 2, and in Luke xvi. 14, where it is applied to the Pharisees.

ἧς τινὲς ὀρεγόμενοι, *which some reaching after....* The image is, perhaps, not strictly correct, for we can hardly *reach after* an ὄρεξις like φιλαργυρία, but it is quite in St Paul's manner; cp. ἐλπὶς βλεπομένη (Rom. viii. 24). For ὀρέγεσθαι see on iii. 1.

ἀπεπλανήθησαν ἀπὸ τῆς πίστεως κ.τ.λ., *have been led astray* (cp. i. 19, iv. 1) *from the faith* &c., i.e. as from a straight path. Struggling out of this they get entrapped among the briars and thorns of the world, and pierce themselves. ἀποπλανᾶν only occurs in the N.T. again in Mark xiii. 22; it is, however, a LXX. word.

καὶ ἑαυτοὺς περιέπειραν ὀδύναις πολλαῖς, *and have pierced themselves through with many sorrows.* περιπείρειν is ἅπ. λεγ. in the Greek Bible; it means to *impale* or *pierce through*, the force of περί arising from the idea of the thing pierced *surrounding* that which pierces. Cp. Philo *in Flacc.* i. ἀνηκέστοις περιέπειρε κακοῖς. ὀδύναι (in N.T. only here and in Rom. ix. 2) stands for the pangs of conscience, the shafts of remorse.

11—16. EPILOGUE. i. PERSONAL ENCOURAGEMENT TO TIMOTHY.

11. σὺ δέ. Emphatic, and in contrast with τινές of *v.* 10.

ὦ ἄνθρωπε θεοῦ. This is not a technical title of office, nor on the other hand is the phrase used quite so generally as in 2 Tim. iii. 17; but it emphatically recalls to the mind of Timothy his position as one entrusted with a Divine message. It is the regular O.T. expression for a prophet, אִישׁ אֱלֹהִים; see 1 Sam. ix. 6; 1 Kings xii. 22, xiii. 1 &c. The N.T. prophets, of whom Timothy perhaps was one (among his other qualifications for his high position), might naturally be thus described.

ταῦτα φεῦγε, *flee these things,* sc. φιλαργυρία and its attendant evils.

δίωκε δὲ δικαιοσύνην. See, for this phrase, Prov. xv. 9; Rom. ix. 30 and 2 Tim. ii. 22, in which last place, as here, it follows φεῦγε, and is followed by πίστιν, ἀγάπην.

The qualities now enumerated fall into three pairs, (i.) δικαιοσύνη and εὐσέβεια, *righteousness* (in the largest sense) and *piety*, linked together again at Tit. ii. 12; these are the ground of all performance of duty to man and to God: (ii.) πίστις and ἀγάπη, *faith* and *love*, the supreme Christian graces: (iii.) ὑπομονή and πραϋπαθία, *patience* and *meekness*, especially necessary in dealing with opponents. ὑπομονή, which in the canonical books of the LXX. stands for *hopeful waiting* or *expectation*, is used often in Ecclus. and always in 4 Macc. (e.g. xvii. 12) for *patient endurance*; it is a favourite word with the Apostle in this sense. St Paul is described by Clement (§ 5) as himself ὑπομονῆς γενόμενος μέγιστος ὑπογραμμός. See further on Tit. ii. 2.

The form πραϋπαθία does not occur elsewhere in the Greek Bible; but we find it in Philo *De Abr.* § 37.

12. ἀγωνίζου τὸν καλὸν ἀγῶνα κ.τ.λ. *Fight the good fight of faith, lay hold* (as a prize) *on eternal life.* The metaphor of life as a gymnastic contest was one which naturally suggested itself to those

who had witnessed the Olympian or Isthmian games which played,
even as late as the Apostolic age, so important a part in Greek
national life. Philo uses the illustration again and again. He notes,
e.g. (*Leg. All.* iii. 71), the *training* and (*Leg. All.* i. 31) the *diet* of the
athletes; he speaks (*de Migr. Abr.* 24) of the *race* and of the *crown*,
which he says is the Vision of God (*de mut. nom.* 12); and in one
striking passage he uses language comparable to that here employed
by St Paul: κάλλιστον ἀγῶνα τοῦτον διάθλησον καὶ σπούδασον στεφανω-
θῆναι...καλὸν καὶ εὐκλεᾶ στέφανον ὃν οὐδεμία πανήγυρις ἀνθρώπων ἐχώρησε
(*Leg. All.* ii. 26). The metaphor is also found in the Ep. to the
Hebrews (xii. 1) and in the Book of Wisdom (iv. 2), and is a favourite
one with St Paul; cp. 1 Cor. ix. 24; Phil. iii. 12, 14 and 2 Tim.
iv. 7 where he says of himself τὸν καλὸν ἀγῶνα ἠγώνισμαι. It is
worth noting that the phrase is found almost verbatim in Euripides:

καίτοι καλόν γ᾽ ἂν τόνδ᾽ ἀγῶν᾽ ἠγωνίσω (*Alcest.* 648).

This contest is τῆς πίστεως, *of faith* (not 'of *the* faith'); it is the personal warfare with evil to which every Christian is called; the καλὴ
στρατεία in i. 18 is, on the other hand, a contest with human
opponents.

ἐπιλαβοῦ. St Paul uses ἐπιλαμβάνεσθαι only here and at *v.* 19; it is
a common LXX. word, and means *to lay hold of.* The aorist imperative marks the *single* act of reaching out for the crown, while the
present ἀγωνίζου marks the *continued* struggle.

τῆς αἰωνίου ζωῆς. This is the 'crown' or βραβεῖον for the victor in
the contest; cp. Jas. i. 12; Rev. ii. 10.

εἰς ἣν ἐκλήθης, *whereunto thou wast called.* Some have found here
an allusion to the voice of the herald calling the combatant into the
arena; but *eternal life* is not the arena of the contest, but the reward.
The metaphor is not to be pressed so closely.

καὶ ὡμολόγησας τὴν καλὴν ὁμολογίαν κ.τ.λ., *and didst confess the
good confession in the presence of many witnesses.* This does not refer
(*a*) to any special moment of *persecution* in Timothy's life (for which
we have no evidence), or (*b*) to his *ordination*; cp. iv. 14; but (*c*), as the
close connexion with the preceding εἰς ἣν ἐκλήθης and the main
thought in the next verse shew, to his *baptism*, as the moment at
which he made his ὁμολογία or confession of faith in the Christian
Revelation.

13. παραγγέλλω σοι ἐνώπιον τοῦ θεοῦ τοῦ ζωογονοῦντος τὰ πάντα.
St Paul charges Timothy in the face of a more awful Witness than
those who stood by and heard his baptismal confession at the first.
ζωογονεῖν (see crit. note) is 'to preserve alive'; the thought of the
prize of eternal life leads up to the thought of Him who is the Source
of all life, *who preserveth all things alive.* The word is perhaps suggested by the thought of Timothy's baptism, when he was 'born
again' of water and the Spirit. He who gives spiritual life in baptism also 'preserves it alive.' ζωογονεῖν does not occur again in
St Paul, but it is found in LXX. (Exod. i. 17, 18; Judges viii. 19;
1 Sam. xxvii. 9) and was known to St Luke (xvii. 33 and Acts vii. 19).

In medical writers it is common in the sense of 'to endue with life' or 'to produce alive[1].'

καὶ Χρ. Ἰη. τοῦ μαρτυρήσαντος ἐπὶ Ποντίου Πειλάτου τὴν καλ. ὁμολ., *and of Christ Jesus who under Pontius Pilate attested the good confession*, sc. the Revelation which He came to bring. Jesus is ὁ μάρτυς ὁ πιστός (Rev. i. 5) and He came that He might *bear witness to the truth* (John xviii. 37); He was thus, strictly, the First Martyr. ἐπί followed by a gen. may mean either (*a*) *in the presence of* (as in Mark xiii. 9), or (*b*) *in the time of* (as in Mark ii. 26); and thus ἐπὶ Ποντίου may be taken as equivalent (*a*) to *coram Pontio*, the publicity of the witness delivered before the imperial authority being the emphatic matter; or (*b*) to *sub Pontio*, as it has been taken in the Apostles' Creed, *in the days of Pontius Pilate*, the reference being merely to the time when the witness in question was given. Taking into account the change of preposition from ἐνώπιον to ἐπί, and the fact that μαρτυρήσαντος is the emphatic word, in contrast with ὡμολόγησας of the preceding verse, we decide for (*b*). Timothy at his baptism had *confessed the good confession* of the Faith of Jesus Christ, which the Lord Himself *attested* with power in the days of Pontius Pilate, not only by His words before His judge, but by His Death and Resurrection.

It seems not improbable that the words of this verse rehearse the phrases of some primitive form of baptismal creed, in which mention was made of God as the Sustainer of Life, of the Passion of Jesus Christ under Pontius Pilate, and of His Second Coming in judgement; cp. 2 Tim. ii. 8 and iv. 1.

14. τηρῆσαί σε τὴν ἐντολὴν κ.τ.λ., *to keep the commandment &c.*, sc. not (*a*) the special commands of *vv.* 11, 12 nor (*b*) vaguely, the Gospel considered as a rule of life, but (*c*) the *baptismal charge*, to which allusion was made in *v.* 12. The words are clearly taken thus in [2 Clem.] § 8: τηρήσατε τὴν σάρκα ἀγνὴν καὶ τὴν σφραγῖδα (sc. of baptism) ἄσπιλον, ἵνα τὴν αἰώνιον ζωὴν ἀπολάβωμεν. And so they are understood by Cyril of Jerusalem, who in quoting *vv.* 13, 14 (*Cat.* v. 13) substitutes τὴν παραδεδομένην πίστιν for ἐντολήν.

ἄσπιλον, *without spot*. We have ἄσπιλον ἑαυτὸν τηρεῖν in Jas. i. 27, and the word occurs 1 Pet. i. 19; 2 Pet. iii. 14, but not elsewhere in the Greek Bible. For ἀνεπίλημπτον see on iii. 2. It is a question whether these two words go with σε or with ἐντολήν; but although the former is a *possible* construction and is favoured by the fact that the words are applied to *persons* elsewhere in the N.T., yet it is more natural to take them with ἐντολή, as they are taken (see above) by Cyril and 2 Clement, in company with the ancient versions. We have ἀνεπίλημπτος applied to τέχνη in Philo (*de Opif.* 22) and to προαίρεσις in Polybius (*Hist.* XIV. 2. 14), so that it is plainly not restricted to persons.

μέχρι τῆς ἐπιφανείας κ.τ.λ., *until the Manifestation &c.*, sc. the Second Advent, which St Paul always kept in the foreground of his thoughts and hopes. There is nothing in *this* passage which suggests

---

[1] See Hobart, *Medical Language of St Luke*, p. 155.

that he expected it soon; indeed καιροῖς ἰδίοις of the next verse shews that he recognised that its time is only known to God.

ἐπιφάνεια is frequently used in the LXX. (esp. 2 Macc.) of manifestations of the Divine glory; it is not found in the N.T. outside the Pastorals save at 2 Thess. ii. 8. The expressions used by St Paul as descriptive of the Second Advent are worth collecting: (i.) ἡ ἡμέρα τοῦ Κυρίου, at 1 Thess. v. 2; 1 Cor. i. 8, v. 5; cp. Phil. i. 10; 2 Tim. i. 12. (ii.) ἡ ἀποκάλυψις τοῦ κυρίου Ἰη., at 2 Thess. i. 7; 1 Cor. i. 7. (iii.) ἡ παρουσία at 1 Thess. ii. 19, iii. 13, iv. 15, v. 23; 2 Thess. ii. 1, 9. (iv.) ἡ ἐπιφάνεια τῆς παρουσίας αὐτοῦ at 2 Thess. ii. 8. (v.) ἡ ἐπιφάνεια αὐτοῦ at 1 Tim. vi. 14; 2 Tim. iv. 1, 8 (it is applied to the Lord's First Coming in 2 Tim. i. 10) and (vi.) ἡ ἐπιφάνεια τῆς δόξης τοῦ μεγάλου θεοῦ καὶ σωτῆρος ἡμῶν Χριστοῦ Ἰησοῦ (Tit. ii. 13). The variety of these shews significantly that the argument, which has been sometimes urged against the genuineness of the Pastorals, resting on the usage in them of ἐπιφάνεια instead of παρουσία, the usual word for the Second Advent in the Thessalonian Epistles, is destitute of any solid ground. In [2 Clem.] 12 and 17 we have the similar phrase ἡ ἡμέρα τῆς ἐπιφανείας τοῦ θεοῦ.

15. ἣν καιροῖς ἰδίοις δείξει, *which He will display in His own seasons*; see on ii. 6, and Acts i. 7, καιροὺς οὓς ὁ πατὴρ ἔθετο ἐν τῇ ἰδίᾳ ἐξουσίᾳ.

The epithets which follow are descriptive of the Eternal Father, and it is not improbable that they and the doxology of *v.* 16 are taken from some liturgical (perhaps even Jewish) formula which had already become stereotyped by use.

μακάριος. See on i. 11.

καὶ μόνος δυνάστης. We have μόνῳ θεῷ in the doxology in i. 17, which should be compared all through with this verse. It does not seem necessary to suppose any special controversial reference to the aeons of Gnostic theology, or to heathen polytheism. The Unity and Sovereignty of God were first principles of the Hebrew religion, and they would fitly be mentioned in an early Christian doxology. Cp. Philo *de sacrificiis Abelis et Caini* 30, περὶ θεοῦ τοῦ ἀγεννήτου καὶ ἀφθάρτου καὶ ἀτρέπτου καὶ ἁγίου καὶ **μόνου μακαρίου.** δυνάστης is not used elsewhere by St Paul; it is frequently applied to *men* in the LXX. and in Luke i. 52; Acts viii. 27, and to *God*, as here, in Ecclus. xlvi. 5, 16 and 2 Macc. xii. 15, iii. 24 (ὁ...δυνάστης ἐπιφανείαν μεγάλην ἐποίησεν). We have the phrase μόνος ἐστὶ δυνάστης in *Orac. Sibyll.* iii. 718.

ὁ βασιλεὺς τῶν βασιλευόντων κ.τ.λ. We have κύριος τῶν κυρίων καὶ βασιλεὺς τῶν βασιλέων in Dan. iv. 34 LXX. (cp. Rev. xvii. 14, xix. 16); and the same phrase (reading βασιλευόντων) in the *Book of Enoch* (ix. 4). *King of kings* was a title commonly assumed by Eastern monarchs; the early Christian writers apply it to God alone. Jehovah is named κύριος τῶν κυρίων in Deut. x. 17; Ps. cxxxvi. 3.

16. ὁ μόνος ἔχων ἀθανασίαν, a fuller statement than the ἀφθάρτῳ of i. 17, inasmuch as ἀθανασία (seemingly not distinguished from ἀφθαρσία in St Paul's phraseology; see 1 Cor. xv. 53, 54) is here declared to be the essential property of God alone. Cp. Wisd. xv. 3, εἰδέναι σου τὸ κράτος ῥίζα ἀθανασίας.

φῶς οἰκῶν, *dwelling in light.* God's dwelling is light (cp. Ps. civ. 2 ἀναβαλλόμενος φῶς ὡς ἱμάτιον) even as He Himself is Light (1 John i. 5), and His messengers are 'angels of light' (2 Cor. xi. 14).

ἀπρόσιτον. This light is *unapproachable.* The word ἀπρόσιτος does not occur elsewhere in the Greek Bible, but it is found in Philo (*de vita Mosis* iii. 2) who uses it of the Mount to which Moses could not approach for the glory of Jehovah (Exod. xxxiii. 17—23). It is this latter passage from Exodus which is behind St Paul's language here, esp.: οὐ γὰρ μὴ ἴδῃ ἄνθρωπος τὸ πρόσωπόν μου καὶ ζήσεται (Exod. xxxiii. 20). Josephus also (*Ant.* III. 5. 1) applies ἀπρόσιτος to God.

ὃν εἶδεν οὐδεὶς ἀνθρώπων οὐδὲ ἰδεῖν δύναται, an expansion of the epithet ἀόρατος in i. 17; cp. Deut. iv. 12; John i. 18; 1 John iv. 12. *We walk by faith not by sight* (2 Cor. v. 7), though the Vision of God is promised to *the pure in heart* (Matt. v. 6; cp. Heb. xii. 14).

ᾧ τιμὴ καὶ κράτος αἰώνιον. Cp. 1 Pet. iv. 11, v. 11; it is just possible that κράτος has been here suggested by the epithet δυνάστης in the preceding verse. But it is, in any case, common in ascriptions. The interjection, as it were, of a doxology in the middle of an argument or discussion is quite in St Paul's manner; see e.g. Rom. i. 25, xi. 36, and i. 17 above.

17—19. ii. Charge to the rich Christians at Ephesus.

17. That some, at least, of the Ephesian Christians were well-to-do is evident from the implication that there were among them the owners of slaves (*v.* 2 above); and that Ephesus in the days of St Paul was a wealthy city we know from many sources.

τοῖς πλουσίοις ἐν τῷ νῦν αἰῶνι, *those who are rich in the present world,* described thus fully to distinguish them from those who lay up treasure εἰς τὸ μέλλον (*v.* 19), though, of course, the two classes overlap. The usual phrase in St Paul (Rom. xii. 2 ; 1 Cor. ii. 6; Eph. i. 21 &c.) and in the Synoptic Gospels (Matt. xii. 32; Luke xvi. 8) for 'the present world' is ὁ αἰὼν οὗτος (see on 1 Tim. i. 17); but in the Pastorals (see 2 Tim. iv. 10 ; Tit. ii. 12) it is ὁ νῦν αἰών. St Paul elsewhere has the similar expression ὁ νῦν καιρός (Rom. iii. 26, viii. 18 ; 2 Cor. viii. 13).

μὴ ὑψηλοφρονεῖν, *not to be high-minded,* i.e. because they are rich; the pride of purse is not only vulgar, it is sinful. Compare Jer. ix. 23 μὴ καυχάσθω ὁ πλούσιος ἐν τῷ πλούτῳ αὐτοῦ and Rom. xii. 16. See crit. note.

μηδὲ ἠλπικέναι ἐπὶ πλούτου ἀδηλότητι, *nor have their hope set on the uncertainty of riches.* The ἀδηλότης of wealth, the familiar fact that it so often takes to itself wings and flies away (Prov. xxiii. 5), is indeed the very reason why we should *not* set our hopes on it. The phrase is thus more forcible, if less precise, than ἐπὶ τῷ πλούτῳ τῷ ἀδήλῳ. Compare Ps. lxii. 10, "If riches increase, set not your heart thereon."

ἀδηλότης does not occur elsewhere in the Greek Bible, but St Paul has ἀδήλως, ἄδηλος in 1 Cor. ix. 26, xiv. 8.

ἀλλ' ἐπὶ θεῷ. For ἐλπίζειν followed by ἐπί with the dative, see on iv. 10 above. The reading is not quite certain here; see crit. note.

τῷ παρέχοντι ἡμῖν πάντα πλουσίως εἰς ἀπόλαυσιν. The true object of hope is the unchangeable God who is the Giver of all good things, *who giveth us all things richly to enjoy.* Riches are a good, if rightly used, and they are the gift of God: cp. iv. 3 where it is said that meats were created εἰς μετάλημψιν. The similar phrase εἰς ἀπόλαυσιν must here be given its full force; riches (as all other gifts of God) are not given to be *possessed* merely, but to be *enjoyed,* and (as is immediately explained in the next verse) to be used for good purposes.

ἀπόλαυσις is a strong word, almost connoting *sensual* enjoyment; it only occurs again in the Greek Bible at Heb. xi. 25. In [2 Clem.] § 10 ἡ ἐνθάδε ἀπόλαυσις is contrasted with ἡ μέλλουσα ἐπαγγελία.

18. ἀγαθοεργεῖν. We have ἀγαθουργεῖν, the contracted form, at Acts xiv. 17 (in St Paul's speech at Lystra); elsewhere in the Greek Bible the word is not found.

πλουτεῖν ἐν ἔργοις καλοῖς, *to be rich in good works,* a play on the meaning of πλουτεῖν. "Men must not compute their riches so much from what they *have,* as from what they *give*" (Bp Beveridge). See the note on ii. 10 above, on ἔργα καλά in the Pastoral Epistles).

εὐμεταδότους εἶναι, κοινωνικοῖς, *ready to impart and to communicate.* Neither εὐμετάδοτος nor κοινωνικός occurs elsewhere in the Greek Bible, although cognate forms of the latter word are common. κοινωνικός seems to express a wider idea than εὐμετάδοτος, which is concerned only with the giving or sharing of worldly goods; there may, however, be a κοινωνία of sympathy which sometimes the rich have peculiar opportunities of shewing. He who is κοινωνικός in the fullest sense will be quick to recognise all the claims of human, and especially of Christian, fellowship. As is often the case, the larger word is placed second, by way of explanation; a kind heart as well as a generous hand is demanded of the rich. This κοινωνία is again directly connected with the doing of good works in Heb. xiii. 16, τῆς δὲ εὐποιίας καὶ κοινωνίας μὴ ἐπιλανθάνεσθε.

19. ἀποθησαυρίζοντας ἑαυτοῖς θεμέλιον καλὸν εἰς τὸ μέλλον, *laying up as treasure for themselves* [that which shall prove] *a good foundation against the time to come.* The thought is quite easy to understand, though expressed with somewhat inexact brevity. The idea of 'treasure in heaven' had already been expounded by our Lord, e.g. Matt. vi. 20; Luke xviii. 22; and the Parable of the Unjust Steward, in particular, enforced the right use of money in view of heavenly rewards (Luke xvi. 9). Cp. Matt. xxv. 34 ff.

ἀποθησαυρίζειν occurs again in the Greek Bible in Ecclus. iii. 4 only.

θεμέλιον καλόν stands in obvious contrast to the ἀδηλότης of riches spoken of in *v.* 17.

ἵνα ἐπιλάβωνται τῆς ὄντως ζωῆς, *that they may lay hold on the life
which is life indeed.* The charge to Timothy himself in *v.* 12 was
ἐπιλαβοῦ τῆς αἰωνίου ζωῆς: here, with a slight but significant change of
expression (see crit. note), a like prospect is held out to those who use
riches aright. *A man's life* (ζωή) *consisteth not in the abundance of
the things which he possesseth* (Luke xii. 15), and the parable of the
Rich Fool shews that the man ὁ θησαυρίζων αὐτῷ καὶ μὴ εἰς θεὸν πλουτῶν
(Luke xii. 21) shall miss here and hereafter τῆς ὄντως ζωῆς, *the life
indeed.* This is the life ἐν Χριστῷ Ἰησοῦ (2 Tim. i. 1).

20, 21. iii. CONCLUDING CHARGE TO TIMOTHY, summarising the main
thought of the Epistle; cp. 1 Cor. xvi. 21.

20. ὦ Τιμόθεε. A solemn and emphatic personal address.

τὴν παραθήκην φύλαξον, *guard the deposit,* sc. the Christian Creed
which has been committed to you in trust, to be transmitted unim-
paired to those who shall come after you. You are to guard the
depositum fidei with jealous care, "quod accepisti non quod ex-
cogitasti" (Vinc. Lir. *Common.* § 22). Cp. i. 18, v. 21; 2 Tim. i. 14,
and (for the main thought) Jude 3; Rev. iii. 15.
παραθήκη is only found in the N.T. again at 2 Tim. i. 12, 14; we
have it in Lev. vi. 2, 4. The rec. reading παρακαταθήκη (see crit. note)
does not differ substantially in meaning. Cp. Philo (*Quis rer. div.
haer.* § 21) who in interpreting λάβε μοι of Gen. xv. 9 goes on: καὶ ἂν
λάβῃς λάβε μὴ σεαυτῷ, δάνειον δὲ ἢ παρακαταθήκην νομίσας τὸ δοθὲν
τῷ παρακαταθεμένῳ καὶ συμβαλόντι ἀπόδος. See on 2 Tim. i. 12.

ἐκτρεπόμενος, *turning away from*; for the word see on i. 6. Cp.
2 Tim. iii. 5.

τὰς βεβήλους κενοφωνίας καὶ ἀντιθέσεις τῆς ψευδωνύμου γνώσεως,
*the profane babblings and oppositions of the knowledge which is falsely
so called.* Observe that βεβήλους (for which see note on i. 9) qualifies
both κενοφωνίας and ἀντιθέσεις, as is indicated by the absence of the
article before the latter word.
κενοφωνία, *empty talk,* only occurs in the Greek Bible here and in
the parallel passage 2 Tim. ii. 16, τὰς δὲ βεβήλους κενοφωνίας περιΐστασο;
it is a forcible word for the ματαιολογία already mentioned in i. 6, or
for the irrelevant ζητήσεις καὶ λογομαχίαι of vi. 4. Cp. iv. 7, τοὺς δὲ
βεβήλους καὶ γραώδεις μύθους παραιτοῦ. In the ἀντιθέσεις τῆς ψευδωνύμου
γνώσεως some have found the Marcionite oppositions between the Old
and New Testaments; but this (see *Introd.* chap. IV., *On the heresies
contemplated in the Pastoral Epistles*) is to read into the text the ideas
of a later age. The phrase probably alludes (to use Dr Hort's words[1])
to "the endless contrasts of decisions, founded on endless distinctions,
which played so large a part in the casuistry of the Scribes as interpreters of the Law." These dialectic subtleties proceed from that
esoteric γνῶσις or technical lore in which the Teachers of the Law
revelled; a γνῶσις only to be described as ψευδώνυμος, for it has not

---

[1] *Judaistic Christianity,* p. 140.

the faith and obedience which are the necessary conditions of gaining that true γνῶσις which is itself *eternal life* (John vii. 17, xvii. 3).

The words ἀντίθεσις and ψευδώνυμος do not occur elsewhere in the Greek Bible, but are common in secular Greek literature.

21. ἥν τινες ἐπαγγελλόμενοι, *which some* (as usual, the false teachers are vaguely hinted at, without specification of individuals) *professing.* For ἐπαγγέλλεσθαι see on ii. 10.

περὶ τὴν πίστιν ἠστόχησαν, *missed their aim in the matter of the faith.* See i. 19; 2 Tim. ii. 18 for a similar use of περί, and for ἀστοχέω on i. 6, ὧν τινὲς ἀστοχήσαντες ἐξετράπησαν εἰς ματαιολογίαν. The aorist ἠστόχησαν points to a definite failure on the part of some; not, as the perfect would, to a continued ἀστοχία apparent at the time of writing. See the note on i. 19.

BENEDICTION.

ἡ χάρις μεθ᾽ ὑμῶν. See the critical note.

The ordinary conclusion of a private letter of the period was ἔρρωσο or ἔρρωσθε, as χαίρειν was the introductory greeting (see note on i. 1). The Epistles of James, 1 John, 2 John have no formal ending, 2 Peter and Jude end in a doxology, and 1 Peter and 3 John with the salutation of *peace* (εἰρήνη). St Paul's usage is quite peculiar; and he calls it the σημεῖον ἐν πάσῃ ἐπιστολῇ (2 Thess. iii. 17). All his letters end with the salutation *The Grace*, ἡ χάρις. In the earlier letters this is put in the form *The grace of the Lord [Jesus Christ] be with you.* When we come to *Ephesians* we find that the word *grace* is used absolutely, and that the words 'of the Lord Jesus,' or the like, are no longer added. And in *Colossians*, 1 *Timothy* and 2 *Timothy* we have simply 'grace (or, rather, the grace) be with you,' and in *Titus* 'the grace be with you all.'

This usage had many imitators afterwards, as e.g. the Ep. to the Hebrews which ends ἡ χάρις μετὰ πάντων ὑμῶν, and the Epistle of Clement of Rome which has the longer form ἡ χάρις τοῦ κυρίου ἡμῶν Ἰησοῦ Χριστοῦ μεθ᾽ ὑμῶν κ.τ.λ. But Ignatius and Polycarp do not follow it; all their letters end with the customary ἔρρωσθε, adding words such as ἐν θεῷ πατρί, ἐν Χριστῷ Ἰησοῦ and the like, which fill it with a Christian meaning.

ANALYSIS OF THE SECOND EPISTLE TO TIMOTHY.

Introductory.   Salutation (i. 1, 2).
                         Thanksgiving for Timothy's faith (i. 3—5).

Charge I.   Be zealous; be courageous; stir up your ordination grace (i. 6—14).
                         The loneliness of St Paul and the faithfulness of Onesiphorus (i. 15—18).
                         Repetition of Charge I. Be strong in Christ's strength (ii. 1—10).
                             (*a*)   The example of the soldier (ii. 3, 4).
                             (*b*)   The example of the athlete (ii. 5).
                             (*c*)   The example of the husbandman (ii. 6).
                         Fragment of a hymn on the glories of martyrdom (ii. 11—13).

Charge II.   Shun vain speculations (ii. 14—16) like those of Hymenaeus and Philetus (ii. 17—22).
                         Follow peace (ii. 22).
                         Take no part in idle controversy (ii. 23—26).
                             The corruptions of the future (iii. 1—9).
                             Timothy is commended for his loyalty and encouraged to endure (iii. 10—14).
                             The uses of Holy Scripture (iii. 15—17).

Charge III.   Be diligent in the duties of your office (iv. 1—5).
                         The end of Paul's course (iv. 6—8).

Invitation.   Come to Rome; I am lonely (iv. 9—12).
                         Instructions (iv. 13).
                         Warning (iv. 14, 15).
                         Paul's loneliness and faith (iv. 16—18).

Epilogue.   Salutations (iv. 19—21).
                         Benediction (iv. 22).

CHAPTER I.

1. Χριστοῦ Ἰησοῦ. Rec. text has Ἰησοῦ Χριστοῦ with AL; but an overwhelming weight of authority, including all the other uncials, supports Χρ. Ἰησοῦ. See crit. notes on 1 Tim. i. 1 and Tit. i. 1.

2. Before Χριστοῦ Ἰησοῦ ℵ* and some cursives insert κυρίου, reading κυρίου Χρ. Ἰησ. τοῦ κυρίου ἡμῶν.

3. θεῷ. D₂*E* and some other authorities add μου, plainly from a reminiscence of Rom. i. 8.

5. λαβών. So ℵ*ACG; the rec. text is λαμβάνων with ℵᶜD₂EKL and the Latin versions.

7. δειλίας. So all the principal manuscripts; some cursives have δουλείας from a reminiscence of Rom. viii. 15. See note *in loc.*

10. Χριστοῦ Ἰησοῦ. So ℵ*AD₂*E* d e and the Sahidic version; while all other MSS. and versions have Ἰη. Χρ., followed by the rec. text. It is possible that the order Χρ. Ἰη. is a corruption suggested by the Χριστῷ Ἰησοῦ of *v.* 9; but it seems better on the whole to adopt this reading, as supported by the earlier authorities.

11. διδάσκαλος ἐθνῶν. ἐθνῶν is omitted by ℵ*A 17, and it is regarded by some critical editors as introduced here from 1 Tim. ii. 7, where it is certainly genuine; it is consequently omitted both by Tischendorf and by WH. But the external evidence for its retention is very strong, including as it does not only all MSS. save those cited, but the witness of the Egyptian, Syriac and Old Latin versions.

13. λόγων ὧν παρ' ἐμοῦ ἤκουσας. Dr Hort (*Notes on Select Readings*, p. 135) held that we must translate "As a pattern of sound words, hold what thou hast heard" (see note *in loc.*) and that thus the attraction in case of ὧν to λόγων offered a very unusual construction. He therefore suggested that ὧν is a primitive corruption of ὅν, and WH accordingly obelise the passage. But for this conjecture there is no manuscript authority.

14. παραθήκην. The Attic παρακαταθήκην is adopted by the rec. text but on poor authority; παραθήκην, the Hellenistic form, is certainly right.

15. Φύγελος. So all uncials except A which has Φύγελλος, the spelling of the rec. text.

16. ἐπαισχύνθη. So ℵᶜACD₂LP; ℵ*K have ἐπῃσχύνθη of the rec. text, a natural grammatical correction of the true reading.

17. σπουδαίως. So ℵCD₂*GP and the old Latin; the rec. text has σπουδαιότερον with D₂ᶜEKL, A reading σπουδαιοτέρως (possibly from a reminiscence of Phil. ii. 28).

18. For κυρίου D₂*E* d e have θεῷ, an attempt to introduce into the text the current interpretation of κυρίου as referring here to God the Father.

1, 2. SALUTATION.

1. For the form of the salutation see the note on 1 Tim. i. 1. διὰ θελήματος θεοῦ is St Paul's usual formula (cp. 1 and 2 Cor. i. 1; Eph. i. 1; Col. i. 1); he never forgets that he is a σκεῦος ἐκλογῆς.

κατ᾽ ἐπαγγελίαν ζωῆς, *according to the promise of life* &c., expressing the aim and purpose of his apostleship; cp. Tit. i. 1. For the expression ἐπαγγελία ζωῆς see on 1 Tim. iv. 8. The life of which godliness has the promise is a life ἐν Χριστῷ Ἰησοῦ; the gift of the Incarnation to man is a life no longer lived in isolated individuality, but 'in Christ,' enriched with the powers and the graces of the Risen Life of Christ.

2. ἀγαπητῷ τέκνῳ. It is γνησίῳ τέκνῳ in 1 Tim. i. 2 and Tit. i. 4; but the change in phrase is hardly to be counted significant. In 1 Cor. iv. 17 Timothy is described as τέκνον ἀγαπητόν μου.

χάρις, ἔλεος, εἰρήνη. See on 1 Tim. i. 2.

3—5. EXPRESSION OF THANKSGIVING FOR TIMOTHY'S FAITH.

3. χάριν ἔχω. See on 1 Tim. i. 12.
The construction is not quite clear, but it seems best to take ὑπόμνησιν λαβών of *v.* 5 as giving the cause of the Apostle's thankfulness, the intermediate phrases beginning ὡς ἀδιάλειπτον expressing the circumstances under which it is displayed. The parallel phrases in Rom. i. 9; Eph. i. 16; 1 Thess. i. 2; Philemon 4 confirm this view.

ἀπὸ προγόνων, *from my forefathers,* perhaps said here with a hint at the difference in Timothy's case, whose paternal ancestors were heathen (cp. *v.* 5). The thought, however, of his religious ancestry is referred to elsewhere by St Paul; cp. Acts xxiv. 14, κατὰ τὴν ὁδὸν ἣν λέγουσιν αἵρεσιν οὕτως λατρεύω τῷ πατρῴῳ θεῷ, and Acts xxii. 3.

ἐν καθαρᾷ συνειδήσει. Cp. Acts xxiii. 1, ἐγὼ πάσῃ συνειδήσει ἀγαθῇ πεπολίτευμαι τῷ θεῷ, and note on 1 Tim. i. 5.

ὡς ἀδιάλειπτον κ.τ.λ., *as unceasing is the remembrance which I make of you in my prayers.* The nearest parallel is Rom. i. 10, ὡς ἀδιαλείπτως μνείαν ὑμῶν ποιοῦμαι πάντοτε ἐπὶ τῶν προσευχῶν μου, but the expression (see above) is a favourite one with St Paul (cp. 1 Thess. i. 2 and iii. 6). It has, indeed, been pointed out[1] that some such phrase was frequently used in Greek letters of the Hellenistic period; e.g. in a letter dated 172 B.C. (*Pap. Lond.* XLII.) we find καὶ οἱ ἐν οἴκῳ πάντες σου διαπαντὸς μνείαν ποιούμενοι. St Paul adopted the customary phraseology of intimate correspondence and charged it with a deep Christian meaning.

νυκτὸς καὶ ἡμέρας. This probably goes with ἐπιποθῶν (as R.V.) rather than with what precedes (as A.V.). Cp. however 1 Tim. v. 5 and see the note there.

---

[1] See Deissmann, *Bibelstudien,* p. 210.

4. ἐπιποθῶν σε ἰδεῖν, *desiring to see thee,* here the natural longing of personal affection. Cp. Rom. i. 9 ; 1 Thess. iii. 6.

μεμνημένος σου τῶν δακρύων, *remembering thy tears,* probably those shed at the last parting of the two friends. Cp. Acts xx. 37.

ἵνα χαρᾶς πληρωθῶ, the desired consequence of the preceding σε ἰδεῖν.

5. ὑπόμνησιν λαβών, *having been put in remembrance,* lit., having received a 'reminder.' ὑπόμνησις (only again in 2 Macc. vi. 17; 2 Pet. i. 13, iii. 1; but cp. ὑπομιμνήσκειν 2 Tim. ii. 14; Tit. iii. 1) is an act of the memory prompted from without; and thus Bengel's suggestion, that there is here an allusion to some news of Timothy which had recently reached St Paul whether by messenger or by letter, is not improbable.

τῆς ἐν σοὶ ἀνυποκρίτου πίστεως, *of the unfeigned faith that is in thee.* For ἐν σοί instead of σου cp. Rom. i. 12, διὰ τῆς ἐν ἀλλήλοις πίστεως; for ἀνυπόκριτος see on 1 Tim. i. 5.

ἥτις. See on 1 Tim. i. 4.

πρῶτον ἐν τῇ μάμμῃ κ.τ.λ. πρῶτον simply means 'before it dwelt in you.' It is likely (though not explicitly stated) that Lois was Eunice's mother. The latter is described in Acts xvi. 1 as *a believing Jewish woman,* and as this was on St Paul's second visit to Lystra it has been supposed that she accepted the gospel on the Apostle's first visit to that place. After the word Ἰουδαίας (Acts xvi. 1) one cursive MS. (25) adds χήρας, and this is confirmed by two or three Latin authorities; the tradition that Eunice was a widow at the time of Timothy's circumcision (although thus slenderly attested) is interesting and falls in with the omission of any mention of Timothy's father in St Paul's letters. It also gives a new significance to the injunctions in 1 Tim. v. 4. But, however this may have been, the faith of both Lois and Eunice is here commended, and it was evidently to their pious care that Timothy owed his instruction in the Scriptures (2 Tim. iii. 15). Whether Lois was a Christian or only a faithful Jewess we cannot tell. The word μάμμη, 'grandmother,' only occurs again in the Greek Bible at 4 Macc. xvi. 9; the more correct Attic form being τήθη.

πέπεισμαι δὲ ὅτι καὶ ἐν σοί, *and* [not only so, but] *I am persuaded* [that it dwells] *in thee also.* We are not to press the adversative force of δέ, as if it meant 'but, notwithstanding all appearances'; it simply connects the clause with what has gone before.

6—14. CHARGE I. BE ZEALOUS; BE COURAGEOUS; STIR UP YOUR ORDINATION GRACE.

6. δι' ἣν αἰτίαν, *for the which cause,* sc. on account of the unfeigned faith inherited and possessed by Timothy, of which the Apostle has just been reminded. The phrase δι' ἣν αἰτίαν does not occur in St Paul outside the Pastorals (2 Tim. i. 12; Tit. i. 13: cp. Heb. ii. 11).

ἀναμιμνήσκω σε, *I put you in remembrance.* It has been supposed by some that here and throughout the Epistle we have allusions to weakness and timidity on the part of Timothy which had come to St Paul's knowledge; but the evidence does not seem sufficient to establish anything more than a very natural anxiety on the part of the older man lest the younger one should faint under his heavy burden. Paul does not here tell Timothy of any new gift; he *reminds* him of that which was already his, and which Timothy knew to be his. See *Introd.* p. xliii.

ἀναζωπυρεῖν κ.τ.λ., *that you kindle into a flame the grace of God &c.* The Divine χάρισμα is a fire which may be extinguished through neglect; cp. 1 Thess. v. 19, τὸ πνεῦμα μὴ σβέννυτε (of the despising of prophesyings). The verb ἀναζωπυρεῖν does not occur again in N.T., but it is found twice in LXX. (Gen. xlv. 27; 1 Macc. xiii. 7, being used *intransitively* in both cases) and was a common Greek word. Cp. Clem. Rom. 27; Ignat. *Eph.* 1.

τὸ χάρισμα τοῦ θεοῦ, ὅ ἐστιν κ.τ.λ., *the gift of God which is in thee through the laying on of my hands.* Cp. carefully 1 Tim. iv. 14 and the note thereon. The χάρισμα is not an ordinary gift of God's grace, such as every Christian may seek and obtain according to his need; but is the special grace received by Timothy to fit him for his ministerial functions.

7. οὐ γὰρ ἔδωκεν κ.τ.λ. *For God did not give us,* i.e. [not all Christians but] you and me, Paul and Timothy, when we were set apart for His service by prayer and the imposition of hands.

πνεῦμα δειλίας, *the spirit of cowardice.* The word δειλία does not occur again in the N.T., but it is common in the LXX. as in all Greek. πνεῦμα does not stand for the natural human temper, but (as generally in St Paul; cp. Rom. viii. 15; 2 Cor. iv. 13; Eph. i. 17) for the human spirit supernaturally affected by the Divine. Of the gifts of the Holy Spirit cowardice is not one; a Christian man, a Christian minister, has no right to be a coward, for God has given him the spirit of *power.* Cp. Isa. xi. 2.

ἀλλὰ δυνάμεως καὶ ἀγάπης καὶ σωφρονισμοῦ, *but of power and love and discipline.* These three graces are specially named, as specially needed for one in Timothy's circumstances; *power* to fulfil his arduous tasks, *love* to suffer gladly all opposition—being ready to believe that for the most part it springs from ignorance—*discipline,* to correct and warn the wayward and careless. Cp. for δύναμις, Rom. xv. 13, ἐν δυνάμει πνεύματος ἀγίου; and again, St Paul's own preaching was ἐν ἀποδείξει πνεύματος καὶ δυνάμεως (1 Cor. ii. 4). For ἀγάπη cp. Rom. xv. 30 &c. σωφρονισμός is a ἅπ. λεγ. in the Greek Bible, but σωφροσύνη and its cognates are favourite words in the Pastorals; see on 1 Tim. ii. 9.

8. μὴ οὖν ἐπαισχυνθῇς. The exhortation is consequent on the assertion of the gift of the Spirit in *v.* 7; as Bengel has it "victo timore, fugit pudor malus."

τοῦ κυρίου ἡμῶν, '*about* our Lord'; cp. τὸ μαρτύριον τοῦ Χριστοῦ (1 Cor. i. 6). See on 1 Tim. i. 14 for the title.

τὸν δέσμιον αὐτοῦ. Cp. Eph. iii. 1 and Philemon 9: 'whom He has bound.' This is not merely a suggestion to Timothy to hasten to Rome; but a general exhortation to courage in upholding St Paul's teaching.

συνκακοπάθησον, 'bravely endure your share of suffering' in company with St Paul and all the martyrs of Christ. The word is only found in the Greek Bible here and at ii. 3.

τῷ εὐαγγελίῳ, dat. *commodi*, 'for the Gospel's sake.'

κατὰ δύναμιν θεοῦ. To be taken with συνκακοπάθησον, 'according to the power which God gives.' It seems better to refer back to the δύναμις of *v.* 7 (cp. 2 Cor. vi. 7) rather than forward to the power of God displayed in the process of salvation of *v.* 9.

9. ἡμᾶς. Primarily in reference to Paul and Timothy, but true generally.

σώσαντος. For the act of σωτηρία as applied to God, see on 1 Tim. i. 1.

καὶ καλέσαντος κλήσει ἁγίᾳ. This calling or *vocation* is always ascribed by Paul to God the Father; cp. Rom. xi. 29; 1 Cor. i. 9; Gal. i. 6 and especially Rom. viii. 28, τοῖς κατὰ πρόθεσιν κλητοῖς οὖσιν.

οὐ κατὰ τὰ ἔργα ἡμῶν. Cp. Tit. iii. 5; a distinctively Pauline idea, and important here as balancing the emphasis laid on good works in the Pastorals. See on 1 Tim. ii. 10.

ἰδίαν, emphatic, as marking the freedom of the Divine purpose.

ἐν Χρ. Ἰη., *in*, [not 'through'], His person.

πρὸ χρόνων αἰωνίων. See Rom. xvi. 25 and Tit. i. 2. The grace of Christ, Incarnate, Crucified, Risen, is part of the eternal purpose of God for man, and since time does not limit the Deity, that which is unfalteringly purposed is described as actually *given*.

10. φανερωθεῖσαν. See note on 1 Tim. iii. 16, and cp. Rom. xvi. 25; Col. i. 26.

ἐπιφάνεια. This word is used here, not as in 1 Tim. vi. 14 of the Second Advent (where see note), but of the whole 'Epiphany' of Christ in the world. Cp. Tit. iii. 4.

τοῦ σωτῆρος ἡμῶν Χρ. Ἰη. Cp. Phil. iii. 20. See critical note for the order Χρ. Ἰη.

τὸν θάνατον. Observe the article; while ζωή and ἀφθαρσία are anarthrous, θάνατον is preceded by τόν, sc. 'that death which we all know and dread.' It, i.e. *physical* death, has been *made of none effect*, for its sharpness is sin (1 Cor. xv. 56), and that has been conquered in the sorrows of the Passion. Cp. Heb. ii. 14 and Rom. v. 12—21.

φωτίσαντος, *brought to light.* Cp. 1 Cor. iv. 5, ὃς καὶ φωτίσει τὰ κρυπτὰ τοῦ σκότους. φωτίζειν is, strictly, to *illuminate*, e.g. John i. 9, ἦν τὸ φῶς τὸ ἀληθινὸν ὃ φωτίζει πάντα ἄνθρωπον κ.τ.λ.; and this is its proper meaning here. In prae-Christian times men had reached after *life and incorruption*; the doctrine of a future life was not first preached by the Apostles of Christ. But that doctrine was *illuminated*, brought into clear light, for the first time, διὰ τοῦ εὐαγγελίου. Yet, exegetically necessary as it is to emphasise this distinction, it is not of much practical importance. As Paley says with his usual sober sense: "It is idle to say that a future state had been discovered already:—it had been discovered, as the Copernican system was, it was one guess among many. He alone discovers who *proves*" (*Moral and Political Philosophy*, v. 9 *sub fin.*). It can hardly be maintained that the doctrine of a future life is demonstrable on grounds of natural religion alone.

διὰ τοῦ εὐαγγελίου. To be connected with φωτίσαντος. By means of the Gospel, life and immortality are brought into full light, for it is through the Gospel that we learn where to seek, and to find, them.

11. εἰς ὃ ἐτέθην ἐγώ, *for which,* sc. for the proclamation of which Gospel, *I was appointed.* Cp. 1 Tim. i. 12 and esp. 1 Tim. ii. 7 where the same three offices are named. See critical note.

12. δι' ἣν αἰτίαν. See on i. 6.

καὶ ταῦτα πάσχω, *I suffer even these things,* sc. bonds and prison.

ᾧ πεπίστευκα, *whom I have believed,* the perfect tense marking the continued πίστις. With the construction cp. John xiii. 18, ἐγὼ οἶδα τίνας ἐξελεξάμην.

τὴν παραθήκην μου. The word is peculiar in the N.T. to the Pastorals (see also 1 Tim. vi. 20), and occurs in the LXX. only in Lev. vi. 2, 4; 2 Macc. iii. 10, 15, the last of which passages presents a parallel to that before us. There were in the treasury at Jerusalem 'deposits' of widows and orphans, and the priests pray that God may keep them safe (διαφυλάξαι) from the spoiler for those who had deposited them. In 1 Tim. vi. 20 and 2 Tim. i. 14 παραθήκη plainly means the doctrine delivered to Timothy to preach; and hence it appears that here τὴν παρ. μου = the doctrine delivered to Paul by God. The Apostle is a prisoner and has no prospect of living much longer, and he expresses his confidence that God will keep safe his doctrine *against that day*, i.e. the day of the final account. Many other meanings for παραθήκη have been suggested, as 'soul,' 'salvation,' 'apostolic office' &c.; but the force of the parallels must be preserved. The connexion with the next verse is also maintained fully by understanding παραθήκη here of the doctrine entrusted to Paul. He knows that he can do little more for the preservation and propagation of the faith; he commends it accordingly to God; and then he solemnly bids Timothy, his spiritual son and successor, to hold fast as a pattern the sound words which he has taught him, to *guard the good deposit.*

13. ὑποτύπωσιν. See note on 1 Tim. i. 16 for the meaning of this word.

ὑγιαινόντων λόγων, *of sound words*; see the note on 1 Tim. i. 10. The usual rendering of this verse *Hold the pattern of sound words which thou hast heard* &c. is not free from difficulty. (1) The emphatic word is ὑποτύπωσιν as its position in the sentence shews, (2) it is used without an article and so seems to have a predicative force, (3) the verb is ἔχε, not κάτεχε; i.e. *hold*, not 'hold fast' (as in 1 Cor. xi. 2, xv. 2; 1 Thess. v. 21). But the difficulty of translating *Hold, as a pattern of sound words, even those which thou hast heard from me* is that we must then suppose ὧν to stand for οὕς governed by ἔχε (see crit. note). On the whole, therefore, we prefer the ordinary rendering.

ἐν πίστει καὶ ἀγάπῃ τῇ ἐν Χρ. Ἰησοῦ. The connexion is again uncertain. (*a*) It seems weak to take this clause with ἤκουσας. (*b*) It is better to take it with ἔχε, *faith* and *love* forming, as it were, the atmosphere in which the 'sound words' are to be preserved; but the order of the words in the sentence does not favour this. Thus (*c*) it has been urged that a period should be placed at ἤκουσας and that ἐν πίστει καὶ ἀγ. κ.τ.λ. are to be taken adverbially with what follows, viz. 'In faith and love guard the good deposit.' But this seems to deprive τὴν καλὴν παραθήκην of the emphasis which its place at the beginning of an injunction gives it. On the whole (*b*) seems best, and the meaning of the whole sentence is: 'Hold as a pattern of sound words, in faith and love, what you heard from me'; cp. ii. 2.

ἐν Χρ. Ἰησοῦ. He is the source and spring of both faith and love; cp. 1 Tim. iii. 13.

14. τὴν καλὴν παραθήκην φύλαξον. See the note on 1 Tim. vi. 20; and for καλήν, a characteristic adjective of the Pastorals, see on 1 Tim. i. 8. Cp. Philo *Quod det potiori insid.* 19 παραδοῦναι...ἐπιστή- μης καλὴν παρακαταθήκην φύλακι πιστῇ.

διὰ πνεύματος ἁγίου τοῦ ἐνοικοῦντος ἐν ἡμῖν, *through the Holy Spirit who dwelleth in us*, sc. in all Christians, but especially in you and me, Paul and Timothy, to whom grace for ministry has been given. Cp. for the phrase as applied to all Christians, Rom. viii. 11.

15—18. The loneliness of St Paul and the faithfulness of Onesiphorus.

15. οἶδας. Note the difference between οἶδας here, signifying general, hearsay, knowledge, which was all that Timothy could have had of St Paul's condition at Rome, and γινώσκεις in *v.* 18, the personal knowledge that he had of the ministrations of Onesiphorus at Ephesus.

ἀπεστράφησάν με πάντες οἱ ἐν τῇ Ἀσίᾳ, *all who are in Asia repu- diated me. Asia* is, as generally in the N.T. (see Acts xvi. 6), the Roman province of that name, embracing the Western parts of what is now called Asia Minor, of which Ephesus was the metropolis. πάντες οἱ ἐν τῇ ᾿Ασίᾳ can hardly mean anything but *all who are* now *in Asia*. Certain Christians (apparently from that province) had been in Rome while St Paul was in bonds but had turned away from him ; they had now returned home, and were probably known to Timothy. Two, *Phygelus and Hermogenes*, are singled out for mention by name, why—we cannot tell; possibly because they were inhabitants of Ephesus and so would come more directly under Timothy's notice. We know nothing further of them; Hermogenes is introduced in company with Demas in the opening sentences of the apocryphal Acts of Paul and Thecla, where he is described as ὁ χαλκεύς and as 'full of hypocrisy,' but such legends are rather to be considered as growing out of the notices in the Pastoral Epistles than as having independent tradition behind them.

16. δῴη ἔλεος. This phrase only occurs here in the N.T.; we have ποιεῖν ἔλεος elsewhere (Luke i. 72, x. 37; James ii. 13). δῴη is the incorrect, late, form for δοίη.

ὁ κύριος, sc. Christ, as appears from *v.* 8 and also from *v.* 18.

τῷ ᾿Ονησιφόρου οἴκῳ, *to the household of Onesiphorus.* Onesiphorus also figures (see above *v.* 15) in the Acts of Paul and Thecla, where he is represented as a householder of Iconium who shewed hospitality to St Paul on his first missionary journey, his wife's name being given as Lectra (see crit. note on iv. 19 below). A martyr called Onesiphorus seems to have suffered at Parium in Mysia between the years 102 and 114 A.D.[1], but there is no ground for identifying him with the friend who shewed kindness to St Paul. See further below on *v.* 18.

ὅτι πολλάκις με ἀνέψυξεν, *for he oft refreshed me,* no doubt with the consolations of his staunch friendship, as well as by bodily relief. ἀναψύχειν does not occur again in the N.T., but cp. ἀνάψυξις (Acts iii. 20).

καὶ τὴν ἅλυσίν μου οὐκ ἐπαισχύνθη, *and was not ashamed of my chain.* St Paul spoke of himself during his first captivity at Rome as being ἐν ἁλύσει (Eph. vi. 20). It is possible that we have here an allusion to the chain by which, according to the prison rules of the time, he was bound to his guard; but it would not be safe to press the singular, so as to insist on this. Onesiphorus was not ashamed of Paul's *bonds*, his state of durance ; this sufficiently brings out the point. Others turned away from the poor prisoner, whether through fear of a like fate at Nero's hands, or through the dislike which many people have to associate with the unfortunate more intimately than is necessary; not so Onesiphorus.

17. ἀλλὰ γενόμενος ἐν ῾Ρώμῃ, *but when he had arrived in Rome.* Cp. Acts xiii. 5.

σπουδαίως ἐζήτησέν με καὶ εὗρεν, *he diligently sought me out and found me.* It was probably no easy task to find one obscure prisoner, among the large numbers in bonds at Rome for various offences.

---

[1] See W. M. Ramsay, *Expository Times* (1898), p. 495.

18. δῴη αὐτῷ ὁ κύριος κ.τ.λ., *may the Lord*, sc. Christ, *grant him to find mercy from the Lord*, sc. God the Father, *in that day*, sc. the Day of Judgement. The repetition ὁ κύριος...παρὰ κυρίου is a little awkward, but probably the phrase δῴη αὐτῷ ὁ κύριος was a common introductory formula, so that the addition παρὰ κυρίου would not occur to the writer as strange. As the first κύριος seems to refer to Christ (see *vv.* 8, 16 above), it is best to take the second κυρίου as referring to God the Father, to whom the function of judgement is given more than once by St Paul (Rom. ii. 5, 16 &c.; but cp. John v. 22).

The question has been much debated whether Onesiphorus was alive or dead at the time of writing, a question which in the absence of fuller information about him it is impossible to answer with certainty. It may be observed, however, that there is no *a priori* difficulty in the way of supposing St Paul to have prayed for him, if he were already dead. Prayer for the dead was admissible among the Jews at the date of the composition of the Second Book of the Maccabees (cir. 100 B.C.), as 2 Macc. xii. 44, 45 establishes beyond question. And that the practice was observed by Christians in the second century becomes apparent as soon as we arrive at a period of which we have adequate knowledge. "Let every friend who observeth this pray for me" are the closing words of the epitaph on the tomb of Abercius, Bp of Hierapolis (160 A.D.)[1], and they are typical of a large number of sepulchral Christian inscriptions in the Catacombs and elsewhere[2]. It cannot be supposed impossible or even improbable that St Paul should have shared in the practice, which the Christian Church seems to have taken over from Judaism. But proof positive we have not got here. Certainly in ch. iv. 19 *the household of Onesiphorus* is saluted without mention of Onesiphorus himself. But this only proves that he was not at Ephesus at the time of writing (it seems a most improbable conjecture that he was actually then at Rome). To speak of a man's οἶκος without specific mention of himself does not necessarily prove that he is dead (cp. 1 Cor. i. 16). A better argument may be based on a comparison of *vv.* 16 and 18. In *v.* 16 St Paul prays for the *household of Onesiphorus*, whereas in *v.* 18 he repeats the same prayer on behalf of the man himself, with the significant addition ἐν ἐκείνῃ τῇ ἡμέρᾳ, which can mean nothing else than the Day of Judgement (see *v.* 12 and iv. 8). This addition seems to betray a feeling that prayer for him in this life, such as has already been made for his οἶκος, would be out of place. On the whole then it seems probable that Onesiphorus was dead when St Paul prayed on his behalf, δῴη αὐτῷ ὁ κύριος κ.τ.λ.[3]

καὶ ὅσα ἐν Ἐφέσῳ διηκόνησεν. Onesiphorus had plainly, from

---

[1] See Lightfoot, *Ignatius and Polycarp*, I. p. 496.
[2] See Warren's *Liturgy of Ante-Nicene Church*, p. 146 ff.
[3] It is curious, however, and the fact is worth noting, that the pseudo-Ignatian writer of the 4th century in the spurious letter to Hero (§ 9) borrows this prayer and applies its words to *living persons*, shewing apparently that at least *he* had not gathered from the passage before us that Onesiphorus was dead.

this, been a Church worker at Ephesus, where his family continued to reside (iv. 19).

βέλτιον σὺ γινώσκεις, *thou knowest*, of thine own personal knowledge, *very well*. βέλτιον is not to be taken as *better than I could tell you*; the comparative is used (as often) as equivalent to a weak superlative.

CHAPTER II.

3. συνκακοπάθησον. The rec. text has σὺ οὖν κακοπάθησον with a few authorities; but the evidence is convincing for συνκακοπάθησον.

Χριστοῦ Ἰησοῦ. The rec. text has Ἰησοῦ Χριστοῦ with D₂ᶜKL; but the order Χρ. Ἰη. has the great weight of authority in its favour.

7. ὅ. So ℵ*ACGP &c.; ἅ, the reading of the rec. text, is supported by ℵᶜD₂EKL, the Latin and the Bohairic versions; it is probably an explanatory correction.

δώσει. This has the preponderance of authorities in its favour, viz. ℵAC*D₂EG, the Latin and the Bohairic versions. δῴη, the reading of the rec. text, is probably a reminiscence of ch. i. 16, 18; it is supported by CᶜKLP &c.

10. αἰωνίου. The Vulgate Latin, with f, *arm*, *aeth*, and the margin of the Harclean Syriac, seem to bear witness to a reading οὐρανίου.

12. ἀρνησόμεθα. So ℵ*AC f and the Bohairic. ἀρνούμεθα, the rec. reading, is supported by ℵᶜD₂EKLP d e; it seems to be a correction of tense due to a misunderstanding of the sequence of thought in the three clauses. See note *in loc.*

13. γάρ. ℵᶜK omit this, as does the rec. text; but the MS. authority is decisive for its retention.

14. θεοῦ. The evidence is here rather evenly balanced between θεοῦ and κυρίου, the rec. reading. θεοῦ is supported by ℵCG f g and the Bohairic; κυρίου by AD₂EKLP d e &c.; but the MS. witness for θεοῦ is confirmed also by the fact that ἐνώπιον τοῦ θεοῦ is a common Pauline phrase, whereas ἐν. κυρίου only occurs once (2 Cor. viii. 21) and then in an O.T. quotation.

λογομαχεῖν. Lachmann is almost alone among critical editors in departing from the rec. text by reading λογομάχει with AC* and the Latins; λογομαχεῖν has the weight of authority in its favour, being supported by ℵD₂EGKLP, the Syriac and the Bohairic versions.

ἐπ᾽ οὐδέν. This is the reading of ℵ*ACP 17; G has ἐπ᾽ οὐδενί. The rec. text has εἰς οὐδέν with ℵᶜD₂EKL.

18. ἀνάστασιν. τὴν ἀνάστ. is read by most authorities and is found in the rec. text; the article is omitted by ℵG 17, and by most recent editors. WH give it a place in their margin.

19. κυρίου. This is read by all the uncials and the versions; χριστοῦ of the rec. text has only scanty cursive authorities in its favour.

21. εὔχρηστον. καί is prefixed in the rec. text, following אᶜC*KLP; א*AD₂*EG omit it. Versions may be cited on both sides, but on such a point their evidence is not very convincing.

22. τῶν ἐπικαλουμένων. Lachmann prefixes πάντων with ACG g (G omits τῶν), the Sahidic and Harclean versions; it is not found in אD₂EKLP, the Bohairic, the Peshito, or the Old Latin for the most part, and probably crept into the text through a reminiscence of 1 Cor. i. 2.

25. πραΰτητι. This is the orthography of the best MSS.; D₂ᵇᶜEKL and some other authorities spell it πραότητι, which is the reading of the rec. text. See crit. note on Tit. iii. 2.

δώῃ. This is the reading of א*ACD₂*G which must be preferred to δῷ the reading of אᶜD₂ᶜEKLP followed by the rec. text.

1—10. Repetition of Charge I. Be strong in Christ's
strength.

1. σὺ οὖν. *Thou therefore*; sc. in reference to the defections of which he had just spoken.

τέκνον μου. See on 1 Tim. i. 2.

ἐνδυναμοῦ, *be strengthened* (passive, not middle, voice). The present tense marks an abiding and continual strengthening. See note on 1 Tim. i. 12.

ἐν τῇ χάριτι τῇ ἐν Χρ. Ἰησ., the sphere within which alone a man can be truly strong.

2. καὶ ἃ ἤκουσας παρ' ἐμοῦ. Cp. i. 13 and the note at that place. Observe that personal strength in the grace of Christ precedes in importance as in time the transmission of the Apostolic deposit of faith.

διὰ πολλῶν μαρτύρων, *through many witnesses*; not only the instruction which St Paul had given orally to Timothy, but the 'sound doctrine' which Timothy had received from him indirectly through the report of others, is to be transmitted to succeeding generations. Many commentators, however, both ancient and modern, take διά here as equivalent to *coram*, 'in presence of,' and examples have been found to illustrate this use of διά where we should expect ἐπί. So it is understood by Chrysostom, πολλῶν παρόντων; and thus the 'many witnesses' are taken to be the presbyters present at Timothy's ordination (see 1 Tim. i. 18, iv. 16, vi. 12). But there is no need thus to strain the meaning of διά or to limit the reference to any single moment in Timothy's life. *Through the intervention of many witnesses* gives a clear and good sense.

ταῦτα παράθου. The delivery of a definite παραθήκη at Ordination is symbolised in our own Office for the Ordering of Priests by the handing a Bible to the newly ordained.

οἵτινες, *quippe qui.*

ἱκανοὶ ἔσονται. Yet these 'faithful men' who are 'able' to teach must needs continually remember ἡ ἱκανότης ἡμῶν ἐκ τοῦ θεοῦ (2 Cor. iii. 5).

ἑτέρους διδάξαι, *to teach others.* The ἐπίσκοπος at this stage of the Church's life needed to be διδακτικός (1 Tim. iii. 2).

3, 4. *a.* THE EXAMPLE OF THE SOLDIER.

3. συνκακοπάθησον. *Take your share of hardship.* See on i. 8, and cp. also the critical note above.

ὡς καλὸς στρατιώτης Χριστοῦ Ἰησοῦ. Cp. 1 Tim. i. 18, and see the note on καλός at 1 Tim. i. 8. A καλὸς στρατιώτης is a soldier 'sans peur et sans reproche.'

4. οὐδεὶς στρατευόμενος, *no one serving as a soldier.*

ἐμπλέκεται ταῖς τοῦ βίου πραγματίαις, *entangles himself with the affairs of life,* sc. the affairs of worldly business, as distinct from the higher life (ζωή) of the soul; see note on 1 Tim. iv. 8. ἐμπλέκειν only occurs again in the N.T. at 2 Pet. ii. 20, where it is also used of entanglement in 'the defilements of the world.' The connexion of this and what follows with *v.* 3 is in the thought that no one, whether *soldier, athlete,* or *husbandman,* can achieve success without toil. *Therefore take* your *share of hardness,* &c. remembering that singleness of purpose and detachment from extraneous cares are essential conditions of successful service; cp. Rom. viii. 8; 1 Cor. vii. 32.

ἵνα τῷ στρατολογήσαντι ἀρέσῃ, *that he may please him who enrolled him as a soldier.* στρατολογεῖν, *to levy a troop,* is not found again in the Greek Bible, but is used by Josephus and Plutarch. Ignatius (*Polyc.* 6) takes up the thought and words of this verse in his exhortation ἀρέσκετε ᾧ στρατεύεσθε.

5. *b.* THE EXAMPLE OF THE ATHLETE.

5. ἐὰν δὲ καὶ ἀθλῇ τις κ.τ.λ., *if any man, again, strive in the games,* &c. See the note on 1 Tim. vi. 12 for the use of this metaphor in St Paul and in Philo. ἀθλεῖν does not occur elsewhere in the Greek Bible, but it is a classical word and is used by Philo in similar contexts.

οὐ στεφανοῦται. The word only occurs again in N.T. at Heb. ii. 7, but it is sufficiently common elsewhere. See 1 Cor. ix. 25; 2 Tim. iv. 8, and notes on 1 Tim. vi. 12.

ἐὰν μὴ νομίμως ἀθλήσῃ, *unless he strive according to the rules.* For νομίμως see on 1 Tim. i. 8. Unless the athlete submit to the rules, whether of preparatory discipline or those by which the actual contest is ordered, he cannot expect the crown. So Epictetus (who taught at Nicopolis about 95 A.D.) speaks of the need of bodily discipline, of eating 'by rule,' to him who would conquer in the Olympic games, applying the illustration as St Paul does here (*Encheiridion* xxix. b).

6. c. THE EXAMPLE OF THE HUSBANDMAN.

6. τὸν κοπιῶντα γεωργὸν δεῖ κ.τ.λ., *the husbandman that laboureth must first*, sc. before him who is lazy and careless, *partake of the fruits.* The emphatic word is κοπιῶντα; as in the preceding verse, the main thought is that labour, discipline, striving are the portion of him who would succeed in any enterprise, be he soldier or athlete or farmer; *E cura quies.* On κοπιᾷν cp. 1 Tim. iv. 10. The *fruits* to which the apostolic labourer may look forward are not here specially in question; *they* are only fully to be reaped in the world to come (Matt. v. 12, xix. 21). The verb μεταλαμβάνειν (cp. 1 Tim. iv. 3) does not occur elsewhere in St Paul's letters; but cp. Acts xxvii. 33, 34.

7. νόει ὃ λέγω. *Understand what I say*, sc. what has just been said about the hardness which the 'good soldier' of Christ must face. νοέω seems to mean 'understand' or 'grasp the meaning of' (as in 1 Tim. i. 7) rather than 'consider'; though no doubt *attention* is a necessary condition of *understanding*.

δώσει γάρ σοι κ.τ.λ., *for the Lord*, sc. Christ, *will give thee understanding in all things.* See critical note on δώσει, and cp. for σύνεσις Eph. iii. 4; Col. i. 9; σύνεσις is the faculty of 'right judgement' and is defined by Aristotle (*Eth. Nic.* VI. 10) as consisting ἐν τῷ χρῆσθαι τῇ δόξῃ ἐπὶ τὸ κρίνειν περὶ τούτων, περὶ ὧν ἡ φρόνησίς ἐστιν, ἄλλου λέγοντος, καὶ κρίνειν καλῶς.

8. Bengel's comment on the verse is, as usual, illuminating. *Paulus exemplo Christi suum, ut solet, exemplum animat.*

μνημόνευε. *Keep in remembrance*, have ever in your thoughts. We have μνημονεύειν with the acc. again in 1 Thess. ii. 9.

Ἰησοῦν Χριστὸν ἐγηγερμένον ἐκ νεκρῶν. *Jesus Christ, as risen from the dead.* The memory of the Risen Lord will inspire with courage and faithfulness; note that it is the Vision of the Risen One, not the Vision of the Crucified, which Timothy is bidden to keep before him. The power of the risen life of Christ is ever in St Paul's mind; cp. Rom. vi. 9, vii. 4.

ἐκ σπέρματος Δαυείδ, *of the seed of David.* Cp. Rom. i. 3 where these two leading thoughts, the true Messiahship of Jesus on the one hand, and His Divine Sonship on the other, as guaranteed by His Resurrection, are placed in juxtaposition in like manner. 'Jesus Christ, risen from the dead'; He is the centre of the New Dispensation. 'Of the seed of David'; here is the pledge that He has fulfilled the hopes of the Old. *Hanc unam genealogiam*, says Bengel, *a Timotheo vult attendi.*

κατὰ τὸ εὐαγγέλιόν μου, *according to my gospel*, i.e. according to the good tidings which I am commissioned to preach. Cp. for the phrase

Rom. ii. 16, xvi. 25. To limit it to the written gospel of St Luke (as Jerome suggested) is to introduce an idea quite foreign to the Apostle's thought.

9. ἐν ᾧ, *in which,* sc. in the preaching of which good tidings.

κακοπαθῶ μέχρι δεσμῶν ὡς κακοῦργος. *I suffer hardship unto bonds, as a malefactor.* Timothy must be ready to take his share of hardship; and St Paul here introduces for his encouragement this notice of his own sufferings.

κακοπαθεῖν (see *v.* 9 and iv. 5) occurs in the N.T. outside this Epistle only at Jas. v. 13.

μέχρι δεσμῶν. This degradation seems to have been deeply felt by St Paul, as was natural in a man of his ardent and generous nature. See Phil. i. 7 and Col. iv. 18, and also 2 Tim. i. 16 with the note thereon. *μέχρι* has the force of *even unto*; the *δέσμοι* were among the worst indignities to which he, a Roman citizen and an innocent man, was subjected.

ὡς κακοῦργος, *as a malefactor,* the word used only occurring again in the N.T. at Luke xxiii. 32, 33, 39. Such an expression suggests that St Paul's second imprisonment was more rigorous than his first (see Acts xxviii. 30, 31). And it has been supposed by some[1] that the phrase *ὡς κακοῦργος* explicitly describes the charge under which Paul lay in prison, and that it refers to the *flagitia* for which Christians were condemned under Nero (Tacitus *Ann.* xv. 44). In 1 Pet. iv. 15 we have in like manner *μὴ γάρ τις ὑμῶν πασχέτω ὡς φονεὺς ἢ κλέπτης ἢ κακοποιός* (cp. 1 Pet. ii. 12). In such phrases indications have been found of the date of writing; for (it is argued) the persecution of Christians with which the writer was acquainted was a persecution instituted *not* against the mere profession of Christianity, but against the Christians as persons convicted of disgraceful crimes (*flagitia*). And as Christianity was not proclaimed a *religio illicita* until the time of Domitian, when the 'Name' was absolutely proscribed, a persecution of the Christians, not *eo nomine* but as *flagitiosi,* such as is suggested to us in the words *ὡς κακοῦργος,* must be ascribed to an earlier date and, probably, to the reign of Nero. The argument is, however, a little precarious; we know too little about the details of the early persecutions to be quite sure of our ground, and, further, the charge of *flagitia* was brought against Christians at all periods, whether early or late.

ἀλλὰ ὁ λόγος τοῦ θεοῦ οὐ δέδεται, *but the Word of God is not bound,* i.e. the Gospel message (see Addit. Note on 1 Tim. iv. 5) is still being preached to the nations, despite the imprisonment of the Apostle of the Gentiles. Others were carrying on the work which he began; and he himself, even if not by speech as during his first imprisonment (Phil. i. 13) yet by letter could do much for the furtherance of the Gospel. The paronomasia will be observed, *δεσμῶν* suggesting *δέδεται* in the next line.

---

[1] E.g. by Prof. Ramsay, *Church in the Roman Empire,* p. 249.

10. διὰ τοῦτο, *wherefore,* sc. because the work is going on, although the worker is bound in chains.

πάντα ὑπομένω, *I endure all things*; in the spirit of that charity of which he had himself said, πάντα ὑπομένει (1 Cor. xiii. 7).

διὰ τοὺς ἐκλεκτούς, *for the elect's sake,* sc. for the sake of all those whom it is God's purpose to bring to a knowledge of the Truth; cp. Rom. viii. 33; Col. iii. 12; Tit. i. 1. The uncertainty implied in the words which follow ἵνα καὶ αὐτοὶ σωτηρίας τύχωσιν shews that it is not in reference to an election to final salvation that St Paul uses the word ἐκλεκτοί; in his Epistles and also in 1 and 2 Peter, the words κλητοί and ἐκλεκτοί are continually used of the whole body of believers, 'chosen' and 'called' by God to the privileges of the Gospel. See esp. Lightfoot on Col. iii. 12 and Hort on 1 Pet. i. 1.

ἵνα καὶ αὐτοὶ σωτηρίας τύχωσιν κ.τ.λ., *in order that they too,* sc. as well as I, *may obtain the salvation* &c. The Apostle's personal confidence is worthy of careful notice; cp. iv. 8.

τῆς ἐν Χρ. Ἰη. μετὰ δόξης αἰωνίου. The consummation of this *salvation which is in Christ Jesus* is *eternal glory.* In 2 Cor. iv. 17 he speaks of αἰώνιον βάρος δόξης as the issue of 'our light affliction which is for the moment.'

11—13. FRAGMENT OF A HYMN ON THE GLORIES OF MARTYRDOM.

11. πιστὸς ὁ λόγος. See notes on 1 Tim. i. 15, iv. 9. Commentators are not agreed as to the reference of this formula here; some, following Chrysostom, hold that it refers to what *precedes,* viz. the motive to patient endurance set forth in *v.* 10. And it is urged that γάρ, which seems to introduce a reason for what has been said, necessitates this explanation and excludes the reference of πιστὸς ὁ λόγος to *vv.* 12, 13. But, on the other hand, there is nothing in the preceding verses of the nature of a formula or aphorism or quotation, and it is to such stereotyped phrases that πιστὸς ὁ λόγος has reference in the other instances of its occurrence. And there can be little doubt that *vv.* 12, 13 are a quotation from a Christian hymn or confession, probably from a hymn on the glories of martyrdom. The antithetical character of the clauses is obvious:—

> εἰ συναπεθάνομεν καὶ συνζήσομεν·
> εἰ ὑπομένομεν καὶ συνβασιλεύσομεν·
> εἰ ἀρνησόμεθα κάκεῖνος ἀρνήσεται ἡμᾶς·
> εἰ ἀπιστοῦμεν ἐκεῖνος πιστὸς μένει·
> ἀρνήσασθαι γὰρ ἑαυτὸν οὐ δύναται.

The last line is, possibly, not part of the quotation, but an explanatory comment added by the writer; but, in any case, this fragment of a hymn is exactly the kind of 'saying' to which the formula πιστὸς ὁ λόγος would apply. The presence of γάρ in the first clause may be variously accounted for. It may actually be a part of the quotation (as is suggested in the text of the Revised Version); or, again, its force may be merely explanatory, 'for, as you remember,' &c.

εἰ συναπεθάνομεν. The words are very close to those of Rom. vi. 8, εἰ δὲ ἀπεθάνομεν σὺν Χριστῷ, πιστεύομεν ὅτι καὶ συνζήσομεν αὐτῷ; but while in that passage the thought is of *baptism* as typifying a death to sin, in this fragment of a hymn the reference seems to be to death by martyrdom. The *ethical* reference of the words here to baptism would, no doubt, give a good sense, but it is not harmonious with the context; the hymn is quoted as an incentive to courage and endurance. The aorist tense, συναπεθάνομεν, should be noted; it points to a single definite act of self-devotion, and in this is contrasted with ὑπομένομεν in the next line, where the present tense marks a *continual* endurance.

καὶ συνζήσομεν, *we shall also live with Him*; not to be interpreted in any figurative or allegorical sense, but literally, of the life of the blessed in heaven.

12. εἰ ὑπομένομεν. We have again a close parallel in the Ep. to the Romans (viii. 17), εἴπερ συνπάσχομεν ἵνα καὶ συνδοξασθῶμεν; cp. Rom. v. 17 and Rev. i. 6. The verb συμβασιλεύειν only occurs in the N.T. here and in 1 Cor. iv. 8.

εἰ ἀρνησόμεθα κ.τ.λ., *if we shall deny Him, He also will deny us,* a reminiscence of our Lord's words recorded in Matt. x. 33, words which may well have been present to the mind of many a martyr for the Name of Christ. The *tense* ἀρνησόμεθα has in this third clause been made *future,* to mark a mere contingency, improbable in itself and to be deprecated.

13. εἰ ἀπιστοῦμεν, ἐκεῖνος πιστὸς μένει. *If we are faithless, He abideth faithful.* The last clause gives a solemn warning; this gives a message of hope. Not every weakness of faith will call down the awful judgement ἀρνήσεται ἡμᾶς; for man's faith in God is not the measure of God's faithfulness to man. He is 'the faithful God' (Deut. vii. 9). ἀπιστεῖν here, as always in the N.T., definitely means *unbelief,* a wavering of faith, not an open act of disloyalty, so much as an inward distrust of God's promises. We have the same thought in Rom. iii. 3 (in a different context), εἰ ἠπίστησάν τινες, μὴ ἡ ἀπιστία αὐτῶν τὴν πίστιν τοῦ θεοῦ καταργήσει; μὴ γένοιτο.

It thus appears that clauses 1, 2, 4 of this remarkable hymn are little more than reproductions of phrases from St Paul's Epistle to the Romans, clause 3 being based on words of Christ. It does not seem an improbable conjecture that the hymn was actually composed at Rome in reference to the earlier persecutions of Christians under Nero, and that it thus became known to St Paul during his second imprisonment in the imperial city. If this be so, he is here, as it were, quoting a popular version of words from his own great Epistle, which had become stereotyped by liturgical use.

ἀρνήσασθαι γὰρ ἑαυτὸν οὐ δύναται, *for He cannot deny Himself*; ἀδύνατον ψεύσασθαι θεόν (Heb. vi. 18). The 'Omnipotence' of God does not include such acts of self-contradiction; omnipotence for a perfectly moral and holy Being is conditioned by that morality and holiness.

14—16. CHARGE II. SHUN VAIN SPECULATIONS.

14. ταῦτα ὑπομίμνησκε, *put them in mind of these things*; sc. remind those over whom you are placed of the need and the reward of courage and endurance. ὑπομιμνήσκω is only used once elsewhere by St Paul, at Tit. iii. 1.

διαμαρτυρόμενος ἐνώπιον τοῦ θεοῦ. See on 1 Tim. v. 21 and critical note above.

μὴ λογομαχεῖν, *not to strive with words*, i.e. not to indulge in controversy. See the note on λογομαχίαι at 1 Tim. vi. 4; the *verb* λογομαχεῖν does not occur again in the Greek Bible.

ἐπ' οὐδὲν χρήσιμον, *which is profitable for nothing*; the words are in apposition to the preceding λογομαχεῖν. χρήσιμος is a ἄπ. λεγ. in the N.T. See critical note. The preposition ἐπί both here and in the next clause marks the *result* rather than the *intention* (which would be expressed by εἰς) of the logomachies which are condemned.

ἐπὶ καταστροφῇ τῶν ἀκουόντων, *to the subversion of them that hear*. καταστροφή does not occur again in the N.T. (in 2 Pet. ii. 6 it is not the true reading), but it is not uncommon in the LXX.; it is used here as almost equivalent to the καθαίρεσις of 2 Cor. xiii. 10, which is the direct opposite of οἰκοδομή.

15. σπούδασον σεαυτὸν δόκιμον παραστῆσαι τῷ θεῷ. *Give diligence to present thyself approved unto God.* For the phrase παριστάνειν τῷ θεῷ cp. 1 Cor. viii. 8; and for a salutary warning as to the true meaning of δόκιμος cp. 2 Cor. x. 18, οὐ γὰρ ὁ ἑαυτὸν συνιστάνων, ἐκεῖνός ἐστιν δόκιμος, ἀλλὰ ὃν ὁ Κύριος συνίστησιν.

ἐργάτην ἀνεπαίσχυντον, *a workman who is not to be put to shame*, sc. by the poor quality of his work. ἀνεπαίσχυντος (ἄπ. λεγ. in the Greek Bible) is thus taken passively by Chrysostom, and the resulting sense seems to be more harmonious with the context than the rendering of the English versions, "that *needeth not* to be ashamed."

ὀρθοτομοῦντα τὸν λόγον τῆς ἀληθείας, *rightly dividing the word of truth*. The exact meaning of ὀρθοτομεῖν here (it does not occur elsewhere in the N.T.) is uncertain. The analogy of the only two places where it is found in the LXX. (Prov. iii. 6, xi. 5) has suggested to some that the metaphor is that of laying down a straight road, the road of Truth, from which heretics diverge on this side and on that. But we cannot read the idea of ὁδός into λόγον where it is not suggested by the context. The image here seems rather to be that of a man *cutting* the λόγος τῆς ἀληθείας into its *right* pattern, the standard provided being the Gospel. This is practically involved in the vaguer rendering given by the Revisers *handling aright the word of truth* (the Vulgate has *recte tractantem*); but the literal and primary meaning of ὀρθοτομεῖν cannot be *to handle aright*. The words at once recall 2 Cor. ii. 17, καπηλεύοντες τὸν λόγον τοῦ θεοῦ, but the metaphor employed there is quite different from that in the writer's mind here.

St Paul offers what amounts to a definition of ὁ λόγος τῆς ἀληθείας in Eph. i. 13, viz. τὸ εὐαγγέλιον τῆς σωτηρίας ὑμῶν ; cp. 2 Cor. vi. 7.

16. τὰς δὲ βεβήλους κενοφωνίας περιΐστασο, *but shun profane babblings*, such being the direct opposite of *the word of truth*, which it is Timothy's business *rightly to divide*. Cp. the parallel passage 1 Tim. vi. 20 and the note thereon. περιϊστάναι is only used by St Paul here and at Tit. iii. 9 (which see).

ἐπὶ πλεῖον γὰρ προκόψουσιν ἀσεβείας, *for they*, sc. the false teachers, *will proceed further in ungodliness*. ἀσεβεία is, of course, the opposite of εὐσεβεία ; see on 1 Tim. ii. 2.   For ἐπὶ πλεῖον cp. iii. 8 and Acts iv. 17.

17—22. THE SPECULATIONS OF HYMENAEUS AND PHILETUS.

17. καὶ ὁ λόγος αὐτῶν, *and their word*, sc. not specifically their 'doctrine' but their 'talk'; cp. 2 Cor. x. 10, xi. 6.

ὡς γάγγραινα, *as a gangrene*.   The word does not occur elsewhere in the Greek Bible, but is used by medical writers of a sore which eats into the flesh.   Cp. the note on *the wholesome doctrine*, 1 Tim. i. 10.

νομὴν ἕξει, *will eat*, lit. 'will have pasture'; cp. John x. 9, the only other place where the word is found in the N.T.   νομή is often used by medical writers of the 'spreading' of a disease, as here; cp. Polyb. I. 81. 6.

ὧν ἐστὶν Ὑμέναιος καὶ Φιλητός. Hymenaeus has been mentioned already, 1 Tim. i. 20 ; but we know nothing further either of him or of Philetus.

18. οἵτινες περὶ τὴν ἀλήθειαν ἠστόχησαν, *who concerning the truth have missed their aim*.   See 1 Tim. i. 6, vi. 21 and the notes there.

λέγοντες ἀνάστασιν ἤδη γεγονέναι, *saying that the Resurrection is already past*.   These persons seem to have interpreted the doctrine of man's Resurrection in an ethical or spiritual sense only. Difficulties about a resurrection of the body were early felt (see 1 Cor. xv. 12 ff.), and such teaching as that of St Paul (Rom. vi. 4; Col. ii. 12) about the analogy between the Lord's Resurrection and the baptized believer's 'newness of life' may have given occasion to heretical speculators to deny that the future bodily resurrection was an article of Christian faith.   A like error is mentioned by Polycarp (§ 7) ὅς...λέγει μήτε ἀνάστασιν μήτε κρίσιν ; there is a warning against it in [2 Clem.] § 9 μὴ λεγέτω τις ὑμῶν ὅτι αὕτη ἡ σὰρξ οὐ κρίνεται οὐδὲ ἀνίσταται : and in the Acts of Paul and Thecla (§ 14) Demas and Hermogenes are introduced as saying ἡμεῖς σε διδάξομεν, ἣν λέγει οὗτος ἀνάστασιν γενέσθαι, ὅτι ἤδη γέγονεν ἐφ' οἷς ἔχομεν τέκνοις. It is probable, however, that this last passage is directly dependent on the verse before us (the reference to the Resurrection being already past is not found in the Syriac version), and therefore it does not furnish additional evidence for the prevalence of the form of error in question.   By the time of Justin (*Dial.* 80) and of Irenaeus (*Haer.* II. 31. 2) an allegorising explanation of the Resurrection was a recognised Gnostic tenet;

but at this early stage in the Church's life, if we judge from the language here employed, we are not to think of the error of Hymenaeus and Philetus as the necessary outcome of a definite heretical system so much as a private blunder based on misinterpretations of the Apostolic doctrine. The mischievous results of such 'vain babblings' were already becoming apparent (*v.* 17).

καὶ ἀνατρέπουσιν τήν τινων πίστιν, *and subvert the faith of some.* ἀνατρέπειν only occurs again in the N.T. at Tit. i. 11, in a somewhat similar context, but it is a common LXX. word.

19. ὁ μέντοι στερεὸς θεμέλιος τοῦ θεοῦ ἔστηκεν. *Howbeit,* despite the subversion of some who are weak in the faith, *the firm foundation of God standeth*; not, as the A.V. has it, "the foundation of God standeth sure," for στερεός is not the predicate here. This θεμέλιος τοῦ θεοῦ, 'foundation laid by God,' as the following words shew, is the Church, which remains firm (cp. 1 Tim. iii. 15) despite the aberrations of individual members; cp. Heb. xii. 28. It is upon this foundation that the οἰκοδομή or 'building up' of the faithful is based; cp. Eph. ii. 20, although the metaphor here is slightly different.

μέντοι is not found again in the Pauline Epistles, but is common in St John. στερεός also is used here only by St Paul (he has στερέωμα in Col. ii. 5), but occurs Heb. v. 12, 14; 1 Pet. v. 9.

ἔχων τὴν σφραγῖδα ταύτην, *having this seal.* As the foundations of the New Jerusalem are said to have upon them the names of the Apostles (Rev. xxi. 14; cp. also vii. 3), so this 'foundation of God' has a double inscription; cp. Deut. vi. 9, xi. 20.

Ἔγνω κύριος τοὺς ὄντας αὐτοῦ. *The Lord knoweth them that are His,* a quotation from Num. xvi. 5, words addressed by Moses in stern reproof to the rebellious Korah and his company, ψευδοδιδάσκαλοι of the Old Covenant. Cp. John x. 14, 27; and, for γινώσκω as used in a sentence of judgement, Matt. vii. 23.

καί· Ἀποστήτω ἀπὸ ἀδικίας πᾶς ὁ ὀνομάζων τὸ ὄνομα κυρίου, *and, Let everyone that nameth the Name of the Lord depart from unrighteousness.* This is not an exact quotation from any part of the O.T.; it resembles, however, several passages, e.g. Is. lii. 11 and (in continuation of the parallel suggested in the previous quotation) Num. xvi. 26; cp. also Is. xxvi. 13. See crit. note.

20. ἐν μεγάλη δὲ οἰκίᾳ. *But,* it must be remembered, although the Church is holy, that *in a great house* &c. The δέ introduces the answer to a possible objection to the suitability of such watchwords for the visible Church. In a great house there are vessels of every kind. The lesson is the same as that in the Parable of the Draw Net (Matt. xiii. 47 ff.); it is noteworthy that this is the only place where St Paul *directly* expresses the thought of the Church embracing evil members as well as good.

οὐκ ἔστιν μόνον κ.τ.λ., *there are not only vessels of gold and silver, but also of wood and of earth, and some unto honour and some unto dishonour.* We have already the idea of vessels 'for honour' and 'for

dishonour,' i.e. for dignified and for ignoble or petty uses, in Rom. ix.
21. "To the former class belonged the *table*, to the latter the *footstool*,
according to Diod. Sic. xvii. 66," is the interesting observation of
Field (*Ot. Norvic.* iii. 130). St Paul's thought however is not merely
of a difference in use between the different vessels, for all service may
be 'honourable' in itself, but of the sorrowful fact that some are
destined εἰς ἀτιμίαν, as unworthy of being εἰς τιμήν ; cp. Wisd. xv. 7.
St Paul has the adjective ὀστράκινος again in 2 Cor. iv. 7 ; cp. Lev.
vi. 28.

21. ἐὰν οὖν τις ἐκκαθάρῃ ἑαυτὸν ἀπὸ τούτων. *If a man therefore purge himself from these.* Quite generally it may be necessary
from time to time to cast out the 'vessels for dishonour'; here
St Paul seems specially to have had in mind Timothy's situation
in respect of the ψευδοδιδάσκαλοι. It will be a stern duty to 'purge
himself' from them. For ἐκκαθαίρειν cp. 1 Cor. v. 7.

ἔσται σκεῦος εἰς τιμήν, *he shall be a vessel unto honour.* (Cp. Acts ix.
15, σκεῦος ἐκλογῆς.) Otherwise, we know that "evil communications
corrupt good manners" (1 Cor. xv. 34).

ἡγιασμένον, *sanctified.* For this word as applied to believers by
St Paul cp. Rom. xv. 16 and Acts xx. 32, xxvi. 18.

εὔχρηστον τῷ δεσπότῃ, *meet for the master's,* or owner's, *use.* See
crit. note. εὔχρηστος is only found again in N.T. 2 Tim. iv. 11;
Philem. 11.

For δεσπότης see on 1 Tim. vi. 1.

εἰς πᾶν ἔργον ἀγαθὸν ἡτοιμασμένον, *prepared unto every good work.*
Cp. ch. iii. 17; Tit. iii. 1; and cp. also 2 Cor. ix. 8; Tit. i. 16. As it
is true that the ἔργα ἀγαθά are prepared of God for us to walk in
(Eph. ii. 10), so it is also true, and equally important to remember,
that God's servants must be on their part prepared for these ἔργα
ἀγαθά.

22. FLEE YOUTHFUL LUSTS : FOLLOW PEACE.

22. τὰς δὲ νεωτερικὰς ἐπιθυμίας φεῦγε, *but flee youthful lusts.* The
injunction may seem inapposite, as addressed to one who presided
over the important Christian community at Ephesus, but it is quite
intelligible when we remember that we have here the words of an old
man writing to one of his disciples. To St Paul, Timothy would
always be 'young,' and exposed to the dangers of youth. The
ἐπιθυμίαι which Timothy is to guard against (*juvenilia desideria* of
the Vulgate) would include all the passions and desires of a young
and vigorous man. See further on 1 Tim. iv. 12. The adjective
νεωτερικός does not occur elsewhere in the N.T.

διώκε δὲ δικαιοσύνην κ.τ.λ. See the note on 1 Tim. vi. 11, where a
similar injunction was affectionately given. Here, as there, *righteousness, faith, love,* are recommended to him ; and St Paul now adds
εἰρήνην μετὰ τῶν ἐπικαλουμένων τὸν κύριον κ.τ.λ. If Timothy is to
' purge himself' from the society of the ' false teachers,' he is not, on
the other hand, to forget the duty of promoting "peace and love

among all Christian people, and especially among them…committed to [his] charge¹." The clause μετὰ τῶν ἐπικαλ. τὸν κύρ. is to be taken in close connexion with εἰρήνην; cp. Rom. xii. 18; Heb. xii. 14. τὸν κύριον is here, of course, Christ; cp. Rom. x. 12; 1 Cor. i. 2. See critical note.

ἐκ καθαρᾶς καρδίας. See note on 1 Tim. i. 5.

23—26. TAKE NO PART IN IDLE CONTROVERSY.

23. τὰς δὲ μωρὰς καὶ ἀπαιδεύτους ζητήσεις παραιτοῦ, *but foolish and ignorant questionings refuse.* The irrelevancy of much of the controversy then prevalent among Christians seems to have deeply impressed St Paul; again and again he returns to this charge against the heretical teachers, that their doctrines are unprofitable and vain, and that they breed strife about questions either unimportant or insoluble. See 1 Tim. i. 4, 7, iv. 7, vi. 4, 20; Tit. iii. 9 &c. The adj. ἀπαίδευτος (*undisciplined*, or *untaught*, and so *ignorant*) does not occur again in the N.T. For παραιτοῦ see on 1 Tim. iv. 7.

εἰδὼς ὅτι γεννῶσιν μάχας, *knowing that they gender strifes.* A seemingly harmless speculation as to obscure problems of theology or sacred history may become directly injurious to true religion, if it issue in verbal controversies. Cp. *v.* 14.

24. δοῦλον δὲ κυρίου οὐ δεῖ μάχεσθαι. *But the Lord's servant* (a title generally applicable to all Christians, as at 1 Cor. vii. 22, but specially appropriate to one who has been entrusted with the oversight of the Lord's family, as Timothy had been) *must not strive,* sc. must not give way to the temptations of controversy with other Christians. In a true sense he is a 'soldier' (*v.* 3) and his course is a 'warfare' (see on 1 Tim. i. 18); but his foes are spiritual powers of evil and not his brothers in the family of Christ.

ἀλλὰ ἤπιον κ.τ.λ., *but,* on the contrary, he must be *gentle toward all, apt to teach, patient of wrong.* ἤπιος, *gentle,* is not found again in the N.T.²; it seems to have special reference to that kindliness of outward demeanour, so important in one who was, as bishop, the *persona ecclesiae,* the representative of the Church to the world. That a bishop should be διδακτικός has been already laid down, 1 Tim. iii. 2, where see the note.

ἀνεξίκακος, a word which does not occur elsewhere in the Greek Bible (cp. ἀνεξικακία Wisd. ii. 19) expresses *patient forbearance.*

25. ἐν πραΰτητι παιδεύοντα τοὺς ἀντιδιατιθεμένους, *in meekness correcting those who are adversely affected.*

πραΰτης is commended again in the list of Christian graces in Tit. iii. 2 (see also on Tit. i. 7), and several times elsewhere in St Paul's Epistles (Gal. v. 23, vi. 1; Eph. iv. 2; Col. iii. 12 &c.). It expresses the Christian's attitude, not to *God* (for this does not enter into the idea) but to *man,* and as a Christian virtue, it is based on the example of Christ, who was Himself, as He said, πραΰς (Matt. xi. 29).

---

¹ See the *Ordering of Priests* in the Anglican Ordinal.
² At 1 Thess. ii. 7, νήπιοι seems to be the true reading.

It is a question whether ἀντιδιατιθεμένους has a *passive* or a *middle* sense. The English versions take it in the latter way as equivalent to 'those who oppose themselves,' which yields a quite satisfactory sense; but, as Field has pointed out, in the only other instance of the occurrence of ἀντιδιατίθεσθαι (in Longinus) it is unquestionably passive, which therefore may rule the present passage. Ambrosiaster renders *eos qui diversa sentiunt*, which agrees with the translation here adopted. The general force of the injunction is not much affected, whichever rendering we adopt; it is comparable to Tit. i. 9, τοὺς ἀντιλέγοντας ἐλέγχειν, although the thought here is rather of a gentle and persuasive exhibition of the error of the false teachers, than of their formal refutation.

μήποτε δώῃ αὐτοῖς ὁ θεός, *if haply God may give to them.* We have adopted the reading δώῃ, as better attested by manuscripts than δῷ of the rec. text (see crit. note); but the optative here is strange (see Blass, *Gram. of N. T. Greek*, § 65. 3). If it is correct, it perhaps suggests the idea of the contingency as more remote than δῷ would indicate. μήποτε does not occur again in St Paul.

μετάνοιαν, *repentance.* It is remarkable how seldom St Paul uses this word (only again in Rom. ii. 4; 2 Cor. vii. 9, 10), although the idea of repentance and reconciliation is continually in his thoughts.

εἰς ἐπίγνωσιν ἀληθείας, *unto knowledge of the truth.* Cp. iii. 7 and see note on 1 Tim. ii. 4.

26. καὶ ἀνανήψωσιν ἐκ τῆς τοῦ διαβόλου παγίδος, *and may return to soberness out of the snare of the devil.* ἀνανήφειν is not found again in the Greek Bible, but we have ἐκνήφειν at 1 Cor. xv. 34. The παγὶς τοῦ διαβόλου here is certainly the snare laid by the devil for the feet of the unwary; the thought of man's great spiritual adversary as a dangerous personal opponent is frequently before St Paul's mind (see Eph. iv. 27, vi. 11). Compare the note on 1 Tim. iii. 6.

ἐζωγρημένοι ὑπ' αὐτοῦ εἰς τὸ ἐκείνου θέλημα. There is a difficulty here as to the reference of the pronouns αὐτοῦ and ἐκείνου. Do they refer to different subjects, and if so, how are they severally to be interpreted? Commentators have given very different answers. (i.) First it may be observed that the rendering of the A.V. which refers both words to ὁ διάβολος, "taken captive by him at his will," is not absolutely inconsistent with the change of pronoun from αὐτός to ἐκεῖνος. We have, e.g., in Wisd. i. 16 συνθήκην ἔθεντο πρὸς αὐτόν, ὅτι ἄξιοί εἰσιν τῆς ἐκείνου μερίδος εἶναι, where the two pronouns seem to refer to the same subject; and other similar examples have been cited. But, nevertheless, such a usage of pronouns is undoubtedly harsh; and further to render εἰς as if it were identical with κατά, calls for justification. We therefore decline to adopt the rendering of the A.V. unless no other will suit the context. (ii.) The Revisers refer αὐτοῦ to the δοῦλος κυρίου of v. 24 and ἐκείνου to θεός of v. 25, translating "having been taken captive by the Lord's servant unto the will of God." But it is surely unnatural and far-fetched to refer αὐτοῦ to an antecedent so far back as v. 24, clause after clause having intervened, and the main thought having changed. (iii.) We prefer to adopt the interpretation suggested in the margin of the R.V. αὐτοῦ relates to the devil, as the position of the words indicates; ἐκείνου relates to God, and the whole sentence runs *may return to soberness from the snare of the devil* (*having been caught by him*) *unto*, i.e. to do, *the will of God*. Thus ἐζωγρημένοι ὑπ' αὐτοῦ merely affords the explanation, logically necessary for the sense, as to how these unwary ones got into the devil's snare, viz. they were taken captive by him; and εἰς τὸ ἐκείνου θέλημα expresses the purpose which they, when rescued, shall strive to fulfil. ἐκ τῆς τοῦ διαβόλου παγίδος is in strict correspondence with εἰς τὸ ἐκείνου θέλημα.

ζωγρεῖν only occurs elsewhere in N.T. at Luke v. 10 where it means 'to catch alive,' as it does here. In medical writers it is often used as equivalent to 'to restore to life.'

CHAPTER III.

1. γίνωσκε. Lachmann reads γινώσκετε with AG g, but nearly all other authorities support the singular γίνωσκε; γινώσκετε, indeed, does not yield any tolerable sense.

6. αἰχμαλωτίζοντες. So the best authorities, ℵACD₂*GP &c.; the rec. text reads αἰχμαλωτεύοντες with D₂ᶜEKL and adds the article τά with a few cursives; the form αἰχμαλωτίζειν is Alexandrian or Macedonian and is condemned by the Atticists, as Ellicott points out, which may account for the variant as a scribe's correction.

8. Ἰαμβρῆς. This is the best supported orthography; but there is a Western reading Μαμβρῆς (Gᶜ d m); Origen refers to a book entitled *Iamnes et Mambres liber*; see exegetical note.

10. παρηκολούθησας. So ℵACG; the rec. text with D₂EKLP and nearly all cursives has the perfect παρηκολούθηκας. See exegetical note.

12. ζῆν εὐσεβῶς. This is the order of ℵAP, the Bohairic and the Harclean; the rec. text has εὐσεβῶς ζῆν with CD₂EGKL, the Peshito, the Latin versions &c., perhaps from confusion with Tit. ii. 12.

14. τίνων. So ℵAC*GP d e g = 'from what teachers,' i.e. Lois and Eunice; the rec. text has τίνος = 'from whom,' i.e. St Paul himself, with CᶜD₂EKL f and the remaining versions. The following clause shews, independently of MS. evidence, that τίνων is the true reading.

15. τὰ ἱερά. The rec. text has the article, following AC*D₂ᶜEKLP; it is omitted by Tischendorf and WH as by ℵCᵇD₂*G 17. It may have come in from the τά a few words further on. Lachmann and Tregelles put it in brackets.

16. καί. This is omitted by the Bohairic, the Peshito, and some MSS. of the Latin Vulgate; but the authority for its insertion is overwhelming.

ἐλεγμόν. So ℵACG; ἔλεγχον, the reading of the rec. text, is found
in the later uncials and in most other authorities. ἐλεγμός and
ἔλεγχος are confused in like manner in *Psalms of Solomon* x. 1 (see
the variants in Ryle and James' edn.).

1—9. THE CORRUPTIONS OF THE FUTURE.

1. In this melancholy forecast the Apostle is describing a recru-
descence of heathenism, with its attendant wickedness, which he assures
Timothy will take place in the 'last days' of the Church, rather than
the prevalence of forms of heresy. The crying evil of those corrupt
times will be that men professing to be Christians (*v.* 5) will yet be
conspicuous for all the worst vices of paganism. The germ of the
evil may be seen in the present (*v.* 5), and he warns Timothy against
the methods of the heretical teachers which will ultimately have such
disastrous results, by perverting the truth and by enfeebling the consciences of those whom they ensnare.

τοῦτο δὲ γίνωσκε calls special attention to the prediction which
follows. See crit. note.

ἐν ἐσχάταις ἡμέραις, *in the last days*, sc. of the present dispensation.
The prospect of the Second Advent of Christ was a vivid reality to
St Paul; he seems at times to have expected it soon (esp. see 1 Thess.
i. 10, 2 Thess. ii.), but at any rate he was not in the habit of contem-
plating the existing order of things as permanent. For the phrase
ἐν ἐσχάταις ἡμέραις, cp. 2 Pet. iii. 3 and Jude 18; and see note on
1 Tim. iv. 1.

ἐνστήσονται καιροὶ χαλεποί, *will ensue troublesome times*, seasons of
trial when it will be hard to keep the path of duty. χαλεπός only
occurs again in N.T. at Matt. viii. 28 (of 'fierce' demoniacs).

2. ἔσονται γὰρ οἱ ἄνθρωποι κ.τ.λ., *for men will be* &c., sc. (as the
presence of the article shews) the generality of men, the members
generally of the Christian communities. The adjectives which follow
are not arrayed in any exact logical sequence; but, nevertheless, as in
the somewhat similar catalogue of Rom. i. 29—31, connexion may be
traced between certain of the vices which are enumerated.

φίλαυτοι, *lovers of self.* The word does not occur elsewhere in the
LXX. or N.T. In Greek thought of an earlier age φιλαυτία had a
good sense, and was expressive of the self-respect which a good man
has for himself (see Aristotle *Nic. Eth.* ix. 8. 7). But a deeper philosophy, recognising the fact of man's Fall, transferred the moral
centre of gravity from self to God; once the sense of sin is truly felt,
self-respect becomes an inadequate basis for moral theory. So Philo
(*de Prof.* 15) speaks of those who are φίλαυτοι δὴ μᾶλλον ἢ φιλόθεοι, in
a spirit quite like that of St Paul.

φιλάργυροι, *lovers of money.* The adjective only occurs again at
Luke xvi. 14. See the note on φιλαργυρία, 1 Tim. vi. 10.

ἀλαζόνες, ὑπερήφανοι, *boastful, haughty*, the former term referring specially to *words*, the latter to *thoughts*. The words are coupled again in the catalogue at Rom. i. 30 (also by Clem. Rom. § 16); Trench (*Synonyms* § 29) has an admirable essay on the difference between them, and on the usage of both words in Greek literature.

βλάσφημοι, *railers*, or evil-speakers, in reference to their fellow men rather than to God. This is the regular force of βλάσφημος and the cognate words in the Pastoral Epistles.

γονεῦσιν ἀπειθεῖς, *disobedient to parents*, a characteristic also mentioned in Rom. i. 30. Cp. what St Paul had said about duty to a widowed parent in 1 Tim. v. 8.

ἀχάριστοι, *without gratitude*. This follows naturally from the last mentioned characteristic, for the blackest form of ingratitude is that which repudiates the claim of parents to respect and obedience. The adjective ἀχάριστος only occurs again once in N.T., at Luke vi. 35.

ἀνόσιοι. See note on 1 Tim. i. 9.

3. ἄστοργοι, *without natural affection*; the adjective only occurs here and in the parallel catalogue Rom. i. 31.

ἄσπονδοι, *implacable*. The word does not occur again in the Greek Bible (it is an interpolation in Rom. i. 31), but is frequent in good authors.

διάβολοι, *slanderers*, or false accusers. See on 1 Tim. iii. 6, 11. The margin of the A.V. suggests here and at Tit. i. 3 the rendering 'makebates,' i.e. 'those who make *baits* or *contentions*.'

ἀκρατεῖς, *without self-control*, in the widest sense, but more particularly in regard to bodily lusts. The adjective only occurs again in the Greek Bible at Prov. xxvii. 20, but St Paul speaks of ἀκρασία in 1 Cor. vii. 5 and we have ἐγκρατής in Tit. i. 8. The ἀκρατής is distinguished from the ἀκόλαστος or deliberate profligate, by the circumstance that he would like to do what is right but finds temptation too strong for him. He is weak and easily led, a man who might well say of himself "Video meliora proboque, deteriora sequor."

ἀνήμεροι, *fierce*. The word is ἅπ. λεγ. in the N.T. and LXX.

ἀφιλάγαθοι, *without love for the good*. The word does not seem to occur elsewhere in Greek literature, but we have φιλάγαθος (Tit. i. 8) in Wisd. vii. 22 and in Philo.

4. προδόται, *traitors*, sc. treacherous in their dealings with their fellows. Cp. Luke vi. 16, where the word is used of Judas, and Acts vii. 52. It is not necessary to suppose any reference to the betrayal of fellow Christians in times of persecution.

προπετεῖς, *headstrong*; cp. Acts xix. 36.

τετυφωμένοι, *besotted*, a form of conceit which is often accompanied by hasty and headstrong action. See on 1 Tim. iii. 6.

φιλήδονοι μᾶλλον ἢ φιλόθεοι. Both words are ἅπ. λεγ. in the N.T. and φιλόθεος does not occur in the LXX. After Wetstein few commentators have omitted to cite an interesting parallel from Philo (*de Agric.* § 19), φιλήδονον καὶ φιλοπαθῆ μᾶλλον ἢ φιλάρετον καὶ φιλόθεον ἀνὰ κράτος ἐργάσηται.

5. ἔχοντες μόρφωσιν εὐσεβείας, *having the form of godliness.* See on 1 Tim. ii. 2.

μόρφωσις is an affectation of, or aiming at, the μορφή of godliness, but not the μορφή itself (cp. Rom. ii. 20). μορφή is that which manifests the essence or inward nature of anything (see Phil. ii. 6) as opposed to the σχῆμα, the outward fashion or bearing; this the semi-pagan teachers of the future will not have. The melancholy thing is that they will affect to have it, although they have repudiated its power over the heart and life (Tit. i. 16), wherein is the real uniqueness of the Gospel (1 Cor. iv. 20). For this use of ἀρνέομαι cp. 1 Tim. v. 8.

καὶ τούτους ἀποτρέπου, *from these turn away;* the καί adds force and speciality to τούτους. Cp. 1 Tim. vi. 20 where ἐκτρέπομαι is used in a like context; ἀποτρέπειν is a ἅπ. λεγ. in the N.T. The injunction shews that these corruptions of the Gospel were not merely contemplated as about to arise in the future, but as already a present danger. This is clearly brought out by the next clause ἐκ τούτων γάρ εἰσιν κ.τ.λ.

6, ἐνδύνοντες εἰς τὰς οἰκίας, *who creep into houses.* The word ἐνδύνοντες is a ἅπ. λεγ. in N.T. ; but we have παρεισεδύησαν in Jude 4.

αἰχμαλωτίζοντες γυναικάρια, *who take captive silly women;* the diminutive form expressing contempt. αἰχμαλωτίζω is Pauline; cp. Rom. vii. 23; 2 Cor. x. 5, and see critical note.

It has been suggested that this characteristic of the false teachers points to their affinity with the later Gnostic heretics, among whom women played an important part. But (as was noticed long ago by Jerome *Ep. ad Ctesiphontem* 133. 4 in a remarkable passage) this is a feature of all heretical systems and has its root deep down in human nature. Women, says Hooker, "are deemed apter to serve as instruments and helps in the cause. Apter they are, through the eagerness of their affection, that maketh them, which way soever they take, diligent in drawing their husbands, children, servants, friends and allies the same way; apter through that natural inclination unto pity, which breedeth in them a greater readiness than in men to be bountiful toward their preachers who suffer want; apter through sundry opportunities, which they especially have, to procure encouragements for their brethren; finally apter through a singular delight which they take in giving very large and particular intelligence, how all near about them stand affected as concerning the same cause" (*Eccl. Pol.* Preface iii. 13). And so a propounder of novel opinions often gains a hearing through having first attracted the attention of women.

σεσωρευμένα ἁμαρτίαις, *laden with sins;* and so they readily give an ear to any impostor who will promise them ease of conscience; they seek peace in spiritual dissipation. The verb σωρεύειν only occurs once again in N.T., in Rom. xii. 20 (a quotation from Prov. xxv. 22).

ἐπιθυμίαις ποικίλαις, *lusts of all kinds*, including not only the desires of the flesh, but the wandering and undisciplined movements of the spirit. ποικίλος does not occur in St Paul outside the Pastorals (cp. Tit. iii. 3). The N.T. meaning of the word 'varied,' 'manifold' is unknown to classical Greek, where it signifies 'elaborate,' 'complicated.' See Hort on 1 Pet. i. 6.

7. πάντοτε μανθάνοντα, *ever learning*; they are full of morbid curiosity.

μηδέποτε. The tendency of the later language (see Blass, *Grammar of N.T. Greek*, § 75. 5) is to employ μή rather than οὐ, and especially with the participle. Hence we cannot lay any stress on the conditional negative μηδέποτε being used here in place of οὐδέποτε.

εἰς ἐπίγνωσιν ἀληθείας, *to a knowledge of the truth*; see note on 1 Tim. ii. 4.

ἐλθεῖν δυνάμενα, they are really *unable* to gain the truth, to such a strait have they brought themselves. Their spiritual sense is dulled, through overmuch curiosity as to the solution of unpractical problems of speculative theology.

It is no wonder that their silly disciples cannot arrive at a perfect knowledge of the truth, which their false teachers withstand. And these latter had prototypes in the earlier history of Israel.

8. ὃν τρόπον δὲ 'Ιαννῆς καὶ 'Ιαμβρῆς ἀντέστησαν Μωϋσεῖ. *For like as Jannes and Jambres withstood Moses.* Whether St Paul derived these names which he gives to the Egyptian magicians who 'withstood Moses' (Exod. vii. 11, 22) from unwritten tradition or from some book now lost to us, it is impossible to say. Origen held (*in Matt.* § 117) that he was quoting from an apocryphal work entitled *Iamnes et Mambres liber* (see crit. note), which is probably the same as a book no longer extant, condemned in the Gelasian decree of 494 under the title *Poenitentia Iamnae et Mambrae*. The names are found in the Targum of Jonathan on Exod. vii. 11. Jewish Haggadoth also described them as sons of Balaam, who either perished in the Red Sea or were killed in the tumult after the episode of the golden calf. The name Jannes meets us several times. E.g. Pliny (*Hist. Nat.* xxx. 1) has "Est et alia factio a Mose et Ianne et Iotape ac Iudaeis pendens, sed multis millibus annorum post Zoroastrem." In the second century Apuleius (*Apol.* p. 544) in like manner mentions Moses and Jannes as Magi who lived after Zoroaster.

οὕτως καὶ οὗτοι ἀνθίστανται τῇ ἀληθείᾳ. *So do these also withstand the truth.* We can hardly lay stress on οὕτως as ascribing to the false teachers pretension to magical arts such as the Egyptian magi practised, although γόητες of *v.* 13 might support this view. ἀνθιστάναι is used of Elymas the sorcerer in a similar context in Acts xiii. 8.

ἄνθρωποι κατεφθαρμένοι τὸν νοῦν, *men corrupted in their mind.* See on 1 Tim. vi. 5. καταφθείρειν is not found elsewhere in N.T., but is a LXX. word.

ἀδόκιμοι περὶ τὴν πίστιν, *reprobate concerning the faith.* For the phrase περὶ τὴν πίστιν see note on 1 Tim. i. 19. ἀδόκιμος we have again in Tit. i. 16; cp. Rom. i. 28; 1 Cor. ix. 27; 2 Cor. xiii. 5; it is a favourite word with St Paul. See on 1 Tim. i. 5.

9. ἀλλ' οὐ προκόψουσιν ἐπὶ πλεῖον. *Notwithstanding they shall not make further progress,* because the hollowness of their pretensions is speedily disclosed. See ii. 16 above.

ἡ γὰρ ἄνοια αὐτῶν κ.τ.λ., *for their senseless folly,* &c. ἄνοια only occurs in N. T. here and at Luke vi. 11.

ἔκδηλος ἔσται πᾶσιν, *shall be openly manifest to all.* Truth *must* prevail in the end, and imposture cannot permanently deceive. ἔκδηλος only occurs again (N.T. and LXX.) in 3 Macc. iii. 19, vi. 5.

ὡς καὶ ἡ ἐκείνων ἐγένετο, even as the folly of the Egyptian magicians became manifest at last; cp. Exod. viii. 18, ix. 11.

10—14. TIMOTHY IS COMMENDED FOR HIS LOYALTY AND ENCOURAGED TO ENDURE.

10. σὺ δὲ. *But thou*; sc. in contrast with the vagaries of the ἑτεροδιδάσκαλοι.

παρηκολούθησας, *didst follow.* The perfect παρηκολούθηκας which is read by some authorities (see crit. note) would clearly indicate a *continual* following of St Paul; but the aorist does not exclude this. In the N.T. the aorist is frequently used where the action is *not* conceived as terminated, and where Classical Greek would prefer the perfect, e.g. Matt. xxiii. 2 ; Mark iii. 21.

μου τῇ διδασκαλίᾳ, *my doctrine*; see note on 1 Tim. i. 10.

τῇ ἀγωγῇ, *conduct,* manner of life. Cp. 1 Cor. iv. 17 where it is said of Timothy ὃς ὑμᾶς ἀναμνήσει τὰς ὁδούς μου τὰς ἐν Χριστῷ. The word ἀγωγή does not occur elsewhere in the N.T., but is found in Esther ii. 20 and 2 Macc. iv. 16 &c.

τῇ προθέσει, *purpose.* This word is always used elsewhere by St Paul for the purposes of God (cp. 2 Tim. i. 9); with the usage here cp. Acts xi. 23.

τῇ πίστει, *faith,* i.e. in the widest sense, indicating his attitude to the Christian revelation generally.

τῇ μακροθυμίᾳ, *long-suffering,* i.e. not only in respect of the false teachers, but in respect of trouble and affliction of every kind; see note on 1 Tim. i. 16.

τῇ ἀγάπῃ, *love,* without which μακροθυμία would be impossible; cp. ἡ ἀγάπη μακροθυμεῖ (1 Cor. xiii. 4). For the history of the word ἀγάπη see note on 1 Tim. i. 5.

τῇ ὑπομονῇ, *brave patience.* See on 1 Tim. vi. 11, where ὑπομονή, as here, follows ἀγάπη in an enumeration of Christian graces, and also note on Tit. ii. 2. The confident assurance with which the

Apostle here claims these graces as his own is in marked contrast with the language of humility which he uses about himself in earlier letters (see on 1 Tim. i. 15); but it must be remembered that he is here writing within sight of death. There can now be no thought of boasting or pride; but with his eyes fixed on the crown laid up for him at the end of his course (iv. 6—8) he speaks frankly out of his experience to his son in the faith about the graces which a Christian apostle most sorely needs.

11. τοῖς διωγμοῖς, τοῖς παθήμασιν, *persecutions, sufferings*, which the mention of ὑπομονή has suggested. He dwells on them parenthetically in this and the next verse.

οἷά μοι ἐγένετο, *such as befell me*; he only gives illustrations, as it were, of what a Christian apostle has to expect.

ἐν Ἀντιοχείᾳ κ.τ.λ. *In Antioch* (sc. of Pisidia, Acts xiii. 50), *in Iconium* (Acts xiv. 2), *in Lystra* (Acts xiv. 19). These persecutions are selected for mention, not necessarily because they were the *first* which St Paul had to endure, or the *most severe* (for he suffered worse things at Philippi), but because they were especially well known to Timothy, who was himself of Lystra (Acts xvi. 2), and must have been matter of common talk in that district when Timothy was a youth.

οἵους διωγμοὺς ὑπήνεγκα, *such persecutions as I endured*, a supplementary clause calling special attention to the fact that these particular persecutions had been endured by him.

καὶ ἐκ πάντων κ.τ.λ. *And* (yet, despite the greatness of the danger) *out of all the Lord* (sc. Christ) *delivered me*. See note on iv. 17, 18.

12. καὶ πάντες δέ, *and, moreover, all*. For καὶ...δέ cp. Rom. xi. 23; 1 Tim. iii. 10.

οἱ θέλοντες, *who are minded*, expressing not a mere passing desire, but the continual bent of the will.

ζῆν εὐσεβῶς. For the order of words see the critical note. εὐσεβῶς only occurs again in the Greek Bible at Tit. ii. 12 (which see) and 4 Macc. vii. 21. See on 1 Tim. ii. 2 for the meaning of εὐσέβεια and its cognates.

ἐν Χριστῷ Ἰησοῦ, *in Christ Jesus*, the sphere of the godly life. 'Life in Christ' is the perpetual theme of St Paul's Epistles, and, however difficult the phrase may be to interpret, it is impossible to doubt that he meant more by it than life lived in obedience to the precepts of Christ, or under the influence of the Gospel of Christ. There is a deep sense in which the baptized believer is *in Christ*, who as the Incarnate Word took human nature into Himself.

διωχθήσονται, *shall be persecuted*. And in such moments of persecution the promise will be recalled, μακάριοι οἱ δεδιωγμένοι ἕνεκεν δικαιοσύνης, ὅτι αὐτῶν ἐστὶν ἡ βασιλεία τῶν οὐρανῶν (Matt. v. 10); cp. John xv. 20.

13. πονηροὶ δὲ ἄνθρωποι, *but* (sc. in contrast with those οἱ θέλοντες ζῆν εὐσεβῶς) *evil men*. Cp. 2 Thess. iii. 2.

καὶ γόητες, *and impostors*, lit. *wizards.* The word does not occur again in the Greek Bible, but we have γοητεία in 2 Macc. xii. 24 in the sense of 'crafty guile.' Its use here is no doubt suggested by the comparison in *v.* 8 of the ἑτεροδιδάσκαλοι to the Egyptian magicians, Jannes and Jambres. It would seem from its employment here that the 'false teachers' whom the Apostle had in his mind professed magical arts, though this is not certain, inasmuch as γόης is not necessarily equivalent to μάγος. (See *Introd.* p. liv.)

προκόψουσιν ἐπὶ τὸ χεῖρον, *will make advance towards the worse.* This is not contradictory of *v.* 9 (which see), for here it is the *intensity*, as there the *diffusion*, of the evil which is in question.

πλανῶντες καὶ πλανώμενοι, *deceiving and being deceived.* The two generally go together. Few men admit to themselves that they are deliberate impostors; the practice of deceit is intolerable unless it be partly hidden from the actor by self-deceit. And, further, πλανώμενοι is strictly *passive*, not *middle*; the deceivers may have themselves been deceived by the teachers who seduced them from the middle way of truth. Cp. Tit. iii. 3.

14. σὺ δὲ μένε κ.τ.λ., *but*, in contrast with all such, *do thou abide in the things which thou hast learned and hast been assured of*; ἐν οἷς ἔμαθες being for ἐν ἐκείνοις ἃ ἔμαθες. ἐπιστώθης is not equivalent to ἐπιστεύθης as the Vulgate *et credita sunt tibi* takes it; πιστοῦν (a LXX. word not found elsewhere in the N.T.) is *to convince, to assure.*

εἰδὼς παρὰ τίνων ἔμαθες, *knowing*, as thou dost, *from whom thou learnedst them.* The critical note shews that there has been a diversity of opinion as to the teachers of Timothy whom the Apostle had in his mind; but it seems plain from the next verse that the primary reference must be to Lois and Eunice, Timothy's earliest instructors, although it is quite possible that St Paul may have also thought of himself as Timothy's father in God.

15—17. The uses of Holy Scripture.

15. καὶ ὅτι, *and that*, not 'because'; ὅτι depends upon εἰδώς.

ἀπὸ βρέφους, *from a babe*; cp. i. 5. It was the custom to teach Jewish children the law at a very early age, and to cause them to commit parts of it to memory.

τὰ ἱερὰ γράμματα οἶδας, *thou hast known the sacred writings.* The reading (see critical note) is uncertain; if we omit the article before ἱερά, it would be necessary to translate 'thou didst know sacred writings,' γράμματα being used as at John v. 47, vii. 16. But τὰ ἱερὰ γράμματα is a quasi-technical expression in Philo (*Vit. Mos.* III. 39 and *Fragm. in Exod.* Mangey's ed. II. 657, and cp. *de Vit. cont.* 3) and in Josephus (*Ant.* Proem. 3 and x. 10. 4) for the Scriptures of the Old Testament[1], and, when this is borne in mind, the manuscript attestation to τά seems amply sufficient.

[1] Of Christian writers, the first to apply this phrase to the N.T. is Clement of Alexandria (*Strom.* I. 20 § 98); he is also the first to call the N.T. θεόπνευστος (*Strom.* VII. 16 § 101).

This is the only place in the N.T. where the epithet ἱερός, *sacer*, 'hallowed' or 'sacred,' as contrasted with *profane* (a quite different adjective from ἅγιος, *sanctus*, 'holy,' which points to the work of the Divine Spirit), is applied to Scripture; but it is frequently so applied both before and after the Apostolic age. Cp. e.g. 2 Macc. viii. 23, τὴν ἱερὰν βίβλον, and Clem. Rom. § 53 τὰς ἱερὰς γραφάς &c.

τὰ δυνάμενά σε σοφίσαι εἰς σωτηρίαν, *which are able to make thee wise unto salvation*. The present participle δυνάμενα expresses the continuous and abiding power of Scripture; it is not only fitted σοφίζειν νήπια (Ps. xix. 8), but it is as valuable to Timothy the bishop as to Timothy the child: cp. Ps. cxix. 98. The words εἰς σωτηρίαν are important, as clearly expressing the *kind* of wisdom which Scripture supplies. The significance of the O.T. is not that it contains an account of the creation of man or the history of the fortunes of Israel; its aim is not *knowledge*, whether scientific or historical, but *wisdom*, and that εἰς σωτηρίαν. σωτηρία, the Salvation of man, is the final purpose of the whole Bible. On this great theme it tells enough to make men wise; it contains "all things necessary to salvation" (Art. vi.), and so candidates for the priesthood are required at ordination to declare in the words of the Apostle their persuasion that "the holy Scriptures contain sufficiently all doctrine required of necessity for eternal salvation through faith in Jesus Christ." "If we be ignorant," say the Translators of our A.V. to their readers, "they will instruct us; if out of the way, they will bring us home; if out of order, they will reform us; if in heaviness, comfort us; if dull, quicken us; if cold, inflame us. *Tolle, lege; tolle, lege.*"

διὰ πίστεως τῆς ἐν Χριστῷ Ἰησοῦ. Faith in Christ Jesus (see 1 Tim. iii. 13) is the instrument, as it were, through which the σωτηρία, expounded in Scripture, may be grasped. And this limiting clause provides at once the link between O.T. and N.T., so that what St Paul said to Timothy about the O.T. may also be applied to the N.T., "the difference between them consisting in this, that the Old did make wise by teaching salvation through Christ that should come, the New by teaching that Christ the Saviour is come" (Hooker, *E. P.* I. xiv. 4).

16. πᾶσα γραφὴ θεόπνευστος κ.τ.λ. We have to fix the meaning of γραφή here, before we examine the construction. Is it simply equivalent to 'writing' or does it mean 'Scripture,' in the special sense in which that word was applied in the Apostolic age to the O.T. as a whole or to passages from it? Despite the absence of the article, the latter meaning seems determined, not only by the context, but by the usage of the word throughout the N.T. In all the passages (some fifty) in which the word occurs (in four without the article, viz. John xix. 37 ἑτέρα γραφή; Rom. i. 2 γραφαὶ ἅγιαι; Rom. xvi. 26 γραφαὶ προφητικαί; 2 Pet. i. 20 πᾶσα προφητεία γραφῆς) it is invariably applied to the O.T., and we therefore must apply it thus in the verse before us. The next point is the true rendering of πᾶσα γραφή. The absence of the article assures us that we must render 'every Scripture' and not (with the A.V.) 'all Scripture'; the thought is not of the O.T. regarded as an organic whole, but of every individual ' Scripture' therein.

We come then to the construction of the sentence, the primary question being, Is θεόπνευστος an epithet attached to the subject γραφή, or is it a predicate? The A.V. and some modern interpreters (Calvin, de Wette, &c.) take it in the latter way, and there is no *grammatical* objection to the translation "Every Scripture is inspired by God and is profitable &c.," the καί being simply copulative. But to introduce at this point a *direct* statement of the θεοπνευστία of the O.T., which is not here questioned, seems quite irrelevant to the context. *V.* 16 is strictly parallel to *v.* 15; the ἱερὰ γράμματα are able to make wise unto salvation; [for] every Scripture inspired by God is profitable also for &c., καί having an *ascensive* force (cp. 1 Tim. iv. 4). It is the *profitableness* of the O.T. which St Paul would press upon Timothy, not its *inspiration*, of which he had been assured from his youth. It is better, therefore, to follow the interpretation of Origen, the Vulgate and Syriac Versions, Luther &c. (also adopted in the older English translations of Wiclif, Tyndale, Coverdale and Cranmer, and in our R.V.), and to render *every Scripture inspired by God is profitable also for teaching* &c.

θεόπνευστος does not occur again in LXX. or N.T., but is a common Greek word; it is well rendered by the Vulgate *divinitus inspirata*, its meaning being passive, *inspired by God*, not active. It supplies no theory as to the manner or measure of inspiration, but felicitously sums up the truth expressed in 2 Pet. i. 21, ὑπὸ πνεύματος ἁγίου φερόμενοι ἐλάλησαν ἀπὸ θεοῦ ἄνθρωποι.

καὶ ὠφέλιμος. See the critical note, and cp. 1 Tim. iv. 8.

πρὸς διδασκαλίαν, *for teaching*, sc. for teaching him who reads it. It is the instruction which it gives to the individual Christian, not the help that it affords to him whose office it is to teach others, that is here in question. For διδασκαλία see on 1 Tim. i. 10.

πρὸς ἐλεγμόν, *for reproof*, or confutation; cp. John xvi. 8. The word does not occur again in N.T.; see critical note. Keble expresses the main idea well:

> "Eye of God's word! where'er we turn
> Ever upon us! thy keen gaze
> Can all the depths of sin discern,
> Unravel every bosom's maze[1]."

πρὸς ἐπανόρθωσιν, *for correction*, sc. in reference to conduct. Like ἐλεγμός, this is ἅπ. λεγ. in N.T. but is a LXX. word.

πρὸς παιδίαν τὴν ἐν δικαιοσύνῃ, *for discipline which is in righteousness*, δικαιοσύνη (see on 1 Tim. vi. 11) being the atmosphere in which the discipline is exercised.

17. ἵνα ἄρτιος ᾖ ὁ τοῦ θεοῦ ἄνθρωπος, *that the man of God may be complete*. The phrase 'man of God' is used quite generally, as in

[1] *Christian Year*, St Bartholomew's Day.

Philo (*de mut. nom.* 3), of any devout person, and has no reference to Timothy's official position; see further on 1 Tim. vi. 11. ἄρτιος is a common Greek word, but does not happen to occur again in the Greek Bible.

πρὸς πᾶν ἔργον ἀγαθὸν ἐξηρτισμένος, *furnished completely unto every good work.* ἐξαρτίζω is not used elsewhere by St Paul, but cp. Acts xxi. 5. See on ch. ii. 21 above.

CHAPTER IV.

1. διαμαρτύρομαι. The rec. text inserts οὖν ἐγώ after διαμ. with D₂ᶜKL.

Χρ. Ἰησοῦ. The rec. text has τοῦ Κυρίου Ἰησοῦ Χρ. with D₂ᶜEKL.

κρίνειν. WH put κρῖναι in their margin on the authority of G 17 and a few other cursives; κρῖναι is the reading adopted in all the early Creeds.

καί. For καί before τὴν ἐπιφάνειαν rec. text has κατά with אᶜD₂ᶜEKLP and the Syriac versions; but καί א*ACD₂*G 17, the Bohairic and most forms of the Latin versions. κατά is a correction of the less easy καί.

2. ἐπιτίμησον, παρακάλεσον. This, the rec. order, is adopted by WH and Lachmann with אᶜACD₂EKLP. The order παρακάλεσον, ἐπιτίμησον is followed by Tischendorf in agreement with א*G, the Bohairic and the Latin versions; WH give it a place in their margin.

3. τὰς ἰδίας ἐπιθυμίας. The rec. text has τὰς ἐπιθυμίας τὰς ἰδίας, following KL.

6. τῆς ἀναλύσεώς μου. So אACGP 17: rec. text has τῆς ἐμῆς ἀναλ. with D₂EKL &c.

7. τὸν καλὸν ἀγῶνα. The rec. text has τὸν ἀγῶνα τὸν καλόν, the MS. authorities being divided almost as in the previous verse.

10. ἐγκατέλιπεν. The rec. text has the aorist here as in *vv*. 13, 16, 20, ἀπέλιπον, ἐγκατέλιπον; the imperfect ἐγκατέλειπεν &c. in these places is adopted by WH, with the aorist in the margin. The aorists, which we adopt with Tischendorf, have for their main support only אD₂* as against ACD₂ᶜGLP for the imperfect; but the itacism ει for ι is very common, and the aorists seem required for the sense.

Γαλατίαν. This is the rec. text, and is adopted by WH. Tischendorf and Tregelles read Γαλλίαν with אC, a few cursives, and some MSS. of the Vulgate; apparently an 'Alexandrian' reading. Γαλατία was early applied to Gaul, and as it was so applied in interpretation of this passage (for which see exegetical note), the gloss Γαλλίαν naturally crept into the text.

13. ἀπέλιπον. See above on *v*. 10.

14. ἀποδώσει. This, the reading of אACD₂*E*G &c., must certainly be preferred to the rec. ἀποδῴη of D₂ᶜKL, which appears to have come in from a reminiscence of i. 16, 18.

15. ἀντέστη. So א*ACD₂*G 17. The rec. ἀνθέστηκε is supported by אᶜD₂ᶜEKLP &c.

16. παρεγένετο. The rec. text has the compound form συμπαρ. with אᶜD₂EKLP; the shorter form is preserved in א*ACG 17.

ἐγκατέλιπον. See on *v.* 10.

17. ἀκούσωσιν. The rec. text has ἀκούσῃ with KL.

18. ῥύσεται. The rec. text prefixes καί; it is omitted by אACD₂* 17, the Bohairic and the Latin versions.

19. Ἀκύλαν. The cursives 46 and 109 are reported to add here: Λέκτραν τὴν γυναῖκα αὐτοῦ καὶ Σιμαίαν καὶ Ζήνωνα τοὺς υἱοὺς αὐτοῦ. These are the names of the wife and sons of Onesiphorus according to the Acts of Paul and Thecla; the clause is evidently a gloss on τὸν Ὀνησιφόρου οἶκον which has got into the text.

20. ἀπέλιπον. See on *v.* 10.

21. πάντες. א* 17 omit this word; and it is accordingly placed in brackets by WH.

22. ὁ κύριος. The rec. text adds Ἰησοῦς Χριστός with אᶜD₂EKLP, the Latin, Syriac and Bohairic versions. א*G 17, which we have seen to be a strong combination in this Ep., omit these words as in text.

The rec. text adds at end ἀμήν with אᶜD₂EKLP and most versions; it is omitted by א*ACG 17 f g.

The subscription printed in the received text is: πρὸς Τιμόθεον δευτέρα, τῆς Ἐφεσίων ἐκκλησίας πρῶτον ἐπίσκοπον χειροτονηθέντα, ἐγράφη ἀπὸ Ῥώμης, ὅτε ἐκ δευτέρου παρέστη Παῦλος τῷ Καίσαρι Νέρωνι. This is found substantially in KL and many other MSS. אC 17 have simply πρὸς Τιμόθεον, D₂E have πρ. Τιμοθ. β´ ἐπληρώθη, G has ἐτελέσθη πρ. Τιμ. β´, P has πρ. Τιμ. β´ ἐγράφει ἀπὸ Ῥώμης. A has πρ. Τ. β´ ἐγράφη ἀπὸ Λαοδικείας. See *Introd.* p. xxxii.

1—5. CHARGE III. BE DILIGENT IN THE DUTIES OF YOUR OFFICE.

1. διαμαρτύρομαι ἐνώπιον τοῦ θεοῦ, *I solemnly charge thee in the sight of God.* See note on 1 Tim. v. 21, and cp. the crit. note above. The oath is fourfold: (1) God, (2) Christ, (3) His Second Coming, (4) His Kingdom.

καὶ Χριστοῦ Ἰησοῦ τοῦ μέλλοντος κρίνειν ζῶντας καὶ νεκρούς. See the passages cited in note on 1 Tim. v. 21, and cp. the crit. note above. The clause κρῖναι ζῶντας καὶ νεκροὺς is found in all the early Creeds, which reproduce the words of this verse; compare Acts x. 42, 1 Pet. iv. 5. The 'quick and the dead' are to be understood literally (cp. 1 Thess. iv. 16, 17); refined interpretations which explain the words of *spiritual* life and death are quite out of place and unnecessary.

καὶ τὴν ἐπιφάνειαν αὐτοῦ, *and by His appearing*, "per adventum ipsius" (Vulg.). τὴν ἐπιφάνειαν and τὴν βασιλείαν in the next clauses are accusatives of adjuration (as at 1 Thess. v. 27); cp. Deut. iv. 26. Through a misunderstanding of this, the rec. text has the correction κατά for καί; see crit. note.   For ἐπιφάνεια see on 1 Tim. vi. 14.

καὶ τὴν βασιλείαν αὐτοῦ, *and by His Kingdom*, the repetition of αὐτοῦ adding emphasis and forbidding us to regard the expression as a hendiadys, 'the manifestation of His Kingdom' or the like.

2. κήρυξον κ.τ.λ.   In the parallel passage, 1 Tim. v. 21, διαμαρτύρομαι κ.τ.λ. is followed by ἵνα with the subjunctive; here it is followed by a series of aorist imperatives. For such general precepts the *present* imperative is usual, but here we have the aorist, as the thought is of a line of conduct to be terminated at a definite epoch which is in view[1], viz. the Second Advent of Christ.

κήρυξον τὸν λόγον, *proclaim the word*, sc. of God (ii. 9).   ὁ λόγος is here used for ὁ λόγος τοῦ θεοῦ, the Divine message of the Gospel, as in Gal. vi. 6, Col. iv. 3 (see Additional Note on 1 Tim. iv. 5).

ἐπίστηθι εὐκαίρως ἀκαίρως, *be instant in season, out of season*, sc. not only in regard to preaching, but to all the duties of your important office.   Paul does not use εὐκαίρως elsewhere (but cp. 1 Cor. xvi. 12 εὐκαιρεῖσθαι), nor ἀκαίρως (but cp. Phil. iv. 10 ἀκαιρεῖσθαι); the oxymoron is rendered well by the Latins, *opportune, importune.*   The precept must be interpreted in practice so as not to do violence to that other precept μὴ δῶτε τὸ ἅγιον τοῖς κυσίν (Matt. vii. 6).

ἔλεγξον, *reprove*, rather than 'bring to the proof,' the marginal alternative of the R.V.; cp. 1 Tim. v. 20.   The apparent parallelism between the clauses of this verse and those of iii. 16 is not to be pressed.

ἐπιτίμησον, παρακάλεσον, *rebuke, exhort* (see crit. note for the order of words).   The verb ἐπιτιμᾶν is not used again by St Paul (cp. 2 Cor. ii. 6 ἐπιτιμία), but it is the regular N.T. word for 'to rebuke.'   For παρακαλεῖν, παράκλησις, see on 1 Tim. i. 3, iv. 13.

ἐν πάσῃ μακροθυμίᾳ.   See note on 1 Tim. i. 16; this and the following διδαχῇ qualify the three preceding imperatives.   Rebuke must be ἐν μακροθυμίᾳ, it being borne in mind that ἡ ἀγάπη μακροθυμεῖ (1 Cor. xiii. 4).

καὶ διδαχῇ.   Rebuke and exhortation must be accompanied with *teaching*, or they will be unprofitable.   Evil and falsehood are less effectually dispelled by controversy than by the presentation of the good and the true.

3. ἔσται γὰρ καιρὸς κ.τ.λ., *for the time will come &c.*; there is need of zeal and instant labour, for the time will come when men will not listen to the truth.   Work therefore while it is day.

---

[1] See this illustrated in Blass, *Grammar of N. T. Greek*, § 58. 2.

ὅτε τῆς ὑγιαινούσης διδασκαλίας οὐκ ἀνέξονται, *when they will not endure the wholesome doctrine*, when there will be a general impatience of the dogmas of the Christian revelation. For 'the wholesome doctrine' see note on 1 Tim. i. 10.

ἀλλὰ κατὰ τὰς ἰδίας ἐπιθυμίας, *but after their own arbitrary lusts.* ἰδίας expresses the caprice with which the men of the future will catch at new theories.

ἑαυτοῖς ἐπισωρεύσουσιν διδασκάλους, *will heap to themselves teachers,* sc. rejecting the teaching of the Church through her ministers. Again the idea of personal caprice is suggested by ἑαυτοῖς. ἐπισωρεύειν, from ἐπὶ, σωρός a mound (cp. iii. 6), is *to heap together,* and is (perhaps) used in an ironical sense. It is ἅπ. λεγ. in the Greek Bible, but is found in Plutarch and other good writers.

κνηθόμενοι τὴν ἀκοήν, *having itching ears,* the admirable rendering of the English versions, ultimately derived from Wiclif; τὴν ἀκοήν is the accus. of nearer definition. κνήθειν (not found elsewhere in the Greek Bible) is 'to scratch,' and in the passive 'to be scratched, or tickled.' The phrase ironically describes those persons (to be found in every age and country) who desire to hear (note that it is not said of the *teachers*) what is new and piquant, rather than what is true.

4. καὶ ἀπὸ μὲν τῆς ἀληθείας τὴν ἀκοὴν ἀποστρέψουσιν κ.τ.λ., *and will turn away their ears from the truth, and will turn themselves aside to the myths.* On the μῦθοι see the notes on 1 Tim. i. 4, iv. 7; the definite article here suggests that it is not myths or fables in general which are in the writer's mind, but *the* myths against which he has previously warned Timothy, as part of the stock-in-trade of the heretical teachers of the future. For the verb ἐκτρέπεσθαι see on 1 Tim. i. 6, v. 15.

5. σὺ δὲ νῆφε ἐν πᾶσιν, *but do you,* in contrast with these aspirants after novelty (cp. iii. 10 above), *be sober in all things.* νήφειν, 'to be sober,' (not 'to be watchful,') is a Pauline word; cp. 1 Thess. v. 6, 8 and 1 Tim. iii. 2 νηφάλιος, 2 Tim. ii. 26 ἀνανήφειν. So Ignatius writes to Polycarp (§ 2) νῆφε ὡς θεοῦ ἀθλητής, sobriety being an important preparatory discipline for him who would be victor in the Christian struggle. It is *possible* that the same idea is here behind St Paul's words, for *vv.* 7, 8 take up the idea of the Christian course as an ἀγών and a δρόμος; but it is not required by the immediate context.

κακοπάθησον, *suffer hardness.* Cp. ch. i. 8, ii. 3.

ἔργον ποίησον εὐαγγελιστοῦ, *do the work of an evangelist.* The title εὐαγγελιστής is only found in N.T. here, Acts xxi. 8; Eph. iv. 11; and it is most probable that it is used of one who performs a distinct *work,* rather than of one who is a member of a distinct *order.* In the list at Eph. iv. 11, *evangelists* are mentioned after *apostles* and *prophets,* and before *pastors* and *teachers,* which would suggest that their function was intermediate between that of the apostles and the *local* ministers of the Christian communities. It was, in short, κηρύσσειν τὸν λόγον (*v.* 2), 'to preach the gospel,' to tell the facts of the Christian story. As a distinct order it does not appear in the Apostolic Fathers or the *Didache*, and we are not to suppose that the office of Timothy was in all respects like that of a εὐαγγελιστής of later times, when the *evangelist* was identical with the ἀναγνώστης or *reader*. In the half-organized condition of the Church which the Pastoral Epistles depict, there would necessarily be an overlapping of function, and the duty of 'preaching the word' would devolve on occasion on every Christian, from the Apostles down. It was truly said "Omnis apostolus evangelista, non omnis evangelista apostolus." And thus Timothy was directed, as a part (though not the whole) of his duty, to 'do the work of an evangelist,' εὐαγγελίζεσθαι, which St Paul counted the main purpose of his own commission (1 Cor. i. 17).

τὴν διακονίαν σου πληροφόρησον, *fulfil thy ministry.* As at 1 Tim. i. 12, (where see note), διακονία is used quite generally, and not in the special sense of 'the office of a deacon'; cp. Rom. xii. 7 and Eph. iv. 12, εἰς ἔργον διακονίας. The force of the verb πληροφορεῖν here should not be mistaken. It is not "make full proof of," as the A.V., or as Calvin "ministerium tuum probatum redde," but simply 'fulfil,' like πληροῦν (as it is in Luke i. 1); cp. Acts xii. 25, πληρώσαντες τὴν διακονίαν, and Col. iv. 17. St Paul elsewhere (Rom. iv. 21, xiv. 5; Col. iv. 12) uses it in the sense of *convince*, but that meaning will not suit the context here or at v. 17.

6—8. THE END OF THE APOSTLE'S COURSE.

6. ἐγὼ γὰρ ἤδη σπένδομαι. *For I am already being poured out,* sc. as a libation. γάρ supplies the connexion with the preceding injunction, which gathers solemnity and emphasis from the fact that St Paul is conscious that this is his last charge; ἐγὼ γάρ is in contrast with σὺ δέ of v. 5. σπένδομαι is correctly rendered *delibor* in the Vulgate; the metaphor is probably suggested by that part of the Jewish ritual in which the sacrifice was accompanied by a drink-offering of wine, σπείσεις σπονδὴν σίκερα κυρίῳ (Num. xxviii. 7). Lightfoot (*in* Phil. ii. 17) notes that Seneca regarded his death in a similar light: "respergens proximos servorum, addita voce libare se liquorem illum Jovi liberatori" (Tac. *Ann.* xv. 64). Ignatius (*Rom.* 2) has the same idea πλέον μοι μὴ παράσχησθε τοῦ σπονδισθῆναι θεῷ, ὡς ἔτι θυσιαστήριον ἕτοιμόν ἐστιν.

The contrast between St Paul's hope of release when writing his letter to the Philippians and his calm expectation of death when engaged on this Epistle comes out well at this point, the verbal similarities of expression being particularly interesting when we remember that Timothy to whom he writes *this* letter was with him when he wrote to the Philippians. At Phil. ii. 17 we have ἀλλὰ εἰ καὶ σπένδομαι ἐπὶ τῇ θυσίᾳ, but the hypothetical is here changed for a categorical statement ἐγὼ γὰρ ἤδη σπένδομαι, *I am already being poured out* (not, as in the A.V., "I am now ready to be offered"). Again in Phil. i. 23 we find τὴν ἐπιθυμίαν ἔχων εἰς τὸ ἀναλῦσαι, but here ὁ καιρὸς τῆς ἀναλύσεώς μου ἐφέστηκεν. And at Phil. iii. 13, 14 he speaks of himself as not yet having apprehended but still pressing forward to the goal, while in *v.* 7 of this chapter he has 'finished his course.'

ὁ καιρὸς τῆς ἀναλύσεώς μου ἐφέστηκεν, *and the time of my departure is come.* The noun ἀνάλυσις does not occur elsewhere in the Greek Bible, but the verb ἀναλύειν is common in the later Apocryphal books in the sense of 'to depart.' Primarily it means 'to unloose,' and so it is used (as at 2 Macc. ix. 1) of breaking up an encampment, and elsewhere (as in Luke xii. 36) of leaving a feast, and again (as in Homer *Od.* xv. 548) of loosing from moorings. There can be no doubt that *departure,* not *dissolution,* is the meaning of ἀνάλυσις here, and that the Vulgate *resolutio* is a wrong translation. Cp. Philo (*in Flaccum* 21), τὴν ἐκ τοῦ βίου τελευταίαν ἀνάλυσιν, and Clement (§ 44) of the blessed dead, τελείαν ἔσχον τὴν ἀνάλυσιν. See crit. note.

ἐφέστηκεν seems to mean *is come* rather than 'is at hand,' as the A.V. has it. It is strictly parallel to ἤδη σπένδομαι, *I am already being poured out.*

7. τὸν καλὸν ἀγῶνα ἠγώνισμαι. See the critical note, and cp. the note on 1 Tim. vi. 12, where the metaphor is discussed. The καλὸς ἀγών would seem from the parallel 1 Tim. vi. 12 to be 'the good fight *of faith,*' but as we have τὴν πίστιν τετήρηκα a little lower down, it is possible that the struggle in the Apostle's thought here is that involved in the due discharge of his Apostolic office.

τὸν δρόμον τετέλεκα, *I have finished the race,* the general metaphor of the games passing into the special one of the race-course. St Paul had thus spoken of his own ministry to the Ephesian elders, ὡς τελειώσω τὸν δρόμον μου καὶ τὴν διακονίαν ἣν ἔλαβον (Acts xx. 24).

τὴν πίστιν τετήρηκα, *I have kept the faith,* viz. the Christian Creed, regarded as a sacred deposit of doctrine. Cp. ch. i. 14 and the note on 1 Tim. i. 19. For the tone and spirit of the Apostle here see the note on ch. iii. 10 above.

8. λοιπὸν ἀπόκειταί μοι κ.τ.λ. *Henceforth is laid up for me the crown of righteousness.*

λοιπὸν is used here (as at Acts xxvii. 20) in its strict sense of *from this time forward, henceforth, for the time that remains*; it is sometimes used in a looser sense to introduce a clause, = 'moreover,' 'finally' &c. (1 Cor. i. 16, iv. 2; 2 Cor. xiii. 11; 1 Thess. iv. 1 &c.).

For the use of ἀπόκεισθαι cp. Col. i. 5, διὰ τὴν ἐλπίδα τὴν ἀποκειμένην ὑμῖν ἐν τοῖς οὐρανοῖς, and 2 Macc. xii. 45.

ὁ τῆς δικαιοσύνης στέφανος, *the crown of righteousness,* sc. (probably) the crown appropriate to the righteous man, and belonging to righteousness. The force of the gen. would thus be quite different from that which it has in 'the crown of life' (Jas. i. 12 ; Rev. ii. 10) or 'the crown of glory' (1 Pet. v. 4). If we take these phrases as strictly parallel, the reward spoken of here would be righteousness, *as* a crown. See the note on 1 Tim. vi. 12.

ὃν ἀποδώσει μοι ὁ κύριος ἐν ἐκείνῃ τῇ ἡμέρᾳ, *which the Lord,* sc. Christ, *will give to me in that day,* sc. the day of the last Judgement.

For ἀποδιδόναι in such a context cp. Rom. ii. 6; ἀπό suggests the idea of requital or reward. For the phrase ἐκείνη ἡ ἡμέρα cp. i. 12, 18 and 2 Thess. i. 10.

ὁ δίκαιος κριτής, *the righteous judge.* The title goes back to Ps. vii. 11; cp. also 2 Macc. xii. 6, 41 and 2 Thess. i. 5.

οὐ μόνον δὲ ἐμοὶ ἀλλὰ καὶ κ.τ.λ. For this form of expression cp. 1 Tim. v. 13 and 3 Macc. iii. 23.

πᾶσι τοῖς ἠγαπηκόσι τὴν ἐπιφάνειαν αὐτοῦ, *to all those who have loved,* and do love, *His appearing.* For ἐπιφάνεια see note on 1 Tim. vi. 14. "The remark of Calvin is gravely suggestive; 'e fidelium numero excludit quibus formidabilis est Christi adventus': thus then we may truly say with Leo, 'habemus hic lapidem Lydium, quo examinemus corda nostra'" (Ellicott).

9—12. INVITATION TO TIMOTHY TO COME TO ROME; THE APOSTLE'S LONELINESS.

9. σπούδασον ἐλθεῖν πρός με ταχέως. *Use diligence* (cp. ii. 15, iv. 21; Tit. iii. 12) *to come to me speedily,* sc. as explained in *v.* 21 πρὸ χειμῶνος. St Paul seems to contemplate that Timothy will come, not by the high seas, but (as appears from *v.* 13) by way of Troas, Philippi, the great Egnatian road from Philippi to Dyrrachium, and thence across to Brundisium. This desire to see Timothy again was probably the immediate occasion of the letter being written.

10. Δημᾶς γάρ με ἐγκατέλιπεν κ.τ.λ., *for Demas forsook me, having loved this present world, and went to Thessalonica.* Demas was with Paul during his first Roman imprisonment and was then counted by him as a συνεργός (Philemon 24), and he is coupled in Col. iv. 14 with Luke the beloved physician, though without any commendatory epithet being applied to him. This last circumstance may be significant, in view of his abandonment of the Apostle through unworthy motives, recorded in the verse before us. It is plain from Col. iv. 11, 14 that Demas was not a Jew, and it is just possible that he was a Thessalonian, and that on his departure from Rome for Thessalonica he went home. The name *Demas* is a contracted form of *Demetrius,* which, as Lightfoot has remarked[1], occurs twice in the list of politarchs of Thessalonica; nothing, however, can be built on this, as the name was a common one. Later tradition (e.g. Epiphanius *Haer.* 51) counts Demas an apostate from the Christian faith, but there is no evidence for this. That St Paul felt his departure keenly is plain; but he ascribes to him nothing worse than desire of ease and disinclination to share the peril which association with one already marked out for martyrdom would involve. The reading ἐγκατέλιπεν (see crit. note) has been adopted with some hesitation; but it seems necessary to the sense and points to a severance of his connexion with St Paul at a definite crisis of which we have no precise information.

[1] *Biblical Essays,* p. 247 n.

ἀγαπήσας τὸν νῦν αἰῶνα. The participle is causal; 'he forsook me, *because* he loved &c.' For the phrase ὁ νῦν αἰών see on 1 Tim. vi. 17; Demas *loved this present world*, and so is markedly contrasted with those who love '*the* ἐπιφάνεια of Christ' (*v.* 8). Polycarp (§ 9) takes up the phrase in his description of Ignatius, Paul and other martyrs, and says of them οὐ γὰρ τὸν νῦν ἠγάπησαν αἰῶνα.

Κρήσκης εἰς Γαλατίαν. It is very doubtful whether the Galatia referred to is *Asiatic Galatia* or *Gaul*, which was generally called Γαλατία by Greek writers in the first century[1]. In favour of the latter view the various readings Γαλλία (see crit. note) and the traditional interpretation of the passage (Eus. *H. E.* iii. 4, Epiphanius, Theodore, Theodoret &c.) must be reckoned with, and the R.V. places *Gaul* in the margin as an alternative translation. Crescens, too (of whom nothing is known save the fact recorded here), was early counted the founder of the Churches of Vienne and Mayence. On the other hand, St Paul elsewhere uses *Galatia* (1 Cor. xvi. 1) and *Galatians* in reference to the Asiatic province and its people; and, further, all the other persons mentioned in this chapter as having left him, went *eastward*. On these grounds, we hold that it is better to understand Γαλατία here of Galatia in Asia. It is worth noting that exactly the same ambiguity meets us in 1 Macc. viii. 2, where the Revisers render ἐν τοῖς Γαλάταις, *among the Gauls*, and where again the context does not determine with certainty the locality intended.

Τίτος εἰς Δαλματίαν. It would seem probable from this that Titus had been at Rome with St Paul for a time during his second imprisonment. Dalmatia is a part of Illyria on the eastern coast of the Adriatic; and this notice harmonises well enough with Titus iii. 12 (see note there).

11. Λουκᾶς ἐστὶν μόνος μετ' ἐμοῦ, *only Luke is with me*; i.e. Luke is the only one of his intimate friends and usual companions who is still with him. St Luke's affection for St Paul is not like that of Demas; he remains with him to the end. During his first imprisonment he was by his side, ὁ ἰατρὸς ὁ ἀγαπητός (Col. iv. 14; cp. Philemon 24), and he now appears again, faithful to the last.

Μάρκον ἀναλαβὼν ἄγε μετὰ σεαυτοῦ. *Having taken up Mark*, sc. on your way hither (cp. Acts xx. 13 for this use of ἀναλαμβάνειν), *bring him with you*. There had been a time (Acts xv. 38) when Paul had little confidence in Mark, because he had turned back to Jerusalem just as the difficulties of Paul's first missionary journey became apparent (Acts xiii. 13). But such feelings of distrust had long since passed away. During the first Roman imprisonment we find him with St Paul at Rome (Col. iv. 10), and he was commended by that Apostle to the Church of Colossae when he should visit it. He is also found in St Peter's company at Rome (1 Pet. v. 13), and he joins in the salutation addressed to Churches in the Asiatic provinces. It is probable that at the time of writing 2 *Timothy* he was somewhere

---

[1] See, for a full discussion, Lightfoot, *Galatians*, pp. 3, 31.

on the coast in the Province of Asia proper, and that thus Timothy could 'pick him up' on his way northward.

ἔστιν γάρ μοι εὔχρηστος εἰς διακονίαν, *for he is useful to me for ministering.* διακονία may be understood either of personal service to St Paul, such as a free man could offer to a captive, a young man to an old one, or else (less probably) of the ministry of the gospel in which Mark could usefully take his part. That he probably had a knowledge of Latin might make his services in either capacity specially valuable at Rome. For the adjective εὔχρηστος cp. ch. ii. 21.

12. Τυχικὸν δὲ ἀπέστειλα εἰς ˝Εφεσον. Tychicus (an ʼΑσιανός, Acts xx. 4) comes before us several times as a trusted emissary of St Paul. Towards the close of Paul's third missionary journey he preceded Paul to Troas (Acts xx. 4). We hear of him again as the bearer of the letters to Colossae (Col. iv. 7, 8, where he is described as ὁ ἀγαπητὸς ἀδελφὸς καὶ πιστὸς διάκονος καὶ σύνδουλος ἐν Κυρίῳ) and to "the Ephesians" (Eph. vi. 21), which were written during St Paul's first captivity at Rome. In Tit. iii. 12 the possibility of his being sent by Paul to Crete is mentioned. And now we learn that among St Paul's last official acts was the sending Tychicus to Ephesus, probably either as the bearer of this second Ep. to Timothy (for ἀπέστειλα may well be an epistolary aorist; cp. Col. iv. 8), or to take Timothy's place during his projected visit to Rome to cheer the Apostle's last days. Either motive for this mission of Tychicus is plausible; neither is certain. But even if both be excluded, there is nothing in the remark 'I sent Tychicus to Ephesus' which can fairly require the inference that Timothy was not at Ephesus at the time of writing. St Paul is explaining how it was that of all his intimate friends only Luke is with him, and among others he mentions that Tychicus has gone to Ephesus, an observation not at all inconsistent (though some have found it so) with the fact that the letter is being sent to Timothy *at* Ephesus.

13. Instructions to Timothy, (14, 15) and a warning.

13. τὸν φελόνην. This is the orthography followed by the best MSS.: the word φελόνης seems to be an incorrect form of φαινόλης = Latin *paenula* (the rendering here of the Latin versions). The meaning of the term has been variously explained. Chrysostom mentions, but does not favour, the translation adopted by the Peshito version, which takes φελόνης as equivalent to γλωσσόκομον or 'a case for books.' And, as a matter of fact, the vellum wrapper with which a papyrus roll was encased to protect it was called a φαινόλης or *paenula.* But to adopt the rendering 'book-cover' here seems to be an entire misapprehension, suggested by the mention of the books and parchments in the next clause of the verse. The primary meaning is that adopted by Chrysostom (*in Phil.* Hom. 1) and Tertullian (*de orat.* 12), viz. that φελόνης = *paenula* = a travelling cloak with long sleeves, such as would be specially desirable in cold weather. From the fact that φαινόλιον is often used (e.g. in the Liturgy of St Chrysostom) for *a chasuble*, some ingeniously perverse commentators have here translated φελόνης thus, and so find Scriptural authority for ecclesiastical vestments! This does not need refutation. φελόνης is *a cloak*, such a large outer cloak as is serviceable in winter (*v.* 21).

ὃν ἀπέλιπον ἐν Τρῳάδι παρὰ Κάρπῳ, *which I left in Troas at the house of Carpus*. Nothing is known of Carpus, beside this notice. The visit to Troas alluded to here could not have been the one recorded at Acts xx. 6, for that was six years before the time of writing, and the language used suggests a recent visit. It must have taken place in the period of freedom between the first and second imprisonments at Rome, to which allusion is also made in *v.* 20. See *Introd.* chap. ii.

καὶ τὰ βιβλία, μάλιστα τὰς μεμβράνας, *and the books, especially the parchments*. μεμβράναι (ἅπ. λεγ. in the Greek Bible) is simply the Latin word *membranae* Graecised, and means the prepared skins of vellum, which gradually superseded papyrus for writing purposes. In the first century vellum would only be used for the more precious codices and documents, papyrus serving for ordinary books and letters, which sufficiently explains the μάλιστα. It is, of course, impossible to determine what these books and parchments contained; we may suppose the Books of the O. T. Scriptures, and (possibly) the diploma of Paul's Roman citizenship, to have been among them, but we have nothing to go on.

Farrar notes an interesting parallel in the history of William Tyndale, who when in captivity at Vilvorde in 1535, wrote to the governor to beg for warmer clothing, a woollen shirt and, above all, his Hebrew Bible, Grammar, and Dictionary[1].

14. Ἀλέξανδρος ὁ χαλκεύς. See note on 1 Tim. i. 20.

πολλά μοι κακὰ ἐνεδείξατο, *did me*, sc. publicly, *much evil*. Cp. for ἐνδείκνυσθαι, 1 Tim. i. 16 &c. It would seem from the context that it was at Rome during the Apostle's imprisonment that Alexander's ill-will had been displayed. The warning in *v.* 15 ὃν καὶ σὺ φυλάσσου would seem to give the reason of his being mentioned. Whether he was now at Ephesus, or whether it was in view of Timothy's meeting him at Rome that the warning was given, we have no means of determining. St Ephraem (on 2 Cor. xii. 7) notes the curious tradition that "Alexander the coppersmith" was Paul's "thorn in the flesh"!

ἀποδώσει αὐτῷ ὁ κύριος κατὰ τὰ ἔργα αὐτοῦ. The reading of the rec. text (see crit. note) would make this an imprecation. As it stands, it is a parenthetical quotation of the familiar words of Ps. lxii. (lxi.) 12 (cp. also Prov. xxiv. 12), and merely amounts to the reflection 'I leave him to God.' St Paul quotes these words in another context at Rom. ii. 6.

15. λίαν γὰρ ἀντέστη τοῖς ἡμετέροις λόγοις, *for he greatly withstood our words*. The aorist (see crit. note) shews that the reference is to a definite act or acts of hostility, rather than to a long-continued attitude

[1] Demaus' *Life of Tyndale*, p. 475.

of ill-will, and thus it is not improbable that the ἡμέτεροι λόγοι which Alexander opposed were part of Paul's ἀπολογία, when on his trial. Another explanation is that the 'words' were 'the words of the Gospel,' which St Paul preached. But this is not really inconsistent with the other hypothesis, for St Paul's ἀπολογία amounted to a κήρυγμα τοῦ εὐαγγελίου (cp. *v.* 17).

16—18. The Apostle's loneliness, and his faith.

16. ἐν τῇ πρώτῃ μου ἀπολογίᾳ κ.τ.λ. Eusebius (*H.E.* ii. 22) refers this to St Paul's first imprisonment, which was followed by release; but what is here told would not suit the circumstances of that less severe trial. The allusion is apparently to what was called in Roman law the *prima actio.* While this was being heard *no man stood forward for him,* whether in friendly sympathy, or (more probably) as his official *patronus* or *advocatus.* Paul had to plead his cause alone. *All deserted him* (the aorist tense ἐγκατέλιπον is again significant); they abandoned him, through fear (see *v.* 10), when the crisis came. *May it not be reckoned to them!* God forgive their weakness!

17. ὁ δὲ κύριός μοι παρέστη, *but,* in contrast to man's unfaithfulness, *the Lord,* sc. Christ, *stood by me.*

καὶ ἐνεδυνάμωσέν με, *and strengthened me.* See, for St Paul's use of this verb, the note on 1 Tim. i. 12.

ἵνα δι' ἐμοῦ τὸ κήρυγμα πληροφορηθῇ, *in order that by me the preaching,* sc. of the Gospel, *might be fulfilled.* For πληροφορέω see on *v.* 5 above; its force here is not 'be fully known,' as the A.V. has it, but 'be fully performed, completed, fulfilled.' How this was true is explained by the next clause καὶ ἀκούσωσιν πάντα τὰ ἔθνη. The opportunity given to St Paul of pleading his cause in the official centre of Rome, the mistress of the nations, was in a sense the 'fulfilling' of the preaching of the Gospel. For ἀκούσωσιν (certainly the right reading) see the crit. note.

καὶ ἐρύσθην ἐκ στόματος λέοντος, *and I was rescued out of the mouth of the lion.* That is, a verdict of *non liquet* was returned at the *prima actio,* and Paul was respited for the time. The phrase is evidently borrowed from the Greek Bible; it was said, e.g., of Daniel that he was rescued ἐκ στόματος τῶν λεόντων; cp. also Ps. xxii. (xxi.) 21; Dan. vi. 20. But interpreters have been anxious to find a more definite allusion in the words ἐκ στόματος λέοντος. Thus (*a*) the λέων has been understood to be the lion of the amphitheatre to whom the martyrs were thrown. The cry *Christianos ad leonem* rises to one's thoughts. But, after all, this was *not* the death with which St Paul was threatened, as the sequel proved. (*b*) The Greek commentators generally understand the λέων to be Nero, and if St Paul's trial really took place before that Emperor (for we have no certainty that Nero was in Rome at this moment), this would give a vivid meaning to ἐκ στόματος λέοντος. A parallel is found in Josephus, where the death of Tiberius is announced to Agrippa in the words τέθνηκεν ὁ λέων (*Antt.* xviii. 6. 10). But the absence of the article here before λέοντος makes this explanation very improbable. (c) *The lion* has been identified with *Satan.* Paul did not yield to weakness or betray the faith at the supreme moment of his trial, and he is thus said to have been rescued from the mouth of the lion, sc. the great ἀντίδικος, the devil, who is ὡς λέων ὠρυόμενος (1 Pet. v. 8). And the fact that there are apparent reminiscences of the phrases in the Lord's Prayer in *v.* 18 gives a certain attractiveness to the identification in *v.* 17 of the *lion* out of whose mouth Paul was *delivered* with the πονηρός, the Evil One. Again, however, the absence of the definite article before λέοντος is a difficulty. We are inclined therefore, on the whole, to take the phrase ῥύεσθαι ἐκ στόματος λέοντος as almost proverbial, as expressive of deliverance out of imminent and deadly peril, such as Daniel's story records; and there is thus no place for the identification of the λέων with any individual adversary, human or diabolical.

18. ῥύσεταί με ὁ κύριος ἀπὸ παντὸς ἔργου πονηροῦ. *The Lord,* sc. Christ, *will deliver me from every evil work.* The change of preposition, ἀπό instead of ἐκ, after ῥύεσθαι is significant. ἐκ was used in *v.* 17 because the Apostle was in the very jaws of the lion, before he was rescued; ἀπό is used here, because the evils contemplated are only potential, and the Apostle has not been actually in their thraldom. ἐκ, in short, indicates *emergence from,* ἀπό, *removal from the neighbourhood of,* a danger [1].

The deliverance of which St Paul speaks thus confidently is not a second deliverance 'from the mouth of the lion'; *that,* he knew, he could not expect. But he will be delivered, if not from bodily pain, yet from 'every evil work,' from the opposition of adversaries without and from the conflict with temptation in his own heart. The prayer ῥῦσαι ἡμᾶς ἀπὸ τοῦ πονηροῦ will be fully answered, but it will be by the gate of martyrdom that deliverance shall come. As Bengel has it: "Decollabitur? liberabitur, liberante Domino." Cp. 2 Cor. i. 9, 10.

καὶ σώσει εἰς τὴν βασιλείαν αὐτοῦ τὴν ἐπουράνιον, *and will save me unto His heavenly kingdom,* a 'praegnans constructio' equivalent to 'save me and bring me to,' &c. The faithful martyr is 'saved' in the highest sense, for ὃς δ᾽ ἂν ἀπολέσῃ τὴν ψυχὴν αὐτοῦ ἕνεκεν ἐμοῦ, οὗτος σώσει αὐτήν (Luke ix. 24). The exact phrase ἡ βασιλεία ἡ ἐπουράνιος does not occur again in St Paul (or, indeed, in the N.T.), but it is quite harmonious with his teaching about the Kingdom of Christ. Cp. 1 Cor. xv. 25; Eph. i. 20; Col. iii. 1, and (for the confident hope here expressed by the Apostle) Phil. i. 23, iii. 20.

ᾧ ἡ δόξα εἰς τοὺς αἰῶνας τῶν αἰώνων, ἀμήν, *to Whom,* sc. to Christ, *be glory for ever and ever, Amen.* That the doxology should be addressed to our Lord, rather than to God the Father (as e.g. at Phil. iv. 20), will not surprise the attentive student of St Paul's theology; cp.

---

[1] This is brought out in Chase's *Lord's Prayer in the Early Church,* pp. 71 ff. The parallel between *vv.* 17, 18 and portions of the Lord's Prayer is fully traced at p. 119 ff. of the same work.

especially Rom. IX. 5. For εἰς τοὺς αἰῶνας κ.τ.λ. see note on 1 Tim. i. 17.

The doxology, which was early added at the end of the Lord's Prayer and is incorporated in the received text of St Matt. vi. 13, deserves careful comparison with the verse before us. In the early part of *v.* 18 we saw that a reflection might be traced of the petition 'Deliver us from the evil one,' and we now find that the thought of the heavenly Kingdom and the glory of Christ is derived from the doxology ὅτι σοῦ ἐστιν ἡ βασιλεία καὶ ἡ δύναμις καὶ ἡ δόξα εἰς τοὺς αἰῶνας. Ἀμήν.

19—21. SALUTATIONS.

19. Ἄσπασαι Πρίσκαν καὶ Ἀκύλαν. Aquila, a Jew of Pontus, and his wife Prisca or Priscilla, are first mentioned in the N.T. at Acts xviii. 2. They had left Rome, in consequence of an edict of Claudius, and had come to Corinth, where St Paul met them and lodged with them, as they were, like him, tent-makers. If they were Christians at this time, as would seem probable, they must have been among the earliest members of the Roman Church. St Paul brought them with him to Ephesus, where he left them (Acts xviii. 19), and where (*v.* 26) they gave instruction to Apollos. Along with 'the Church in their house' they send salutations to the Corinthian Christians from Ephesus in 1 Cor. xvi. 19; and we find them again at Rome when St Paul wrote his Epistle to the Romans (xvi. 3). We gather from the verse before us that they returned to Ephesus. Like many Jews of the time, Aquila evidently travelled a great deal, probably for the purposes of his trade. From the fact that Prisca's name precedes that of Aquila in four out of the six places where they are mentioned, it suggests itself that she was a more important person than her husband. It may be that she was a member of a good Roman family, but it seems more probable that both Aquila and Prisca were freed members of some great household. It has been pointed out, e.g., that Priscilla was a name of the women of the Acilian gens. But such identifications hardly admit of proof[1].

καὶ τὸν Ὀνησιφόρου οἶκον. See the critical note, where the traditional names of the wife and sons of Onesiphorus are given. Cp. also the note on i. 16, 17 above.

20. Ἔραστος ἔμεινεν ἐν Κορίνθῳ, *Erastus abode in Corinth*, sc. at some epoch in the interval between the first and second imprisonments, of which we have no information. Erastus was the name of the treasurer (οἰκονόμος) of Corinth, when St Paul wrote to the Romans (xvi. 23); and also of an emissary sent with Timothy from Ephesus to Macedonia (Acts xix. 22). We cannot be sure whether we have here notices of different persons or of one and the same man. It seems however unlikely that the Erastus, whose abiding in Corinth is communicated here to Timothy as a piece of information, was a

[1] A full and interesting note on Aquila and Priscilla will be found in Sanday and Headlam's *Romans*, p. 420 ff.

permanent official of that city; it is more probable that he was Timothy's companion on the journey mentioned in Acts xix. 22.

Τρόφιμον δὲ ἀπέλιπον ἐν Μιλήτῳ ἀσθενοῦντα, *but Trophimus I left* (not 'they left,' as some have rendered) *at Miletus sick.* Of Trophimus we know only what is told here and at Acts xx., xxi. He was a Gentile Christian of Ephesus, who, in company with Tychicus (Acts xx. 5, cp. *v.* 12 above), preceded Paul to Troas. He was seen at Jerusalem in St Paul's society, which led to the riot, in consequence of which Paul was apprehended (Acts xxi. 29). The episode mentioned in this verse must be referred to St Paul's journey in the Levant between his first and second imprisonments (see above *vv.* 12, 13).

The motive for this mention of Erastus and Trophimus, both of whom had connexions with Ephesus, may possibly have been that the Apostle wished to explain that *their* absence from his side at this juncture was not due to unfaithfulness.

21. σπούδασον πρὸ χειμῶνος ἐλθεῖν, *do thy diligence to come before winter*, when travelling would be difficult; cp. Matt. xxiv. 20. See *v.* 9 above.

ἀσπάζεταί σε. The verb in the singular followed by the names of a number of individuals who send salutations is the construction adopted also at Rom. xvi. 21, 23.

Εὔβουλος. Of this person nothing further is known. The names which follow are those, seemingly, of prominent members of the Roman Church; they are not among Paul's intimate friends, for of these 'only Luke' was with him (*v.* 10).

Πούδης καὶ Λίνος καὶ Κλαυδία. Linus is the only one of these three who can be identified with certainty. He was the first bishop of Rome after Apostolic days (Iren. *Haer.* III. 3), and governed the Roman Church, according to tradition, for twelve years after the death of St Peter and St Paul. He seems to be described in *Apost. Const.* VII. 46 as the son of Claudia (Λίνος ὁ Κλαυδίας), but it is probable that this is a mere guess resting on the juxtaposition of their names in this verse.

With the names of Pudens and Claudia modern ingenuity has been very busy. It has been assumed that they were husband and wife, and that they are identical with a dissolute friend of Martial called Aulus Pudens and a British maiden called Claudia Rufina, whose marriage is recorded in an epigram of Martial which appeared in A.D. 88 (*Epigr.* IV. 13). The chronological data are plainly inconsistent with this identification, and indeed the names Pudens and Claudia are sufficiently common to make such speculations highly uncertain. Another husband and wife with these names are recorded, e.g., in an inscription quoted by Lightfoot[1] (*C.I.L.* VI. 15066).

Ingenuity has gone a step further. On an inscription discovered at Chichester it is recorded that one Pudens built a temple there to

---

[1] Lightfoot's *Clement*, I. p. 79, where a full discussion of the matter will be found.

Neptune, with the sanction of the British king Claudius Cogidubnus, and it has been assumed that this Pudens was the Pudens mentioned by Martial, and that his wife Claudia was the daughter of Claudius Cogidubnus. Thus by a series of hypotheses, none of which is susceptible of proof, we reach a direct connexion between early British Christianity and the teaching of St Paul! It is sufficient to say that we know nothing for certain of the Pudens and Claudia mentioned in the verse before us, and that, inasmuch as the name of Linus is interposed between them, it is even improbable that they were husband and wife.

καὶ οἱ ἀδελφοὶ πάντες.   See the crit. note, and cp. 1 Cor. xvi. 20.

22. BENEDICTION.

22. ὁ κύριος μετὰ τοῦ πνεύματός σου.   This is a personal benediction addressed to Timothy, as the Apostle's last word, and it is followed by the σημεῖον ἐν πάσῃ ἐπιστολῇ, viz. ἡ χάρις μεθ᾽ ὑμῶν, on which see the note on 1 Tim. vi. 21. The form of this personal blessing, however, is not quite like anything elsewhere found at the end of St Paul's Epistles (cp. Rom. xv. 33). The nearest parallel to it is perhaps the conclusion of the so-called Epistle of Barnabas, ὁ κύριος τῆς δόξης καὶ πάσης χάριτος μετὰ τοῦ πνεύματος ὑμῶν. It is worth while to compare the words with Gal. vi. 18 and Philem. 25; *there* the presence of 'the grace of the Lord,' *here* the presence of 'the Lord of grace,' is invoked.

ANALYSIS OF THE EPISTLE TO TITUS.

Introductory. Salutation (i. 1—4).

I. *The duties of Titus in reference to the appointment of* πρεσβύτεροι (i. 5).
The qualifications of an ἐπίσκοπος (i. 6—9).

II. *The heretical teachers* and Titus' duty in regard to them (i. 10—16).

III. *Titus' positive teaching* (ii. 1) as regards
  (i) aged men (ii. 2),
  (ii) aged women (ii. 3),
  (iii) young wives (ii. 4, 5).
  (iv) young men (ii. 6—8),
  (v) slaves (ii. 9, 10).
The doctrinal ground of the preceding exhortations (ii. 11—14).
Titus to speak with authority (ii. 15).

IV. *The attitude of Christians to their heathen neighbours and rulers* (iii. 1, 2).
We have no reason for pride, but rather for thankfulness (iii. 3—7).

V. *Final injunctions.*
  (a) Maintain good works (iii. 8).
  (b) Avoid controversy (iii. 9).
  (c) Shun obstinate heretics (iii. 10, 11).

Invitation. Come to me to Nicopolis (iii. 12).
Speed on their journey Zenas and Apollos (iii. 13).
Final charge to the Christians at Crete (iii. 14).

Epilogue. Salutations and
Benediction (iii. 15).

CHAPTER I.

1. Ἰησοῦ Χριστοῦ. Χριστοῦ Ἰησοῦ is the order of A, the Bohairic and Harclean Syriac Versions. Practically all the other authorities support Ἰη. Χριστοῦ, the reading of the rec. text. See crit. note on 1 Tim. i. 1.

4. χάρις καὶ εἰρήνη. This, the usual form of salutation in St Paul's letters (see exegetical note on 1 Tim. i. 2), is supported by ℵC*D₂EGIP and most of the versions; the rec. text (following the analogy of 1 Tim. i. 2 and 2 Tim. i. 1) reads χάρις ἔλεος εἰρήνη with ACᵇKL.

Χριστοῦ Ἰησοῦ. So ℵACD₂*I d e and the Bohairic; the reading of the rec. text κυρίου Ἰησοῦ Χριστοῦ (D₂ᶜEGKLP f g and the Syriac versions) probably arose from a tendency to assimilate the salutation to St Paul's usual form, it not having been observed that here that form is modified by the addition of the words τοῦ σωτῆρος (see exegetical note and note on 1 Tim. i. 2).

5. ἀπέλιπον. So ℵ*D₂*; cp. 2 Tim. iv. 20. WH prefer ἀπέλειπον with ACGI. The rec. text has κατέλιπον with ℵᶜD₂ᶜEK. κατέλειπον is the reading of LP. See exegetical note, and on ch. iii. 13.

ἐπιδιορθώσῃ. This, the rec. reading, is supported by ℵCD₂ᵇEᵇIKLP; AD₂*EG* have ἐπιδιορθώσῃς, which probably arose from assimilation to καταστήσῃς.

10. πολλοί. The rec. text inserts καὶ after πολλοί with D₂EGKL d e f g; but it is unnecessary for the sense and must be omitted as not found in ℵACIP, the Syriac or the Bohairic versions.

ἐκ τῆς περιτομῆς. So ℵCD₂*I, but the rec. text, following the remaining uncials, omits τῆς, perhaps through a reminiscence of ἐκ περιτομῆς (without the article) at Rom. iv. 12; Gal. ii. 12; Col. iv. 11.

11. After χάριν the cursive 109 inserts the gloss τὰ τέκνα οἱ τοὺς ἰδίους γονεῖς ὑβρίζοντες ἢ τύπτοντες ἐπιστόμιζε καὶ ἔλεγχε καὶ νουθέτει ὡς πατὴρ τέκνα, which has no apparent relation to the context. It was probably a gloss about the duties of children, originally appended to *v.* 8 of the next chapter, as advice on the management of *children* would come in appropriately after the discussion of the duties of *wives* and before the consideration of the duties of *slaves* (as in Eph. v., vi.).

12. εἶπέν τις. So the rec. text with the majority of MSS.; ℵ*G f g and the Bohairic version insert δὲ after εἶπεν.

13. ἐν τῇ πίστει. ℵ* omits ἐν, but the authority for its insertion is overwhelming.

15. πάντα. The rec. text (with ℵᶜD₂ᶜKL) adds μέν, possibly because of the δέ in the next clause (cp. Rom. xiv. 20); but it is omitted by ℵ*ACD₂*E*GP and the Latins.

μεμιαμμένοις. This is the spelling of the best MSS.; D₂ᵇᶜE have μεμιασμένοις as in the rec. text.

1—4. SALUTATION.

1. Παῦλος δοῦλος θεοῦ. St Paul does not use this expression else-where, and it is thus an unlikely expression to be used by a forger. Paul calls himself 'the slave of Christ Jesus' or 'of Christ' at Rom. i. 1; Phil. i. 1; Gal. i. 10, which is also the phrase used in 2 Pet. i. 1; Jude 1. St James (i. 1) uses the longer phrase 'a slave of God and of the Lord Jesus Christ.' Cp. Acts xvi. 17; 2 Tim. ii. 24 and Rev. xv. 3.

ἀπόστολος δὲ Ἰησοῦ Χριστοῦ. δέ signifies *and further* &c., this additional specification of his office being specially desirable in an official letter like the present. See on 1 Tim. i. 1, and see the crit. note.

κατὰ πίστιν ἐκλεκτῶν θεοῦ, *according to the faith of God's elect.* κατά cannot mean simply *secundum* (Vg.), for the standard of St Paul's apostleship was something higher even than the faith of the elect. It seems, as in the somewhat similar phrase κατ' ἐπαγγελίαν ζωῆς of 2 Tim. i. 1, to convey the idea of *purpose*, though not so strongly as there; cp. Rom. i. 5. For St Paul's use of the word 'elect' see on 2 Tim. ii. 10.

καὶ ἐπίγνωσιν ἀληθείας τῆς κατ' εὐσέβειαν, *and the knowledge of the truth which is according to godliness.* κατά, in *this* clause, does not convey any suggestion of *purpose*, but of *concomitance* and intimate connexion; it is only in a life of godliness (see on 1 Tim. ii. 2 for εὐσέβεια) that the 'knowledge of the truth' can be fully learnt (see on 1 Tim. vi. 3). For the expression ἐπίγνωσις ἀληθείας see on 1 Tim. ii. 4. The purpose of St Paul's apostolic mission was to perfect the knowledge of the truth, no less than to promote the faith of the elect, of God's chosen.

2. ἐπ' ἐλπίδι ζωῆς αἰωνίου, *in hope of life eternal.* This is the hope in which the labours of the Apostolic ministry are cheerfully endured; cp. 1 Tim. i. 16, vi. 12, and for ἐπί with the dat. see on 1 Tim. iv. 10 and v. 5.

ἣν ἐπηγγείλατο ὁ ἀψευδὴς θεὸς πρὸ χρόνων αἰωνίων, *which* (sc. ζωὴ αἰώνιος) *God, Who cannot lie, promised before times eternal.* The 'promise of life' occupies a prominent place in the salutation here, as at 2 Tim. i. 1; for the 'life' of which 'godliness has the promise,' see on 1 Tim. iv. 8.

The adj. ἀψευδής only occurs elsewhere in the Greek Bible at Wisd. vii. 17; see Heb. vi. 18; Rom. iii. 4 for the thought of God's abiding truth. Cp. also John xiv. 6, where He Who is *the Truth* declares Himself also to be *the Life.*

πρὸ χρόνων αἰωνίων has been understood by some commentators to mean simply 'from ancient times,' and the allusion would thus be to the dim revelations of ζωὴ αἰώνιος which had been vouchsafed in the centuries long precedent to the Incarnation. But it seems better to take the phrase as at 2 Tim. i. 9, *before times eternal.* The promise was made before time was, in the eternal purpose of God.

3. ἐφανέρωσεν δέ. We should expect *but which* (sc. the ζωή) *He manifested*; but the construction suddenly changes and the object of ἐφανέρωσεν is τὸν λόγον αὐτοῦ, the contrast being between the promise of life before times eternal, and the manifestation of the Divine Word in the fulness of time (cp. Eph. i. 10).

For φανερόω see on 1 Tim. iii. 16.

καιροῖς ἰδίοις, *in its own,* sc. appropriate, *seasons.* See the note on the same phrase at 1 Tim. ii. 6 (cp. 1 Tim. vi. 15). Here we render *in its own seasons* rather than (as at 1 Tim. vi. 15) 'in *His* own seasons'; because the point is not the freedom of the Divine choice, but the 'seasonableness' of the Divine Advent.

τὸν λόγον αὐτοῦ. *His word,* sc. the saving message of the Gospel, and not the Incarnate Logos, as appears by the defining ἐν κηρύγματι which follows. See Additional Note on 1 Tim. iv. 5.

ἐν κηρύγματι, *in the message,* sc. the content of the message, not the act of proclaiming it. See on 1 Tim. ii. 7 for Paul's office as κῆρυξ.

ὃ ἐπιστεύθην ἐγώ. St Paul continually repeats this thought, that the preaching of the Gospel is not a self-chosen occupation, but that he has been *entrusted* with it. See Gal. ii. 7; 1 Tim. i. 11; 2 Tim. i. 11.

κατ' ἐπιταγὴν τοῦ σωτῆρος ἡμῶν θεοῦ, *according to the commandment of God our Saviour,* i.e. God the Father. See for this interesting phrase on 1 Tim. i. 1.

4. Τίτῳ γνησίῳ τέκνῳ. *To Titus, true child.* See on 1 Tim. i. 2. It seems not improbable from the application of this phrase to Titus that he had been converted to the faith by St Paul; but we have no certain information on the point. See Gal. ii. 1 ff.

κατὰ κοινὴν πίστιν, *after a common faith,* corresponding to ἐν πίστει of 1 Tim. i. 2. The κοινὴ πίστις is the sphere of their spiritual relationship; cp. κοινὴ σωτηρία in Jude 3.

χάρις καὶ εἰρήνη. Cp. the critical note, and see on 1 Tim. i. 2.

ἀπὸ θεοῦ πατρὸς κ.τ.λ. See the critical note. The exact title Χριστοῦ Ἰησοῦ τοῦ σωτῆρος ἡμῶν does not occur in the salutation of any other of the Pauline Epistles; and is only found elsewhere 2 Tim. i. 10; Tit. ii. 13, iii. 6; 2 Pet. i. 1, 11, ii. 20, iii. 18. Cp. Phil. iii. 20.

5. THE DUTIES OF TITUS IN REFERENCE TO THE APPOINTMENT OF πρεσβύτεροι.

5. τούτου χάριν, *for this cause,* sc. the reason introduced by ἵνα. He reminds Titus of what he had previously explained to him.

ἀπέλιπόν σε. See the crit. note; the aorist seems to give better sense than the imperfect. καταλείπειν is used much oftener in the N.T. than ἀπολείπειν, and may have got into the text as more familiar to scribes; if there is *any* difference in meaning, καταλείπειν is the stronger verb of the two and indicates a more permanent 'leaving behind.'

ἐν Κρήτῃ. This cannot have been on the occasion mentioned Acts xxvii. 7 ff., which is the only visit of St Paul to Crete of which we have any account; we refer this visit therefore (see *Introd.* p. xxxii.) to the period of liberty between the Apostle's two imprisonments at Rome.

ἵνα τὰ λείποντα ἐπιδιορθώσῃ, *that thou thyself shouldest further* (ἐπί = insuper) *set in order the things that are defective*; i.e. as Bengel paraphrases " quae ego per temporis brevitatem non potui expedire." ἐπιδιορθοῦν does not occur again in the Greek Bible; the use of the middle voice here (the true reading, see crit. note) perhaps implies that the needful corrections are to be made by Titus himself, and not through the agency of others.

καὶ καταστήσῃς κατὰ πόλιν πρεσβυτέρους, *and appoint presbyters in every city.* So it was said of Paul and Barnabas χειροτονήσαντες δὲ αὐτοῖς κατ' ἐκκλησίαν πρεσβυτέρους (Acts xiv. 23); Clement uses the verb καθιστάναι in a similar context: κατὰ χώρας οὖν καὶ πόλεις κηρύσσοντες καθίστανον τὰς ἀπαρχὰς αὐτῶν, δοκιμάσαντες τῷ πνεύματι, εἰς ἐπισκόπους καὶ διακόνους τῶν μελλόντων πιστεύειν (§ 42). For the use of κατὰ cp. Luke viii. 1; Acts xv. 21, xx. 23. The injunction does not, of course, imply that there is to be only *one* presbyter in each city, but simply provides for the due establishment and organisation of the presbyterate in the Christian communities. In this work Titus is to take the initiative in Crete; it is *his* duty.

ὡς ἐγώ σοι διεταξάμην, *as I gave thee charge,* ὡς including the *mode* of selection of presbyters as well as the duty of establishing them in every city.

6—9. The qualifications of an ἐπίσκοπος.

6. εἴ τις ἐστὶν ἀνέγκλητος. *If any man has nought laid to his charge.* No suggestion as to the scarcity of such persons can be founded on the form of the sentence εἴ τις κ.τ.λ.; cp. e.g. 2 Cor. xi. 20. The list of qualifications, negative and positive, which follows, should be compared with the list in 1 *Timothy*; see on 1 Tim. iii. 2 ff.

μιᾶς γυναικὸς ἀνήρ. As at 1 Tim. iii. 2, this is desirable because the ἐπίσκοπος is to be ἀνέγκλητος; see the note on that passage.

τέκνα ἔχων πιστά, *having believing children*; the emphasis is on πιστά. It is not the fact that the ἐπίσκοπος has children that is important, but that if he has children they should be professing Christians and of good behaviour. See 1 Tim. iii. 4, 5 and the notes thereon.

It has been suggested that this qualification marks the fact that Christianity had been established for some time in Crete, as Christians of the second generation are contemplated, and that thus it corresponds (in a measure) to μὴ νεόφυτον of 1 Tim. iii. 6. But this is to miss the point, which is merely a further provision that the ἐπίσκοπος shall be ἀνέγκλητος. We have no knowledge as to when the Gospel reached

Crete; quite possibly it was carried there by some of those Cretans who heard it preached on the Day of Pentecost (Acts ii. 11).

μὴ ἐν κατηγορίᾳ ἀσωτίας, *who are not accused of dissoluteness.* For ἀσωτία cp. Eph. v. 18 and 1 Pet. iv. 4; the Prodigal Son lived ἀσώτως (Luke xv. 13). The word signifies every kind of riotous and profligate living. ἄσωτος γάρ, says Aristotle, ὁ δι' αὐτὸν ἀπολλύμενος (*Nic. Eth.* IV. 1. 5).

ἢ ἀνυπότακτα, *or insubordinate.* See, for the reason of this, 1 Tim. iii. 5 and the note thereon. For the word ἀνυπότακτος see on 1 Tim. i. 9.

7. δεῖ γὰρ τὸν ἐπίσκοπον ἀνέγκλητον εἶναι, *for the ἐπίσκοπος must be ἀνέγκλητος.* See *Introd.* chap. v. for the significance of the titles πρεσβύτερος and ἐπίσκοπος in the Pastoral Epistles. For the singular τὸν ἐπίσκοπον see on 1 Tim. iii. 2.

ὡς θεοῦ οἰκονόμον, *as God's steward,* as steward of the οἶκος θεοῦ (1 Tim. iii. 15). The commission of the ἐπίσκοπος is, in the end, from God and not from man; he is God's steward, the steward of His mysteries (1 Cor. iv. 1) and of His manifold grace (1 Pet. iv. 10), not, be it observed, the steward of the Christian community. It is to God, not to man, that he is responsible for the due discharge of his office.

μὴ αὐθάδη, *not self-willed.* αὐθάδης only occurs once again in N.T., viz. τολμηταί, αὐθάδεις (2 Pet. ii. 10); it signifies *self-satisfied* and so *self-willed, arrogant.* Field notes that Aristotle (*Magn. Moral.* I. 28) counts σεμνότης as the mean between αὐθάδεια and ἀρέσκεια, i.e. between arrogance on the one hand and over-complaisance of manner on the other, an interesting observation. σεμνότης is mentioned as one of the qualities of the ἐπίσκοπος at 1 Tim. iii. 4 (see also on 1 Tim. ii. 2).

μὴ ὀργίλον, *not irascible,* 'not soon angry' as the A.V. felicitously renders. ὀργίλος is a ἅπ. λεγ. in the N.T.; Aristotle reckons πραΰτης as the mean between ὀργιλότης and that incapacity for being roused to anger which he calls ἀοργησία (*Nic. Eth.* IV. 5); see on 2 Tim. ii. 25. In the *Didache* (§ 3) we have the precept μὴ γίνου ὀργίλος.

μὴ πάροινον, μὴ πλήκτην. See on 1 Tim. iii. 3.

μὴ αἰσχροκερδῆ. See on 1 Tim. iii. 8, where μὴ αἰσχροκερδεῖς is a note of the διάκονοι. The corresponding qualification for the ἐπίσκοπος in 1 *Timothy* is ἀφιλάργυρον (see on 1 Tim. iii. 3). See also on *v.* 11 below.

8. ἀλλὰ φιλόξενον. We now come to the positive qualifications, the first-named of which, φιλοξενία, stands in sharp contrast to αἰσχροκέρδεια. See on 1 Tim. iii. 2.

φιλάγαθον, *a lover of good;* whether 'of good *things*' or 'of good *persons*' is not clear, but probably it ought to be taken in its widest meaning, as including both. See note on ἀφιλάγαθοι, 2 Tim. iii. 3.

σώφρονα. See on 1 Tim. ii. 9 and iii. 2.

δίκαιον, ὅσιον. These important qualifications are not mentioned in the corresponding list in 1 Tim. iii. From Plato onward δικαιοσύνη and ὁσιότης were counted as complementary to each other, the former being expressive (in its largest sense) of duty to our fellow men, the latter of duty to God, the two together including the sum of moral excellence. But anything like a sharp division between them, as if a man could discharge his duty to his neighbour in all its fulness, while neglecting his duty to God, or *vice versâ*, would be utterly foreign to the central thought of Christianity, which refuses thus to divorce the religious from the secular life. For the association of the two words or their cognates, as here, cp. Luke i. 75; Eph. iv. 24; 1 Thess. ii. 10.

ἐγκρατῆ, *continent*, and generally, one who is master of himself. The distinction between the σώφρων and the ἐγκρατής, as presented in the Ethics of Aristotle, was that while the ἐγκρατής is able to endure pain which ought to be endured, the σώφρων is able as well to resist unlawful pleasure, a harder task. The distinction is between him who *endures*, and him who *overcomes*, for conscience' sake. The σώφρων is moderate in the enjoyment of what is *lawful*; the ἐγκρατής refrains from what is *unlawful*. The word ἐγκρατής does not occur again in the N.T., but cp. 1 Cor. vii. 9; Gal. v. 23 for ἐγκρατεύεσθαι and ἐγκράτεια.

9. ἀντεχόμενον τοῦ κατὰ τὴν διδαχὴν πιστοῦ λόγου, *holding by the faithful word which is according to the doctrine.*

ἀντέχεσθαι is a difficult word; it is used of "holding to" one of two masters in Matt. vi. 24; Luke xvi. 13, and of "laying hold of" and so "supporting" the weak in 1 Thess. v. 14; and again in Prov. iii. 18 wisdom is said to be a tree of life τοῖς ἀντεχομένοις αὐτῆς "to them that lay hold upon her," from which it seems that *holding by* is a legitimate rendering here.

The phrase πιστοῦ λόγου suggests the 'Faithful Sayings' of the Pastoral Epistles (see on 1 Tim. i. 15). κατὰ τὴν διδαχήν must mean 'in accordance with the [Apostolic] doctrine,' διδαχή being taken objectively, and not in the active sense of 'teaching.' Hence the whole clause indicates the function of the ἐπίσκοπος as the guardian of the 'deposit of faith' (cp. 1 Tim. vi. 20).

ἵνα δυνατὸς ᾖ καὶ παρακαλεῖν, *in order that he may be able both to exhort.* For the distinction between διδασκαλία and παράκλησις see on 1 Tim. iv. 13.

ἐν τῇ διδασκαλίᾳ τῇ ὑγιαινούσῃ. For this metaphor, often recurring in the Pastoral Epistles, see on 1 Tim. i. 10; ἐν indicates the *sphere*, as it were, in which the exhortation will take place. If the ἐπίσκοπος hold not by the 'word which is faithful,' his 'doctrine' will not be 'wholesome' and thus his 'exhortation' will be ill-founded and probably ineffective, if not misleading.

καὶ τοὺς ἀντιλέγοντας ἐλέγχειν, *and to convict the gainsayers.* A firm grasp of the truth is the indispensable preparation for him who would undertake to dispel error. The ἀντιλέγοντες are cavillers at the truth, primarily the heretical teachers of Crete, but there are those in every age who satisfy themselves with like negations. Cp. 2 Tim. iv. 2 ἔλεγξον...παρεκάλεσον.

10—16. THE HERETICAL TEACHERS AND TITUS' DUTY IN REGARD TO THEM.

10. **εἰσὶν γὰρ πολλοὶ ἀνυπότακτοι.** *For* (in reference to the precept τοὺς ἀντιλέγοντας ἐλέγχειν) *there are many insubordinate persons,* sc. among the ἀντιλέγοντες. For ἀνυπότακτος see on 1 Tim. i. 9. See the critical note.

ματαιολόγοι καὶ φρεναπάται, *vain talkers and deceivers.* The word ματαιολόγος does not occur again in the Greek Bible; cp. the note on ματαιολογία at 1 Tim. i. 6. In like manner φρεναπάτης is ἅπ. λεγ., but we have φρεναπατᾶν, Gal. vi. 3.

μάλιστα οἱ ἐκ τῆς περιτομῆς, *specially they of the circumcision,* sc. the Judaizing Christians in Crete. μάλιστα shews that the heretical troublers of Titus were not *all* from among these Judaizers, but that it was from them that he was to expect the most serious opposition. Titus, being an uncircumcised Greek, would probably be personally unwelcome to Jews, of whom there were large numbers in Crete (see Josephus *Ant.* XVII. 12. 1, Philo *ad Caium* 36); but quite apart from that, we have seen already (*Introd.* p. xlviii.) that the forms of heresy contemplated in the Pastoral Epistles had their roots in Judaism, and that therefore the ἀντιλέγοντες would naturally be ἐκ τῆς περιτομῆς. See crit. note.

11. **οὓς δεῖ ἐπιστομίζειν,** *whose mouths must be stopped,* the felicitous translation of Tyndale, followed by A.V. and R.V. ἐπιστομίζειν does not occur elsewhere in the true text of the N.T. (or the LXX.), but it is the reading at Luke xi. 53 of three cursive manuscripts (for ἀποστοματίζειν), and was the reading followed by Jerome at that place and rendered by him *os eius opprimere.*

οἵτινες, *inasmuch as they,* 'quippe qui'; cp. 1 Tim. i. 4.

ὅλους οἴκους ἀνατρέπουσιν, *subvert whole households.* For ἀνατρέπειν see on 2 Tim. ii. 18, and for οἶκος used as equivalent to 'household' cp. 1 Tim. iii. 4; 2 Tim. ii. 16.

διδάσκοντες ἃ μὴ δεῖ, *teaching things which they ought not.* In the N.T. we generally have οὐ in relative sentences with the indicative, even where the classical language would require μή; this verse is an exception to the general rule[1].

αἰσχροῦ κέρδους χάριν, *for sake of base gains.* Tyndale's "filthy lucre," which has been followed in all our English versions, does not seem to bring out the exact point here, which is not that money is a despicable thing in itself, but that to teach ἃ μὴ δεῖ for the sake of money is disgraceful and dishonourable, a prostitution of the high

[1] See Blass, *Grammar of N. T. Greek,* § 75. 3.

gifts of a teacher, and that all 'gain' so acquired is 'base.' See
1 Tim. iii. 8 for αἰσχροκερδής.

In like manner the heretical teachers of 1 Tim. vi. 5 'suppose that
godliness is a way of gain': and no doubt greed for his wages is a mark
of the hireling shepherd always (John x. 12). But there may have
been special reason for mentioning it in a letter to the Chief Pastor
of Crete. Livy (XLIV. 45) speaks of "Cretenses spem pecuniae secuti,"
and Plutarch (*Paul. Aemil.* 23) and Polybius (VI. 46) bear similar
testimony to their love of money.

12. εἶπέν τις ἐξ αὐτῶν ἴδιος αὐτῶν προφήτης, *one of themselves*, sc.
the Cretans, *a prophet of their own, said.* The philosopher here quoted
by St Paul is Epimenides, a Cretan who flourished about 600 B.C.;
Plato calls him θεῖος ἀνήρ, and Diogenes Laertius (I. x. 11) reports
that the Cretans used to offer sacrifice to him ὡς θεῷ.

For the gen. αὐτῶν after ἴδιος, which might be thought redundant
(but the usage is classical), cp. Acts xxiv. 23; 2 Pet. iii. 3, 16.

Κρῆτες ἀεὶ ψεῦσται, κακὰ θηρία, γαστέρες ἀργαί. This hexameter
comes from the περὶ χρησμῶν of Epimenides ; it is quoted by Callima-
chus in his *Hymn to Zeus*, and (as Farrar observes) was a well-known
verse in antiquity, because it gave rise to the syllogistic puzzle known
as 'the Liar' (Farrar, *St Paul*, p. 661).

The Cretans had a bad reputation and were reckoned among the
τρία κάππα κάκιστα of the Greek world, the Cappadocians and Cilicians
being associated with them in this unenviable notoriety. Polybius
(VI. 47. 5) speaks of their mendacity; indeed, κρητίζειν was a euphe-
mism for 'to lie,' as Suidas records.

γαστέρες ἀργαί, *idle gluttons.* Tyndale's rendering "slow bellies,"
which has been reproduced in many English versions, does not indicate the true sense of ἀργαί, *idle*, as at 1 Tim. v. 13 (see note thereon).
Cp. "venter tardus" of Juvenal (*Sat.* iv. 107).

St Paul elsewhere quotes Aratus (Acts xvii. 28) and Menander
(1 Cor. xv. 33), but it is plain that these references, along with the
one before us, are quite insufficient to establish the wide acquaintance
with Greek literature which some have claimed for him in consequence.
It is by no means improbable that he was a man of liberal education,
as well as large experience and profound intellect, but two or three
hackneyed quotations will not go far to prove it. The skilful application of the quotations in each case is the interesting point to notice.

13. ἡ μαρτυρία αὕτη ἐστὶν ἀληθής. *This witness is true.* St Paul
deliberately assents to the truth of the proverbial judgement upon the
Cretan character. It was a serious thing to say, and especially significant in a letter which became part of the Canonical Scriptures
received at a later date by the Cretan Church.

δι' ἣν αἰτίαν ἔλεγχε αὐτοὺς ἀποτόμως. *For which cause*, sc. on
account of these evil traits of character, *rebuke them sharply*, sc. not,
to be sure, the Cretans generally, but the heretical teachers described
in *v.* 9 as οἱ ἀντιλέγοντες.

ἀποτόμως only occurs again in the Greek Bible 2 Cor. xiii. 10; Wisd. v. 22 (cp. Rom. xi. 22).

ἵνα ὑγιαίνωσιν ἐν τῇ πίστει, *in order that they may be sound in the faith.* ἡ πίστις is here, plainly, used objectively, as equivalent to 'the Christian faith' (see on 1 Tim. i. 19); for the metaphor of 'soundness,' 'wholesomeness,' as applied to doctrine, see on 1 Tim. i. 10.

14. μὴ προσέχοντες Ἰουδαϊκοῖς μύθοις, *not giving heed to Jewish fables.* See on 1 Tim. i. 4 and *Introd.* chap. IV.

καὶ ἐντολαῖς ἀνθρώπων ἀποστρεφομένων τὴν ἀλήθειαν, *and commandments of men who turn away from the truth.* As the next verse shews, these commandments were probably of a ceremonial or ritual character (cp. 1 Tim. iv. 3, and the note at that place, and Col. ii. 16, 22). Such ἐντολαὶ ἀνθρώπων (Isa. xxix. 13) must not be permitted to usurp the authority of Divine revelation or of the moral law (cp. Matt. xv. 9). To pay undue attention to questions of this kind tends to distract the mind from the contemplation of the great problems of life.

15. πάντα καθαρὰ τοῖς καθαροῖς. *For the pure all things are pure.* τοῖς καθαροῖς is a *dat. commodi,* and conveys the sense *not* that all things are pure *in the judgement* of the pure, but that all things are pure *for their use.* St Paul had said the same thing before, Rom. xiv. 20 (the whole chapter is a commentary on its meaning), πάντα μὲν καθαρά, ἀλλὰ κακὸν τῷ ἀνθρώπῳ τῷ διὰ προσκόμματος ἐσθίοντι; cp. also 1 Tim. iv. 4; Matt. xv. 11 and Luke xi. 41.

τοῖς δὲ μεμιαμμένοις καὶ ἀπίστοις οὐδὲν καθαρόν, *but for the defiled and unbelieving nothing is pure.* If it is true *omnia munda mundis,* it is also true *omnia immunda immundis.* "Honi soit qui mal y pense." See again Rom. xiv. 23 and the other references given in last note.

The intimate connexion between moral purity and soundness in the faith (cp. Acts xv. 9, τῇ πίστει καθαρίσας τὰς καρδίας αὐτῶν), which is so often assumed in the Pastorals (see esp. on 1 Tim. i. 5), is here again indicated; the 'defiled and unbelieving' form one class, not two, as the absence of the article before ἀπίστοις shews. Cp. 1 Tim. iv. 3.

ἀλλὰ μεμίανται αὐτῶν καὶ ὁ νοῦς καὶ ἡ συνείδησις, *but both their mind and their conscience are defiled.* See for νοῦς and συνείδησις the notes on 1 Tim. i. 5, vi. 5.

16. θεὸν ὁμολογοῦσιν εἰδέναι. *They confess that they know God.* There is here no hint of Gnostic pretensions to esoteric knowledge of deity. It was ever the boast and the pride of Judaism that it was the religion of the One True God, in contrast to the religions of τὰ ἔθνη τὰ μὴ εἰδότα τὸν θεόν (1 Thess. iv. 5; cp. also Gal. iv. 8; 2 Thess. i. 8). And so far the heretical Judaisers at Crete were right; their confession, so far, was a 'good confession' (1 Tim. vi. 12).

τοῖς δὲ ἔργοις ἀρνοῦνται, *but they deny Him by their works*; they acted as if this Supreme Being was a mere metaphysical abstraction, out of all moral relation to human life, as if He were neither Saviour nor Judge. Cp. 2 Tim. ii. 12, and see note on 1 Tim. ii. 10.

βδελυκτοὶ ὄντες, *being abominable.*
βδελυκτός is not found again in the N.T.; in Proverbs xvii. 15 (LXX.) the man who perverts moral distinctions is described as ἀκάθαρτος καὶ βδελυκτὸς παρὰ θεῷ (cp. Ecclus. xli. 5; 2 Macc. i. 27 for other occurrences of the word).

καὶ ἀπειθεῖς. Cp. Rom. xi. 32; Tit. iii. 3. The two ideas of *disobedience* to Jehovah and *abominableness* in His sight go together in Judaism; these Judaisers, putting in the forefront of their teaching the Unity of God and claiming for themselves a special knowledge of God as His peculiar people, were yet disobedient to His word and so abominable in His sight.

καὶ πρὸς πᾶν ἔργον ἀγαθὸν ἀδόκιμοι, *and unto every good work reprobate.* For the form of the expression cp. 2 Tim. iii. 17; Tit. iii. 1; for ἀδόκιμος see on 2 Tim. iii. 8.

CHAPTER II.

3. ἱεροπρεπεῖς. So the rec. text with the great majority of uncials (and the margin of the Harclean version); CH** 17, the Syriac, Latin, and Bohairic versions support ἱεροπρεπεῖ, and take it as qualifying καταστήματι.

μὴ οἴνῳ. This is the reading of the rec. text (adopted by Tischendorf and Lachmann), and it is supported by nearly all the· available MSS. and versions. But the important group ℵ*AC 73 read μηδὲ οἴνῳ, and this is printed by Tregelles and WH; μὴ οἴνῳ is the reading in the parallel passage 1 Tim. iii. 8.

4. σωφρονίζουσιν. This is the reading adopted by Tischendorf and Tregelles, and it is supported by the strong combination ℵ*AGHP. We have printed it in the text, in accordance with the rules laid down for the direction of editors of the *Cambridge Greek Testament* (p. v.). But that ἵνα should be followed by the present indicative (see, however, 1 Cor. iv. 6; Gal. iv. 17) seems improbable, and we concur with WH and the rec. text in preferring σωφρονίζωσιν, which is read by ℵcCD₂EKL, the cursives, and the Greek Fathers generally.

5. οἰκουργούς. So the best MSS., ℵ*ACD₂*EG, seem to require us to print; also Clement (§ 1), in a passage which recalls this verse, has τὰ κατὰ τὸν οἶκον σεμνῶς οἰκουργεῖν ἐδιδάσκετε. Of the word οἰκουργός only one other instance has been produced, and that from Soranus, a medical writer of the second century. The rec. text with the bulk of MSS. (ℵcD₂cHKLP) and Fathers has οἰκουρούς, which certainly gives more point to the whole passage. The Latin and Syriac Versions both seem to support it, the Vulgate rendering being *domus curam habentes.* See exegetical note.

7. ἐν τῇ διδασκαλίᾳ ἀφθορίαν. This is undoubtedly the true reading and is found in ℵ*ACD₂*E*KLP; G has ἀφθονίαν. The rec. text has ἀδιαφθορίαν with ℵcD₂cE**L and cursives.

After σεμνότητα the rec. text adds ἀφθαρσίαν, with D₂ᶜE**KL and about 30 cursives; instead of which C and a few other authorities have ἀγνείαν. But neither addition is sufficiently well supported to entitle it to a place in the text.

8. λέγειν περὶ ἡμῶν φαῦλον. The rec. text has ὑμῶν for ἡμῶν (with A and the Bohairic version), and also places λέγειν directly before φαῦλον (with KL and a considerable number of authorities). But the mass of uncial evidence is overwhelmingly in favour of the text as printed.

9. ἰδίοις δεσπόταις. This is the order of the rec. text, as well as of recent editors; it is supported by אCGKL, Chrysostom, Theodoret &c. The order δεσπόταις ἰδίοις is found in AD₂EP and the Latin authorities (versions and Fathers).

10. μὴ νοσφιζομένους. WH give μηδέ a place in their margin, on the authority of CᵇD₂*G 17; אAC*D₂ᶜEKLP &c. have μή.

πᾶσαν πίστιν. There is some confusion about the order. The reading of the text has the weight of uncial authority, viz. אᶜACD₂EP and d e, on its side; and it is in favour of this, as Ellicott points out, that in St Paul (except Eph. iv. 19) where πᾶς is in connexion with an abstract and anarthrous substantive, it always *precedes* the noun. The rec. text has πίστιν πᾶσαν with KL (so also Chrysostom, Theodoret, and the Latin Vulgate). It is remarkable that א* 17 omit πίστιν altogether, and 17 for the following ἀγαθήν has ἀγάπην; WH, in consequence, place πᾶσαν ἐνδεικνυμένους ἀγάπην in their margin, as a reading of which it is quite *possible* that the others may be corruptions. See exegetical note.

τὴν διδασκαλίαν τήν. The second τήν is wanting in rec. text as it is in KLP and some other authorities; *ins.* אACD₂EG 17, Chrysostom and Theodoret.

ἡμῶν. The rec. text has ὑμῶν, apparently through a printer's error, for it has no MS. support.

11. σωτήριος. The rec. text with CᶜD₂ᵇᶜEKLP and the great mass of authorities (MSS. and Fathers) inserts ἡ before σωτήριος (with a view of suggesting that σωτήριος is *subject*, not predicate); it is omitted by אAC*D₂*G, the Syriac, Latin and Bohairic versions and is, in fact, unnecessary. א*G read σωτῆρος, and G prefixes τοῦ.

13. Χριστοῦ Ἰησοῦ. This order is supported by א*G g and the Bohairic version, a strong combination; but the rec. reading (adopted by the R.V. and placed in the margin by WH) has, seemingly, the weight of evidence in its favour, viz. אᶜACD₂EKLP and *all* the other authorities (MSS., versions and Fathers). See exegetical note.

1—10. Titus' positive teaching, as regards various classes
of persons.

1. σὺ δὲ λάλει. *But do thou,* in contrast with the ματαιολόγοι
(as at 1 Tim. vi. 11; 2 Tim. iii. 10, iv. 5), *speak,* i.e. speak out boldly
and plainly.

ἃ πρέπει τῇ ὑγιαινούσῃ διδασκαλίᾳ, *which befit* (cp. 1 Tim. ii. 10)
the sound doctrine, sc. in contrast with the μῦθοι and ἐντολαὶ ἀνθρώπων
of i. 14. For ἡ ὑγ. διδασκαλία see on 1 Tim. i. 10.

i. *Aged men.*

2. πρεσβύτας. The word πρεσβύτης is common in the LXX. (see
note on 1 Tim. v. 1 and cp. the parallel use there of πρεσβύτερος), but
only occurs again in the N.T. at Luke i. 18 and Philem. 9 (in which
last place it is probably for πρεσβευτής, 'an ambassador'). It simply
means *an old man,* and is not a title of office.

νηφαλίους εἶναι, *should be temperate,* not only in the use of wine,
though this would be included (cp. the parallel μηδὲ οἴνῳ πολλῷ δεδουλωμένας in *v.* 3), but generally. See on 1 Tim. iii. 2, 11 and
2 Tim. iv. 5.

σεμνούς, *grave.* See on 1 Tim. ii. 2, iii. 4 and Tit. i. 7 above.

σώφρονας. See on 1 Tim. ii. 9, iii. 2 and Tit. i. 8 above.

ὑγιαίνοντας τῇ πίστει. The similar phrase ἵνα ὑγιαίνωσιν ἐν τῇ πίστει
(ch. i. 13 above) would suggest that ἡ πίστις was here to be taken
objectively (see on 1 Tim. i. 19), but it will be observed that the
defining preposition ἐν is lacking here, and further the words which
follow shew that πίστις, ἀγάπη, ὑπομονή are here a triad of Christian
graces, and that therefore πίστις must be taken subjectively. The
old men are to be bidden 'to be sound in their faith.'

With the phrase ὑγιαίνοντας τῇ πίστει cp. τὸν ἀσθενοῦντα τῇ πίστει
(Rom. xiv. 1).

τῇ πίστει, τῇ ἀγάπῃ, τῇ ὑπομονῇ. For the intimate connexion
between πίστις and ἀγάπη see on 1 Tim. i. 14.

πίστις and ὑπομονή are coupled at 2 Thess. i. 4; Rev. xiii. 10, and
the relation between them is described thus by St James (i. 3), τὸ δο-
κίμιον ὑμῶν τῆς πίστεως κατεργάζεται ὑπομονήν.

ἀγάπη and ὑπομονή are grouped in 2 Thess. iii. 5.

The three graces πίστις, ἀγάπη, ὑπομονή are also placed in juxtaposition, 1 Thess. i. 3; 1 Tim. vi. 11 (where Timothy is bidden to
pursue them), and 2 Tim. iii. 10 (where St Paul speaks of his own
example in respect of them); and they form three of the eight graces
enumerated in the catalogue 2 Pet. i. 6, 7, πίστις being the beginning,
ἀγάπη the end, and ὑπομονή an intermediate stage, of the Christian
course as there described. Ignatius (*Polyc.* 6) thus distinguishes
them as parts of the Christian's equipment, ἡ πίστις ὡς περικεφαλαία,
ἡ ἀγάπη ὡς δόρυ, ἡ ὑπομονὴ ὡς πανοπλία. See further on 1 Tim. vi. 11;
2 Tim. iii. 10.

ii. *Aged women.*

3. πρεσβύτιδας. πρεσβῦτις, *an aged woman,* is only found again in the Greek Bible at 4 Macc. xvi. 14. It is interesting to find Epiphanius (*Haer. Collyr.* 79, n. 3) using the word of the most venerable of the Church Widows (see 1 Tim. v. 9), who were quite distinct from the Deaconesses; he distinguishes the πρεσβῦτις carefully from the πρεσβύτερις or woman 'elder.' Here, however, the term πρεσβῦτις is used just as πρεσβυτέρα was in 1 Tim. v. 2; it was not yet a distinct office. But we have in this and the corresponding passage in 1 *Timothy* the beginnings of what came to be an organised ministry in a later age.

ὡσαύτως. See on 1 Tim. ii. 9.

ἐν καταστήματι, *in demeanour*; as compared with καταστολή *dress* of 1 Tim. ii. 9, it points rather to a habit of mind than to outward appearance, as also it does at 3 Macc. v. 45, the only other place where the word κατάστημα is found in the Greek Bible. Of the Bishop of Tralles Ignatius says that his κατάστημα was itself μεγάλη μαθητεία (*Trall.* 3), and this, no doubt, is the idea here also.

ἱεροπρεπεῖς, *reverend,* or as the A.V. has it "as becometh holiness"; the R.V. "reverent" does not seem to hit the sense, which has reference rather to the effect upon others of their decorous demeanour than to their own respect for sacred things. Yet it is hard to distinguish the two, and the parallel passage 1 Tim. ii. 10 ὃ πρέπει γυναιξὶν ἐπαγγελλομέναις θεοσέβειαν in some measure countenances the *subjective* sense of the word here.

μὴ διαβόλους. See on 1 Tim. iii. 6, 11.

μηδὲ οἴνῳ πολλῷ δεδουλωμένας, *nor enslaved to much wine,* a stronger expression than the corresponding one, 1 Tim. iii. 8 (see note thereon), which applies to *deacons.* The 'slavery of sin' is a familiar thought with St Paul (Rom. vi. 18, 22 &c.), and in the case of no sin is the bondage more conspicuous than in the case of drunkenness. It may have been specially necessary to warn the Cretans, γαστέρες ἀργαί (i. 12), against it.

καλοδιδασκάλους, *teachers of that which is good,* sc. not in the public assemblies of Christians (1 Tim. ii. 12, where see note), but in private ministrations, such as those of Lois and Eunice (2 Tim. iii. 15) and those contemplated in the next verse. For the form of the word καλοδιδάσκαλος (ἅπ. λεγ. in the Greek Bible) see the note on ἑτεροδιδασκαλεῖν (1 Tim. i. 3), and for the force of καλός see on 1 Tim. i. 8.

4. ἵνα σωφρονίζωσιν τὰς νέας, *that* (this is the reason why they should be καλοδιδάσκαλοι) *they may train the young women,* sc. primarily the young *married* women, as the context shews. The demeanour of Titus himself to these members of his flock would, no doubt, be the same as that recommended to Timothy (1 Tim. v. 2; see note thereon). See critical note.

The verb σωφρονίζειν is ἄπ. λεγ. in the Greek Bible; see on 2 Tim. i. 9 and on 1 Tim. ii. 9.

iii. *Young wives.*

φιλάνδρους εἶναι, *to be lovers of their husbands.* The word does not occur again in LXX. or N.T.; we have in Plutarch (*Praec. conj.* 38) φίλανδροι καὶ σώφρονες γυναῖκες.

φιλοτέκνους, *lovers of their children.* The word is not found again in N.T.; we have it in 4 Macc. xv. 4, 5 and (coupled with φίλανδροι) in Plutarch (*Mor.* p. 769).

5. σώφρονας, *soberly discreet;* see on 1 Tim. ii. 9, iii. 2 and Tit. i. 8 above.

ἁγνάς, *chaste,* probably in its primary sense. See on 1 Tim. iv. 12, v. 22; cp. 2 Cor. xi. 2.

οἰκουργούς, ἀγαθάς. Some excellent critics, e.g. Lachmann, Tregelles and Weiss, remove the comma, and treat ἀγαθάς as qualifying the word which precedes it. This, however, is to disturb the rhythm of the sentence, and is not in accordance with the ancient interpretations of the passage. We shall see that ἀγαθάς may very well be taken absolutely, as all the words preceding it are taken.

The question then arises, Are we to read οἰκουργούς or οἰκουρούς? Diplomatic evidence certainly favours the former, and the passage quoted in the critical note from Clement of Rome may also be alleged to support the opinion that οἰκουργούς was the primitive reading. But the resultant meaning (apparently, for it was an extraordinarily rare word, as the crit. note shews) *workers at home* is not very impressive. And when we remember that the alternative reading οἰκουρούς, *keepers at home,* supplies an attribute of good wives by which Greek writers generally set great store (Field supplies a large number of apt illustrations) we are much tempted to hold that it was the word used by St Paul. Wetstein quotes Philo, *de Exsecr.* 4, and the words are worth reproducing as illustrating the whole passage before us: γυναῖκας ἃς ἠγάγοντο κουριδίας ἐπὶ γνησίων παιδῶν σπορᾷ, σώφρονας οἰκουροὺς καὶ φιλάνδρους. Another passage from Philo (*de Prof.* 27) is interesting. Of a virtuous wife he says κοσμιότητι καὶ σωφροσύνῃ καὶ ταῖς ἄλλαις διαπρέπουσιν ἀρεταῖς, ἑνὶ προσέχουσαν ἀνδρὶ καὶ τὴν ἑνὸς οἰκουρίαν ἀγαπῶσαν καὶ μοναρχίᾳ χαίρουσαν. In short, οἰκουρούς is the word we should naturally expect in such a catalogue from a writer in St Paul's circumstances; οἰκουργούς is of very doubtful meaning, nor is it supported by such overwhelming external evidence as to require its adoption. Hence we are disposed to hold by the A.V. *keepers at home* (or perhaps 'keepers of their homes') in preference to the R.V. *workers at home.*

ἀγαθάς. The Vulgate translates *benignas,* ἀγαθός thus having an absolute meaning akin to what it has at Matt. xx. 15; 1 Pet. ii. 18, and (according to the most probable interpretation) Rom. v. 7, where it is contrasted with δίκαιος. ἀγαθάς means here, then, *kind* (the rendering of the R.V.) or *kindly.*

ὑποτασσομένας τοῖς ἰδίοις ἀνδράσιν, *submitting themselves, each to her own husband,* advice which St Paul had given before in almost identical words (Eph. v. 22; Col. iii. 18). See for this unemphatic use of ἴδιος on 1 Tim. vi. 1, and cp. *v.* 9 below.

Whatever may be thought of the ' subjection of women ' there can be no doubt that St Paul's belief was that the man is, and ought to be, ' head of the wife ' (Eph. v. 23). See on 1 Tim. ii. 11.

ἵνα μὴ ὁ λόγος τοῦ θεοῦ βλασφημῆται. Quoted as in Rom. ii. 24 (cp. also 1 Tim. vi. 1) from Isa. lii. 5. Christianity has undoubtedly emancipated woman from the state of degradation in which Greek civilisation and Hebrew prejudice were alike content to leave her; but the first preachers of the Gospel sanctioned no sudden revolution in domestic life any more than in civic life. For Christianity was a religious movement before it became either a social or political movement; and it was the constant fear of its early exponents that it might be misinterpreted as loosening the bonds of society and of the state, and that so *the Word of God,* i.e. the Gospel (see Addit. Note on 1 Tim. iv. 5), *might be blasphemed.* See on 1 Tim. vi. 1.

iv. *Young men.*

6. τοὺς νεωτέρους ὡσαύτως παρακάλει σωφρονεῖν, *the younger men likewise exhort to be sober-minded.* It will be observed that Titus is not directed, as Timothy was (1 Tim. v. 1, where see the note), to exhort the νεώτεροι as ἀδελφοί, probably because he was himself a man in middle life. See on 1 Tim. ii. 9; the references there given shew that *specially* great stress is laid in this Epistle on the virtue of σωφροσύνη and the need of σωφρονισμός.

7. περὶ πάντα σεαυτὸν παρεχόμενος τύπον καλῶν ἔργων, *in all things shewing thyself an example of good works.* The use of the reflexive pronoun along with the middle voice of the verb makes the personal application of the injunction more pointed. Example is better than precept, and Titus is to set an example in his own person. For the use of τύπος cp. 1 Tim. iv. 12, and the note thereon; and for the stress laid on καλὰ ἔργα in the Pastorals and the significance of the adjective καλός see on 1 Tim. ii. 10.

It will be remembered that these words, together with those of *v.* 8 and of *v.* 12, form the substance of one of the solemn questions which are put to a bishop before his consecration.

ἐν τῇ διδασκαλίᾳ ἀφθορίαν, σεμνότητα, *in thy teaching* (shewing) *uncorruptness, gravity.* These two attributes have reference to the qualities of the teacher, rather than to the content of the doctrine taught; the character of *that* is defined by the words which follow. σεμνότης (see on 1 Tim. ii. 2) is peculiarly a quality of persons, not of doctrine; and ἀφθορία (ἅπ. λεγ. in N.T.) well expresses the single-mindedness and sincerity which a teacher of sacred things should exhibit. It signifies his whole-heartedness, while σεμνότης rather has reference to his outward demeanour.

ἡ διδασκαλία here is to be taken actively, *thy teaching,* and not (as in the A.V. and R.V.) in the objective sense of *the doctrine taught.* It has been pointed out in the note on 1 Tim. i. 10, that it is used in both senses in the Pastoral Epistles, but here the context as well as the close juxtaposition of the verb παρακαλεῖν (παράκλησις *exhortation* being contrasted with διδασκαλία *instruction,* as at 1 Tim. iv. 13) seems to require us to translate *teaching,* as Wiclif's version has it.

The A.V. has at the end of this verse the additional attribute *sincerity,* the rendering of ἀφθαρσίαν of the rec. text. But as the critical note shews, it is a later gloss, and not entitled to a place in the text at all.

8. λόγον ὑγιῆ ἀκατάγνωστον, *sound discourse that cannot be con- demned.* The two qualities which the λόγος or 'discourse' of one in the position of Titus should have are (1) that it be ὑγιής (see the note on 1 Tim. i. 10), and (2) that it be ἀκατάγνωστος or *irreprehensible.* The word ἀκατάγνωστος occurs again in the Greek Bible only once, at 2 Macc. iv. 47 where it means 'uncondemned'; here it means rather 'not open to just rebuke.' In fact, every faithful teacher has fre- quently to declare 'doctrine' against which some of his hearers rebel and which they are only too ready to 'condemn.' But the true standard of ὑγιεία or *soundness* is not derived from a comparison of the opinions of the taught, but is the Apostolic deposit of faith, as officially and authoritatively interpreted by the Church.

ἵνα ὁ ἐξ ἐναντίας ἐντραπῇ, *in order that he of the contrary part,* sc. the ματαιολόγος, *may be put to shame,* and so his vain talk be silenced. The positive presentation of truth, of the 'sound doctrine,' is the best means of combating error; falsehood dreads the light and is— generally—discredited as soon as the light of truth is allowed to play on it, without any direct controversial attack. Chrysostom interprets ὁ ἐξ ἐναντίας of the *devil,* but this is to introduce an idea quite foreign to the context, as indeed the next clause sufficiently shews.

μηδὲν ἔχων λέγειν περὶ ἡμῶν φαῦλον, *having no evil thing to say of us.* φαῦλος is in the N.T. always applied to evil *deeds* rather than evil *words*; and so the point of this clause is that the opponents of St Paul's 'sound doctrine' have nothing scandalous to report of his conduct or of that of Titus.

v. *Slaves.*

9. δούλους ἰδίοις δεσπόταις ὑποτάσσεσθαι. Exhort (going back to παρακάλει of *v.* 6) *slaves to be in subjection to their masters.* The corresponding injunctions in 1 Tim. vi. 1 ff. should be compared with what follows; ἴδιος is used without special emphasis here, as in that place. The article before ἰδίοις is dropped, apparently because of the anarthrous δούλους which precedes[1]. See critical note.

ἐν πᾶσιν εὐαρέστους εἶναι, *to give satisfaction to them in all things.* εὐάρεστος, *well-pleasing,* is a favourite adjective with St Paul; but everywhere else he uses it in reference to God the Father or Christ.

---

[1] See Blass, *Grammar of N. T. Greek,* § 48. 8.

μὴ ἀντιλέγοντας, *not gainsaying*; it is wider than Tyndale's
"not answering again," which is preserved in the A.V. ἀντιλέγειν
here has reference to all kinds of opposition, whether of words or
deeds.

10. μὴ νοσφιζομένους, *not purloining*; for νοσφίζεσθαι cp. Acts v. 3;
2 Macc. iv. 32. Tyndale's "neither be pickers" gives the sense exactly; the allusion is to the petty thefts which are always possible for
a dishonest servant.

ἀλλὰ πᾶσαν πίστιν ἐνδεικνυμένους ἀγαθήν, *but shewing all good
fidelity*, sc. shewing good faith on every possible occasion; see note
on the *extensive* force of πᾶς in St Paul, at 1 Tim. i. 15. πίστις here
=*fidelitas*, the fidelity which slaves owe to their masters, servants to
those who employ them.

ἵνα τὴν διδασκαλίαν κ.τ.λ., *that they may adorn the doctrine of God
our Saviour in all things*, sc. in every department and call of duty.
κοσμεῖν 'to adorn,' is used of the 'setting' of a jewel; and so, here,
'the doctrine of God our Saviour' is, as it were, 'set off,' and exhibited
in a favourable light to the unbelieving world, by the conduct of
those who, in whatever station, profess belief in it. For the title
'our Saviour' as applied to God the Father, see note on 1 Tim. i. 1
and cp. 1 Tim. iv. 10.

11—14. DOCTRINAL GROUND OF THE PRECEDING EXHORTATIONS.

11. ἐπεφάνη γὰρ ἡ χάρις τοῦ θεοῦ σωτήριος πᾶσιν ἀνθρώποις, *for
the grace of God appeared bringing salvation to all men*. ἡ χάρις
τοῦ θεοῦ is the whole favour of God, revealed in the Person of Christ;
in this brief sentence we have at once a declaration of the Incarnation (ἐπεφάνη; cp. iii. 4) and the Atonement (σωτήριος; cp. the Name
Jesus, Matt. i. 21). The aorist ἐπεφάνη points to a definite manifestation in time of the unfailing grace of God, i.e. to the Nativity
and the Advent of our Lord.

For the adj. σωτήριος, which does not occur again in the N.T., cp.
Amos v. 22 σωτηρίους ἐπιφανείας ὑμῶν οὐκ ἐπιβλέψομαι. The absence
of the article before σωτήριος (see crit. note) shews that it is not
attached to the subject χάρις, but is connected with the predicate; it is
as bringing salvation that this grace has visited us, not 'the saving
grace of God has appeared.'

The construction and order of the words require us to take πᾶσιν
ἀνθρώποις with σωτήριος, not with ἐπεφάνη, as the A.V., following
Wiclif and the Rheims Version, has done. Tyndale has rightly *that
bringeth salvation unto all men*, sc. whether Jew or Greek, bond or free.
It is the Universality of the Atonement (cp. 1 Tim. ii. 4) which is the
thought in the second clause of the verse; it is not indeed easy to
attach any exact sense to the rendering "appeared unto all men."
Even yet, after nineteen centuries of Christian Missions, 'the grace
of God' is still unknown to multitudes of those whose nature the
Lord took upon Himself; it has not yet 'appeared' to them.

12. παιδεύουσα ἡμᾶς, ἵνα κ.τ.λ., *schooling us, in order that* &c. This is the point of stress in the whole paragraph. The ground of the foregoing exhortations to fulfil our several duties lies here, that "the grace of God appeared...schooling (*or* disciplining) us" for right living. The final cause of the Revelation in Christ is not *creed*, but *character.*

ἵνα ἀρνησάμενοι τὴν ἀσέβειαν καὶ τὰς κοσμικὰς ἐπιθυμίας, *in order that having denied ungodliness and worldly lusts* &c. The aorist participle seems to point to a definite act of renunciation, such as is made at Baptism, which is everywhere in the N.T. contemplated as the beginning of the Christian life. It is grammatically possible to take ἀρνησάμενοι as coextensive in time with ζήσωμεν which follows, and to translate *denying* (as A.V. and R.V.), the continual denials of the Christian course being thus described. But a reference to the baptismal vow (see on 1 Tim. vi. 12 and cp. 1 Pet. iii. 21) seems to be intended. ἀσέβεια (2 Tim. ii. 16) is, of course, the opposite of εὐσέβεια; see on 1 Tim. ii. 2. The *worldly desires* which we are called on to 'deny' include the lusts of the flesh, but are not confined to these; ἡ ἐπιθυμία τῆς σαρκὸς καὶ ἡ ἐπιθυμία τῶν ὀφθαλμῶν καὶ ἡ ἀλαζονία τοῦ βίου are all ἐκ τοῦ κόσμου (1 John ii. 16).

σωφρόνως καὶ δικαίως καὶ εὐσεβῶς ζήσωμεν, *we should live soberly and righteously and godly.* The three adverbs, taken together, express the Christian ideal of life (cp. the language of the General Confession), and they are so used in the Form for Adult Baptism and also in that for the Consecration of Bishops (see above on *v.* 7). In a rough way they may be considered as pointing respectively to our duties to *ourselves*, to our *neighbours*, and to *God*, but anything like a sharp division is not to be pressed (see on ch. i. 8). For σωφροσύνη see on 1 Tim. ii. 9 and for εὐσέβεια on 1 Tim. ii. 2.

ἐν τῷ νῦν αἰῶνι, *in the present world.* For this phrase see on 1 Tim. vi. 17.

13. προσδεχόμενοι τὴν μακαρίαν ἐλπίδα κ.τ.λ., *looking for the blessed hope*, &c. Note that the connexion of this with what goes before shews that this attitude of expectation is not only a privilege and a consolation, but a *duty*. *Hope* 'abides' no less than *faith* and *love* (1 Cor. xiii. 13). The ἐλπίς is almost regarded as something objective, not only *spes* but *res sperata*; cp. Acts xxiv. 15 ἐλπίδα...ἣν ...προσδέχονται (in a speech of Paul's). It is called μακάριος as containing in itself the fulness of bliss (see on 1 Tim. i. 11).

καὶ ἐπιφάνειαν τῆς δόξης, *and appearing of the glory.* The A.V. "glorious appearing" (derived from Tyndale, all the other English versions having preserved the true rendering) is a quite unjustifiable hendiadys, and impoverishes the sense. The absence of the article before ἐπιφάνεια requires us to connect it closely with ἐλπίδα; it is, indeed, the emphatic word in the sentence. The strength in which the Christian life is to be lived is the grace revealed in the First Advent (the Epiphany of *v.* 11); the hope to which it presses is the glory of the Second Advent (the Epiphany of *v.* 13).

τοῦ μεγάλου θεοῦ καὶ σωτῆρος ἡμῶν Χριστοῦ 'Ἰησοῦ. The rendering
of this verse has been the subject of much dispute. (1) The older
English versions distinguish two Persons in the clause to which we
have come, and understand τοῦ μεγάλου θεοῦ of God the Father
(cp. 2 Pet. i. 1). (2) On the other hand the R.V. (though placing
the other rendering in the margin) translates *of our great God and
Saviour Jesus Christ* (see, however, the critical note for the order).
(*a*) *Primâ facie*, it might be thought (and it has often been urged)
that the omission of the article before σωτῆρος requires us to think of
θεοῦ and σωτῆρος as being part of one conception, and that therefore
the rendering of the R.V. is demanded inexorably by the ordinary
rules as to the use of the definite article. But, in fact, σωτήρ is one
of those quasi-technical words which speedily became anarthrous
(see on 1 Tim. i. 1); and further it might possibly be, that, as τοῦ
μεγάλου qualifies θεοῦ, so σωτῆρος is qualified by the following ἡμῶν.
The point cannot be decided on grammatical grounds alone. (*b*) Again
it has been supposed by some that interpretation (2), as being that
adopted (with fair unanimity) by the Greek Fathers and as being
therefore the traditional interpretation of the early Eastern Church,
has strong claims upon us on this ground alone. Against that,
however, a fact of exactly opposite significance may be set, viz. that
the early translations of the N.T., Latin, Syriac, Egyptian and
Armenian, seem to adopt interpretation (1). Patristic interpretation
is not decisive when the evidence of the Versions is the other way.
And, again, we must always remember that the Fathers were far
better theologians than critics. Their judgement on a point of
doctrine may be trusted with much readier confidence than the
arguments by which they support that judgement. That St Paul
would not hesitate to call Christ by the awful title *God* need not
be doubted (see Acts xx. 28; Rom. ix. 5 in particular), and the
Fathers were right in asserting this quite plainly. But whether
he does so at this point or not is a question of exegesis, not of
doctrine; the dogma of our Lord's Godhead does not rest only on
one or on twenty texts.

Tradition, then, does not settle the problem before us any more
than grammar, and we ask next (*c*) What is the general usage of
the Pastoral Epistles as to the combination of the words θεός and
Χριστός? To this there can be only one answer. From a comparison
of 1 Tim. i. 1; Tit. i. 4, iii. 4—6 (see also 1 Tim. ii. 3—5) it will be
perceived that the habit of the writer of these letters is to use θεός of
God the Father (the epithet σωτήρ being frequently applied to Him:
see on 1 Tim. i. 1); ἀπὸ θεοῦ πατρὸς καὶ Χριστοῦ 'Ἰησοῦ τοῦ σωτῆρος
ἡμῶν (Tit. i. 4) is his usual method of coupling the Eternal Father
and His Son our Lord. Hence there is *some* ground for distinguishing
the terms in the same way in the verse before us. But (*d*) we have
not yet examined the context, and this will lessen our confidence in
the conclusion to which (*c*) would point. For (*a*) the application of
the adj. μέγας to θεός is unique in the N.T. (cp. Neh. ix. 32 and esp.
Dan. ii. 45); and this remarkable choice of epithet may suggest that
θεός is used in a special connexion with special motive. In other

words μέγας is somewhat pointless (in *this* context) if applied to God
the Father; but τοῦ μεγάλου θεοῦ has remarkable significance if it be
understood of God the Son, with whose Second Advent the verse is
concerned. It calls attention to the *glory* of that Appearing which
shall be. (β) ἐπιφάνεια is habitually used by Paul of our Lord Jesus
Christ, and not of God the Father, as a rule. Against this the
expression in this very Epistle (iii. 4) ἡ χρηστότης καὶ ἡ φιλανθρωπία
ἐπεφάνη τοῦ σωτῆρος ἡμῶν θεοῦ (sc. God the Father), has been set;
but this latter Epiphany was that of the First Advent, not of the
Second, and in reference to the *Second* Advent (which is here in
question) ἡ ἐπιφάνεια is exclusively and perpetually applied to Christ.
(γ) The full phrase ἡ ἐπιφάνεια τῆς δόξης perhaps is more applicable
to the glory of the Son (Matt. xxv. 31) which shall be revealed at the
Last Day (1 Pet. iv. 13), than to the glory of the Father; but yet
Matt. xvi. 27 shews how easy it would be to press a consideration of
this kind too far.

On the whole, then, though with great hesitation, we prefer the
rendering of the Revised Version (2) for the reasons assigned under
head (d); but it must not be supposed that the rendering of the
Authorised Version is less doctrinally significant. In both cases
our Lord's equality in glory with the Eternal Father is asserted in a
fashion which would be out of the question if the writer did not
believe that He was in truth the Almighty and Infinite God; the only
difference is that what is only implied, according to the one translation,
is explicitly stated by the other.

14. ὃς ἔδωκεν ἑαυτὸν ὑπὲρ ἡμῶν, *Who gave Himself for us.* This is
the phrase in which St Paul again and again describes the efficacy of
the Lord's Atonement; cp. Rom. viii. 32; Gal. i. 4, ii. 20; Eph. v. 25,
and see on 1 Tim. ii. 6.

ἵνα λυτρώσηται ἡμᾶς ἀπὸ πάσης ἀνομίας, *in order that He might
redeem us from all iniquity.* The final cause of the Atonement is
represented in *v.* 14 as (a) *negative* (Redemption), (b) *positive*
(Sanctification). In this clause we have its negative purpose described; it is to redeem us from all sin (all sin is ἀνομία, 1 John iii. 4,
and ἀνομία here stands for violation of the moral law in general).
The *rationale* of the Atoning Efficacy of the Lord's Death is illustrated
in the N.T. by various metaphors, such as *Ransom, Reconciliation,
Sacrifice.* Here (as at 1 Tim. ii. 6) the metaphor of *emancipation from
slavery,* ransom from the bondage of sin, is adopted, the language
used being taken from Ps. cxxix. (cxxx.) 8 καὶ αὐτὸς (sc. ὁ κύριος)
λυτρώσεται τὸν Ἰσραὴλ ἐκ πασῶν τῶν ἀνομιῶν αὐτοῦ, where this
'plenteous redemption' is sung as the work of the Messiah who
was to come (cp. also Ezek. xxxvii. 23). This was the metaphor
which (possibly because of its adoption by our Lord Himself, Matt.
xx. 28; Mark x. 45) was most frequently dwelt on by the early
Church; and from Irenaeus to Anselm the one theory of the Atonement, which was popularly regarded as orthodox, was that which
set forth the Lord's Death as a 'ransom' paid to the devil, into
whose bonds man had fallen. The metaphor of 'redemption from

evil' was all too soon hardened into a theory of 'ransom from the Evil One.' See Westcott *Hebrews*, p. 295, and Abbott *Ephesians*, p. 11.

What has been said above (on 2 Tim. iv. 17) as to the usage of ἀπό and ἐκ after verbs of deliverance suggests that the change of the ἐκ of the Psalm into ἀπό is not without significance; redemption ἐκ πάσης ἀνομίας would only indicate deliverance from all the acts of lawlessness of which man had been guilty; ἀπό indicates a complete deliverance from the neighbourhood and company of sin, whether original or actual.

καὶ καθαρίσῃ ἑαυτῷ λαὸν περιούσιον κ.τ.λ., *and might purify to Himself a peculiar people,* i.e. a people for His own possession. This is the *positive* purpose of the Atonement; not only *ransom* from sin (not to speak of deliverance from the pains of hell), but *sanctification* to a good life. The two things go together; cp. 2 Cor. vii. 1. In this clause St Paul again uses the language of the LXX. to express the sacred truths which have been committed to him to teach; λαὸς περιούσιος is the equivalent of עַם סְגֻלָּה, 'a people of possession' (Exod. xix. 5; Deut. vii. 6, xiv. 2, xxvi. 18), the phrase used by St Peter being λαὸς εἰς περιποίησιν (1 Pet. ii. 9; cp. Mal. iii. 17). περιούσιος is usually represented in the Vulgate by *peculiaris* or *in peculium,* whence Tyndale's rendering "peculiar people" is derived; but in this verse (Tit. ii. 14) curiously enough the Vulgate has *acceptabilem.* The original Hebrew shews that the word περιούσιος is almost identical with the classical ἐξαίρετος, 'chosen out,' as it were for God's purposes; and this is the proper sense of the adj. *peculiar* which has gained, from this and parallel passages, a permanent place in our language[1].

ζηλωτὴν καλῶν ἔργων, *zealous of good works.* See on 1 Tim. ii. 10 for the place which 'good works' occupy in the theology of the Pastoral Epistles. For the word ζηλωτής cp. Acts xxii. 3; 1 Cor. xiv. 12; Gal. i. 14.

15.   TITUS TO SPEAK WITH AUTHORITY.

15. ταῦτα λάλει, *these things,* sc. what has gone before, *speak;* cp. 1 Tim. vi. 2.

καὶ παρακάλει καὶ ἔλεγχε μετὰ πάσης ἐπιταγῆς, *and exhort and reprove with all authority.* The duties both of παράκλησις, *exhortation* (1 Tim. iv. 13), and of ἐλεγμός (2 Tim. iii. 16) are frequently commended to Timothy and Titus in the Pastorals (see on 2 Tim. iv. 2). They are to be carried out μετὰ πάσης ἐπιταγῆς *with all authority.* "I verily believe," says Bp Beveridge, "that the non-observance of this hath been, and still is, the principal reason why people receive so little benefit by hearing of sermons as they usually do. For they look upon sermons only as popular discourses, rehearsed by one of their fellow-creatures, which they may censure, approve, or reject, as themselves seem good." It is not presumptuous, it is a plain duty,

---

[1] See Lightfoot, *Revision of the N. T.* Appendix II., for a full discussion of the word περιούσιος.

for the minister of the Gospel to speak μετὰ πάσης ἐπιταγῆς. For the word ἐπιταγή see on 1 Tim. i. 1, and cp. 2 Cor. viii. 8.

μηδείς σου περιφρονείτω, *Let no man despise thee.* This is in close connexion with the previous injunction to exhort and rebuke with all authority; the corresponding direction to Timothy (1 Tim. iv. 12) springs out of a different context, and is suggested by the thought of Timothy's 'youth.' See on 1 Tim. v. 1 and Titus ii. 6.

CHAPTER III.

1. The rec. text inserts καὶ between ἀρχαῖς and ἐξουσίαις, on the authority of D₂ᶜE**KLP, most other MSS., and a general consensus of versions and Fathers. It is omitted by modern editors, chiefly because of the lack of uncial evidence, it not being found in אACD₂* EG 17 or g.

2. **πραΰτητα.** This is the orthography of ACP (see crit. note on 2 Tim. ii. 25); the spelling of the rec. text πραότητα is supported here by אᶜD₂EGKL &c.

5. **ἅ.** This reading is guaranteed by the majority of the uncials, viz. אAC*D₂*G, and by 17; the rec. text has ὧν, an obvious correction, with CᵇD₂ᶜEKLP and many cursives and Fathers.

τὸ αὐτοῦ ἔλεος. So אAP 17 and the preponderance of patristic testimony; instead of the neuter, the rec. text has τὸν αὐτοῦ ἔλεον with D₂ᵇKL.

λουτροῦ. A stands alone in inserting τοῦ before λουτροῦ.

7. **γενηθῶμεν.** This is the reading of א*ACD₂*GP 17 &c.; the rec. text has γενώμεθα with אᶜD₂ᶜEKL and the majority of cursives.

8. **θεῷ.** The rec. text, following the majority of the cursives, prefixes τῷ; but all the uncials omit it.

καλά. The rec. text, following D₂ᶜEKLP, prefixes τά; but it is not found in אACD₂*G and a considerable number of cursives.

9. **ἔρεις.** So אᶜACKLP and all the versions (except the Aethiopic); but the rec. text has ἔριν with א*D₂EG *aeth.* See critical note on 1 Tim. vi. 4.

10. **καὶ δευτέραν νουθεσίαν.** This, the rec. reading, is supported by אACKLP and the great majority of MSS. and versions, and is indubitably the primitive reading; but the variants (νουθεσίαν καὶ [ἢ] δευτέραν D₂ᶜG g, and νουθεσίαν καὶ δύο D₂*E d e) are curious, and point to early corruption. The various readings do not affect the meaning.

13. **Ἀπολλώ.** This, the rec. spelling, has the authority of CD₂*ᶜEH** KLP d e f, and is adopted by Tregelles and Lachmann; Tischendorf and WH print Ἀπολλών with אD₂ᵇH* (cp. 1 Cor. iv. 6).

λείπῃ. So ACD₂ᶜEGLP &c. (with the rec. text), followed by Tregelles, Lachmann and WH; Tischendorf prefers λίπῃ with אD₂* and some cursives, and WH give a place to this reading in their margin. See on ch. i. 5.

15. The rec. text adds at the end ἀμήν with the great bulk of manuscripts and versions, and the Greek Fathers; but Tischendorf, Tregelles and WH omit it with the important group ℵ*ACD₂* 17 d and the Latin Fathers.

The subscription printed in the rec. text is:

Πρὸς Τίτον, τῆς Κρητῶν ἐκκλησίας πρῶτον ἐπίσκοπον χειροτονηθέντα, ἐγράφη ἀπὸ Νικοπόλεως τῆς Μακεδονίας. This is found in K and in some cursives, and substantially the same colophon is preserved in HL.

ℵC 17 have simply πρὸς Τίτον; D₂E add to this ἐπληρώθη, G has ἐτελέσθη ἐπιστολὴ πρὸς Τίτον; AP have πρ. Τίτον ἐγράφη ἀπὸ Νικοπόλεως. See *Introd.* p. xxxii., and note on *v.* 12 below.

1, 2. THE ATTITUDE OF CHRISTIANS TO THEIR HEATHEN NEIGHBOURS AND RULERS.

1. ὑπομίμνησκε αὐτούς. *Put them in mind* (cp. 2 Tim. ii. 14) &c. The injunctions which follow would not be novel to the Cretan Christians; but, though familiar, they will bear repetition.

ἀρχαῖς ἐξουσίαις ὑποτάσσεσθαι, *to be subject to rulers, to authorities,* a very necessary injunction to men who might be apt to presume on their possession of the true faith, so as to offend the pagan government under which their lot was cast. It is said by Polybius (VI. 46. 9) that the Cretans were notorious for their seditious character, and it has been supposed that St Paul had this revolutionary spirit of theirs in his mind; but the qualities which he proceeds to mention in the next verse do not seem to have any such special reference, and, as a matter of fact, he addressed like counsel to the Romans (xiii. 1); cp. also 1 Tim. ii. 1—3, where the Ephesian Christians are directed to pray for 'all in authority.'

πειθαρχεῖν, *to be obedient,* sc. to the civil law and to the magistrates; St Paul never underrates the duties of *citizenship.*

πειθαρχεῖν is not found anywhere else in St Paul's writings, but it occurs in a speech of his (Acts xxvii. 21).

πρὸς πᾶν ἔργον ἀγαθὸν ἑτοίμους εἶναι, *to be ready unto every good work;* for, as he explains in the parallel passage Rom. xiii. 3, 'rulers are not a terror to good works but to evil.' See on 2 Tim. ii. 21.

2. μηδένα βλασφημεῖν, *to speak ill of no man* (cp. Jude 8); not an easy precept to observe, if we are surrounded by persons whose principles of faith and conduct we believe to be quite unsound and mistaken. See on 2 Tim. iii. 2.

ἀμάχους εἶναι, ἐπιεικεῖς, *not to be contentious, to be forbearing.* These two adjectives are coupled again among the qualifications of the ἐπίσκοπος at 1 Tim. iii. 3, where see the note.

πᾶσαν ἐνδεικνυμένους πραΰτητα πρὸς πάντας ἀνθρώπους, *shewing all meekness to all men.* For the form of the sentence cp. ch. ii. 10 above; and for πραΰτης see on 2 Tim. ii. 25. We see here that the exhibition of this grace is not to be reserved for the intercourse of fellow Christians; it is to be displayed *to all men*, as a mark of the followers of Him who was Himself πραΰς (Matt. xi. 29).

3—7. WE HAVE NO REASON FOR PRIDE, BUT RATHER FOR THANKFULNESS.

3. ἦμεν γάρ ποτε καὶ ἡμεῖς κ.τ.λ. *For we ourselves were once &c.* Before we became Christians we were even as these very heathen.

ἀνόητοι, *foolish*, senseless; cp. Gal. iii. 1.

ἀπειθεῖς, *disobedient*, sc. to God. There is a general parallelism between the evil qualities enumerated in this verse, and those against which the Cretans are warned in *v.* 2; thus ἀπειθεῖς corresponds to πειθαρχεῖν, but the disobedience which the Apostle has now in his mind is not disobedience to earthly rulers. Cp. all through the mournful catalogue in Rom. i. 30 f.

πλανώμενοι may mean either *deceived* (as the English versions have), or 'going astray,' *errantes* (Vg.). The former seems preferable (cp. πλανώμενοι at 2 Tim. iii. 13, where it is certainly passive), but the intransitive meaning might be supported by such passages as Matt. xviii. 12; Heb. v. 2.

δουλεύοντες ἐπιθυμίαις καὶ ἡδοναῖς ποικίλαις, *slaves to divers lusts and pleasures.* It is curious that the common Greek word ἡδονή occurs nowhere else in St Paul's writings. For ποικίλος see on 2 Tim. iii. 6.

ἐν κακίᾳ καὶ φθόνῳ διάγοντες, *living in malice and envy.* κακία, no less than φθόνος, expresses an internal malignity, which is admirably expressed by the word *malice.* We have the full phrase βίον διάγειν at 1 Tim. ii. 2.

στυγητοί, μισοῦντες ἀλλήλους, *hateful, hating one another.* The word στυγητός does not occur again in the Greek Bible; we have it in Philo (*de Dec. Orac.* 24).

4. ὅτε δὲ ἡ χρηστότης καὶ ἡ φιλανθρωπία ἐπεφάνη τοῦ σωτῆρος ἡμῶν θεοῦ. *But when the kindness of our Saviour God and His love toward man appeared*, sc. at the Advent of Christ (cp. John iii. 16). Thus *vv.* 4—8 are appointed as the Evening Second Lesson for Christmas Day.

The combination of χρηστότης καὶ φιλανθρωπία, *benignitas et humanitas* (Vulg.) is very common in Greek, as Field has shewn by many examples.

χρηστότης is a specially Pauline word, not occurring in the N.T. outside St Paul's writings; he applies it to *man* at 2 Cor. vi. 6; Gal. v. 22; Col. iii. 12, and uses it, as here, of an attribute of *God* at Rom. ii. 4, xi. 22; Eph. ii. 7. It signifies the *graciousness* of the Divine love for man; the yoke of Christ is called χρηστός (Matt. xi. 30).

φιλανθρωπία in Greek generally means simply kindness to *individuals* in distress (e.g. 2 Macc. vi. 22), and does not involve the thought of mankind at large, as the English word *philanthropy* does. However, when φιλανθρωπία is used of superior beings (e.g. 2 Macc. xiv. 9) and especially when it is used of God it has this widest range. The two attributes χρηστότης καὶ φιλανθρωπία are here in striking contrast to the στυγητοί, μισοῦντες ἀλλήλους of the last verse; love of man for man is best engendered by the thought of God's all-embracing love.

For the epithet σωτήρ, here applied to God the Father, see on 1 Tim. i. 1.

5. οὐκ ἐξ ἔργων τῶν ἐν δικαιοσύνῃ ἃ ἐποιήσαμεν ἡμεῖς, *not by works done in righteousness which we did ourselves.* This is the side of St Paul's teaching so prominent in the Second Group of his Epistles (cp. Rom. ix. 11; Gal. ii. 16 &c.). No more pregnant statement of the doctrines of the Gospel is found anywhere in his writings than we find in these verses. See on 1 Tim. ii. 10 and 2 Tim. i. 9.

For the reading ἅ see the critical note.

ἀλλὰ κατὰ τὸ αὐτοῦ ἔλεος ἔσωσεν ἡμᾶς, *but according to His own mercy He saved us.* The position of αὐτοῦ makes it emphatic, and marks its contrast with ἡμεῖς of the preceding clause.

That man's salvation is 'according to' God's mercy is deep-rooted in the O.T.; cp. Ps. cviii. 26, σῶσόν με κατὰ τὸ μέγα ἔλεός σου.

διὰ λουτροῦ παλινγενεσίας καὶ ἀνακαινώσεως πνεύματος ἁγίου, *through the washing of regeneration and renewal of the Holy Spirit.*

That the 'washing of regeneration' is the Water of Baptism is undoubted; see Eph. v. 26 καθαρίσας τῷ λουτρῷ τοῦ ὕδατος. It is the instrument (διά) of salvation (cp. 1 Pet. iii. 21 ὃ καὶ ὑμᾶς ἀντίτυπον νῦν σώζει βάπτισμα), the means, that is, through which we are placed in a 'state of salvation,' in union with the mystical Body of Christ; cp. Gal. iii. 27. For λουτρόν 'washing,' cp. Cant. iv. 2; Ecclus. xxxiv. 25.

Two constructions are grammatically possible. (1) διά may govern λουτροῦ and also ἀνακαινώσεως, 'through the washing of regeneration and through the renewing of the Holy Spirit,' as the margin of the R.V. and, by its punctuation, the A.V., suggest. So it is taken by Tyndale, "by the fountain of the New Birth and with the renewing of the Holy Ghost"; and, of ancient versions, the Peshito also takes the words thus. Indeed D₂*E*G d e g bear witness to the insertion in the text of διά before ἀνακαινώσεως. Or, (2) we may take ἀνακαινώσεως (with the Greek Fathers generally) as a second genitive after λουτροῦ, the meaning being 'through a washing which was a washing of regeneration and of renewal of the Holy Spirit.' This is the rendering of the Vulgate, "per lavacrum regenerationis et renovationis Spiritus sancti," and of the Bohairic and Armenian versions, and is adopted by the R.V. Both (1) and (2) being admissible in grammar, (2) seems to preserve better the balance of the sentence, and to bring out better the double function, as it were, of the baptismal water, which is not only the instrument of the New Birth (cp. John iii. 5), but a pledge of the abiding grace of the Holy Ghost. It is this second aspect of baptismal grace,

the Renovation of the Spirit, which is prominent in Confirmation.
παλινγενεσία is, as it were, a 'new creation' (cp. Matt. xix. 28, the
only other place where the word is found in the N.T.); ἀνακαίνωσις
(cp. Rom. xii. 2) is the daily renewal of grace which the Holy Spirit
gives; cp. 2 Cor. iv. 16.

The Christmas Day Collect (while leaning to interpretation (1)
above) supplies a good devotional paraphrase, where we pray that
"we being regenerate, and made God's children by adoption and
grace, may daily be renewed by His Holy Spirit."

6. οὗ ἐξέχεεν ἐφ' ἡμᾶς πλουσίως, *which,* sc. the Holy Spirit, *He,* sc.
God the Father, the subject of the whole sentence, *poured out upon us
richly.*

By the ordinary rules of attraction, οὗ is attracted into the case of
the immediately preceding genitive, to which it refers.

The verb ἐκχέειν is the verb used to signify the outpouring of the
Holy Spirit in Acts ii. 17 (Joel iii. 1) and 33. In the former passage
the occasion was the Day of Pentecost; here the reference is to that
outpouring of grace in baptism which is always pledged to the
penitent and faithful soul: cp. Acts ii. 38.

διὰ 'Ιησοῦ Χριστοῦ τοῦ σωτῆρος ἡμῶν. This is closely connected
with the preceding ἐξέχεεν, and not, of course, with the more distant
ἔσωσεν of *v.* 5. The co-operation of all three Persons of the Blessed
Trinity in the work of grace is tersely and pregnantly expressed in
this short verse. If the Father is σωτήρ (*v.* 4, see on 1 Tim. i. 1), so
also the Son is σωτήρ, in a sense undreamed of under the Old
Covenant.

7. ἵνα δικαιωθέντες τῇ ἐκείνου χάριτι, *in order that, having been
justified by His grace* &c. The ἵνα has its full *telic* force; this heirship
now spoken of is the final purpose of that rich outpouring of the
Holy Spirit just described.

The mention of justification in such a context is characteristically
Pauline; cp. Rom. iii. 24 δικαιούμενοι δωρεὰν τῇ αὐτοῦ χάριτι, a parallel
which determines the reference (which grammar does not forbid) of
ἐκείνου to God the Father.

κληρονόμοι γενηθῶμεν, *we might be made heirs,* sc. heirs of all the
evangelical promises in Christ. κληρονόμοι is used thus absolutely by
St Paul; cp. e.g. Rom. iv. 14, viii. 17; Gal. iii. 29.

κατ' ἐλπίδα ζωῆς αἰωνίου, *according to the hope of life eternal.* See
on ch. i. 2 for this phrase. The heirship is κατ' ἐλπίδα ζωῆς αἰωνίου,
for if there were no such hope, then the heirship would be vain and
disappointing; cp. Heb. ix. 15.

8—11. FINAL INJUNCTIONS. (*a*) MAINTAIN GOOD WORKS.

8. πιστὸς ὁ λόγος. The 'faithful saying' in question is certainly
to be found in the preceding *vv.* 4—7; it has even been supposed by
some that we have here a fragment from a hymn on the way of
salvation (see on 1 Tim. iii. 16; 2 Tim. ii. 10), but there is not

sufficient evidence to confirm the hypothesis. No nobler statement of doctrine is found anywhere in the Pauline Epistles than these verses present.

καὶ περὶ τούτων βούλομαί σε διαβεβαιοῦσθαι, *and concerning these things I will* (see on 1 Tim. ii. 8) *that thou affirm confidently.* See for διαβεβαιοῦσθαι on 1 Tim. i. 7.

ἵνα φροντίζωσιν καλῶν ἔργων προΐστασθαι οἱ πεπιστευκότες θεῷ, *that they who have believed God may be careful to maintain good works.* Right belief must exhibit its fruits in life; this is the continual burden of St Paul's exhortations in the Pastoral Epistles; see on 1 Tim. ii. 10. φροντίζειν does not happen to occur again in the N.T., but it is frequent in the LXX. For the translation *maintain good works* the R.V. gives the marginal alternative "profess honest occupations." There is no doubt that this is an admissible meaning for προΐστασθαι, and 'honest trades' would give a very good sense to the injunction here, and again at *v.* 14. But the usage of the phrase καλὰ ἔργα in the Pastorals (see on 1 Tim. ii. 10) is decisive for the rendering *good works* here, as in the other instances of its occurrence; and προΐστασθαι may very well mean 'be forward in,' 'be foremost in the practice of' (see 1 Thess. v. 12, and 1 Tim. iii. 4, 5, 12). We therefore retain with confidence the ordinary rendering of the words.

ταῦτά ἐστιν καλὰ καὶ ὠφέλιμα τοῖς ἀνθρώποις. *These things,* sc. the preceding injunctions, *are good and profitable unto men.* For ὠφέλιμος see on 1 Tim. iv. 8.

9. (b) AVOID CONTROVERSY.

9. μωρὰς δὲ ζητήσεις καὶ γενεαλογίας καὶ ἔρεις καὶ μάχας νομικὰς περιΐστασο, *but shun foolish questions and genealogies and strifes and fightings about the law.*

The corresponding advice in the Epistles to Timothy will be found 1 Tim. i. 4 ff., vi. 4, and 2 Tim. ii. 23, where see the notes. The language descriptive of the forms of heresy to be avoided, and of the dangers resulting from idle and irrelevant speculations, is remarkably similar in all three Epistles. See *Introd.* chap. IV. For περιΐστασο cp. 2 Tim. ii. 16.

εἰσὶν γὰρ ἀνωφελεῖς καὶ μάταιοι, *for they are unprofitable and vain.* The word ἀνωφελής does not occur elsewhere in St Paul; cp. Heb. vii. 18. Ellicott notes that, although the adjective μάταιος is treated here and at James i. 26 as of two terminations, as in Attic Greek, yet the feminine form is found 1 Cor. xv. 17; 1 Pet. i. 18. The simple adj. μάταιος does not occur again in the Pastorals, but the false teachers are called ματαιολόγοι (Tit. i. 10) and their doctrine ματαιολογία (1 Tim. i. 6).

10, 11. (c) SHUN OBSTINATE HERETICS.

10. αἱρετικὸν ἄνθρωπον μετὰ μίαν καὶ δευτέραν νουθεσίαν παραιτοῦ. *A man that is heretical after a first and second admonition avoid.* We must be careful not to read into the adjective αἱρετικός all that it

came to imply at a later stage of the Church's life. The essence of
the idea of αἵρεσις in St Paul (see 1 Cor. xi. 19; Gal. v. 20) is that
wilful 'choosing' for oneself, which is the root of division and schism.
The duty of the Christian teacher, in his view, is to 'guard the
deposit' of doctrine which has been entrusted to him, and to refrain
from vain and irrelevant speculations on matters where our only
possible source of knowledge is revelation. The αἱρετικὸς ἄνθρωπος, on
the other hand, is the man who is always trying to strike out a new
line, and who is a cause of faction in the Church. αἱρετικός, thus,
means rather 'one who causes divisions' than 'one who holds false
doctrine,' a meaning which the word did not connote until a later
date.

παραιτεῖσθαι (see on 1 Tim. iv. 7) has no reference to anything like
formal excommunication; the counsel here offered to Titus is simply
to avoid persons who cause strife by their unedifying disputations and
theories.

11. εἰδὼς ὅτι ἐξέστραπται ὁ τοιοῦτος. *Knowing*, as you do, *that
such an one is perverted.*

ἐκστρέφεσθαι does not occur again in the N.T., but cp. Deut. xxxii.
20; Amos vi. 12.

The use of τοιοῦτος is thoroughly Pauline; cp. 1 Cor. v. 5; 2 Cor.
ii. 6; Gal. vi. 1.

καὶ ἁμαρτάνει ὢν αὐτοκατάκριτος, *and sinneth, being self-condemned.*
This principle is difficult to carry into practice. There is nothing
more common, or more lamentable, in theological controversy than
the assumption that a theological opponent is at heart dishonest
and 'self-condemned.' It is not possible to believe that any justification for this temper of mind is to be found in St Paul's words here
or in 1 Tim. iv. 2, where he speaks of the "speakers of lies who are
branded in their conscience." At the least it may be laid down that for
anyone possessed of a less keen insight into character than was given
to St Paul for his special work, it is not only unseemly, but presumptuous and wicked to impute hypocrisy to those who seem to be
'heretically' minded. That may indeed be true; but we can never be
sure of it, and it is probably far less often true than we are prone to
believe. In all men the power of self-deceit is so strong that self-
condemnation is very unusual. αὐτοκατάκριτος is ἅπ. λεγ. in the
Greek Bible.

12, 13. INVITATION. COME TO ME TO NICOPOLIS: SPEED ON THEIR
JOURNEY ZENAS AND APOLLOS.

12. ὅταν πέμψω Ἀρτεμᾶν πρὸς σὲ ἢ Τυχικόν. *Whenever I shall
have sent Artemas or Tychicus to thee*, sc. probably to supply the place
of the Chief Pastor of Crete during the absence of Titus. We learn from
2 Tim. iv. 12 that, at a later date, Tychicus, who was a trusted friend
of the Apostle, was sent to Ephesus; so there is just a slight probability that it was Artemas who was sent to Crete, but we do not really
know anything certain of the course of events (see *Introd.* p. xxxii.). Of

Artemas we have no knowledge; though there is a late tradition that he was bishop of Lystra.

For the construction of ὅταν with the aor. subj. see on 1 Tim. v. 11.

σπούδασον ἐλθεῖν πρός με εἰς Νικόπολιν, ἐκεῖ γὰρ κέκρικα παραχειμάσαι. *Use diligence* (cp. 2 Tim. ii. 15, iv. 9, 21) *to come to Nicopolis, for there I have determined to winter.*

There were at least three cities called Nicopolis, in Cilicia, in Thrace, and in Epirus respectively. Of these the third seems in every way more likely to be the city where St Paul proposed to winter (see *Introd.* p. xxxii.) than either of the other two. It was an important place, built by Augustus after the battle of Actium, and deriving its name 'the City of Victory' from that event. The use of ἐκεῖ ('there' not 'here') plainly indicates that the Apostle was *not* at Nicopolis at the time of writing. Despite this, the colophon appended to *v.* 15 of the rec. text reports that the Epistle was written ἀπὸ Νικοπόλεως τῆς Μακεδονίας (see crit. note), which makes the further mistake of identifying the Nicopolis of this verse with the Macedonian or Thracian city of that name.

See further on 2 Tim. iv. 10, where Titus is said to have gone to Dalmatia, a notice which agrees well enough with the present verse if, as we have assumed, the Nicopolis in Epirus on the Ambracian Gulf is the place whose name is recorded. It is worth adding that, as no such city is mentioned anywhere else in connexion with St Paul's history, the detail has the appearance of truth, and is extremely unlikely to be the invention of a forger of a later age, who would be careful to confine his allusions to places already associated with the name of St Paul.

For the construction of κέκρικα followed by an infinitive cp. 1 Cor. v. 3, vii. 37.

13. Ζηνᾶν τὸν νομικὸν καὶ Ἀπολλὰ σπουδαίως πρόπεμψον κ.τ.λ. *With diligence* (cp. 2 Tim. i. 17) *set forward on their journey Zenas the lawyer and Apollos, that nothing may be wanting to them.*

The duty of speeding fellow-Christians on their journeys, of giving them a good 'send-off,' as we say, is often mentioned by St Paul; cp. Rom. xv. 24; 1 Cor. xvi. 6, 11; 2 Cor. i. 16, and see also 3 John 6. It is, in fact, a point of hospitality, on which so much stress is naturally laid in these early years of the Church's life.

Of Zenas we know nothing further, not even whether the epithet ὁ νομικός is intended to describe him as skilled in *Roman* or *Hebrew* law. The Gospel use of the term (Luke vii. 30) might seem to favour the latter interpretation, but there is no certainty. He was by late tradition counted the author of apocryphal *Acts of Titus.*

Of Apollos, on the other hand, we hear several times. He is the learned and eloquent Alexandrian whom we find (Acts xviii. 24) at Ephesus receiving instruction from Priscilla and Aquila, and then proceeding to Corinth, where all too soon parties arose claiming respectively Apollos and Paul as their leaders (1 Cor. iii. 4 &c.). Jerome accounts for the presence of Apollos in Crete by supposing that he had retired thither until the unhappy controversies among the Corinthians should have died out. But this is not a probable account of the matter.

14. FINAL CHARGE TO THE CHRISTIANS AT CRETE.

14. μανθανέτωσαν δὲ καὶ οἱ ἡμέτεροι καλῶν ἔργων προΐστασθαι. *And let our people also,* sc. the Christian brethren at Crete, *learn to maintain good works.* Although the letter is primarily for Titus, yet it also has words of counsel for his flock. Probably a letter like this would be read aloud when the brethren were assembled for public worship.

For καλῶν ἔργων προΐστασθαι see on *v.* 8 above; here it is directly connected with what follows, viz:

εἰς τὰς ἀναγκαίας χρείας, ἵνα μὴ ὦσιν ἄκαρποι, *for necessary uses, that they be not unfruitful.* The definite article τάς is significant, viz. such necessary uses as may present themselves from time to time.

For χρεία cp. Eph. iv. 28; Phil. iv. 16; and for ἄκαρπος cp. 1 Cor. xiv. 14.

15. SALUTATIONS.

15. ἀσπάζονταί σε οἱ μετ᾽ ἐμοῦ πάντες. *All that are with me salute thee.*

This exact form of salutation is not used elsewhere by St Paul (though cp. 2 Tim. iv. 21), which again may be urged as a point in favour of the genuineness of the letter, a forger not being likely to introduce unfamiliar features.

Cp. Gal. i. 2, οἱ σὺν ἐμοὶ πάντες ἀδελφοί; it is worth remarking that σύν is not once found (save in composition) in the Pastoral Epistles, its place being always supplied by μετά[1].

ἀσπασαι τοὺς φιλοῦντας ἡμᾶς ἐν πίστει. *Salute them that love us in faith.* ἐν πίστει seems to be used as at 1 Tim. i. 2, their πίστις being as it were the bond which unites Paul and the Cretan Christians.

BENEDICTION.

ἡ χάρις μετὰ πάντων ὑμῶν. *The Grace,* sc. of our Lord, *be with you all.* This ⸓ the σημεῖον ἐν πάσῃ ἐπιστολῇ (2 Thess. iii. 17). See on 1 Tim. vi. 21.

---

[1] In like manner, σύν is very rare in St John's Gospel, and never occurs in his Epistles or in the Apocalypse.

INDEX GRAECITATIS

Words marked * are peculiar in N.T. to the Pastoral Epp.
——————— † are not found in the LXX.[1]
——————— ‡ are not in any other of the Pauline Epp.
——————— § are peculiar in N.T. to the Pauline Epp.

*†ἀγαθοεργεῖν, 1 Tim. vi. 18
ἀγάπη, 1 Tim. i. 5 &c.
ἀγιάζειν, 1 Tim. iv. 5; 2 Tim. ii. 21
ἀγιασμός, 1 Tim. ii. 15
*ἀγνεία, 1 Tim. iv. 12, v. 2
ἀγνός, 1 Tim. v. 22; Tit. ii. 5
*ἀγωγή, 2 Tim. iii. 10
ἀγωνίζεσθαι, 1 Tim. iv. 10, vi. 12; 2 Tim. iv. 7
*†ἀδηλότης, 1 Tim. vi. 17
§ἀδιάλειπτος, 2 Tim. i. 3; Rom. ix. 2
ἀδόκιμος, 2 Tim. iii. 8; Tit. i. 16
§ἀθανασία, 1 Tim. vi. 16; 1 Cor. xv. 54
ἀθετεῖν, 1 Tim. v. 12
*†ἀθλεῖν, 2 Tim. ii. 5
*αἰδώς, 1 Tim. ii. 9
*†αἱρετικός, Tit. iii. 10
*†αἰσχροκερδής, 1 Tim. iii. 8; Titus i. 7; cp. 1 Pet. v. 2
§αἰσχρός, Tit. i. 11
‡αἰτία, 2 Tim. i. 6, 12; Tit. i. 13
αἰχμαλωτίζειν, 2 Tim. iii. 6
*ἀκαίρως, 2 Tim. iv. 2
*ἀκατάγνωστος, Tit. ii. 8; 2 Macc. iv. 47 only
*ἀκρατής, 2 Tim. iii. 3
§ἀλαζών, 2 Tim. iii. 2; Rom. i. 30

*ἄλλως, 1 Tim. v. 25
§ἀλοᾷν, 1 Tim. v. 18; 1 Cor. ix. 9, 10 (from Deut. xxv. 4)
ἅλυσις, 2 Tim. i. 16
*†ἄμαχος, 1 Tim. iii. 3; Tit. iii. 2
‡ἀμελεῖν, 1 Tim. iv. 14
*†ἀμοιβή, 1 Tim. v. 4
ἀνάγνωσις, 1 Tim. iv. 13
*ἀναζωπυρεῖν, 2 Tim. i. 6
†§ἀνακαίνωσις, Tit. iii. 5; Rom. xii. 2
*†ἀνάλυσις, 2 Tim. iv. 6; cp. 2 Macc. ix. 1
ἀναμιμνήσκειν, 2 Tim. i. 6
*†ἀνανήφειν, 2 Tim. ii. 26
ἀναστρέφειν, 1 Tim. iii. 15
ἀναστροφή, 1 Tim. iv. 12
*ἀνατρέπειν, 2 Tim. ii. 18; Tit. i. 11
*ἀναψύχειν, 2 Tim. i. 16. Cp. ἀνάψυξις, Acts iii. 19
*†ἀνδραποδιστής, 1 Tim. i. 10
*ἀνδροφόνος, 1 Tim. i. 9; 2 Macc. ix. 28 only
§ἀνέγκλητος, 1 Tim. iii. 10; Tit. i. 6, 7
*ἀνεξίκακος, 2 Tim. ii. 24
*†ἀνεπαίσχυντος, 2 Tim. ii. 15
*†ἀνεπίλημπτος, 1 Tim. iii. 2, v. 7, vi. 14
ἀνέχεσθαι, 2 Tim. iv. 3
*†ἀνήμερος, 2 Tim. iii. 3
ἀνθιστάναι, 2 Tim. iii. 8, iv. 15

[1] No account is taken in this index of the occurrence of words in the versions of Aquila, Symmachus, &c.

ἀνόητος, 1 Tim. vi. 9 ; Tit. iii. 3
‡ἄνοια, 2 Tim. iii. 9 ; Luke vi. 11
ἀνομία, Tit. ii. 14
ἄνομος, 1 Tim. i. 9
*ἀνόσιος, 1 Tim. i. 9 ; 2 Tim.
    iii. 2
ἀντέχεσθαι, Tit. i. 9
*†ἀντιδιατίθεσθαι, 2 Tim. ii. 25
*†ἀντίθεσις, 1 Tim. vi. 20
ἀντίκεισθαι, 1 Tim. i. 10, v. 14
‡ἀντιλαμβάνεσθαι, 1 Tim. vi. 2 ;
    Luke i. 54 ; Ac. xx. 35
ἀντιλέγειν, Tit. i. 9, ii. 9
*†ἀντίλυτρον, 1 Tim. ii. 6 ; cp.
    Matt. xx. 28
ἀνυπόκριτος, 1 Tim. i. 5 ; 2 Tim.
    i. 5
†‡ἀνυπότακτος, 1 Tim. i. 9 ; Tit.
    i. 6, 10 ; Hebr. ii. 8 ; cp. Rom.
    xiii. 1, 5
‡ἀνωφελής, Tit. iii. 9 ; Hebr. vii.
    18
*ἀπαίδευτος, 2 Tim. ii. 23
*ἀπέραντος, 1 Tim. i. 4
ἀπέχεσθαι, 1 Tim. iv. 3
ἀπιστεῖν, 2 Tim. ii. 13 ; ἀπιστία,
    1 Tim. i. 13 ; ἄπιστος, 1 Tim.
    v. 8 ; Tit. i. 15
*†ἀπόβλητος, 1 Tim. iv. 4
*†ἀπόδεκτος, 1 Tim. ii. 3, v. 4
*†ἀποδοχή, 1 Tim. i. 15, iv. 9
*ἀποθησαυρίζειν, 1 Tim. vi. 19
‡ἀπόλαυσις, 1 Tim. vi. 17 ; Hebr.
    xi. 25
‡ἀπολείπειν, 2 Tim. iv. 13, 20 ;
    Tit. i. 5
ἀπολογία, 2 Tim. iv. 16
*ἀποπλανᾶν, 1 Tim. vi. 10 ; Mark
    xiii. 22
ἀποστερεῖν, 1 Tim. vi. 5
ἀποστρέφειν, 2 Tim. i. 15, iv. 4 ;
    Tit. i. 14
ἀποτόμως, Tit. i. 13 ; 2 Cor. xiii.
    10
*ἀποτρέπειν, 2 Tim. iii. 5
*†ἀπρόσιτος, 1 Tim. vi. 16
ἀπωθεῖν, 1 Tim. i. 19
ἀπώλεια, 1 Tim. vi. 9
‡ἀργός, 1 Tim. v. 13 ; Tit. i. 12
‡ἀργυροῦς, 2 Tim. ii. 20

‡ἀρνεῖσθαι, 1 Tim. v. 8 ; 2 Tim.
    ii. 12, 13, iii. 5 ; Tit. i. 16,
    ii. 12
†§ἀρσενοκοίτης, 1 Tim. i. 10 ; 1 Cor.
    vi. 9
*†ἄρτιος, 2 Tim. iii. 17
ἀσέβεια, 2 Tim. ii. 16 ; Tit. ii.
    12
ἀσεβής, 1 Tim. i. 9
†ἄσπιλος, 1 Tim. vi. 14 ; Jas. i.
    27 ; 1 Pet. i. 19 ; 2 Pet. iii.
    14
*†ἄσπονδος, 2 Tim. iii. 3
§ἄστοργος, 2 Tim. iii. 3 ; Rom. i.
    31
*ἀστοχεῖν, 1 Tim. i. 6, vi. 21 ;
    2 Tim. ii. 18
ἀσωτία, Tit. i. 6
§ἀτιμία, 2 Tim. ii. 20
‡αὐθάδης, 2 Pet. ii. 10 ; Tit. i. 7
*†αὐθεντεῖν, 1 Tim. ii. 12
†§αὐτάρκεια, 1 Tim. vi. 6 ; 2 Cor.
    ix. 8
*†αὐτοκατάκριτος, Tit. iii. 11
§ἀφθαρσία, 2 Tim. i. 10
ἄφθαρτος, 1 Tim. i. 17
*ἀφθορία, Tit. ii. 7
*†ἀφιλάγαθος, 2 Tim. iii. 3
†‡ἀφιλάργυρος, 1 Tim. iii. 3 ; Hebr.
    xiii. 5
§ἀφορμή, 1 Tim. v. 14
‡ἀχάριστος, 2 Tim. iii. 2 ; Luke
    vi. 35
*ἀψευδής, Tit. i. 2

*βαθμός, 1 Tim. iii. 13
βαρεῖσθαι, 1 Tim. v. 16
*βδελυκτός, Tit. i. 16
‡βέβηλος, 1 Tim. i. 9, iv. 7, vi. 20 ;
    2 Tim. ii. 16 ; Hebr. xii. 16
*βέλτιον, 2 Tim. i. 18
‡βίος, 1 Tim. ii. 2 ; 2 Tim. ii. 4
*βλαβερός, 1 Tim. vi. 9
βλασφημεῖν, 1 Tim. i. 20, vi. 1 ;
    Tit. ii. 5, iii. 2 ; βλασφημία,
    1 Tim. vi. 4 ; βλάσφημος, 1 Tim.
    i. 13 ; 2 Tim. iii. 2
‡βραδύνειν, 1 Tim. iii. 15 ; 2 Pet.
    iii. 9
‡βρέφος, 2 Tim. iii. 15

ἐπιγινώσκειν, 1 Tim. iv. 3
ἐπίγνωσις, 1 Tim. ii. 4; 2 Tim.
ii. 25, iii. 7; Tit. i. 1
*†ἐπιδιορθοῦν, Tit. i. 5
ἐπιεικής, 1 Tim. iii. 3; Tit. iii. 2;
Phil. iv. 5; cp. 2 Cor. x. 1
‡ἐπίθεσις, 1 Tim. iv. 14; 2 Tim.
i. 6; Acts viii. 18; Hebr. vi. 2
ἐπιθυμία, 1 Tim. vi. 9; 2 Tim.
ii. 22, iii. 6, iv. 3; Tit. ii. 12,
i ii. 3
‡ἐπιλαμβάνεσθαι, 1 Tim. vi. 12, 19
‡ἐπιμελεῖσθαι, 1 Tim. iii. 5; Luke
x. 34, 35
*ἐπίορκος, 1 Tim. i. 10; cp. Matt.
v. 33
*†ἐπιπλήττειν, 1 Tim. v. 1; cp.
2 Macc. vii. 33
ἐπιποθεῖν, 2 Tim. i. 4
‡ἐπισκοπή, 1 Tim. iii. 1
ἐπίσκοπος, 1 Tim. iii. 2; Tit. i. 7
‡ἐπίστασθαι, 1 Tim. vi. 4
*†ἐπιστομίζειν, Tit. i. 11 (where
see note)
*†ἐπισωρεύειν, 2 Tim. iv. 3
§ἐπιταγή, 1 Tim. i. 1; Tit. i. 3,
ii. 15
‡ἐπιτιθέναι, 1 Tim. v. 22
‡ἐπιτιμᾶν, 2 Tim. iv. 2
ἐπιτρέπειν, 1 Tim. ii. 12
‡ἐπιφαίνειν, Tit. ii. 11, iii. 4;
Luke i. 79; Acts xxvii. 20
§ἐπιφάνεια, 1 Tim. vi. 14 (where
see note) &c.
ἐπουράνιος, 2 Tim. iv. 18
§ἔρις, 1 Tim. vi. 4; Tit. iii. 9
*†ἑτεροδιδασκαλεῖν, 1 Tim. i. 3,
vi. 3
†εὐαγγελιστής, 2 Tim. iv. 5
‡εὐεργεσία, 1 Tim. vi. 2; Acts
iv. 9
‡εὐκαίρως, 2 Tim. iv. 2; Mark
xiv. 11; cp. 1 Cor. xvi. 12
*†εὐμετάδοτος, 1 Tim. vi. 18
‡εὐσέβεια, 1 Tim. ii. 2 (where see
note) &c.
‡εὐσεβεῖν, 1 Tim. v. 4; Acts xvii.
23
*εὐσεβῶς, 2 Tim. iii. 12; Tit. ii.
12

εὐχαριστία, 1 Tim. ii. 1, iv. 3, 4
§εὔχρηστος, 2 Tim. ii. 21, iv. 11

‡†ζήτησις, 1 Tim. vi. 4; 2 Tim.
ii. 23; Tit. iii. 9
‡ζωγρεῖν, 2 Tim. ii. 26; Luke v. 10
‡ζωογονεῖν, 1 Tim. vi. 13; Luke
xvii. 33; Acts vii. 19 only

‡ἡδονή, Tit. iii. 3
*†ἤπιος, 2 Tim. ii. 24
*ἤρεμος, 1 Tim. ii. 2
‡ἡσύχιος, 1 Tim. ii. 2; 1 Pet.
iii. 4

*†θεόπνευστος, 2 Tim. iii. 16
*θεοσέβεια, 1 Tim. ii. 10
‡θηρίον, Tit. i. 12
θλίβειν, 1 Tim. v. 10

ἴδιος, 1 Tim. ii. 6 &c.; (very often
in Paul; 15 times in 1 Cor.)
*ἱεροπρεπής, Tit. ii. 3
§ἱερός, 2 Tim. iii. 15; 1 Cor. ix.
13
‡ἱματισμός, 1 Tim. ii. 9
*†'Ιουδαϊκός, Tit. i. 14; cp. Gal.
ii. 14

καθαρίζειν, Tit. ii. 14
καθαρός, 1 Tim. i. 5, iii. 9; 2 Tim.
i. 3, ii. 22; Tit. i. 15; Rom.
xiv. 20
κακία, Tit. iii. 3
‡κακοπαθεῖν, 2 Tim. ii. 9, iv. 5;
Jas. v. 13
‡κακοῦργος, 2 Tim. ii. 9; Luke
xxiii. 32, 33, 39
*†καλοδιδάσκαλος, Tit. ii. 3
καλός, 1 Tim. i. 8 (where see
note)
*καταλέγεσθαι, 1 Tim. v. 9
καταργεῖν, 2 Tim. i. 10 (24 times
in Paul)
*κατάστημα, Tit. ii. 3
*καταστολή, 1 Tim. ii. 9
*†καταστρηνιάζειν, 1 Tim. v. 11
*καταστροφή, 2 Tim. ii. 14
*καταφθείρειν, 2 Tim. iii. 8
καταφρονεῖν, 1 Tim. iv. 12, vi. 2

*νοσεῖν, 1 Tim. vi. 4
‡νοσφίζεσθαι, Tit. ii. 10; Acts v. 2, 3
§νουθεσία, Tit. iii. 10
νοῦς, 1 Tim. vi. 5; 2 Tim. iii. 8; Tit. i. 15

*†ξενοδοχεῖν, 1 Tim. v. 10
‡ξύλινος, 2 Tim. ii. 20; Rev. ix. 20

§ὀδύνη, 1 Tim. vi. 10; Rom. ix. 2
§οἰκεῖν, 1 Tim. vi. 16
§οἰκεῖος, 1 Tim. v. 8
*†οἰκοδεσποτεῖν, 1 Tim. v. 14, but οἰκοδεσπότης is common in the Synoptic Gospels
οἰκονομία, 1 Tim. i. 4
οἰκονόμος, Tit. i. 7
*†οἰκουργός, Tit. ii. 5 or *†οἰκουρός
§ὄλεθρος, 1 Tim. vi. 9
ὁμολογεῖν, 1 Tim. vi. 12; Tit. i. 16
ὁμολογία, 1 Tim. vi. 12, 13
*ὁμολογουμένως, 1 Tim. iii. 16
ὀνειδισμός, 1 Tim. iii. 7
ὁπτεσθαι, 1 Tim. iii. 16
*ὀργίλος, Tit. i. 7
‡†ὀρέγεσθαι, 1 Tim. iii. 1, vi. 10; Hebr. xi. 16
*ὀρθοτομεῖν, 2 Tim. ii. 15
‡ὅσιος, 1 Tim. ii. 8; Tit. i. 8
§ὀστράκινος, 2 Tim. ii. 20; 2 Cor. iv. 7

παγίς, 1 Tim. iii. 7, vi. 9; 2 Tim. ii. 26
†§παλινγενεσία, Tit. iii. 5; Matt. xix. 28
παράβασις, 1 Tim. ii. 14
†παραγγελία, 1 Tim. i. 5, 18
παραγίνεσθαι, 2 Tim. iv. 16
‡παραδέχεσθαι, 1 Tim. v. 19; Acts xvi. 21, xxii. 18
*παραθήκη, 1 Tim. vi. 20; 2 Tim. i. 12, 14
‡παραιτεῖσθαι, 1 Tim. iv. 7, v. 11; 2 Tim. ii. 23; Tit. iii. 10
παρακαλεῖν, 1 Tim. i. 3, ii. 1,

v. 1, vi. 2; 2 Tim. iv. 2; Tit. i. 9, ii. 6, 15
παράκλησις, 1 Tim. iv. 13
‡παρακολουθεῖν, 1 Tim. iv. 6; 2 Tim. iii. 10
†παραχειμάζειν, Tit. iii. 12
παρέχειν, 1 Tim. i. 4, vi. 17; Tit. ii. 7
*†πάροινος, 1 Tim. iii. 3; Tit. i. 7
*†πατρολῴης, 1 Tim. i. 9
‡πειθαρχεῖν, Tit. iii. 1; Acts xxvii. 21
πειρασμός, 1 Tim. vi. 9
‡†περίεργος, 1 Tim. v. 13; Acts xix. 19
‡περιέρχεσθαι, 1 Tim. v. 13; Acts xix. 13; xxviii. 13
‡περιιστάναι, 2 Tim. ii. 16; Tit. iii. 9; Acts xxv. 7
*περιούσιος, Tit. ii. 14
*†περιπείρειν, 1 Tim. vi. 10
‡περιποιεῖσθαι, 1 Tim. iii. 13; Acts xx. 28
περιτομή, Tit. i. 10
*περιφρονεῖν, Tit. ii. 15
πίστις, 1 Tim. i. 2, 19 (where see note)
πιστός, 1 Tim. i. 12 &c.
*πιστοῦσθαι, 2 Tim. iii. 14
πλανᾶν, 2 Tim. iii. 13; Tit. iii. 3
πλάνος, 1 Tim. iv. 1
§πλάσσειν, 1 Tim. ii. 13; Rom. ix. 20
*†πλέγμα, 1 Tim. ii. 9; cp. 1 Pet. iii. 3
*†πλήκτης, 1 Tim. iii. 3; Tit. i. 7
πληροῦν, 2 Tim. i. 4
πληροφορεῖν, 2 Tim. iv. 5, 17
πλουτεῖν, 1 Tim. vi. 9, 18
πλοῦτος, 1 Tim. vi. 17
‡ποικίλος, 2 Tim. iii. 6; Tit. iii. 3
‡πολυτελής, 1 Tim. ii. 9
πονηρός, 1 Tim. vi. 4; 2 Tim. iii. 13, iv. 18
*πορισμός, 1 Tim. vi. 5, 6
πόρνος, 1 Tim. i. 10
*πραγματεία, 2 Tim. ii. 4
*†πραϋπαθία, 1 Tim. vi. 11
πραΰτης, 2 Tim. ii. 25; Tit. iii. 2

‡πρεσβυτέριον, 1 Tim. iv. 14; Luke xxii. 66; Acts xxii. 5

πρεσβύτερος, 1 Tim. v. 1, 2, 17, 19; Tit. i. 5

πρεσβύτης, Tit. ii. 2

*πρεσβῦτις, Tit. ii. 3

‡προάγειν, 1 Tim. i. 18, v. 24; Acts xxv. 26

*πρόγονοι, 1 Tim. v. 4; 2 Tim. i. 3

‡πρόδηλος, 1 Tim. v. 24, 25; Hebr. vii. 14

‡προδότης, 2 Tim. iii. 4; Luke vi. 16

πρόθεσις, 2 Tim. i. 9, iii. 10

§προϊστάναι, 1 Tim. iii. 4, 5, 12; Tit. iii. 8, 14

§προκοπή, 1 Tim. iv. 15; Phil. i. 12, 25

†προκόπτειν, 2 Tim. ii. 16, iii. 9, 13

*†πρόκριμα, 1 Tim. v. 21

§προνοεῖν, 1 Tim. v. 8

‡προπετής, 2 Tim. iii. 4; Acts xix. 36

προσδέχεσθαι, Tit. ii. 13

‡προσέρχεσθαι, 1 Tim. vi. 3

προσεύχεσθαι, 1 Tim. ii. 8

προσευχή, 1 Tim. ii. 1, v. 5

‡προσέχειν, 1 Tim. i. 4, iii. 8, iv. 1, 13; Tit. i. 14

*†πρόσκλισις, 1 Tim. v. 21; cp. 2 Macc. iv. 14, xiv. 24

‡προσμένειν, 1 Tim. i. 3, v. 5

προφητεία, 1 Tim. i. 18, iv. 14

προφήτης, Tit. i. 12

‡πυκνός, 1 Tim. v. 23; Acts xxiv. 26

*†ῥητῶς, 1 Tim. iv. 1

σάρξ, 1 Tim. iii. 16

σατανᾶς, 1 Tim. i. 20, v. 15

§σεμνός, 1 Tim. iii. 8, 11; Tit. ii. 2; Phil. iv. 8

*σεμνότης, 1 Tim. ii. 2, iii. 4; Tit. ii. 7; 2 Macc. iii. 12 only

*†σκέπασμα, 1 Tim. vi. 8

σκεῦος, 2 Tim. ii. 20, 21

‡σοφίζειν, 2 Tim. iii. 15; 2 Pet. i. 16

†σπαταλᾶν, 1 Tim. v. 6; Jas. v. 5

§σπένδεσθαι, 2 Tim. iv. 6; Phil. ii. 17

σπέρμα, 2 Tim. ii. 8

σπουδάζειν, 2 Tim. ii. 15, iv. 9, 21; Tit. iii. 12

σπουδαίως, 2 Tim. i. 17; Tit. iii. 13

‡στερεός, 2 Tim. ii. 19; Hebr. v. 12, 14; 1 Pet. v. 9

στέφανος, 2 Tim. iv. 8

‡στεφανοῦν, 2 Tim. ii. 5; Hebr. ii. 7

στόμα, 2 Tim. iv. 17

*†στόμαχος, 1 Tim. v. 23

§στρατεία, 1 Tim. i. 18; 2 Cor. x. 4

στρατεύεσθαι, 1 Tim. i. 18; 2 Tim. ii. 4

‡στρατιώτης, 2 Tim. ii. 3; Acts xxvii. 31 &c.

*†στρατολογεῖν, 2 Tim. ii. 4

*†στυγητός, Tit. iii. 3

στύλος, 1 Tim. iii. 15

§συμβασιλεύειν, 2 Tim. ii. 12; 1 Cor. iv. 8

συναποθνήσκειν, 2 Tim. ii. 11

συνείδησις 1 Tim. i. 5 (where see note)

σύνεσις, 2 Tim. ii. 7

§†συνζῆν, 2 Tim. ii. 11

*†συνκακοπαθεῖν, 2 Tim. i. 8, ii. 3

σφραγίς, 2 Tim. ii. 19

‡σωματικός, 1 Tim. iv. 8; Luke iii. 22

§σωρεύειν, 2 Tim. iii. 6; Rom. xii. 20 (Prov. xxv. 22)

σωτήρ, 1 Tim. i. 1, ii. 3, iv. 10; 2 Tim. i. 10; Tit. i. 3, ii. 10, 13, iii. 4, 6

σωτηρία, 2 Tim. ii. 10, iii. 15

*σωτήριος, Tit. ii. 11; cp. Eph. vi. 17; Acts xxviii. 28

†σωφρονεῖν, Tit. ii. 6

*†σωφρονίζειν, Tit. ii. 4

*†σωφρονισμός, 2 Tim. i. 7

*σωφρόνως, Tit. ii. 12

‡σωφροσύνη, 1 Tim. ii. 9, 15;
Acts xxvi. 25 only
*σώφρων, 1 Tim. iii. 2; Tit. i.
8, ii. 2, 5

ταχέως, 1 Tim. v. 22; 2 Tim.
iv. 9
τάχιον, 1 Tim. iii. 14
*†τεκνογονεῖν, 1 Tim. v. 14
*†τεκνογονία, 1 Tim. ii. 15
*†τεκνοτροφεῖν, 1 Tim. v. 10
τηρεῖν, 1 Tim. v. 22, vi. 14;
2 Tim. iv. 7
τιμή, 1 Tim. i. 17 &c.
τύπος, 1 Tim. iv. 12; Tit. ii. 7
*†τυφοῦσθαι, 1 Tim. iii. 6, vi. 4;
2 Tim. iii. 4

§ὑβριστής, 1 Tim. i. 13; Rom. i.
30
‡ὑγιαίνειν, 1 Tim. i. 10, vi. 3;
2 Tim. i. 13, iv. 3; Tit. i. 9,
13, ii. 1, 2
‡ὑγιής, Tit. ii. 8
*ὑδροποτεῖν, 1 Tim. v. 23; Dan.
i. 12 only
ὑπερήφανος, 2 Tim. iii. 2
§ὑπεροχή, 1 Tim. ii. 2; 1 Cor.
ii. 1
*†ὑπερπλεονάζειν, 1 Tim. i. 14
ὑπόκρισις, 1 Tim. iv. 2
ὑπομένειν, 2 Tim. ii. 10, 12
‡ὑπομιμνήσκειν, 2 Tim. ii. 14;
Tit. iii. 1
‡ὑπόμνησις, 2 Tim. i. 5; 2 Pet.
i. 13; 2 Macc. vi. 17 only
ὑπομονή, 1 Tim. vi. 11; 2 Tim.
iii. 10; Tit. ii. 2
*ὑπόνοια, 1 Tim. vi. 4
§ὑποταγή, 1 Tim. ii. 11, iii. 4
ὑποτάσσειν, Tit. ii. 5, 9, iii. 1
§ὑποτιθέναι, 1 Tim. iv. 6; Rom.
xvi. 4
*†ὑποτύπωσις, 1 Tim. i. 16;
2 Tim. i. 13
ὑποφέρειν, 2 Tim. iii. 11
‡ὕστερος, 1 Tim. iv. 1; Matt.
xxi. 31

†§ὑψηλοφρονεῖν, 1 Tim. vi. 17;
Rom. xi. 20

φανερός, 1 Tim. iv. 15
φανεροῦν, 1 Tim. iii. 16; 2 Tim.
i. 10; Tit. i. 3
φαῦλος, Tit. ii. 8
*†φελόνης, 2 Tim. iv. 13
φθόνος, 1 Tim. vi. 4; Tit. iii. 3
*φιλάγαθος, Tit. i. 8; Wisd. vii. 22
only
*†φίλανδρος, Tit. ii. 4
‡φιλανθρωπία, Tit. iii. 4; Acts
xxviii. 2
*φιλαργυρία, 1 Tim. vi. 10
‡φιλάργυρος 2 Tim. iii. 2; Luke
xvi. 14
*†φίλαυτος, 2 Tim. iii. 2
φιλεῖν, Tit. iii. 15
*†φιλήδονος, 2 Tim. iii. 4
*†φιλόθεος, 2 Tim. iii. 4
‡†φιλόξενος, 1 Tim. iii. 2; Tit. i.
8
*φιλότεκνος, Tit. ii. 4
φιμοῦν, 1 Tim. v. 18 (from Deut.
xxv. 4)
*φλύαρος, 1 Tim. v. 13
*†φρεναπάτης, Tit. i. 10
*φροντίζειν, Tit. iii. 8
φῶς, 1 Tim. vi. 16
φωτίζειν, 2 Tim. i. 10

‡χαλεπός, 2 Tim. iii. 1; Matt.
viii. 28
*χαλκεύς, 2 Tim. iv. 14
χαρά, 2 Tim. i. 4
χάρισμα, 1 Tim. iv. 14; 2 Tim.
i. 6
‡χειμών, 2 Tim. iv. 21
‡χείρων, 1 Tim. v. 8; 2 Tim. iii.
13
χήρα, 1 Tim. v. 3 ff.
χρεία, Tit. iii. 14
χρῆσθαι, 1 Tim. i. 8, v. 23
*χρήσιμος, 2 Tim. ii. 14
§χρηστότης, Tit. iii. 4
χρόνος, 2 Tim. i. 9; Tit. i. 2
‡χρυσίον, 1 Tim. ii. 9
‡χρυσοῦς, 2 Tim. ii. 20

Thornapple Commentaries

Baker Book House, Box 6287, Grand Rapids, Michigan 49506